ROBERT MANNING
STROZIER LIBRARY.

AUG 24 1994

Tallahassee, Florida

Non-Natural Social Science: Reflecting on the Enterprise of *More Heat than Light*

Annual supplement to volume 25

History of Political Economy

Edited by Neil de Marchi

Duke University Press   Durham and London   1993

Copyright © 1993 by Duke University Press
Printed in the United States of America
on acid-free paper ∞
ISBN 0-8223-1410-X
This is the 1993 annual supplement to
History of Political Economy, ISSN 0018-2702.

Contents

Introduction *Neil de Marchi* 1

Part 1 Disciplinary History and the Use of Metaphor

Analogy, Homology, and Metaphor in the Interactions between the Natural Sciences and the Social Sciences, Especially Economics
I. Bernard Cohen 7

What's So Wrong with Physics Envy? *Margaret Schabas* 45

Interpreting the Triumph of Mathematical Economics
Theodore M. Porter 54

A Method to Mirowski's Mad Use of Metaphor *Steve Fuller* 69

Part 2 Economic Problems and Mathematical Formalism

Neoclassical Economics as Mathematical Metaphysics
Jack Birner 85

More Light on Integrability, Symmetry, and Utility as Potential Energy in Mirowski's Critical History *D. Wade Hands* 118

Paul Ehrenfest and Jan Tinbergen: A Case of Limited Physics Transfer
Marcel Boumans 131

Part 3 The Mirowski Thesis and Three Generations of Neoclassicals

"Procrustean Beds and All That": The Irrelevance of Walras for a Mirowski Thesis *Albert Jolink* 159

Remaking the Mathematician as an Economist: Knut Wicksell and the Mittag-Leffler Circle *Clifford G. Gaddy* 175

What Was Abandoned Following the Cambridge Capital Controversies? Samuelson, Substance, Scarcity, and Value
Avi J. Cohen 202

Part 4 Perspectives on Constructivist History

Modernism in Economics: An Interpretation beyond Physics
Arjo Klamer 223

Chalk and Cheese: Mirowski Meets Douglas and Bloor
Robert J. Leonard 249

What Mirowski's History Leaves Out *A. W. Coats* 271

History through the Lens of "Social" Value Theory
Neil de Marchi 283

After Mirowski, What? *E. Roy Weintraub* 300

Part 5 The Enterpriser Responds

The Goalkeeper's Anxiety at the Penalty Kick *Philip Mirowski* 305

Index 351

Contributors 371

Non-Natural Social Science

Introduction

Neil de Marchi

This volume of essays is the fourth in the Annual Supplement series of *HOPE* and stems from a conference held at Duke University in March 1991 to explore the enterprise represented by *More Heat than Light* and some of the historical challenges it poses. At the time, Philip Mirowski's book had been available for more than a year, and versions of various chapters had been in circulation for much longer than that. His argument that neoclassical economic theory had put "utility" in place of "energy" and borrowed both the field metaphor and the mathematics adapted by physicists to show how particles are positioned according to the principle of least energy, was somewhat familiar. So too was his criticism that economists, at the time of borrowing, had failed to attend to the conservation of energy and had therefore bequeathed a set of flawed foundations to those who would later erect the structure of modern economics.

Familiar did not necessarily mean well understood. One barrier to understanding was the fact that even to appreciate the argument, one needed a fair grasp of some nineteenth-century physics and an understanding of conservative and nonconservative systems. These are not part of the background of most historians of economics.

Furthermore, if true, the argument constituted a radically new reading of the so-called marginalist revolution, an episode that most historians probably thought they had understood pretty well. And not only that. Mirowski challenged both the substance and the commonly accepted way of writing the history. For him, "substance" could not even be said to exist independently of "way of writing." That struck some as too radical by half. Mirowski's history of the "marginal revolution" was not a story about the "discovery" of marginal utility, told as if, like other concepts deemed important stones in the foundation of modern economic analysis, marginal utility had been waiting around to be noticed, picked up, and cemented into position. The contingency of history, to him, involved much more than whether and why individual X or Z had, or had failed to, notice (what was *really* there all along). There was more to it than nuggets and dross, winners and also-rans.

From this point difficulties, and possibly readers' resistances, seem to proliferate. Since, for Mirowski, marginal utility is a construct, so too is any history about it. And since, in his history, utility was just the economist's name for another concept, "energy," that had originated elsewhere, we are back at the first-mentioned barrier to understanding. Historians had readily accepted that the adjective (as Terence Hutchison put it) was more revolutionary than the noun in the switch to marginal utility. Hence the introduction of the calculus had seemed a plausible adjunct to the strictly economic part of the marginal revolution tale. But again, such extradisciplinary borrowing is not innocent, in Mirowski's view; even mathematical concepts and techniques, being constructs, are necessarily more than neutral, and carry baggage from their original contexts. Seeing a connection between the concept of the marginal, and that of a first derivative, seems innocence itself once one is told that actually Laplace's dream and Hamiltonian determinism are being sneaked in. But if mathematics is not just a neutral language, this also puts in question the notion, shared by many economists and possibly not a few historians of economics, that progress in economics can be guaranteed, and possibly also measured, simply by our convergence in technique toward the "hard" sciences.

All those difficulties were apparent to readers of the chapters already in circulation. Once *More Heat* appeared, however, it was plain that the argument about energy and utility was the easy part to appropriate. The language of the book—not just "metaphor," but oddities like "lineamentric" and such devices as "the chrystalline trialectic" of page 107 (as Mirowski calls it in his comment in this volume)—as well as almost parenthetic invocations of Mary Douglas and of Durkheim and Mauss, and the contrasting major role given to the obscure Emil Meyerson, was bound to befuddle. Then too, the book was full of startling historical propositions, some intriguing but little more than working possibilities (industrial progress followed the path of dissemination of Italian bookkeeping methods), some very peculiar (Adam Smith disdained both peasant and farm). These have annoyed some historians. Finally, the tone of the book was not just critical but angry, and this struck some as unnecessary if not unseemly.

These difficulties and resistances have evoked strong reactions, many of them negative, possibly hiding a lot of uncertainty about how the book should be approached. They also extend to others of Mirowski's writings. One such reaction is illustrated by a comment in a recent review of Rita McWilliams Tullberg's edited collection *Alfred Marshall in Retrospect* (1990). The reviewer, Denis O'Brien, clearly felt affronted by Mirowski's essay "Smooth Operator: How Marshall's Demand and Supply Curves Made Neoclassicism Safe for Public Consumption but Unfit for Science." This is surely a title chosen to reassure the nervous and please all those who gathered to celebrate Marshall. O'Brien writes of this essay that it "can only be described as an extraordinary tirade . . . an account of nineteenth-century economics, garnished with references to nineteenth-century physics, neither of which I was able to recognize except in the sense that one can 'recognize' the image in fairground mirrors" (1991, 42). There is no doubt that in that essay, as in *More Heat*, Mirowski constructs, and deploys under the banner of a crusader, a battering ram on behalf of strict theoretical coherence, flattening whoever would seem to defend anything less, no matter their stature. O'Brien decided that, all in all, "it seems best to pass by without comment."

That might be an adequate response if Mirowski could be considered badly read or flippant in his approach to the written record and casual about the archival materials bearing on his themes, or if his critical standpoint could be dismissed as mere spleen. But none of those possible accusations would stick. If anything, their opposite is truer. That does not guarantee that his history is satisfactory—whatever that means— much less superior. But he is not arguing that his is the only, or the true interpretation; just that it bears thinking about. If the measures are the number of interesting questions formulated and provocative propositions adumbrated, or the freshness of the approach devised, he has to be taken very seriously.

It was in that vein that the conference was organized. Mirowski himself seems to have expected that the conference would turn up new historical studies that would test his theses and at the same time help transform into real people the rather disembodied and driven minds that populate his narrative. That seemed premature. There was still too much confusion as to what he was really about. The papers therefore are, for the most part, attempts to understand and assess the Mirowski enterprise. The historical studies he hoped for will certainly follow. The premise of the conference was that working through the implications of *More Heat* for constructing history will yield more in the long run than assuming that the enterprise itself is well understood and can be evaluated simply by checking particular points for "veracity." One of the unsettling things about *More Heat* is precisely that it requires a reconsideration of what historical veracity might be. The essays in this volume, then, are a set of early efforts to test, not what *More Heat than Light* has said, but what it might mean for making histories of economics.

Is such reflection really necessary? Yes, for the health of economics as a discipline. Because the number of our theories is not restricted by our data, and because our data are not so much givens as themselves matter for discussion, economics is never far from causal narrative. That point needs to be driven home again and again. And who is better fitted to do it than historians? Yes, for the health of history of economics. History of economics has lived too long in the shadow cast by one particular audience, our own economist colleagues. This has meant that what is selected to be examined, and the way it is treated, tend to be heavily weighted by what has become part of the modern economics canon—witness Mirowski's quote from Niehans's recent *History of Economic Thought* (1990) in his comment below. One of Philip Mirowski's most refreshing challenges is that he asks us whether we want to go on living in penumbral obscurity.

References

Mirowski, Philip. 1989. *More Heat than Light: Economics as Social Physics, Physics as Nature's Economics*. Cambridge: Cambridge University Press.

———. 1990. Smooth Operator: How Marshall's Demand and Supply Curves Made Neoclassicism Safe for Public Consumption but Unfit for Science. In Tullberg 1990.

Niehans, Jurg. 1990. *A History of Economic Thought*. Baltimore: The Johns Hopkins University Press.

O'Brien, Denis. 1991. Review of *Alfred Marshall in Retrospect* (Tullberg 1990). *Marshall Studies Bulletin* 1:41–45.

Tullberg, Rita McWilliams, ed. 1990. *Alfred Marshall in Retrospect*. Aldershot: Edward Elgar.

Part 1 Disciplinary History and the Use of Metaphor

Analogy, Homology, and Metaphor in the Interactions between the Natural Sciences and the Social Sciences, Especially Economics

I. Bernard Cohen

1. Some Historical Interactions between the Natural and the Social Sciences

The study of the interactions between the natural sciences and the social sciences has been a grossly neglected field of study.[1] Although many prominent social scientists—economists, sociologists, political scientists, historians, and others—have been making extensive use of one or several of the natural sciences ever since the seventeenth century, this feature of historical development is conspicuously absent from the historical record concerned with the social sciences. Of course, there are a few notable exceptions, among them the relations between neoclassical economics as it came into being in the late nineteenth century and rational mechanics plus energy physics (and also the interactions of other parts of economics with the natural sciences).[2] Some recent studies by historians of science interested in economics and other social sciences give hope that this particular part of the historical record may attract more serious attention from scholars.[3]

---

1. I use the term "natural sciences" to include the usual physical and biological sciences, plus the earth and atmospheric sciences and mathematics. In earlier presentations of my research I used the simple term "sciences" as an abbreviated version of "physical and biological sciences plus mathematics." This procedure aroused hostile criticism from sociologists, who claimed that to discuss the relations between the "sciences" and the "social sciences" introduced a pejorative tone concerning "social sciences," which were thus said to be not "sciences."

2. Examples are the works of Philip Mirowski, Roy Weintraub, Neil de Marchi, Claude Ménard, Arjo Klamer, and others who are represented in Cohen 1993d and also in a similar volume, edited by Mirowski, *Natural Images in Economics* (1993).

3. Among others whose work has been especially helpful are Theodore Porter, Timothy Alborn, Camille Limoges, Margaret Schabas, and Norton Wise.

For the historian of science, it is not surprising that the influence of the new science on the various social sciences began in the early days of the Scientific Revolution. A notable example from the early seventeenth century is the work of Hugo Grotius (or de Groot). In his correspondence with Galileo, Grotius expressed his admiration for the mathematical sciences of nature that Galileo had so notably advanced, and he declared himself to be a follower of Galileo's method. He conceived his celebrated treatise on international law, *De jure belli et pacis* (1625), in the spirit and manner of a work on geometry, that is, in the style of Galileo. This aspect of Grotius's presentation, however, is not even mentioned in the article on Grotius in either the older *Encyclopaedia of the Social Sciences* (1931) or the more recent *International Encyclopedia of the Social Sciences* (1968). A current reprint of the English version of Grotius's treatise even omits altogether the preface in which Grotius explicitly states that his model had been classical geometry. The question must then arise as to whether I am stressing an aspect of Grotius's thought that is not truly relevant, since historians of political science and of international law seem to have paid so little attention to it. In fact, this aspect of Grotius's treatise—that he conceived it in the style of Greek geometry—is a most significant feature, since it determined that he would deal with abstract cases rather than either the disputes of his own age or examples drawn from the historical record—an aspect of his presentation for which he has been roundly criticized over the centuries.

The situation is somewhat the same for James Harrington's politico-social thought, expressed in his *Oceana* (1656) and other writings. Harrington's ideas assumed significant proportions in the eighteenth century, when they influenced many of the American founding fathers and to some degree became embodied in the American Constitution. Although Harrington expressly founded his system on the basis of the new Harveian physiology, even making use of Harvey's studies of animal generation, and wrote of his work as a political anatomy, this feature is not even noted in one of the above-mentioned encyclopedias and is barely alluded to in the other. Historians of political and social theory have not critically scrutinized Harrington's political and social ideas from the point of view of their relation to the main scientific currents of his times.

The example of Leibniz is even more striking. Although as a young man Leibniz published an essay on a mathematical demonstration of a method for selecting a king for Poland, this work is not even mentioned in standard presentations of political thought. It is an index of the low state of studies of the interactions of the natural and the social sciences that there is not even a passing reference to this essay in a recent volume devoted to Leibniz's political writings (Riley 1972).

Even when the scientific component of social thought is introduced, as in the case of George Berkeley's Newtonian social thought, the significance is apt to be lost because of a lack of understanding of the precise nature of Newtonian natural philosophy. Thus Berkeley's perfectly correct presentation of the Newtonian explanation of planetary orbital motion—as a combination of a continual central accelerating force and an undiminished initial component of linear inertial motion along a tangent—is reduced to the incorrect form of a "balance" between centripetal and centrifugal forces (e.g., Sorokin 1928), a standard elementary textbook error that persisted into the early twentieth century and that essentially denies the significance of the Newtonian revolution in celestial dynamics.

2. Identity

In studying the interactions between the natural sciences and the social sciences, whether economics, political science, history, sociology, or any other, I find it helpful to distinguish four levels of interaction, with metaphor and identity at the extremes, and analogy and homology in an intermediate position.

Let me begin with identity: a belief that there is a relation of identity and not mere similarity between a social system and one from the natural sciences. An example would be a belief that the state is actually a machine or that society is actually an organism. An example of the latter is the sociology of Paul von Lilienfeld in the nineteenth century, based on the firm conviction that society is an organism, of which the human individuals are the cells. The title of the first volume of Lilienfeld's five-volume opus *Thoughts on the Social Science of the Future* (1873–81) boldly declared his thesis: *Human Society as a Real Organism.* In the opening of this work, Lilienfeld issued his challenge: "*Human society is, like natural organisms, a real being, is nothing more than a continuation of nature, is only a higher expression of the same forces that underlie all natural phenomena:* This is the argument, this is the thesis, which the author has set himself to accomplish and to prove" (1881, 5:v).

Lilienfeld's contemporary Herbert Spencer left his readers in no doubt concerning his own views on this subject. "What is a society?" he asked, in one of the opening chapters of his *Principles of Sociology* (1897). His unambiguous reply (given in the title of the next chapter) was, "an organism." Another nineteenth-century social thinker of the "identity" persuasion was Otto Bluntschli, who went to the extreme of endowing society and its institutions with sex.[4]

A similar kind of identity is found in beliefs that the social system or the economic system is a machine or is endowed with machine-like parts. Such a concept appears in the economic writings of François Quesnay of the physiocratic school of economic thought, even though his system of economics was based on an organismic model. That is, although Quesnay conceived that economic life is like the circulation of the bloodstream in humans and animals, he also introduced "wheels and pumps which push the mass of commodities from stage to stage" (Stark 1962, 170–71).

The reverse situation occurs when a natural scientist considers an organism to be a social entity. A primary instance of this line of thought occurs in the writings of Rudolf Virchow, the mid-nineteenth-century founder of the doctrine of "cellular pathology" (Ackerknecht 1953). Believing that every plant and animal is an aggregate of cells, which are the fundamental life-units, Virchow concluded that all structural and functional properties of organisms are determined by relations among individual cells. Thus, he wrote, "the composition of a larger body, the so-called individual, always amounts to some kind of social institution."[5] In referring to the cells as providing the "living organism" with a "multiplicity of vital foci," Virchow explained that every organism "is a free state of individuals with equal rights though not with equal endowments, which keeps together because the individuals are dependent upon one another and because there are certain centers of organization without whose integrity the single parts cannot receive their necessary supply of healthful nourishing material" (Temkin 1949, 167–94, esp. 175). This example shows that considerations of identity are not limited to social scientists but may arise in the thought of natural scientists.

---

4. Further information concerning Lilienfeld, Spencer, and Bluntschli in relation to the belief that society *is* an organism may be found in Cohen 1993d, ch. 1, esp. n. 149; Stark 1962; and Sorokin 1928.

5. Virchow, we may note, was not the only nineteenth-century biologist to use social institutions in scientific discourse. Thomas Henry Huxley used a social comparison in describing the sponge, which—he said—represents a kind of subaqueous city, "in which the people are arranged about the streets and roads, in such a manner, that each can easily appropriate his food from the water as it passes along."

3. Analogy and Homology

Most social scientists, however, have not taken the extreme position of identity. They usually have argued from analogy or homology or have made use of metaphor. The literature on the social sciences, both primary documents and secondary sources, does not customarily make use of all three of these terms, most historical exegeses dealing only with analogy and metaphor. These two terms—analogy and metaphor—are generally not carefully distinguished from each other and are even used in a confusing way as synonyms, while metaphor sometimes becomes the equivalent of model. I believe that the exact nature of the interactions between the natural sciences and the social sciences is masked by such a lack of clear distinction between analogy and metaphor and that it is frequently useful to keep separate the concepts of analogy and homology.

Let me begin with analogy and homology, reserving for last (sections 10 and 11) the question of metaphor. From the point of view of the dictionary, *analogy* may be used correctly for various kinds of similarity, but I have found it most useful to follow the lead of biological scientists and to use *analogy* for a similarity that depends primarily on relations of functions and to use *homology* for a similarity that depends primarily on structure.

Structure, as expressed in a homology, may range all the way from anatomical features to the form of equations and can even encompass concepts and laws. Structural comparisons in biology produce anatomical homologies. For example, the forearm of a human is a homologue of the foreleg of a horse and of a bat, and of the flipper of a seal and the wing of a bird, all of which exhibit the same structure. In the nineteenth century the economist and sociologist Henry Carey believed he had found a law which was a social homologue of the Newtonian law of universal gravity, that is, a law having the identical form as the Newtonian law. His ability to formulate this law depended on his invention or introduction of social concepts which would be homologues of Newton's three fundamental physical concepts: force, mass, and distance. Carey was depending on a fundamental axiom, that identically formal laws must occur in the universe of nature and in the social realms. He took as granted that the formal structure of relations between fundamental parameters must be exactly the same in celestial physics and in sociology (see Cohen 1993d and below).

When we shift our attention from homologies to analogies, however, we find that analogous parts may not necessarily be homologues.[6]

This usage is not strictly limited to the life sciences but has found application in the physical and earth sciences as well. For example, David Brewster wrote about "a property of sound which has its analogy also in light" (1843, 181). John Tyndall discussed the "analogy between a river and a glacier moving through a sinuous valley" (1861, 285). Using two sciences, John Lubbock Avery observed that there "seem to be three principal types" of ants, thus "offering a curious analogy to the three great phases" in "the history of human development": "the hunting, pastoral, and agricultural" (1879, 4:137).

On the plane of interaction between the social sciences and the natural sciences, a social analogue of Newton's law of universal gravity would be any law that performs the same organizing and explanatory functions for understanding social phenomena that the law of gravity does for terrestrial and celestial phenomena. An example would be the basic social law announced by the early nineteenth-century sociologist Charles Fourier (1971, 30). Fourier claimed that his law was the equivalent in sociology of Newton's law in physics, even though the form was in no way similar, much less identical. Here, then, is an example of a social analogue that is definitely not a homologue. Whereas Carey's law was put forth as an analogue of Newton's law that was also a homologue, Fourier's law was an analogue of Newton's law without being a homologue.

4. The Use of Analogies

Analogies constitute a primary instrument of interaction between the natural sciences and the social sciences.[7] These interactions are very much like the interactions between one branch of the natural sciences and another. Such interactions arise from a recognition that an idea, concept,

---

6. In Darwinian evolution, analogy is the result of parallel adaptation, the way in which different organisms in separate but parallel evolutionary stages have developed, independently of one another, different ways of "adapting themselves to the same external circumstances" or needs. An example is given by an organ of vision, in which a lens concentrates light on special sensitive tissue. Konrad Lorenz has noted that this "invention" has been made independently by animals of four different phyla, in two of which (the vertebrates and the cephalopods) this kind of "eye" has "evolved into the true image-projecting camera through which we ourselves are able to see the world."

7. Some important insights into the use of analogies are given in the writings of Claude Ménard (e.g., 1988), and especially the chapter by Ménard and Camille Limoges in Mirowski 1993.

law, theory, system of equations, method of investigation, mathematical tool, or any other element of one subject is similar in its function to some element in another and thus has properties enabling it to be introduced usefully into that other subject. Analogy has always had the important role of being a tool of discovery, that is, of reducing a problem to another that has already been solved, or of introducing some element or elements that have proved their worth in a quite different area of knowledge. Jeremy Bentham once said that hints from analogies constituted one of the most important tools available for scientific discovery (Mack 1962, 275–81).

Another traditional use of analogy is to provide a source of justification for a novel or radical method or theory. An example would be to defend the introduction of higher mathematics (e.g., the calculus) into economics on the analogy that the calculus had been used successfully in rational mechanics.

Yet another use of analogy is to make a difficult or strange idea seem reasonable and hence acceptable to the scientific community or to help in explaining an abstruse concept, as in all general presentations of relativity theory. For example, Sigmund Freud was hesitant in presenting in full one of his radical and difficult concepts (introduced only as a "suspicion" in 1900 in his *Interpretation of Dreams*), that human beings have two different memory systems, one of which "receives perceptions but retains no permanent trace of them," while the other preserves these "traces of the excitations" in " 'mnemic systems' lying behind the perceptual system" (Freud 1953–74, 19:228).[8] In 1926, emboldened by his encounter with a mechanical device called the "Mystic Writing-Pad," which seemed to simulate the main features of his concept, Freud described his ideas about human memory in full, suggesting that this writing pad could be considered an analogue of his "hypothetical structure of our perceptual apparatus."[9] Analogy was always an important part of Freud's thinking. Best known of Freud's analogues are those he drew from literature, notably Greek tragedies, in formulating and describing (and even naming) concepts. Freud was consciously aware that

---

8. When he wrote *Beyond the Pleasure Principle* (1920), Freud understood more clearly (as he phrased it in 1924) that "the inexplicable phenomenon of consciousness arises in the perceptual system *instead of* the permanent traces" (Freud 1953–74, 19:228). See also 5:540, 18:25. In the latter, Freud notes that this distinction had already been made by Breuer.

9. This mechanical analogue served two functions often found in the use of analogues: (1) to make his earlier hypothetical conjecture seem reasonable enough for him to set forth his ideas in full, and (2) to make his difficult concept of the structure of memory understandable and thus acceptable to the psychoanalytic community.

in his cultural and anthropological studies—e.g., *Totem and Taboo* and *Moses and Monotheism*—"we are only dealing with analogies," and he fully recognized how dangerous it is, "not only with men but also with concepts, to tear them from the sphere in which they have originated and been evolved" (Freud 1953–74, 21:144). It was by invoking an analogy that Freud "likened religion to a collective obsessional neurosis, or allowed that Hamlet suffered unduly from an Oedipus complex" (Kaplan 1988, 260).

Analogies also serve science in exhibiting the validity of a conclusion that seems untestable. In discussing the stability of the solar system in his *Système du monde*, Laplace had to argue that certain observed variations are not secular but periodic; they seem to be secular only because they have a period extending over millions of years. Laplace showed that the system of Jupiter's satellites is a dynamical analogue of the solar system, the satellites displaying in their motions the same perturbations as the planets. Since the satellites exhibit all the phases of their mutual gravitational perturbations within a few centuries, the periodic nature of the oscillations can be verified, thus making it likely by analogy that the similar variations in the planetary motions are also periodic (Jevons [1887] 1958, 638; based on Laplace's *System of the World*).

Both Charles Darwin and his contemporary James Clerk Maxwell made eloquent use of analogies. Darwin's basic concept of a "struggle for existence" was presented in his *Origin of Species* (1849) on the basis of analogy with Malthus's principles of population. Malthus's two laws dealt only with human populations, for which an unchecked population would naturally increase in an exponential ratio, while the available food supply could be increased by human intervention only in an arithmetic ratio. By analogy Darwin inferred that all populations of organic beings—human, animal, plant—would naturally increase exponentially so that—as he wrote—"more individuals are produced than can possibly survive," with the result that "there must be a struggle for existence." The analogy, Darwin noted, was not exact since in the plant and animal world, unlike the human world of agriculture, "there can be no artificial increase in food." Nor in the plant and animal world is there exercised that "prudential restraint from marriage" which Malthus found to exert a moral rein on human population growth (Darwin 1964, ch. 10, 63).[10]

---

10. Darwin drew on the argument from analogy in other parts of *Origin*. The concept of natural selection was introduced in analogy with man's process of "artificial" selection in

This example embodies the use of analogy rather than generalization, since the latter is an extension of some property to more individuals of the same kind, whereas analogy is the attribution of some property to something that is similar.

Maxwell not only made extensive use of analogies but wrote eloquently about their role in science. His discussions of analogy remain today perhaps the best introduction to this subject (Nagel 1961, 107–17). One example of his use of analogies occurred in relation to the theory of heat. The "laws of the conduction of heat in uniform media, he wrote, "appear at first sight among the most different in their physical relations from those relating to attractions." Even so, he concluded, we "have only to substitute *source of heat* for *centre of attraction, flow of heat* for *accelerating effect of attractions* at any point, and *temperature* for *potential*," and the result is that "the solution of a problem in attractions is transformed into that of a problem of heat." So very exact is this analogy that "if we knew nothing more than is expressed in the mathematical formulae, there would be nothing to distinguish between the one set of phenomena and the other"—despite the fact that the conduction of heat "is supposed to proceed by an action between contiguous parts of a medium, while the force of attraction is a relation between distant bodies" (Maxwell [1890] 1965, 1:156). We should take note that once Maxwell had justified his method, he proceeded to use it in elaborating a mathematical theory of "lines of force" (in Faraday's sense) by making use of an analogy with the "mathematical formalism" of the motion of an incompressible and imponderable fluid.[11]

---

breeding pigeons, horses, dogs, and various ornamental and useful plants. A classic use of analogy, as opposed to generalization, occurs in the final chapter of *Origin*, in Darwin's presentation of the theory of common descent. He first concluded that all animals had "descended from at most only four or five progenitors, and plants from an equal or lesser number." This led him to remark, "Analogy would lead me one step further, namely, to the belief that all animals and plants have descended from one prototype." He was aware, as he wrote, that "analogy may be a deceitful guide." Yet he found the evidence for common descent to be very persuasive, noting that "all living things have much in common, in their chemical composition, their germinal vesicles, their cellular structure, and their laws of growth and reproduction." This evidence justified his inference "from analogy that probably all the organic beings that have ever lived on this earth have descended from one primordial form, into which life was first breathed."

11. This was the occasion for Maxwell to make what may be considered the classic statement about the use of what he called "physical analogies" in science. According to Maxwell, "physical analogies" provide a means "to obtain physical ideas without adopting a physical theory." Ernest Nagel (1961, 109) has explained that Maxwell meant that he could obtain

5. The Use of Analogies and Homologies in the Social Sciences, Especially Economics

Two primary areas of nineteenth-century natural science which have provided analogies for the social sciences are mathematical physics (notably the new rational mechanics plus energy physics), which had a profound influence on economics, and the cell theory (and related aspects of the life sciences), which gave new form as well as content to theories of social morphology and behavior. These two subject areas illustrate very different aspects of the ways in which social sciences draw on the natural sciences.

Philip Mirowski has shown how rational mechanics plus energy physics provided a rich source of conceptual homologues for a rising marginalist (or neoclassical) economics, together with analytical tools such as Lagrangian virtual displacements and Hamiltonian functions, even analogous equations and principles of minimization and maximization. Additionally he has observed that while producing a social science with an external appearance of physics, the founders of neoclassical economics wholeheartedly adopted the "metaphor" of mathematical physics, clearly hoping to give the social science of economics a legitimation (especially in the opinion of natural scientists) and some measure of the value system of "hard" science (see sections 10 and 11 below). Economists of this school have continued to draw on a body of knowledge well-established by the end of the nineteenth century. Apparently they have not been under the necessity of encompassing within their theoretical structures any later developments such as quantum physics or relativity. An outsider may well be astonished that neoclassical or post-neoclassical economics displays so little effect of all the later, dramatic revolutions in the very subjects—rational mechanics and energy physics—that provided its principal analogies and metaphors. For example, there seems to have been no effect on economics of today's radical conclusion that the conservation of energy can no longer be considered an independently true principle or that energy itself is no longer believed to be subject to continuous variation but acts in quantized steps. Perhaps this paradox is to be explained by the conclusion of Mirowski

---

physical ideas without invoking a "theory formulated in terms of some particular model of physical processes." In other words, by "physical analogies" he implied no more than "that partial similarity between the laws of one science and those of another which makes each of them illustrate the other."

and other critics of neoclassical economics that the energy metaphor was only imperfectly understood by the founders, who apparently were not aware that their adopted energy model was flawed because they did not take account of the conservation law.

Ernest Nagel (1961, ch. 6, section 1), using a terminology that is somewhat different from that used above, has divided analogies into two classes: "formal" and "substantive." A substantive analogy is one in which a theory or a system is constructed on the model of another system which contains known laws (1961, 107–17). Examples are the kinetic theory of gases (patterned on the known laws of the interaction of elastic spheres such as billiard balls), electron theory (in which the analogy is with macroscopic electrostatically charged bodies), and atomic structure (where the model is the solar system). A formal analogy is based on a structure of abstract relationships rather than a "more or less visualizable set of elements." Neoclassical economics illustrates the use of such formal analogies.

This kind of example in economics, however, goes far beyond a mere creative transfer of concepts and principles, mathematical expressions, and other tools of the arsenal of mathematical physics. Economics, and to some degree the other social sciences, may illustrate the fundamental manner in which analogy may lead an investigator to identify some region (or regions) of one discipline that is undeveloped and for which an important key is furnished by the "corresponding truths" in some other discipline (Jevons [1887] 1958, 631). This proposition becomes more universally valid when we extend Jevons's "corresponding truths" to include successful methods and formal techniques (e.g., equations).

To an outsider, economics and mathematical physics seem at first sight to be extremely different. Economics deals with such human and moral or ethical factors as greed, profit, cost, value, utility, need, and good, which do not seem susceptible of universal definition and which therefore appear to be wholly different from such abstract concepts of physics as force, field, distance, speed, and kinetic and potential energy, which seem to lend themselves "naturally" to mathematical treatment. But analogies between very different subjects are not unusual in the history of science: "No two sciences might seem at first sight more different in their subject matter than geometry and algebra," Jevons once wrote, since one deals with "forms in space (circles, squares, triangles, parallelograms, . . .) and the other with abstract symbols and number" (1958, 631). Yet as Jevons pointed out, a crucial step in the development of modern mathematics was the recognition of analogies between these two branches of mathematics. He described Descartes's great breakthrough as a demonstration of a "most general kind": that equations may be represented by curves or figures in space, and vice versa, and "that every bend, point, cusp or other peculiarity in the curve indicates some peculiarity in the equation." Jevons found it "impossible to describe in any adequate manner the importance of this discovery" (632). This kind of analogy occurs frequently in the social sciences, notably in economics. In his *Theory of Political Economy* (1911) Jevons took note of the "objections made to the general character of the [differential] equations" he had employed, defending his position by making an analogy between economics and physics, declaring that economics is similar to physics insofar as "the equations employed do not differ in general character from those which are really treated in many branches of physical science." [12] The example he chose to develop was the use of the principle of virtual velocities (or virtual displacements) applied to the lever, where there is a homology of equations; that is, the equations for the case of the lever "have exactly the form of the equations of exchange [in economics]" ([1911] 1965, 105). He even introduced a diagram in order to "put this analogy of the theories of exchange and of the lever in the clearest possible light."

The same kind of likeness of theories was invoked by Léon Walras in his "Economique et mécanique" (1909), where he argued that identical differential equations appear in his analysis of economics and in two examples from mathematical physics: the equilibrium of a lever and the motion of planets according to gravitational celestial mechanics (see also Mirowski and Cook 1990).[13] Here we see yet another instance of the exactness of homology set forth by Maxwell with respect to theory of heat.

---

12. It has even been suggested, by Jevons ([1887] 1958, 633) on the authority of Lacroix, that "the discovery of the Differential calculus was mainly due to geometrical analogy, because mathematicians, in attempting to treat algebraically the tangent of a curve, were obliged to entertain the notion of infinitely small quantities."

13. Francis Ysidro Edgeworth (1881, 9, 12) proposed the same kind of analogy between his "mathematical psychics" (as he called his brand of economics) and mathematical physics, declaring that "every psychical phenomenon is the concomitant, and in some sense the other side of a physical phenomenon." He had no doubt that " 'Mécanique Sociale' may one day take her place along with 'Mécanique Céleste,' throned each upon the double-sided height of one maximum principle, the supreme pinnacle of moral as of physical science."

6. The Use of Analogies and Homologies by Pareto, Fisher, and Marshall

Vilfredo Pareto, writing as an economist, invoked what I would call an exact homology in the example of "the equations which determine [economic] equilibrium." On seeing these equations, he wrote, a writer trained in mathematical physics (as he was) would observe: "These equations do not seem new to me; I know them well, they are old friends. They are the equations of rational mechanics." Because the equations are the same, he concluded, "pure economics is a sort of mechanics or akin to mechanics" (Pareto 1953, 3:185).[14]

Pareto envisioned a double role for mathematics in economics and in social science in general. Mathematics provides a means of analogically transferring the basic equations of physics to economics. Mathematics also provides a primary tool to deal with such problems as the "mutual dependence of social phenomena" in conditions of equilibrium; here mathematical analysis enables us to make precise "how the variations of any one of these [conditions] influence the others," an assignment in which "we really need to have *all* the conditions of the equilibrium." In the "existing state of our knowledge," he remarked, only mathematical analysis can "tell us if this requirement is observed" ([1898] 1966, 103–5).

This led Pareto to some remarks on the proper role of analogies and the dangers of using them in social science. Since "the human intellect proceeds from the known to the unknown," he wrote, we can make progress in our thinking by basing our ideas of an area in the "unknown" on analogies drawn from an area of the "known." For example, "extensive knowledge of the equilibrium of a material system" helps us to "gain a conception of economic equilibrium," and this in turn "can help us to form an idea of social equilibrium" ([1898] 1966, 103–5).[15] He warned, however, that in "such reasoning by analogy there is . . . a pitfall to be avoided." That is, the use of analogies "is legitimate, and perhaps highly useful, as long as what is involved is only the elucidation of the sense of a given proposition." We are led into grave errors, how-

---

14. For a discussion of Pareto's point of view see Mirowski, *MHL*, 221–22; Ingrao 1991, 1993.

15. This text is selected from Pareto's *Cours d'économie politique* (1898) 2: sections 580, 588–90.

ever, if we try to use analogies to prove a proposition or even "establish a presumption in its favor." Analogies, he added, serve—in addition to guiding research and discovery—primarily to clarify the meaning of propositions.

Here we have an example that proves the thesis of Mirowski's *More Heat than Light*, that Jevons—and such other leading architects of the marginalist revolution—based their economics on the mathematics of a post-Newtonian rational mechanics (i.e., incorporating principles of Lagrange and Laplace plus the methods of Hamilton) combined with the doctrines of energy. Jevons and other founders of the marginalist revolution believed firmly in the homology of their concepts in economics and the concepts found in physics, a factor which was bound up with the fundamental axiom that the laws of one could be directly translated into the other. Jevons, for example, stated *expressis verbis* that the "notion of value is to our science what that of energy is to mechanics." He even adopted directly from Maxwell the technique of dimensional analysis (M,L,T) and showed that "the *dimensions of commodity*, regarded merely as a physical quantity, will be *the dimensions of mass*" ([1911] 1965, 65). The homology extended ultimately to Newton's law of gravity: Jevons declared that "utility is an attraction between a wanted being and what is wanted" and is "just" like "the gravitating force of a material body" (Jevons 1981, 80). In a similar vein, Léon Walras wrote in his *Elements of Pure Economics* (1954) that "the pure science of economics is a science which resembles the physico-mathematical sciences in every respect."[16]

Pareto was fully convinced that the "equilibrium of an economic system offers striking similarities with that of a mechanical system," but he was also aware that there are special pitfalls for those who study political economy without "a knowledge of pure mechanics" ([1898] 1966, 105). Firm in his conviction that an analysis of a mechanical system is of the greatest help in giving "a clear idea of the equilibrium of an economic system," he drew up a table for "those who have not studied pure mechanics" and who would need help in understanding the argument. In this table (see figure 1) he placed in parallel columns some major concepts and principles of physical mechanics and their counterparts in economics. He warned, however, that in making such a table of "analogies

---

16. Similar sentiments were expressed by Edgeworth (1881); for details see Cohen 1993d, ch. 1.

existing between mechanical and social phenomena," the "analogies do not prove anything: they simply serve to elucidate certain concepts which must then be submitted to the criterion of experience" (104).

Another example of the extreme homology between economics and rational mechanics is found in Irving Fisher's *Mathematical Investigations into the Theory of Value and Prices* (1926). It should be noted that Fisher was rather well trained in mathematics and physics (as Jevons and Walras were not), having been one of the small group of students who worked for their Ph.D.'s under J. Willard Gibbs. In the style of Pareto, with whom he was in correspondence, Fisher also drew up a complete set of homologies from physical mechanics and economics. Fisher's table, however, goes beyond Pareto's to the degree that it is not limited to conceptual homologue pairs (a particle and an individual; space and commodity; energy and utility) but is extended to general principles and even includes the property of concepts being scalars or vectors.

Mirowski found, however, that despite Fisher's parade of dynamical analogies and homologies, he apparently took "most of his analogies . . . from hydrostatics rather than from fields of force" (*MHL*, 229). Mirowski notes that in his (unpublished) essay "My Economic Endeavors" Fisher boasted of having pioneered in "hydrostatic and other mechanical analogies." Mirowski presents a critique of Fisher's table, beginning with the "incorrect" identification "of a particle with an individual." Like other "neoclassical economists," Fisher—according to Mirowski—made a serious blunder in not appreciating the principle of conservation of energy, which would imply for an economic system that "the sum of total expenditure and the sum of total utility in a closed trading system must be equal to a constant."[17] The general failure to carry the physical analogy to its full logical conclusion—that is, to take cognizance of the conservation law—may now be seen to be a fundamental fault that comes from an incomplete understanding of the physics metaphor of energy and field that lies at the very foundation of neoclassical economics.

One of the difficulties in using analogies, particularly in the social sciences, is that there may be more than one analogy for the same problem. The problem of multiple analogies, along with the concomitant need for a decision concerning which one to choose, has long plagued the social

---

17. On Fisher's manuscript, preserved in the Sterling Library, Yale University, see Mirowski (*MHL*, 228–29, 409n.).

Mechanical Phenomena	Social Phenomena
Given a certain number of material bodies, the relationships of equilibrium and movement between them are studied, any other properties being excluded from consideration. This gives us a study termed *mechanics*.	Given a society, the relationships created amongst human beings by the production and exchange of wealth are studied, any other properties being excluded from consideration. This gives us a study termed *political economy*.
This science of mechanics is divisible into two others:	This science of political economy is divisible into two others:
1. The study of material points and inextensible connections leads to the formulation of a pure science—rational pure mechanics, which makes an abstract study of the equilibrium of forces and motion.	1. The study of *homo economicus*, of man considered solely in the context of economic forces, leads to the formulation of pure political economy, which makes an abstract study of the manifestations of ophelimity.
Its easiest part is the science of equilibrium. D'Alembert's principle enables dynamics to be reduced to a problem of statics.	The only part we are beginning to understand clearly is that dealing with equilibrium. A principle similar to D'Alembert's is applicable to economic systems; but the state of our knowledge on this subject is still very imperfect. Nevertheless, the theory of economic crises provides an example of the study of economic dynamics.
2. Pure mechanics is followed by applied mechanics which approaches a little more closely to reality in its consideration of elastic bodies, extensible connections, friction, etc.	2. Pure political economy is followed by applied political economy which is not concerned exclusively with *homo economicus*, but also considers other human states which approach closer to real man.
Real bodies have properties other than mechanical. Physics studies the properties of light, electricity and heat. Chemistry studies other properties. Thermodynamics, thermochemistry and the like sciences are concerned specifically with certain categories of properties. These sciences all constitute the physico-chemical sciences.	Men have further characteristics which are the object of study for special sciences, such as the sciences of law, religion, ethics, intellectual development, esthetics, social organisation, and so on. Some of these sciences are in an appreciably advanced state; others are extremely backward. Taken together they constitute the social sciences.
Real bodies with only pure mechanical properties do not exist.	Real men governed only by motives of pure economics do not exist.

Exactly the same error is committed *either* by supposing that in concrete phenomena there exist solely mechanical forces (excluding, for example, chemical forces), *or* by imagining, on the other hand, that a concrete phenomenon can be immune from the laws of pure mechanics.	Exactly the same error is committed *either* by supposing that in concrete phenomena there exist solely economic motives (excluding, for example, moral forces), *or* by imagining, on the other hand, that a concrete phenomenon can be immune from the laws of pure political economy.
The difference between practice and theory arises precisely from the fact that practice has to take account of a mass of details which theory does not deal with. The relative importance of primary and secondary phenomena will differ according to whether the viewpoint is that of science or of a practical operation. From time to time, attempts are made to synthesise all the phenomena. For example, it is held that all phenomena can be ascribed to:	
The attraction of atoms. The attempt has been made to reduce to unity all physical and chemical forces.	Utility, of which ophelimity is only a type. The attempt has been made to find the explanation of all phenomena in *evolution*.

Figure 1 Pareto's table of parallels between elements of mechanics and economics

Reprinted from Pareto 1966, 106–7 (originally in French, Pareto 1898, 2: section 592).

sciences. It arose in a dramatic fashion in 1898 in Alfred Marshall's discussion of "mechanical and biological analogies in economics" (Pigou 1925, 312–18).[18] After a discussion of dynamics and statics in relation to economics, Marshall—who was well trained in physics and mathematics—expressed deep skepticism about the analogy with physics. He concluded that while there is "a fairly close analogy between the earlier stages of economic reasoning and the devices of physical statics," there is not "an equally serviceable analogy between the later stages of economic reasoning and the methods of physical dynamics" (Pigou 1925, 214). At the later stages, he argued, "better analogies are to be got from biology than from physics." Accordingly, "economic reasoning should start on methods analogous to those of physical statics, and should gradually become more biological in tone." This need for shifting analo-

---

18. This was part of Marshall's article "Distribution and Exchange" in the *Economic Journal* for March 1898.

gies was apparently very important for Marshall. Analogies, he wrote, "may help one into the saddle, but are encumbrances on a long journey" (Pigou 1925, 214). That is, it is "well to know when to introduce them, it is even better to know when to stop them off." Another way of expressing this philosophy is that "in the later stages of economics, when we are approaching nearly to the conditions of life, biological analogies are to be preferred to mechanical" (Marshall 1885, 13–14; Pigou 1925, 154).[19] On the title page of Marshall's *Principles of Economics* there is a biological apothegm taken directly from Darwin's *Origin of Species*: "Natura non facit saltum."[20]

The great achievements in physics in the nineteenth century, followed by the dramatic revolutions that occurred in the early years of the twentieth century, have often tended to obscure the fact that in the late nineteenth century there was a general cognizance of great achievements in the biological sciences and extraordinary progress in medicine. One result was a vigorous school of social thought based on an exact analogy with the life sciences (Cohen 1993d). A number of social scientists came to believe that a new great age of biology was taking the place of the older great age of physics. This point of view was expressed dramatically by Marshall in his inaugural lecture in Cambridge University in 1885. At "the beginning of the nineteenth century," he said, "the mathematico-physical group of sciences was in the ascendant." But now, at last, "the speculations of biology [have] made a great stride forwards." The discoveries in biology, he continued, now attract "the attention of all men as those of physics had done in earlier years." The result was that the "moral and historical sciences of the day have . . . changed their tone, and Economics has shared in the general movement" (Marshall 1885, 12–14; Pigou 1925, 154).

7. The Problem of Mismatched Homology

In the middle of the nineteenth century the French economist Léon Walras and the American economist and sociologist Henry C. Carey proposed laws which can be considered analogues of Newton's to the degree to which both were intended to serve the same basic function in

---

19. Developments in the natural sciences themselves are also relevant; cf. Marshall's lecture of 1885, cited in the following paragraph.

20. On Marshall's use of biological analogies see the chapter by Camille Limoges and Claude Ménard in Mirowski 1993; see also Niman 1991.

sociology or economics that Newton's law serves in rational mechanics and celestial dynamics. Carey's law was presented as a kind of corollary to a general principle of social gravitation: "Man tends of necessity to gravitate towards his fellow-man." His corollary is that "the greater the number [of men] collected in a given space the greater is the attractive force there exerted" (Carey 1858, 1:42–43). Like Newton's law, Carey's expresses a property of "attractive force." Carey's force, considered in terms of the number of men in two places, appears to be formally equivalent to Newton's force as directly proportional to two masses. That is, a force is posited as proportional to a product of two variables, so that there is a homology between the two laws. In Carey's social law, however, the force varies inversely with distance, whereas in Newton's physical law the force varies inversely with the square of the distance.[21] The two laws do not, therefore, have the same form; there is not a perfect fit. I have called this kind of failure in homology the "problem of mismatched homology" in imitation of Alfred North Whitehead's concept of the fallacy of misplaced concreteness (Whitehead 1931, ch. 4, pp. 82, 85).[22]

21. Carey's exact words are "Gravitation is here, as everywhere else in the material world, in the direct ratio of the mass, and in the inverse one of the distance." Later (1860, 3: ch. 55, p. 466), when he recapitulates his physics and social science, he begins by stating "simple laws which govern matter in all its forms, and which are common to physical and social science." The first of these reads: "All particles of matter gravitate towards each other—the attraction being in the direct ratio of the mass, and the inverse one of the distance." Incidentally, it may be observed that Carey also misunderstood the Newtonian explanation of orbital or curved motion, under the action of a centripetal force, such as a planet moving under the action of the sun's gravity plus its own component of inertia. Carey says: "All matter is subjected to the action of the centripetal and the centrifugal forces—the one tending to the production of local centres of action, the other to the destruction of such centres, and the production of a great central mass, obedient to but a single law." We may take note that Carey also introduced ratios other than direct and inverse proportion. Thus, he wrote, "the motion of society, and the power of man, tend to increase in a geometrical ratio" (1858, 1:389).

22. Although "fallacy" is often used in a narrow technical sense to denote a flaw (or type of flaw) that "vitiates a syllogism," a primary meaning in every dictionary I have consulted (*OED*, its supplement, and its 2d ed.; *The Concise Oxford Dictionary*; and *Webster's New International*, 2d and 3d eds.) is a misleading argument or a delusion or error, or some unsoundness or delusiveness or disappointing character of an argument or belief. *The American Heritage Dictionary* gives, as the first meaning, "An idea or opinion founded on mistaken logic or perception; a false notion"; other meanings include "the quality of being deceptive" and "incorrectness of reasoning or belief." The only example given is a "romantic fallacy, that Shakespeare was superhuman." This example displays features in common with two frequently encountered uses of "fallacy" today: John Ruskin's notion of the "pathetic fallacy" (in which inanimate objects are supposed to have human emotions) and W. K. Wimsatt and Monroe Beardsley's "intentional fallacy" (overstressing the author's intentions in assessing a literary work). These usages are somewhat similar to Whitehead's "fallacy of misplaced concreteness."

Fowler (*Modern English Usage*) inveighs against using "fallacy" and "fallacious" as mere

In Carey's law, furthermore, the number of men is but a poor homologue for Newtonian mass. The salient characteristic of Newtonian or classical physics, the concept of mass was invented by Newton himself. Newtonian mass is an invariant property of any body or sample of matter; it does not change when the body is heated or chilled, bent or twisted, stretched or compressed, or transplanted to another location—whether another spot on earth or some place out in space or even on the moon or on another planet. In this feature mass differs from a local property such as weight, which varies with latitude on earth and also with transplantation to the moon or to another planet.[23] Although Carey's concept fails as a homologue of Newton's mass, it does have the same function in his law that Newton's concept has in the law of universal gravity, that is, it shows society functioning in a way that is similar to the way in which Newton shows matter functioning. In short, the two concepts are used analogously even though they are not homologous.

Let me now turn to Walras's law. Early in his career, in 1860, Walras wrote a short work, "The Application of Mathematics to Political Economy," in which he essayed a Newtonian law of economics: that "the price of things is in inverse ratio to the quantity offered and in direct ratio to the quantity demanded" (see Jaffé 1973, 115–39). This law may be considered an analogue of the Newtonian law of gravity in the sense that it would have the same important role in market theory that the Newtonian law has for the theory of planetary motion, that is, it shows commercial objects functioning in a way similar to the way in which Newton shows matter functioning. But even if the two laws are analogues

---

"long variants" of "falsehood" and "false." Though he illustrates various types of fallacy in logic, Fowler is silent on other (and acceptable) uses. This deficiency is repaired in Nicholson's American revision, which goes beyond Fowler's discussion of "fallacy in logic" by observing that, additionally, "fallacious" (and, by implication, "fallacy") can be used legitimately for "misleading," "disappointing, delusive"—as in "fallacious hopes" or "a fallacious peace." The *Encyclopedia of Philosophy* divides fallacies into three classes: fallacies in the strict sense (formal or logical fallacies), fallacies in nondeductive reasoning and in observation, and fallacies in discourse.

23. This concept of mass has two separate aspects: one (inertial mass in post-Einstein terminology) is a measure of a body's resistance to being accelerated or being made to undergo a change in "state"; the other (gravitational mass) is a measure of a body's response to a given gravitational field (i.e., the weight). For details see Cohen 1980. Newton described some experiments (using "gold, silver, lead, glass, sand, common salt, wood, water, and wheat") in book 3, prop. 6, of the *Principia*. He did not, of course, use such terms as "gravitational mass" or "inertial mass" but rather proved that for all such materials the ratio of the "weight" to "quantity of matter" (or mass) was the same.

in the sense of being functionally equivalent, they are not genuine homologues. The failure of homology has two factors. First of all, Walras's law depends on a simple inverse ratio (the price is inversely proportional to the quantity offered), whereas Newton's law invokes the ratio of the inverse square (the force is inversely proportional to the square of the distance). Second, Walras's law involves a direct proportion of a single quantity or parameter (quantity demanded), whereas Newton's law uses the direct proportion of two quantities (the masses). Furthermore, Walras's law posits a price that is proportional to a "quantity" divided by another "quantity" of the same kind or dimensionality, that is, to a dimensionless quotient or pure numerical ratio. Clearly, whatever other characteristics this law has, it fails because it exemplifies mismatched homology (Mirowski and Cook 1990, 189–224).

Mismatched homology is a characteristic feature of another current of social thought of the nineteenth century and its twentieth-century overtones, the attempts to produce organismic depictions of society. This feature occurs in the writings of such diverse authors as Thomas Carlyle, Johann Caspar Bluntschli, Paul von Lilienfeld, Albert E. Schäffle, René Worms, A. Lawrence Lowell, Theodore Roosevelt, Herbert Spencer, and Walter B. Cannon (see, e.g., Roosevelt 1910 and 1926, 12:25–60; Lowell 1937, 119–32; and discussion below). It appears as a prominent feature in Thomas Carlyle's analysis of the problems of society in *Sartor Resartus* (1836). An example is provided by his discussion of the social analogy of the skin:

> For if Government is, so to speak, the outward SKIN of the Body Politic, holding the whole together and protecting it; and all your Craft-Guilds, and Associations for Industry, of hand or of head, are the Fleshly Clothes, the muscular and osseous Tissues (lying *under* such SKIN), whereby Society stands and works;—then is Religion the inmost Pericardial and Nervous Tissue, which ministers Life and warm Circulation to the whole. Without which Pericardial Tissue the Bones and Muscles (of Industry) were inert, or animated only by a Galvanic vitality; the SKIN would become a shrivelled pelt, or fast-rotting raw-hide; and Society itself a dead carcass,—deserving to be buried. ([1836] 1969, 1:172; see also Roe 1921; Hale 1971, 134–35)

Carlyle seems to have been obsessed with such organismic comparisons drawn from the realms of anatomy and medicine. For him, England was "in sick discontent," writhing "powerless on its fever bed," and the evils of his contemporary world were a kind of "Social Gangrene" ([1843] 1969, 10:137, 29:129).

A similar extravagance occurs in the organismic conception of society proposed by the Russian sociologist Paul von Lilienfeld in a comparison between the intellectual and moral state of a hysterical woman and a condition of society.[24] According to Lilienfeld, women suffering from hysteria are "mobile in their sentiments," and "they pass very easily from tears to laughter, from excessive joy to sadness, from passionate tenderness to haughty rage, from chastity to wanton purposes and lewd ideas." Such women "love publicity, and to get themselves talked about they employ every means: denunciation, simulation of infirmities or sicknesses, and the revolver." They find joy in pretending to be "victims of anything; they say they have been violated." In order to "achieve their goals they deceive everyone: husband, family, confessor, examining magistrate, and their doctor" (1896, 59).

The reader who is uninitiated in the literature of organismic sociology may wonder what social manifestations could possibly present similar symptoms. Lilienfeld develops the comparison by presenting a series of correspondences which clearly must be characterized as homologues even if he himself refers to analogy. He begins by observing that the symptomatic behavior of women suffering from hysteria is "perfectly analogous to the manner in which the population of a large city behaves during a financial crisis or on the occasion of civil disturbances." He finds in the behavior of such women "a faithful picture of the agitation of parties during elections." And when we consider the past, he asks (59–60), do we not find the same confused and disordered pattern of behavior, "caused by convulsive and contradictory reflexes of the social nervous system," during "all the religious, economic, and political revolutions with which humanity has been assailed?" This complex nesting of mismatched homologies needs no comment.

Further examples of mismatched homology from two very different authors, one from the nineteenth and one from the twentieth century, speak loudly for themselves in illustration of the excesses which are typical of this pitfall. The first author, Herbert Spencer, was a self-educated sociologist or philosopher who absorbed the language of science and

---

24. On Lilienfeld's life and career see Becker 1933. As most people are aware (because of the interest Sigmund Freud and Josef Breuer had in the subject), hysteria was of major psychiatric interest in the nineteenth century. As physiological foundation for his comparisons, Lilienfeld used (and quoted) the work of Dr. Edmond Dupouy (ca. 1845–1920).

used his knowledge of science in constructing his systems of psychology and sociology; the second, Walter Bradford Cannon, was an eminent scientist who, on several occasions, dabbled in sociology. Spencer seems to have indulged in analogies and homologies to a degree that might cause a late-twentieth-century reader to wonder how his writings could ever have gained the enormous popular appeal that history records.[25]

A favorite target for Spencer's critics has been his correlation of "internuncial agencies" in animals and in societies. He compared the "lowest races," such as the Bushmen, to the protozoa, which he described in great detail, as if he had been writing a textbook of elementary biology. Just as in one there is "nothing beyond an undifferentiated group of individuals, forming the germ of a society," he wrote (Spencer 1897, 2: para. 221), so in the other (a "homogeneous group of cells") there is only "the initial stage of animal and vegetable organization." From protozoa Spencer turned to polyps, which he again described at great length, declaring a parallel between them and "the majority of aboriginal tribes." Next came the hydra, similarly treated and then presented as compared with peoples who break off into splinter groups when the population becomes too great for the original territory. This led him to descriptions of more complex marine animals and their parallels in more advanced social organization.[26] The limit of mismatched homology may have been reached when Spencer elsewhere referred to the two great national schools of France—the Ecole Normale and the Ecole Polytechnique—as "a double gland" intended "to secrete engineering faculty for public use" (1896, 3:427–28).

Walter Cannon is a more interesting example than Spencer to the degree that he was not only a trained, practicing scientist but was one of the foremost scientific investigators of his time, a world-renowned authority on physiology. Cannon (1932) had the clever idea that some aspects of his own research into the self-regulating processes in the human body might find parallels in the analysis of society. So he sought in the "social body" for the equivalent ("in a functional sense") of the fluid matrix

---

25. Robert J. Richards (1987) has made a careful study of Spencer's ideas, based on extensive reading and analysis; in particular he has given us a new understanding of the relation of Spencer's social views and biological concepts to the main currents of thought in these areas in Spencer's lifetime.

26. It is perhaps notable that although J. D. Y. Peel, in his biography of Spencer (1971, 178), thought that this latter group of homologies between forms of marine life and stages of society was "helpful," he omitted the textbookish descriptions of every one of the forms of life from his reprint of Spencer's essay (1972, 61–63).

which is responsible for homeostasis in humans and animals. Unfortunately he introduced extravagant homologies, of which one was the system of "canals, rivers, roads and railroads, with boats, trucks and trains serving like the blood and lymph, as common carriers," on which "the products of farm and factory, of mine and forest, are borne to and fro" (314).

Cannon's essay into sociology illustrates the risks of using homologies. On the level of general analogy, his suggestion that society might resemble an organism could be original and instructive, at least insofar as suggesting that the stability of a society is caused by certain self-regulating mechanisms. We may agree with the sociologist Robert Merton, however, that Cannon made the mistake of introducing "substantive analogies and homologies between biological organisms and social systems." Merton went so far as to describe Cannon's result an "unexcelled . . . example of the fruitless extremes to which even a distinguished mind is driven." This comment is all the more significant in that it occurs in Merton's essay "Manifest and Latent Functions" (1968, ch. 3, 101n., 102–3), in which he finds "Cannon's logic of procedure in physiology" to be a model for the sociological investigator, recommending to his readers the text proper of Cannon's book *The Wisdom of the Body* while warning them about its "unhappy epilogue on social homeostasis."[27]

---

27. In 1941 Cannon returned to this topic, choosing it as the subject of his presidential address to the American Association for the Advancement of Science, delivered in December of that year. In preparing the new version Cannon sought help and advice from a sociologist—Merton himself, a junior colleague at the time—who sent him a list of books and articles on the subject of society as an organism. Cannon now withdrew his earlier comparisons of cells and human members of society, and he declared that comparisons of "the body physiologic and the body politic" had been discredited in the past because they mistakenly had concentrated on "minutiae of structure." He came out strongly against what he considered to be absurd (we would say "mismatched") homologies. We are "not illuminated," he said, "by a likening of manual laborers to muscle cells, manufacturers to gland cells, bankers to fat cells, and policemen to white corpuscles." He accordingly would not be concerned with structures, but would rather examine "functional accomplishments in physiological and social realms."

In his presentation of the nation's equivalent of the body's fluid matrix, Cannon now omitted canals and boats (although he kept the rivers) and added "all the factors, human and mechanical, which produce and distribute goods in the vast and ramifying circulatory system which serves for economic exchange." In less florid prose than before, he said: "Into this moving stream, products of farms and factories, of mines and forests, are placed at their source, for carriage to other localities."

8. Incorrect Science

One of the problems that beset the use of the natural sciences in advancing the social sciences is that the science being applied may be wrong. A conspicuous example is again provided by the American sociologist Carey, who sought to build a science of society on physical principles centering on Newtonian celestial mechanics. I have introduced Carey's ideas earlier as an example of the problem of mismatched homology, in reference to the concept of mass and the form of his law. Carey also made a grave error in stating the law of universal gravity, wrongly believing that the force between two gravitating masses is inversely proportional to the distance between them rather than inversely proportional to the square of the distance between them (Carey 1858, 42–43). Although this error stands out like a sore thumb to anyone who is even slightly familiar with elementary physics, it has not been noted by historians of social science and even by Carey's critics (see Sorokin 1928; Stark 1962).

Of course, an argument can be made that Carey's system would not have been in any way different—certainly no better or no worse—if he had used the correct Newtonian law. That is, since he was developing his subject mathematically, he was only using the law of gravity in the manner of a general likeness in which any error in fact or mismatch of homology might be deemed irrelevant. But Carey himself insisted that there is an isomorphism between the laws of the physical universe and the laws of society, which would condemn his own sociology for falsely claiming to be based on the Newtonian principles of nature.

A striking example of incorrect science appears in Montesquieu's celebrated *Spirit of the Laws* (1748). In discussing the "principle of monarchy," he wrote, "it is with this kind of government as with the system of the universe." That is, "there is a power that constantly repels all bodies from the center, and a power of gravitation that attracts them to it" (1949, book 3, section 7). This notion of a "power of gravitation" that "attracts" all bodies to a center is, of course, Newtonian. But Newton's explanation of the "system of the universe" expressly denied any such balance of centripetal and centrifugal forces.

A somewhat similar example occurs in Adam Smith's *Wealth of Nations*, where it is said that the "natural price" is "the central price, to which the prices of all commodities are continually gravitating" ([1776]

1976, book 1, ch. 7). Often cited as an instance of Smith's Newtonianism, this use of gravity seems to be a case of incorrect science. The use of the words "all" and "continually gravitating" define the context of Newtonian universal gravitation. But a central feature of Newtonian gravitation theory is that all bodies mutually gravitate toward one another. Hence, the "natural price" would by analogy have to "gravitate" to the "actual prices" or the "prices of all commodities." This example, however, shows that creative innovation in the social sciences need not slavishly follow the natural science which was the point of inspiration. (This aspect of creativity is discussed, in reference to Smith and others, in Cohen 1993d, ch. 1.)

9. Inappropriate Analogy

Not all analogies are equally useful. The extreme case occurs when an analogy is so inappropriate that it never serves to advance the subject. Two analogies that have frequently been used in considering the state or society illustrate this problem. One is taken from the biological or life sciences, the other from the physical sciences. One is part of the organismic analogy of the state as the body politic; the other is the Newtonian analogy of the state or society as a physical science. We have seen how, in our own century, Cannon conceived that his own researches might give the organismic analogy a new life. But he did not provide any significant new insights into the theory of society; his ideas did not in any way advance the science of society. Nor, to my knowledge, have any successors made fruitful use of his general analogy. The only possible conclusion is that since the analogy has proved to be unfruitful, it is insofar inappropriate for the advance of sociological knowledge or understanding. If an analogy does not provide a gauge of the validity of a social theory or system or concept, or does not introduce some new insight that advances a social science, then the analogy—being of no use to that social science—must be deemed inappropriate.[28]

The notion that gravitational cosmology or the Newtonian system of the world could provide an analogy for society or for the ordering of the state goes back to the days of Newton himself. One of his disciples, J. T.

---

28. Of course, one reason why an analogy may be inappropriate is that it is actually mismatched homology. Another reason might be that the analogy did not advance the subject to the same degree as a rival one.

Desaguliers, the author of a standard Newtonian textbook, embodied his hopes in a poem,[29] *The Newtonian System of the World, the Best Model of Government* (1728). I know of no political theorist, no practical politician or political leader, and no natural or social scientist who has ever made use of this curious presentation. Here then is an example of a useless analogy, an illustration of an inappropriate analogy.

A similar example of inappropriate analogy, also associated with Newton, is the attempt to replicate Newtonian science in the domain of human affairs. This occurs in a work by a contemporary of Newton's, the Scots mathematician John Craig, whose *Theologiae Christianae Principia Mathematica* (1699) is a direct emulation of Newton's *Philosophiae Naturalis Principia Mathematica*.[30] Craig's aim was to devise a Newtonian law in a social context, the realm of reliability of testimony. The subject he explored was the degree of credence that may be assigned to the testimony of successive witnesses, a topic of major significance in the context of reported miracles. Craig came up with an ingenious Newtonian answer: the reliability of such testimony varies inversely as the square of the time from that testimony to the present, just as the Newtonian gravitational force decreases as the square of the distance. This law is plainly another example of inappropriate analogy.[31]

Despite the hopes of many social scientists, Newton's physics— i.e., the physics he expounded in the *Principia*—has never provided a useful analogy for economics, political science, or sociology. Although post-Newtonian rational mechanics (with non-Newtonian additions by d'Alembert, Euler, Lagrange, Laplace, and Hamilton) proved useful for economics, especially when combined with energy physics, Newtonian rational mechanics by itself was never sufficient to provide a useful model for the social sciences. The reason, I believe, is that the Newtonian system is built on a set of abstractions and conditions that are not realizable in the world of experience. Even the Newtonian sys-

---

29. Henry Guerlac once described it as one of the worst in the English language.

30. A translation of some major extracts by Anne Whitman has been published (without the translator's name) as "Craig's Rules of Historical Evidence" (Craig 1964). Craig once suggested to Newton a minor modification of the *Principia*; see Cohen 1974.

31. For two centuries and more, Craig's book with its Newton-like laws has usually been presented as an example of the kind of aberration to which Newtonian science may lead. The entire book can, in fact, be considered an extended example of the problem of inappropriate analogy. Yet a recent study by Stephen Stigler (1986) has shown that Craig made a serious contribution to applied probability, in that "his formula for the probability of testimony was tantamount to a logistic model for the posterior odds."

tem of the world is an abstract concept to the extent that it cannot be embodied in a mechanical model or picture, in the sense that is possible for the Cartesian system of vortices or even the complex machinery of the Ptolemaic world of epicycles or the Aristotelian universe of nesting spheres. In fact it was on account of this feature that some of Newton's contemporaries rejected the celestial physics of the *Principia*, criticizing Newton specifically for having deserted the "mechanical philosophy." In any case the record of history shows that Newton's physics, despite centuries of hope and effort, has never yielded an analogy of permanent value to social science. This conspicuous failure leaves no other choice than to conclude that there is some important lack of fit between the laws of social behavior and the Newtonian laws of motion and between any general system of social action and the Newtonian cosmology based on the general law of universal gravity. The Newtonian analogy must be deemed inappropriate for the social sciences. We shall see (section 11, below) a comparable example from the biological sciences put forth in an inappropriate analogy for economics.

10. The Role of Metaphor

The role of analogy in the development of the natural sciences and social sciences has been recognized for centuries, and some philosophers and historians of science have begun to make a distinction between analogy and homology. But the role of metaphor is still a subject of uncertainty and debate, at least as far as the sciences are concerned.

A metaphor is often a fiction, a fictive comparison or contrast, an attribution of some property or function to an object or concept to which it does not properly apply. Aristotle defined metaphor as the assignment of a name to something to which it does not belong, but the term has generally assumed a larger range than mere names. Some common metaphors are "root of a problem," "falling into error," "food for the mind," "plowing through the waves," "footing the bill," and "volley of oaths." In each such case our attention is attracted by an attribution which is contrary to experience or knowledge: problems are not like plants and have no roots; making a mistake does not involve a physical descent; the mind is not an organic being requiring physical nourishment; and so on. But metaphors need not be fictive; a metaphor may express something that is rare or uncommon but not necessarily impossible. Examples are "to be as mad [angry] as a wet hen," or "once in a blue moon."[32] In all these examples, metaphor appears as a rhetorical device to attract the attention of a reader or listener. One of the features of the great seventeenth-century revolution which produced modern science was a program of conscious elimination of all rhetorical flourishes, including metaphor, so that science would appear in "plain" or unadorned language with no eye- or ear-catching metaphors to distract the reader or auditor from the logic of induction or deduction or the evidence of experiment and critical observation. Metaphor and rhetoric were limited to the confines of oratory, literature, and theology.

In recent decades, however, the study of metaphor has ceased to be a topic of purely literary or theological interest and has become a concern of philosophers, psychologists, and social scientists. Back in 1931 the critic John Middleton Murray began an essay on metaphor by observing that "discussions of metaphor—there are not many of them—often strike us at first as superficial." Some four and one-half decades later, in a commentary on Murray's remark, the philosopher Max Black observed that as of 1977 "both comments would be inappropriate" (Ortony 1979, 19). As evidence against the quantitative part of Murray's comment, Black pointed to W. A. Shibles's bibliography (1971), which lists some four thousand titles of books and articles on this subject. Mark Johnson has remarked that we are now "in the midst of a metaphormania" and calls attention to Wayne Booth's estimate that if the rate of increase of scholarly interest in metaphor from 1940 to 1978 were to be sustained, by the year 2039 there would be "more students of metaphor than people" (1981, ix).

The literature on the social sciences, and notably economics, manifests a constantly increasing concern for metaphor, especially in relation to the impacts of mathematics and the natural sciences. This literature, however, is especially confusing to an outsider for the reason that the term *metaphor* is used in a variety of different (and unspecified) ways and often appears as a synonym for analogy. The lack of clear distinction between metaphor and analogy has historical roots that go back to classical Greece. The word *metaphor* sets forth its meaning in the

---

32. The expression "blue moon" refers to an actual astronomical event, the appearance of a thirteenth new moon in a given year. Since there are a little more than twelve lunar months in a year, a blue moon occurs with a frequency of some three or four years. Thus "a blue moon," like "wet hen," refers to a rare but not impossible event.

sense of its Greek roots, stemming back to *metapherein* (from *meta*, the equivalent of the Latin *trans*, plus *pherō* from the verb "to bear") and so being the exact equivalent of our Latin-originating word *transfer*, of which the roots are *trans* ("across") and *ferre* ("to bear"). Etymologically, the meaning of *metaphor* could thus encompass the use of analogy as well as the rhetorical figure of speech. Aristotle wrote that analogy is a special kind of metaphor that takes the form of a four-part ratio: we may take note that the Greek word *analogia* stems from *an(a)* ("according to") plus *logos* ("ratio," "proportion"). Aristotle had in mind a ratio expressed in the form "as evening is to day, so old age is to life." Transposing the terms in a way not permissible by the strict rules of deductive logic yields the analogy "evening is the old age of day, while old age is the evening of life."[33] Jevons gave this ratio in terms of a prime minister's being the pilot of a state.

In the literature on economics, in particular in the writings of Philip Mirowski, the word *metaphor* appears in various meanings and senses. Sometimes it is used interchangeably with *analogue* (in the sense in which *analogue* is customarily used by philosophers and historians of science); at other times, it is used in a general way to characterize a part of science as a whole; at still other times, it may be used as a synonym for *model*. Donald McCloskey takes language a step further in a bold declaration that the mathematical equations of economics are its "metaphors." We may applaud Mirowski's riposte (*MHL*, 144) concerning the "subversive" character of McCloskey's "idea that mathematical expressions [in economics] are 'merely' rhetorical." At the same time, however, we must note here yet another sense Mirowski gives to "metaphor," in this case a synonymy being put forth between metaphor and rhetoric.

Since a metaphor is a means of attributing some property or quality to something to which it does not ordinarily belong, there is function of metaphor in every interaction between the natural sciences and the social sciences. By making this function specific, we may indeed do honor to Mirowski's research and even, to some degree, rescue a major part of his real achievement from the problems of loose usage. I have mentioned the fact that one of the main points Mirowski makes in *More Heat than Light* is that some important founders of neoclassical economics—e.g., Jevons, Walras, Edgeworth, Pareto, and Fisher—based

---

33. More strictly, "as evening is to life, so old age is to day."

that subject on physics, in particular, certain aspects of post-Newtonian rational mechanics plus some aspects of the new energy physics. Unlike Mirowski, who goes on to explore the deficiencies in this process of transfer, I myself have been more concerned with the actual act of transfer and its allied transformations (see Cohen 1992). What did these founders actually have in mind?

In the preface to the second edition of his *Theory of Political Economy* Stanley Jevons defended the introduction of the calculus into economics (it was very elementary calculus, as Mirowski and others have quite correctly observed) on the grounds that differential equations had long been used with signal success in rational mechanics. As I read what Jevons had to say on this subject, it is obvious that he is making several points at once. He is declaring that the experience of rational mechanics shows that the use of the calculus is appropriate in "science" and that this form of mathematics may be expected to be as beneficial to economic science as it has been for the science of rational mechanics. So much for analogy. Jevons is also taking pride in showing that the form of equations is the same in both domains, introducing what I would call the factor of homology. But he is also making another point: that the reason why economics can be treated mathematically in the same way as rational mechanics is that economics is "like" rational mechanics, which is the reason why there is a parallelism of concepts and a homology of equations. Léon Walras makes the same point in his *Elements of Pure Economics* (1954, 41), and he does so rather explicitly in his essay on "mechanics and economics" (see above; and Mirowski 1990), where he boasts that laws of the same form (that is, the identical differential equations) occur in both domains, implying directly that the two are similar. And as we have seen, this similarity (analogy and homology) appears in extreme form in actual tables of corresponding concepts and principles from economics and rational mechanics drawn up by Vilfredo Pareto and by Irving Fisher.

This kind of parallelism goes far beyond any mere analogy (similarity in function) or homology (similarity in form of concept or equation) between the two disciplines. There is, additionally, the transfer to economics of the values of what was reckoned in the nineteenth century to be the paradigmatic science: rational mechanics, the science established by Isaac Newton, which obtained its name from the preface written by Newton for his great *Principia* (published in 1687). Such a transfer of values, which goes beyond the formal transfer of concepts, equations, laws, and principles, is well described as *metaphor*. That is, the founders of neoclassical economics not only introduced into their subject the specific analogues and homologues that Mirowski has delineated for us in critical perspective; they also adopted the metaphor of rational mechanics or mathematical physics—attributing to their own endeavors, and to their subject at large, the values associated with the great branch of the exact sciences that they were attempting to emulate.

11. Analogy, Homology, Metaphor—A Case History from Economics

One reason for a separation of metaphor and analogy in considering social sciences is that the one makes use of the images and language of the natural sciences as a rhetorical flourish, whereas the other attempts to glean from one or other of the natural sciences some feature or features that may be of use in solving a puzzle or a problem. That is, the purpose of a metaphor drawn from one of the natural sciences may be no more than to attract the attention of the reader or hearer. Often the aim may be to make a presentation seem "scientific" by introducing terminology or even concepts or principles or laws from the natural sciences. By contrast, an analogy suggests to a natural or social scientist a concept or method or theory that may inspire the creation of a new concept or method or theory that will actually advance the subject or serve as illustration. But a metaphor, as a scientistic rhetorical flourish, may only obscure the logic of the argument by introducing extraneous considerations.

Thus far we have restricted our attention to analogies that have proven to have been potentially useful, noting the types of problems that plague analogical reasoning in the social sciences. But there are also analogies which, even though based on correct natural science, may prove to be purely metaphorical and even misleading, producing confusion and obfuscation rather than illumination. We may see this feature of analogies as a central issue in a fairly recent intellectual exchange in the domain of economics. This example serves to illustrate a fundamental distinction between analogy and metaphor.

In 1950 Armen A. Alchian published "Uncertainty, Evolution and Economic Theory," an article which brought a response by Edith Penrose (1952) on the proper use of biological analogies in economics. Penrose admitted, at the outset, that economics "has always drawn heavily on the natural sciences for analogies designed to help in the understanding of economic phenomena." Yet she was not concerned with analogies in general but rather with what she saw as a deleterious effect of using "sweeping analogies" in economics, their tendency to frame "the problems they are designed to illuminate" in so special a way that "significant matters are inadvertently obscured." Concentrating on "theories of the firm," she focused her attention on three biological analogies used by economists: the life cycle, natural selection (or viability), and homeostasis.

In the course of her critique Penrose stressed an important distinction between two uses of analogies in economics that has features in common with the typology I have been presenting. One use is to advance our understanding by referring a not fully understood economic phenomenon to an analogous one in some other science which is presumably better understood. The other, which she calls a "purely metaphorical analogy," uses such resemblances "to add a picturesque note to an otherwise dull analysis" and to help the reader in following a difficult argument or in dealing with a strange concept or principle (1952, 807). That is the traditional role of rhetorical metaphor.

I need not go into details of Penrose's argument,[34] but I note that she acknowledges that Alchian's analysis is not a crude evolutionism but is rather "very modern in its emphasis on uncertainty and statistical probabilities." Among the conclusions on which she focuses her criticism are that "successful innovations—regarded by analogy as 'mutations'—are transmitted by imitation to other firms" and that the "economic counterparts of genetic heredity, mutations, and natural selection are imitation, innovation, and positive profits." She concludes by observing that "natural selection is substituted for purposive profit-maximizing behavior just as in biology natural selection replaced the concept of special creation of species" (1952, 812).

I transpose her argument into the typological language I have been using here, observing that as she has called attention to a set of proposed bio-economical homologies in analyzing Alchian's presentation, Penrose makes the case that on every level of homology (although she does not use this term) there is a misfit between biology and economics. For example, she detects a serious error in treating "innovations" as

---

34. For details see the useful analysis by Neil Niman (1993), a presentation which I have found extremely helpful in understanding this issue.

homologues (her term is "analogues") of "biological mutations," since the latter involve an alteration of the "substance of the hereditary constitution" whereas innovations rather tend to be "direct attempts by firms to alter their environment." Her conclusion is that introducing the biological analogy has hindered rather than advanced Alchian's stated purpose of exploring "the precise role and nature of purposive behavior in the presence of uncertainty and incomplete information."

In his reply to her critique Alchian (1953) asserted that his theory of the firm "stands independently of the biological analogy" and that "every reference to the biological analogy" was "merely expository" and "designed to clarify the ideas in the theory." That is, evolutionary biology did not contribute anything essential to the argument. It would then seem that in this instance the use of concepts from the natural sciences was intended as a rhetorical flourish, an example of metaphor. We may note, however, that in her rejoinder Penrose (1953) reasserted her position that, even so, "the biological analogy places the whole problem in a misleading frame of reference."[35] She concludes by insisting that wholly apart from the merits of one or other position with respect to the theory of the firm, the introduction of the analogy of natural selection hinders rather than furthers understanding. Only the future will tell whether this conclusion has general validity or whether it applies only to the example under consideration.

This article draws on material treated in a different manner in the introductory chapter of Cohen 1993d. My research in this area during the past six years has been made possible by the generous support of the Richard Lounsbery Foundation of New York. I acknowledge, in particular, the encouragement I have received from its president, Alan F. McHenry.

References

Ackerknecht, Erwin Heinz. 1953. *Rudolph Virchow: Doctor, Statesman, Anthropologist*. Madison: University of Wisconsin Press. Reprinted New York: Arno Press, 1981.

Alchian, Armen A. 1950. Uncertainty, Evolution and Economic Theory. *Journal of Political Economy* 57:211–21.

———. 1953. Biological Analogies in the Firm: Comment. *American Economic Review* 43:600–603.

35. Penrose (1953) quotes from Alchian's original article to the effect that the "suggested approach embodies the principles of biological evolution and natural selection."

Avery, John Lubbock. 1879. *Scientific Lectures*. London: Macmillan.
Becker, Howard. 1933. Lilienfeld-Toailles, Pavel Fedorovich. In *Encyclopaedia of the Social Sciences* 9:373–74. New York: Macmillan. Reprinted 1937.
Boumans, Marcel. 1993. Paul Ehrenfest and Jan Tinbergen: A Case of Limited Physics Transfer. In Mirowski 1993.
Brewster, David. 1843. *Letters on Natural Magic*. New York: Harper.
Cannon, Walter. 1932. *The Wisdom of the Body*. New York: Norton. 2d ed., 1939.
———. 1941. The Body Physiologic and the Body Politic. *Science* 93:1–10.
Carey, H. C. 1858–60. *Principles of Social Science*. 3 vols. Philadelphia: Lippincott.
Carlyle, Thomas. 1836. *Sartor Resartus*. London: James Munroe.
———. 1843. *Past and Present*. London: Chapman & Hall.
———. [1896–99] 1969. *The Works of Thomas Carlyle*. 30 vols. Edited by H. D. Traill. London: Chapman & Hall. Reprinted New York: AMS Press.
Cohen, I. Bernard. 1974. Isaac Newton, the Calculus of Variations, and the Design of Ships. In *For Dirk Struik: Scientific, Historical, and Political Essays in Honor of Dirk J. Struik*, edited by Robert S. Cohen, J. J. Stachel, and M. M. Wartofsky, 169–87. Boston Studies in the Philosophy of Science, 15. Dordrecht and Boston: D. Reidel.
———. 1980. *The Newtonian Revolution: With Illustrations of the Transformation of Scientific Ideas*. Cambridge, London, and New York: Cambridge University Press.
———. 1993a. Newton and the Social Sciences, with Special Reference to Economics: Or, The Case of the Missing Paradigm. In Mirowski 1993.
———. 1993b. Some Interactions of the Natural Sciences and the Social Sciences. In *Essays in Honor of Allen G. Debus*, edited by Katharine Parsell and E. N. Thierman. Cambridge and New York: Cambridge University Press.
———. 1993c. *Science and the Founding Fathers: New Aspects of the Political Thought of Jefferson, Franklin, Adams, and Madison*. New York: Norton.
———, ed. 1993d. *The Natural Sciences and the Social Sciences: Some Critical and Historical Perspectives*. Boston Studies in the Philosophy of Science. Dordrecht and Boston: Kluwer Academic Publishers.
Craig, John. 1699. *Theologiae Christianae Principia Mathematica*. London: Impensis Timothei Child.
———. 1964. Craig's Rules of Historical Evidence. *History and Theory: Studies in the Philosophy of History*. Beiheft 4. The Hague: Mouton.
Darwin, Charles. [1849] 1964. *The Origin of Species*. London: John Murray. Reprinted Cambridge: Cambridge University Press.
Desaguliers, John Theophilus. 1728. *The Newtonian System of the World, the Best Model of Government*. Westminster: A. Campbell.
Edgeworth, F. Y. 1881. *Mathematical Psychics: An Essay on the Application of Mathematics to the Moral Sciences*. London: Kegan.
Fisher, Irving. 1926. *Mathematical Investigations in the Theory of Value and Prices*. New Haven: Yale University Press.
Fourier, Charles. 1971. *Harmonian Man: Selected Writings of Charles Fourier*.

Edited by Mark Poster, with translations by Susan Hanson. Garden City, N.Y.: Doubleday/Anchor.

Freud, Sigmund. 1953–74. *The Standard Edition of the Complete Psychological Works of Sigmund Freud*. 24 vols. Translated under the general editorship of James Strachey. London: Hogarth Press and Institute of Psycho-analysis.

Hale, David George. 1971. *The Body Politic: A Political Metaphor in Renaissance English Literature*. The Hague and Paris: Mouton.

Ingrao, Bruna. 1991. L'analogia meccanica nel pensiero di Pareto. In *Pareto oggi*, edited by G. Busino. Bologna: Il Mulino.

———. 1993. Physics and Pareto's Economics. In Mirowski 1993.

Ingrao, Bruna, and Giorgio Israel. 1990. *The Invisible Hand: Economic Equilibrium in the History of Science*. Cambridge: MIT Press.

Jaffé, William. 1973. Léon Walras's Role in the "Marginal Revolution" of the Late 1870s. In *The Marginal Revolution in Economics: Interpretation and Evaluation*, edited by R. D. Collison Black, A. W. Coats, and Craufurd D. W. Goodwin. Durham: Duke University Press.

Jevons, W. Stanley. 1878. *Political Economy*. 2d ed. London: Macmillan.

———. [1887] 1958. *The Principles of Science: A Treatise on Logic and Scientific Method*. New York: Dover. (A reprint of the 2d and final edition.)

———. [1911] 1965. *The Theory of Political Economy*. New York: Augustus Kelley. (A reprint of the 5th edition.)

———. 1981. *Papers and Correspondence of William Stanley Jevons*. Vol. 7. Edited by R. D. Collison Black. London: Macmillan, with the Royal Economic Society.

Johnson, Mark, ed. 1981. *Philosophical Perspectives on Metaphor*. Minneapolis: University of Minnesota Press.

Kaplan, Donald H. 1988. The Psychoanalysis of Art: Some Ends, Some Means. *Journal of the American Psychoanalytic Association* 36:259–302.

Leamer, Edward S. 1987. Economic Metaphors. In *Recent Advances in Econometrics*, edited by T. Bewley. Cambridge and New York: Cambridge University Press.

Lilienfeld, Paul. 1873–81. *Gedanken über die Socialwissenschaft der Zukunft*. Vols. 1–4, 1873–79. Mitau: E. Behre. Vol. 5, 1881. Hamburg: Gebr. Behre; Mitau: E. Behre.

———. 1896. *La pathologie sociale*. Paris: V. Giard & E. Brière.

Lowell, A. Lawrence. 1937. An Example from the Evidence of History. In *Factors Determining Human Behavior* (Harvard Tercentenary Conference of Arts and Sciences, 1936), 119–32. Cambridge: Harvard University Press.

McCloskey, Donald N. 1990. *If You're So Smart: The Narrative of Economic Expertise*. Chicago and London: University of Chicago Press.

Mack, Mary P. 1962. *Jeremy Bentham: An Odyssey of Ideas, 1748–1792*. London: Heinemann.

Marshall, Alfred. 1885. *The Present Position of Economics: An Inaugural Lecture Given in the Senate House at Cambridge, 24 February, 1885*. London: Macmillan. Reprinted in Pigou 1925, 52–74.

Maxwell, James Clerk. [1890] 1965. On Faraday's Lines of Force. In *The Scientific*

Papers of James Clerk Maxwell, edited by W. D. Niven. Cambridge: Cambridge University Press. Reprinted New York: Dover.

Mayr, Ernst, and W. B. Provine, eds. 1980. *The Evolutionary Synthesis: Perspectives on the Unification of Biology*. Cambridge: Harvard University Press.

Ménard, Claude. 1988. The Machine and the Heart: An Essay on Analogies in Economic Reasoning. *Social Concept* 4:81–95.

Merton, Robert K. 1968. *Social Theory and Social Structure*. New York: Free Press.

Mirowski, Philip. 1984. Physics and the "Marginalist Revolution." *Cambridge Journal of Economics* 8:361–79.

———. 1988. *Against Mechanism: Protecting Economics from Science*. Totowa, N.J.: Rowman & Littlefield.

———. 1989a. *More Heat than Light: Economics as Social Physics, Physics as Nature's Economics*. Cambridge and New York: Cambridge University Press. [Citations are abbreviated *MHL*.]

———. 1989b. On Hollander's "Substantive Identity" of Classical and Neoclassical Economics. *Cambridge Journal of Economics* 13:471–77.

———, ed. 1993. *Natural Images in Economics: Markets Read in Tooth and Claw*. Proceedings of a Symposium at Notre Dame on "Natural Images and Economics," October 1991. Cambridge and New York: Cambridge University Press.

Mirowski, Philip, and Pamela Cook. 1990. Walras' "Economics and Mechanics": Translation, Commentary, Context. In *Economics as Discourse*, edited by Warren J. Samuels. Boston, Dordrecht, and London: Kluwer.

Montesquieu, Charles Louis de Secondat. 1949. *The Spirit of the Laws*. Translated by Thomas Nugent. New York: Hafner.

Nagel, Ernest. 1961. *The Structure of Science: Problems in the Logic of Scientific Explanation*. New York and Burlingame: Harcourt Brace & World.

Nelson, R., and S. Winter. 1982. *An Evolutionary Theory of Economic Change*. Cambridge: Harvard University Press.

Niman, Neil B. 1991. Biological Analogies in Marshall. *Journal of the History of Economic Thought* 13:19–36.

———. 1993. The Role of Biological Analogies in the Theory of the Firm. In Mirowski 1993.

Oppenheimer, Robert. 1956. Analogy in Science. *American Psychologist* 11:127–35.

Ortony, Andrew, ed. 1979. *Metaphor and Thought*. Cambridge, London, and New York: Cambridge University Press.

Pareto, Vilfredo. 1953. On the Economic Phenomenon: A Reply to Benedetto Croce. Translated by F. Priuli. In *International Economic Papers*, edited by Alan Peacock, Ralph Turvey, and Elizabeth Henderson. London: Macmillan.

———. [1898] 1966. *Cours d'économie politique*. Lausanne: F. Rouge. Translated by Derick Mirfin in *Sociological Writings*, edited by S. E. Finer. Oxford: Basil Blackwell.

Peel, J. D. Y. 1971. *Herbert Spencer: The Evolution of a Sociologist*. New York: Basic Books.

———. 1972. *Herbert Spencer on Social Evolution.* Chicago: University of Chicago Press.
Penrose, Edith Tilton. 1952. Biological Analogies in the Theory of the Firm. *American Economic Review* 42:804–19.
———. 1953. Rejoinder. *American Economic Review* 43:603–9.
Pigou, A. C., ed. 1925. *Memorials of Alfred Marshall.* London: Macmillan.
Richards, Robert J. 1987. *Darwin and the Emergence of Evolutionary Theories of Mind and Behavior.* Chicago and London: University of Chicago Press.
Riley, Patrick. 1972. *The Political Writings of Leibniz.* Cambridge: Cambridge University Press.
Roe, Frederick W. 1921. *The Social Philosophy of Carlyle and Ruskin.* New York: Harcourt Brace.
Roosevelt, Theodore. 1910. *Biological Analogies in History.* New York: Oxford University Press; London: Henry Frowde.
———. 1923–26. *The Works of Theodore Roosevelt.* New York: Scribner's.
Shibles, Warren A. 1971. *Metaphor: An Annotated Bibliography.* Whitewater, Wis.: Language Press.
Smith, Adam. [1776] 1976. *An Inquiry into the Nature and Causes of the Wealth of Nations.* The Glasgow Edition of the Works and Correspondence of Adam Smith. Oxford: Oxford University Press.
Sorokin, Pitirim A. 1928. *Contemporary Sociological Theories.* New York and London: Harper.
Spencer, Herbert. 1896. *Essays Scientific, Political, and Speculative.* 3 vols. New York: D. Appleton.
———. 1897. *The Principles of Sociology.* New York: D. Appleton.
Stark, Werner. 1962. *The Fundamental Forms of Social Thought.* London: Routledge & Kegan Paul.
Stigler, Stephen. 1986. John Craig and the Probability of History: From the Death of Christ to the Birth of Laplace. *Journal of the American Statistical Association* 81:879–87.
Temkin, Oswei. 1949. Metaphors of Human Biology. In *Science and Civilization*, edited by Robert C. Stauffer. Madison: University of Wisconsin Press.
Thoben, H. 1982. Mechanistic and Organistic Analogies in Economics Reconsidered. *Kyklos* 35:292–306.
Tyndall, John. 1861. *The Glaciers of the Alps.* Boston: Ticknor & Fields.
Walras, Léon. 1909. Economique et mécanique. *Bulletin de la Société Vaudoise des Sciences Naturelles* 45:313–25.
———. 1954. *Elements of Pure Economics.* Translated by William Jaffé. London: Allen and Unwin for the American Economic Association and the Royal Economic Society.
———. 1990. Economics and Mechanics. In *Economics as Discourse*, edited by Warren J. Samuels. Boston, Dordrecht, and London: Kluwer.
Whitehead, Alfred North. 1931. *Science and the Modern World.* New York: Macmillan.

What's So Wrong with Physics Envy?

Margaret Schabas

As a contribution to the history and philosophy of economics, Philip Mirowski's *More Heat than Light* has justly achieved much recognition. Few scholars have swept over so much material with such agility and finesse. His grasp of the primary and secondary literature alone is most impressive, and his confidence in passing judgments on the past is almost as bold as Joseph Schumpeter's. The book is very readable although the prose deviates from the conventional academic style. Almost every page is filled with more alliterations than your average poem, not to mention enough new vocabulary to significantly improve your game of Scrabble. The more serious problem, however, is what to make of it all. The more passages I read and reread, the more bewildered I become. The book tugs in all sorts of directions. But implicit throughout is the view that virtually every economist since the end of the last century (and arguably since the Enlightenment) has been engaged in an immense conspiracy to dupe the public and other fellow economists.

This sociological thesis notwithstanding, Mirowski definitely downplays the social context in his detailed account of the history of physics and economics. In fact he subscribes to a very strict internalist history. His explanations of ideas, events, and actions follow with a deductive rigor that would make Carl Hempel grin. We learn, for example, that Marx did not publish his work on the transformation of values into prices while alive because he had made the "blunder" of imposing "one conservation principle too many" (*MHL*, 185). And the advent of Freudianism, it is purported, was sufficient to silence any appeals by economists to a subjective psychology (235). Countless more examples can be found to illustrate that the history given here is grossly oversimplified. But there is no need to go on. Once the conspiracy to promote economics as social physics is granted, everything else falls into place with an inexorable logic.

And yet, our author insists, history is nothing more than a bunch of metaphors. There is no ultimate foundation to any of our knowledge claims. Only the metaphors impose constraints, both methodological and substantive. Adopting a metaphor is like boarding a train. The tracks only go certain places, and the key to a good journey is to make sure that all of the theoretical baggage that you took on board initially arrives intact. "Scientific metaphors should set in motion research programs that strive to render explicit the totality of the attendant submetaphors" (279).

If there is no granite rock under those railroad tracks, then how do we establish criteria for judging one line of inquiry as superior to another? Does Mirowski in fact need some Archimedean point after all to make his evaluations? If physics and economics share a primal metaphor of body, motion, and value, then why make such a fuss about their formal similarities or the temporal priority of one set of insights over another? In fact, if there really are only a handful of metaphors out there (and from reading the book I'm convinced that one of them has to be food), then what's so wrong with one discipline copying (either in part or in full) that of another? Must we really place all of the blame on economists if they have been held "hostage" to physics, and an outmoded physics at that?

At least it is easy to locate the central motive for writing the book: neoclassical economics is rotten to the core, and it's high time we did something about it. Until now most critics of contemporary economics have chipped away at the foundations in only a piecemeal fashion. No one, to the best of my knowledge, has called for such a complete overhaul as forcefully as Philip Mirowski. What we have here is a full-scale indictment of the economics profession, and the promise that once justice is served, genuine economic knowledge will emerge and flourish.

A few contributions to economics receive praise. Marx, for example, was "an epoch-making economist because he combined the metaphor of a value substance in motion with the metaphor of the body in motion in the concept of labor" (179). But he was also aware of the pitfalls of drawing analogies to physical properties and states, though not enough to avoid the temptation of imposing one conservation principle too many. The Institutionalists are paid homage from time to time, and Thorstein

Veblen is almost deified. Other recent developments, game theory for example, promise to avoid the slavish imitation of physics.

The real culprits in the story are the neoclassical economists, for adhering so strictly to mid-nineteenth-century physics. But at least they owned up to all of this. The "robbery" was carried out in "brazen daylight" (9), and the points of similarity were acknowledged: "neoclassicals did not imitate physics in a desultory or superficial manner; no, they copied their models mostly term for term and symbol for symbol, and said so" (3). Unfortunately, neoclassical economists failed to invest in a diverse portfolio. By placing all their bets on energetics, first in the 1870s and then, more fervently, in the 1930s and 1940s, they now find themselves bankrupt. Because of the facile equivalences between utility and energy, and the prolonged investment in the mathematics of Lagrangian and Hamiltonian analysis, economists are left building castles in the air. Worst of all, they have no place to go. The physics metaphor "cannot seriously be repudiated or relinquished, because there is nothing else that can hold the neoclassical research program together" (368).

To grasp the extent to which energetics has infiltrated economic theory, the author prescribes a crash course in physics and devotes about one-fourth of the book to teaching the economist-reader what she needs to know. Unfortunately, so much of the presentation of the material on physics is testimony to Mirowski's latent desire to dazzle us with his own mastery of the queen of the sciences. With such a serious task at hand, however, not to mention the central message that economists need to mature past the stage of physics envy, this display of mental gymnastics is somewhat self-defeating. In my view the exposition would have been much improved if chapter 2 had been shortened considerably. There is no need to retell the history of thermodynamics in so much depth and detail unless one is making original contributions to the subject. And not only does Mirowski rely heavily on secondary sources, but he presents the material as though there is not one iota of controversy among historians of physics. This seems very much at odds with his unrelenting efforts to challenge orthodoxy in the community of historians of economics.

Mirowski first walks us through the metaphysical debates of the Cartesians, Leibnitzians, and Newtonians, particularly the controversy over *vis viva*. But the most critical turning point in the history of physics, he submits, came with the formulation of thermodynamics in the middle decades of the nineteenth century. Theories of heat, mechanical work, electricity and magnetism, and light were all brought under the rubric of the concept of energy. So powerful was this unifying concept that, as Mirowski remarks, "if it [energy] did not exist, we would have had to invent it" (101). In fact, he insists, that is just what we did. Energy turns out to be just another metaphor that underwent extensive metamorphosis. It started out as a substance, was transformed into a "mathematical artifact of a field," and then ended up as "just another way to express a symmetry" (11).

With the demise of energetics came the renunciation of the Laplacean dream of a world entirely comprehended by mathematical equations. Mirowski views this entire episode as one motivated by that worst of human flaws, hubris. But, quite remarkably, physicists were soon able to swallow their pride and make the necessary adjustments. Poincaré led the way, with his program to "diversify and fissure" (88). Since then, energy has retreated into the background, as physicists have come to terms with the very "topsy-turvy world" that we in fact inhabit. It is a "frightening and demoralizing place," with "chaos whereever one turns" (140). But, for some reason that is never spelled out, it is a world worth inhabiting, even emulating.

It seems that this conceptual revolution was sparked by successive failures to formulate a single unifying principle that would capture the immense range of phenomena in the physical world. Actually, Mirowski equivocates on this point. He suggests in one place that almost as soon as the energetics program solidified, physicists had found "more change in the world than the energy concept would permit" (133). This marked its decline. But elsewhere, he contends, the rise and decline of energy had nothing to do with empirical results: "Since the world never pointed to the energy concept in the first place, it seems a little tendentious to assert that the world pointed to its demise. . . . Energy was . . . the expression of a specific world view, one bound up with Laplacean determinism, temporal symmetry, a reductionist conception of the body, and the exchange of equivalents" (133). One of the most glorious eras in the history of physics was grounded in little more than hot air.

Mirowski spends so much time and effort (I hesitate to say energy) on the subject in order to demonstrate to economists that physics is not what meets the eye. As he remarks after his long chapter on physics:

> I'll wager that prior to this moment, the reader harbored the conviction that it was *physics* that constituted a tranquil and reassuring body of commonsense wisdom, whereas economics was nothing more than a cacophony of groundless claims, wishful thinking, smoke and mirrors

and vanity. But after the last chapter, the dollar, the accelerometer, and the mirror are all starting to look the same. (140)

Both physics and economics are, at bottom, just a "House of Mirrors." And the reason so many of us are still "lost in the funhouse" is that we fail to see that conservation principles are at the focal point of both disciplines. The upshot of this exposé, it would seem, is that physicists have done a brilliant job of snowing not only the laity, but most professional economists. If that were something economists could only grasp, then they would be able to bury a false idol and move on to their proper business. Mirowski aspires to be the therapist who will purge the "collective neoclassical neurosis with . . . the physics metaphor" (243).

But is physics in fact something to cease worshiping? In so many passages, we gather that it is the physicists who have the correct grasp of the world, or rather that handful of metaphors that make up the world of cognition:

> No one who examines the historical record could maintain that physicists have been lax or unimaginative in their explanations and elaborations of all the vertexes of the pyramid—and yes, they have not just confined themselves to motion. Physicists have in the past displayed a dynamism and flexibility with regard to the meaning of their metaphors for which they can rightfully be proud. (108)

They have an uncanny knack for stretching the vertexes of the energy pyramid apart with the utmost consistency and sense of balance. Physicists like Helmholtz and Poincaré also displayed an ability to respond to outside stimuli; they instinctively knew when to put aside a particular theory and move on to another. They were even able to see past the Laplacean dream and, in the case of Poincaré, to grasp the fundamental randomness of the universe.

What gives physicists this versatility that economists so lack? Not, it seems, the subject matter, since for Mirowski biologists and economists have an equally legitimate claim on the body-motion-value metaphor. The real reason, it seems, is that for Mirowski physicists are honest inquirers. They try to make the most of what the world presents, and don't engage in robbery or other criminal practices. Because of their good intentions, they are more imaginative, flexible, and self-critical. Physicists are the virtuous purveyors of the truth, whereas economists are unimaginative and basically devious. Perhaps handling money necessarily corrupts.

At bottom, *More Heat than Light* is a morality tale, as the author hints at one point (293). Over and over again, physicists display the proper virtues in pushing forward the frontiers of knowledge, whereas economists do not. Paul Samuelson, for example, is severely impugned for "trying to suppress the negative components of the energetics metaphor by attempting to suppress the metaphor itself" (279). Mind you, not all neoclassical economists harbored such a "conscious intent to deceive" (366). The very success of their program, however, attests to their guilt, whether consciously motivated or not. In the spirit of George Washington, telling the truth, owning up to the limitations of the metaphors one employs, is paramount in the scientific enterprise:

> What matters for our present purposes is not that any particular metaphor has flaws, but rather that the appropriate research community responds to those flaws in a responsible, systematic, and scientific manner, and acknowledges that metaphors have consequences for the content and conduct of inquiry. (279)

Why have physicists alone succeeded in acting in an honest fashion? Mirowski never really tells us. But the answer, even if we remain within his framework, is not difficult to find. It's because they work with more than metaphors. Physics is not just a game of Scrabble. As several philosophers of science have recently emphasized, experimentation provides nonpropositional knowledge that survives theory shifts.[1] Much ink has been spilt to diminish the thrust of Popperian falsificationism, but even such opponents do not entirely silence the right of nature to shout yes or no.[2]

Obviously this is not the time or place to take on the realism/instrumentalism debate. But I think it is worth pointing out that Mirowski is implicitly assuming that empirical findings can arbitrate between competing theories. Otherwise, why would the energetics movement have declined? What was to be gained by renouncing the very theory that would put the capstone on the Laplacean dream? Clearly, the gain came in the form of greater empirical accuracy. The world really is more messy and complicated than Laplace envisioned. Mirowski only concedes this on the very last page of the book. But, at bottom, this is why so many economists find themselves in a pickle. Their metaphors simply don't

---

1. See Hacking 1983; Franklin 1986; Galison 1987.
2. See, e.g., Lakatos 1981.

resonate with the salient features of our world. It's not a question of where the metaphors came from, but whether or not they latch up with the "heterogeneous and asymmetric" phenomena of the external world (401). It is ultimately on empirical grounds that Mirowski deems physics a success and economics a failure.

Appropriating metaphors is not an innocent activity: "the metaphorical inspiration of neoclassical economics [was not] just a harmless artifact of the context of discovery" (3). For one, an energetics-based theory of economics meant that "all vestiges of value substances just had to go" (280). And once value is deprived of its material base, "analysis stumbles in a labyrinth of incoherence" (162). The reason, it seems, is that value is necessarily linked to body, through the energy pyramid. Once body and value are severed, there is no foundation left. Manifestations of this confusion are found in many regions of the field. Try as they might, economists cannot solve the problem of the integrability of utility functions. And when it comes to production theory, they are reduced to childish tantrums: we find "the wringing of hands and the gnashing of teeth whenever the topic of production was broached" (284). The most daunting problem of all seems to be finding the analogues for the invariance properties of modern physics. Peering deep into the social realm, our author declares that they don't exist.

There is another dimension to this glorification of physics and condemnation of economics. For Mirowski, metaphors are essentially vehicles for power. Allegiances to certain metaphors, and the repudiation of others, are tantamount to a conspiracy against innocent bystanders. The real source of Mirowski's complaint with neoclassical economists is that they have influence over the lives and well-being of people. Masquerading as a science just like physics is not innocent stuff if you deprive children of school lunches or wreak havoc on the Chilean economy. There is no reason for Mirowski to have such a strong dislike for neoclassical economics if it is just elaborate storytelling.

Why, then, doesn't he call a spade a spade? Why does he cloud the power play with a veneer of moralizing about good comportment when using metaphors? The reason, quite simply, is that it would sound too much like good old-fashioned Marxism: neoclassical economics is an elaborate apology for capitalism. Mirowski is to be praised for such a clever disguise. By addressing them at their own level, his message might just appeal to mainstream economists. He may well be far more effective by psychoanalyzing their physics envy than waxing on in grandiose terms about the material base and ideological superstructure of capitalism. If so, I take my hat off to him. But let's be perfectly clear that that is what he's up to here.

Owning up to the political subplot helps me to understand why Mirowski is so favorably disposed toward physicists. He presents them as the layperson imagines them: basically honest and apolitical. Certainly he never casts aspersions on them for being successful, the way he does on economists. His lengthy discourse on the history of physics suggests rather that science is devoid of political import. Helmholtz, Poincaré, and Einstein were drawn to their profound insights solely by scientific factors. Physics is in essence just an attempt to "reify a notion of causality in the Meyersonian sense" (142). Only once, in passing, does he note that "we owe to this physics the ability to destroy our world in a space of minutes" (140).

If Mirowski is to purchase the discourse of social constructivism, then he must also own up to the enormous power wielded by the physics profession. Looking to theoretical content or mathematical technique is a red herring. What's wrong with physics envy is that physicists have managed to conceal the immense social power which they now possess.[3] Ironically it was Veblen, Mirowski's hero, who predicted the rise of this techno-aristocracy. By contrast, economists from Hobbes to Keynes have always been upfront about the power of political economy. Mirowski's most fundamental grievance, it seems to me, is that economists lack the sophistication to cloak their power. In their clumsy and slipshod fashion, economists never managed to fool anyone by marching under the banner of science.

Is the physics envy of economists cause for despair? Not necessarily. Let us take our cue not from Jorge Luis Borges, but from Bernard Mandeville and his delightful *Fable of the Bees*. Envy, he maintained, is not only riveted in human nature, but essential for keeping the world together: "Envy and Emulation have kept more Men in Bounds, and reform'd more Ill Husbands from Sloth, from Drinking, and other evil Courses, than all the Sermons that have been preach'd since the time of the Apostles."[4] Envy, in short, is one of those private vices that turns out to be a public benefit. Imagine how wayward and fickle economists might have been had they not been kept in line by envy?

3. Some recent studies of the political dimensions of the physical sciences are Forman 1987, Kevles 1990, and Leslie 1990.
4. Mandeville 1924, 138–39.

Is it time for a divorce, now that Mirowski has unveiled the scandalous intimacy of physics and economics? I think not. Physics and economics are both attempts to make sense of a single world, whether it be made of Platonic tetrahedrons or an incompressible jelly. As long as fair exchanges are made (and yes, let's continue to carry them out in broad daylight), the more trade the better. Mirowski's book may actually help to knock physics off its pedestal. If economists can be patient and become more confident about what insights they have already achieved, then time may be on their side. They have ultimately done less to deceive than physicists manage to pull off any old day of the week.

References

Forman, Paul. 1987. Behind Quantum Electronics: National Security as a Basis for Physical Research in the United States, 1940–1960. *Historical Studies in the Physical and Biological Sciences* 18:149–229.

Franklin, Allan. 1986. *The Neglect of Experiment*. Cambridge: Cambridge University Press.

Galison, Peter. 1987. *How Experiments End*. Chicago: University of Chicago Press.

Hacking, Ian. 1983. *Representing and Intervening*. Cambridge: Cambridge University Press.

Kevles, Daniel. 1990. Cold War and Hot Physics: Science, Security, and the American State, 1945–56. *Historical Studies in the Physical and Biological Sciences* 20:239–64.

Lakatos, Imre. 1981. History of Science and Its Rational Reconstructions. Reprinted in *Scientific Revolutions*, edited by Ian Hacking. Oxford: Oxford University Press.

Leslie, Stuart W. 1990. Profit and Loss: The Military and MIT in the Postwar Era. *Historical Studies in the Physical and Biological Sciences* 21:59–85.

Mandeville, Bernard. 1924. *The Fable of the Bees*. London: Oxford University Press.

Mirowski, Philip. 1989. *More Heat than Light*. Cambridge and New York: Cambridge University Press. [Citations are abbreviated *MHL*.]

Interpreting the Triumph of Mathematical Economics

Theodore M. Porter

1. Mirowski and the Metaphysical Hubris of Economists

To me, a historian, Philip Mirowski's *More Heat than Light* seems a dazzling historical critique of neoclassical economics. Economists have praised it as a landmark work of history. Mirowski thus has succeeded brilliantly in defying the specialists. He also defies current academic fads. Dissatisfied with Foucault, and with the postmodern outlook that deconstructs explanations and narratives, he has found his inspiration in Emile Meyerson's 1908 investigation of the *intellectus ipse, Identity and Reality*. By no means has his perspective been defined by a single source. His book makes creative use of an astonishing variety of sources. A historian of science like myself certainly cannot chastise him for failing to attend to research in our discipline; he has, on the contrary, placed himself among the most successful of scholars working to break down the barriers between science studies and historical research on economics.[1] Still, in one crucial respect Mirowski's interpretations look quite archaic from the standpoint of the historian of science. For this is a book in which concepts make their own history. Human individuals are mere mouthpieces. Political and intellectual cultures are invisible. Disciplinary institutions and scientific practices are nowhere in evidence.

Mirowski has written a story of metaphysical hubris, one that simul-

---

1. Other notable recent works that effectively combine studies of economics with those of mathematics and the sciences include Ingrao and Israel 1990, Schabas 1990, Cartwright 1989, and Wise 1989–90.

taneously exemplifies some of this hubris. He reduces the whole history of economics, from Aristotle to Samuelson and beyond, to the working out of a central metaphor of conservation, viewed as a fundamental structure of human, or at least Western, thought. The historical evolution of physics, economics, and even biology is understood here in terms of a triad of concepts, "body, motion, and value." That triad supports the notion of energy, forming a pyramid and, more crucially, implying that the links of economics with physics and biology are anything but fortuitous. They are deep and inescapable; they structure, at a minimum, the whole history of mathematization in science.

From theoretical declarations like these one might suppose that the book is a monolith, wholly lacking in historical contingencies. This would be wrong. Mirowski has not spun this story entirely out of his own head. He has engaged effectively with his materials, making his work richer and at the same time less consistent than one would expect from a pure work of grand theory. I suggest that *More Heat than Light* contains at least three frameworks of interpretation. The first is a matter of interdisciplinary influences—more precisely, interdisciplinary copying. We can call it mimesis. The undoubted star here is Walras, who was able to summarize his program for economics under the title "Economique et méchanique."[2] As Mirowski shows, Walras got his mathematics from textbooks of mechanics. He considered the analogies of his work to mechanics to be the highest justification for mathematical economics. And the tone of his dealings with physicists like Poincaré can only be called sycophantic. There are other moments, too, when physics seems to provide the main incentive to new work in economics. Mirowski deals very effectively with Paul Samuelson from this point of view. The introduction of game theory is another key point at which economics intersects with physics (Ingrao and Israel 1990; Weintraub 1992).

But can one really say that neoclassical economic theory had no alternative to "unabashed and shameless imitation" of physics (*MHL*, 368)? Mirowski's story sometimes proceeds as if the economists had no disciplinary structures, no textbooks, no research traditions, of their own—as if every time physics sneezes, economics comes down with pneumonia. The protagonists of his story seem to worry about nothing else except keeping track of the latest in physics, and undertaking instantly to adjust their economics accordingly. This is unbelievable, for at least two

2. Now, at last, translated into English in Mirowski and Cook 1990.

reasons. One—and Mirowski is aware of this—is that few economists have any appreciable knowledge of physics (though, to be sure, some very important ones have been emigrés and interlopers from physics). The other is that economists are capable of considerable satisfaction regarding the achievements of their field, and have made this sufficiently believable that others, like political scientists and sociologists, scramble to copy them. The story of the economists' dependency on physics is an important one, for which Mirowski deserves much credit. But it ought to be a story of selective borrowing, sometimes pseudo-borrowing, and only very rarely of simple imitation. And the story needs to be set firmly in the context of economic strategies and institutions, and not depend on a sequence of stick figures who know nothing except that they will freeze if isolated from the reflected glow of physics.

Mirowski's second framework of interpretation is the one for which he credits Meyerson. We might call it metaphor, but a better term is reification. Meyerson saw science, and indeed all thought, as thoroughly antipositivistic. To explain, for Meyerson, is to identify something as cause. It is, in fact, to find stability underlying change, to comprehend causes in a way that makes them somehow equal to their effects. Hence conservation principles are especially typical of scientific reasoning. On this basis Mirowski treats the "discovery" of energy conservation in physics as even more epochal for physics than it actually was. His exaggeration has some relevance to the main line of his story, for he holds that the economists copied energy physics just as soon as energy conservation became available as an intellectual resource. And indeed this would make the timing almost exactly right for Jevons and Walras. But potential theory, and the mathematics of constrained maximization, were in place, and available even in textbooks, some decades earlier.[3] Especially important for Walras was Louis Poinsot's *Eléments de statique* of 1842. Doubtless there was copying here, but it was not prompt.

Still, energy conservation can very reasonably be seen as the central development of nineteenth-century physics, and the Meyersonian perspective contributes usefully to an understanding of it. On the basis of a reasonable success in interconverting electricity, mechanical energy, and heat at constant ratios, physicists justified belief in a conserved entity,

---

3. The important distinction between potential theory and energy physics was greatly clarified for me by discussion at the March 1991 conference at Duke University where this paper was first presented. See Wise 1991.

soon named "energy," which was taken to underlie the phenomena. The doctrine of energy conservation was a triumph of reification. Mirowski handles this issue admirably. But his point of view cannot be sustained as a framework for the whole history of economics. In a characteristically unwieldy chapter on political economy from Aristotle to Marx, Mirowski finds himself obliged to chastise first William Petty, then Turgot, then Quesnay for failing to recognize the need for conservation laws. Finally, to everyone's relief, conservation of value appears on the scene with Adam Smith. Mirowski is interested mainly in its destiny, which is to break down and be replaced by a field concept of value analogous to field theory in electricity. But here the centrality of conservation principles breaks down as well. For as Mirowski shows so clearly, the conservation of value, or rather of income plus utility, was not welcomed into economics. Economists had no use for it. It was rather an embarrassment. It arrived, unwanted, attached to the mathematics that economists borrowed from potential theory in mechanics. Possibly a conservation law applying to income plus utility was unavoidable, since this is the correlate of kinetic plus potential energy; but economists have taken great pains to avoid it nonetheless. Mirowski may be right in arguing that this is the Achilles' heel of neoclassical economics. But then neoclassical economics becomes the Achilles' heel of his argument, for economists have not wanted to reify their conservation principles.

The third form of explanation Mirowski offers is his own masterpiece of metaphysics. This is his attempt to understand the development of all forms of scientific thought in terms of an expanding pyramid with the concepts of body, motion, and value at the base, and energy at the summit. Since he seems to regard this model as the deepest and most fruitful perspective from which to view his story, it is not a little unfortunate that I have been wholly unable to understand it. Doubtless this explains why I find it forced and unconvincing whenever he invokes this threefold "simplex" to make sense of any particular episode in his narrative. And there are other obvious objections. For example, it seems clear that the element of "body" is quite absent from neoclassical economics. The "consumer depicted by Figure 1"[4] in any number of economics books looks for all the world like a standard-format graph comparing demand curves.

---

4. Mohring 1968, 257–58. It should be clear that I do not wish to single this author out for ridicule.

Nor am I content with the relation of this level of explanation to the other two. The "simplex" seems calculated to entail the overwhelming need of conservation principles, but I cannot see how. And the requirement that all sciences proceed simultaneously through "anthropometric," "lineamentric," and "syndetic" stages reduces all interdisciplinary interactions to the most negligible of epiphenomena. This scheme demands that every science must develop more or less as it has, even had the disciplines been isolated from one another. The reciprocal imitation of economists and physicists then must be regarded as a false correlation, a consequence of parallel developmental processes. Everything takes place as it must in this new monadology, even if we do not find here the best of all possible worlds.

At the core of this book, then, I find a tension bordering on contradiction. But I do not wish to rest my critique of *More Heat than Light* mainly on what I have identified as internal inconsistencies. I object, rather, to the common premise underlying all three lines of interpretation: that the history of these interactions between physics and economics was dictated in its most essential features by a few all-embracing concepts. Let me sketch a different model for doing history of economics.

2. Toward a Cultural History of Economic Practice

"The best way to talk about science is to examine how people have done it," writes Mirowski (*MHL*, 8). Alas, flesh-and-blood people in concrete political, social, and cultural situations are nowhere to be found between the covers of *More Heat than Light*. My program for history of economics in the wake of that book is to take them more fully into account. And so, inspired by Mirowski's pyramid, I here unveil my own magical triad of concepts for understanding the triumph of quantification in science: *identity, language,* and *community*. They do not dictate a unique line of development in all scientific disciplines. They do provide a valuable approach for understanding the forms that knowledge takes in different contexts.

The problem of scientific identity has recently gained attention as a result of some new work on Galileo by Mario Biagioli (1990). He argues that patronage was in some ways the key social institution of early modern science. Even claims to objectivity, he suggests, were bound up with the particular circumstances of a patronage relationship. Reliable support from a very great patron like Cosimo II of Florence enabled Galileo to suppress the utilitarian aspect of his work and present it as pure and disinterested. And the identity of science, the prestige of scientific knowledge, long depended on its relations to powerful figures in the larger society. In the case of the Academy of Science in Paris, founded in the 1660s, a key element was the patronage of the king. In England it may have been more important that rich and powerful people participated in the work of natural philosophy. They did so in some cases by carrying out their own research, but most essentially by witnessing and certifying notable experiments and observations.

The transition to modern science involved a shift towards more self-contained scientific bodies. Scientific identities became increasingly tied to particular kinds of scientific communities. Those communities need not be equivalent to formally constituted bodies, though the new scientific societies helped to define science in terms of communities of inquiry. Still, it is clearly crucial that natural philosophy made claims to universal knowledge, truth that was not confined to any particular place or any particular society. Experimenters, especially, faced the considerable problem of making knowledge that would transcend the local circumstances of its production. For this purpose, the community to which scientific work was addressed had to extend beyond those members of an academy in a particular city who might potentially witness an important experiment. Hence it was necessary to create an effective and appropriate rhetoric, what Steven Shapin calls a "literary technology" (Shapin and Schaffer 1985, ch. 2). In short, community is intimately bound to language.

Shapin and Simon Schaffer, writing about Robert Boyle's seventeenth-century experiments with the air pump, emphasize the notion of virtual witnessing. Boyle wrote with notorious prolixity, providing abundant and often irrelevant details and appearing to report his results in the order he obtained them. He thus reported some failures as well as his successes. This, combined with careful attention to vivid, corroborative detail, makes his readers feel almost as if they were present in the laboratory as witnesses to the experiment. The authority of his reported results could thereby extend out to a much larger community, including all those interested in natural philosophy who were able to buy or borrow his publications.

Vividness and candor, though, are not notable traits of modern scientific prose. Experimental papers are now written first of all for a community of fellow investigators. It is generally supposed that the acceptance of experimental results depends on the possibility of replication. But the dogma of replication has been exploded by recent sociology of science, and it is undoubtedly true that researchers very rarely try to duplicate exactly the reported work of others. And yet the form of scientific community implied by the doctrine of replication is in fact rather close to the one that now prevails. Scientific papers are written above all for the consumption of other researchers engaged with similar problems or using similar methods. Although they will rarely try to replicate previous results, they will judge published work mainly on the basis of the contribution it makes to their own research. What seems consistent with what is done by other members of a research community will be accepted; what provides directions for new lines of research may be highly influential; but what seems puzzling, inexplicable, or pointless in the context of the research others are doing may be challenged, and will more likely be ignored. The scientific research paper, in any event, is written not simply to convince its readers, but to induce other specialists to put its methods and conclusions to work.

Thus even if we are skeptical of claims to replication, the problem of communicating results in such a way that others can perform related work remains a central problem of working science. And this is no small difficulty. Every successful laboratory depends on a wealth of craft skills, of tacit knowledge. Such knowledge does not travel easily. Yet somehow it is made to travel, as we know from the enormous success of the natural sciences in diffusing both theoretical commitments and experimental programs across wide barriers of geography, politics, and language. How is this done? The new sociology of experimentation emphasizes the importance of personal contact, the transportation of people and equipment between laboratories. Another way in which experimental networks are promoted is the standardization of equipment, made possible through mass production. But the diffusion of science is not wholly, probably not even mainly, a matter of material technologies and craft skills. The ideal of a research community based on knowledge shared through what I am loosely calling replication demanded a reconception of what would count as scientifically interesting. A model scientific fact could no longer be some singular occurrence, vividly described to excite the wonder of the reader. A solid fact had to be under good experimental control, something that the author could demonstrate at will and that might be accessible even to distant readers. Finally, literary technologies must be given a prominent place in this story. A particularly important one is quantification (Porter 1992a). Quantitative rules have been a powerful instrument of standardization, in economics and the natural sciences alike.

The use of quantification to render a richly textured and intuitive local knowledge more homogeneous and detached is wonderfully illustrated in a book that Mirowski has also made good use of, Witold Kula's *Measures and Men* (1986). Mirowski emphasizes the movement away from body as the basis for measuring, the transition from anthropometric measures to standardized, conventional ones. My point is a related one. The move to rigid, conventional measurements accompanied a shift of power from local communities to centralized institutions, the state. In Old Regime Europe, Kula shows, almost every measurement involved a qualitative judgment: a bushel of grain would be heaped if the grain were judged of low quality, or if the social position of the recipient entitled him to demand it. The normal measure of land was not a fixed, objective area, but the amount that could be plowed in a day or that absorbed a certain amount of seed when planted by a very experienced sower. That is, measurement was fundamentally subjective. In addition, different measures were used for different kinds of products, and all of these varied from region to region, often from village to village. In a world of face-to-face contact this subjectivity could be negotiated, and it seems not to have constituted a great obstacle to economic exchange. But for agents of the centralized state, all these "soft" and variable measures were uninterpretable.

The imposition of the metric system showed what harmony of interests prevailed between modern science and the modern state. Both depend on a certain kind of objectivity, the replacement of the ineffable and the subjective with fixed, uniform rules. The literary technologies of science now embrace a host of such rules. One of the more extreme examples is the methodology of statistics, which has too often been treated as a set of obligatory recipes for reaching conclusions from scientific data (McCloskey 1985; Gigerenzer et al. 1989). Inevitably the rules do more than determine how results can be presented. They help to define what should count as good scientific research in the first place. They determine what parts of the natural world are worthy of investigation and how it is permissible to interpret them.

Mirowski, who is keenly alert to what is newest and most radical in studies of the natural sciences, makes virtually no use of these studies of laboratories and experiments in *More Heat than Light*.[5] The reason can be readily surmised. Experimentation has almost no place in neoclassical economics. The nearest thing to an economic laboratory is the computer, where vast quantities of econometric data are processed and, sometimes, compared with theoretical predictions. But one might well apply to theoretical economics a remark that William Petty made about the city of London: that it is a head far too big for its body (England). Neoclassical economics is a lot more like eighteenth-century rational mechanics than it is like experimental physics. How does the new literature on craft skills, replication, communication, and networks apply to a largely theoretical research tradition?

If we recall that a key problem of the literature on experimentation is to explain how the private, craft skills of the laboratory are made into a kind of public knowledge, suitable to support a research community, the relevance is easy to see. We can readily situate the ideology of economics in terms of the debate on the air pump depicted by Shapin and Schaffer. Economics has taken its stand firmly with Thomas Hobbes. Hobbes, as Shapin and Schaffer show, was a sharp and persistent critic of Boyle's experimental research with the air pump. He argued that experiment can never serve as an adequate basis for science, for public knowledge. It cannot because the laboratory is inescapably a private space. Its privacy is partly a matter of physical location: only a select few can witness any particular experiment, and everyone else must take it on faith. Further, true experimental demonstration is impossible, since a critic can always place in the foreground one of the myriad details that the experimenter has dismissed as secondary and uninteresting. Against Boyle and the Royal Society Hobbes held up the ideal of logical and mathematical demonstration. Here is truly public knowledge, because the whole train of reasoning can be put on paper, and made accessible to every competent reader. Hobbes, of course, did not defeat the experimentalists. But in a way he was vindicated by the astonishingly vehement and persistent debates that divided the early experimental community about the meanings, and even the outcomes, of their most important experiments. It was easier to form a research community in mathematics, or rational mechanics. There, the fiercest controversies concerned priorities of discovery. Mathematicians were much more nearly in agreement than experimentalists about the standards of adequate demonstration.

---

5. He does relate economics to science studies in Mirowski and Sklivas 1991.

For obvious reasons, having to do above all with the politically charged character of their subject matter, political economists faced grave obstacles to the formation of a research community. A total faith in mathematics and quantification has gone a long way toward overcoming divisions about practical matters.[6] The understanding I am proposing is, in a way, the obverse of George Stigler's (1973) argument about the sociological factors that aided the triumph of marginalism. He emphasized the usefulness of mathematics in excluding amateurs from economic science (see also Coats 1967; Maloney 1985). I am suggesting that a rigidly mathematical research methodology facilitated the solidification of a research tradition within the economic profession.[7] This understanding is not inconsistent with Mirowski's argument that economists have characteristically entertained an excessive reverence for the achievements of physics, or even with his claim that they copied much of their mathematics from physics. But I prefer to see their unyielding commitment to mathematical theory as something other than evidence of timeless beliefs and deep metaphysical commitments. Mathematics might almost be seen as an alternative to belief, a set of conventions that work *because* they constrain and obscure debate about those issues which, to outsiders, clearly matter most.[8] Indeed the point may be made, more temperately, about other disciplines as well. Nancy Cartwright (1989) remarks that mathematical simplicity in physics as well as economics "is gained only at the cost of misrepresentation," that it is "an artefact of too narrow a focus." To be sure, economists' faith in mathematics is real enough. But such faith may be more consequence than cause of mathematical practice.

To argue this way is to emphasize the role of quantification as an economic rhetoric. This is right, but it might also be misleading. Even economists are now aware of the inescapability of rhetoric, thanks to Donald McCloskey (1985). But as Mirowski (1987) points out, McClos-

---

6. Mary Morgan (1990, 6) remarks that in the early meetings of the econometricians, quantitative enthusiasm and methodological agreement overshadowed obvious political differences and created an almost euphoric sense of common purpose. Kurt Danziger (1990) provides especially compelling illustrations of the ways in which quantitative formalism can provide the basis for a coherent disciplinary discourse.

7. Weintraub (1991) shows how the mathematical formalism of stability analysis has delimited a crucial area of theoretical discussion in neoclassical economics.

8. See Furner 1975 for the sharp political debates that preceded the triumph of mathematical economics in America. On quantitative positivism see Heilbron 1982; also my forthcoming essay "The Death of the Object: *Fin-de-siècle* Philosophy of Physics" in Ross (forthcoming).

key has presented the implications of rhetoric for economics in a form that is far too unthreatening to the complacency of economists. By speaking a less technical and rebarbative prose, McCloskey suggests, economists would only make their arguments more interesting, intelligible, and influential. This is unbelievable. Mirowski offers an apt paraphrase of Heinrich Hertz on James Clerk Maxwell: neoclassical economics *is* neoclassical mathematics. If, in the wake of a rhetorical revolution, plain prose became the language of choice for expert discussion of economies, the field of economics would rapidly become unrecognizable to those who know it today. I am convinced that sharply discrepant visions of economic order and economic morality would come to the surface and would fracture the now almost unified discourse of modernist, neoclassical economics.[9] Policy discussion is of course tolerated, but it is consigned to the periphery of the field. At the center must be scientific rigor, enforced with great severity, especially upon the young, by doctoral committees, journal reviewers, and tenure boards.

My program for the new history of economics, then, would require historians to be far more attentive to matters of language, community, and identity, to the implications for economic theory and methods of the ways that economists form consensus and make shared knowledge. The rigidity and rigor of an overwhelmingly mathematical language should be understood not as a consequence of too many economists thinking too uncritically about physics, but in cultural terms, as a rather strict set of norms that regulate this particular scientific community. At the same time, my argument might well be taken to imply that economists have evaded all the really important issues, and hence that the history of economics is not really of much consequence except for a few benighted souls who are overly impressed by the mindless pursuit of rigor. In fact I do believe something like this—but with important qualifications. No historian without a severely underdeveloped organ of irony could sneer at economists for the irrelevance of their discourse to modern life. The issue needs to be posed differently. How can we reconcile the prominence of economists in modern public life with the prevailing unworldliness of their professional discourse?

I do not propose to attempt an answer to that question here, but only to flag its importance. It is, to me, astonishing that historians of economics

---

9. A. W. Coats has argued that with the triumph of marginalism, theory replaced ideology as the glue that held the economics profession together. See the citation in Maloney 1985, 217.

since Schumpeter have accepted so unquestioningly the reigning dogma of the current neoclassical orthodoxy, that what really matters in modern economics is mathematical theory. One can find numerous studies of the policy influence of Adam Smith or the Ricardians, but policy studies are decidedly outside the mainstream of the history of modern economics. There are, to be sure, a few laudable exceptions to the dominance of theory and methodology in history of recent economics.[10] Even these exceptional works, though, have scarcely begun to account for the coexistence, indeed alliance, of mathematical abstraction and policy influence in the contemporary economics discipline. There is a great need for careful scrutiny of the relation of the economics discipline to economic policy, and the uses of economics in administration. I would add that the French literature is better in this regard and that the estimable works on French economics by François Etner (1987) and Hervé Dumez (1985) deserve to be better known among anglophone historians than they currently are.

One area of scholarship that would provide an excellent model for a more engaged history of economics, and of which historians of economics (and of natural science) seem to be completely oblivious, is the sociology and history of accounting. There is now an effective movement of accounting scholars who are well informed about modern science studies and who have a sophisticated appreciation of the social role of quantification as a tool for coordinating and legitimating decisions. I have tried to call that work to the attention of historians of science because of its relevance to current discussions of objectivity.[11] Historians of economics could benefit equally from what historians of accounting say about quantification and objectivity. In addition, the subject matter of history of economics ought to overlap with that of history of accounting a lot more than it currently does. Budgeting methods, input-output analysis, cost-benefit analysis, and a host of other governmental and corporate financial methods involve economic ideas and expertise. They do not, to be sure, amount to unproblematical applications of pure

---

10. A few distinguished examples: Winch 1969, Goodwin 1981, Barber 1985, Alchon 1985, Furner and Supple 1990, and Coats 1981. Also admirable for its attention to statistical practice among economists is Morgan 1990.

11. See Porter 1992b. Interested readers can find their way into the accounting literature by examining the last ten years or so of the journal *Accounting, Organizations, and Society*. Among the most interesting authors in history and sociology of accounting are Anthony Hopwood (editor of the journal), Stuart Burchell, Ruth Hines, Anne Loft, Peter Miller, Ted O'Leary, Michael Power, and Nikolas Rose.

economic theory (Fourquet 1980; Ashmore, Mulkay, and Pinch 1989). Precisely for this reason, it is of the greatest importance that historians of economics pay more attention to them.

That is, historians need to be alert also to the public language of economics, to the rhetorical strategies economists use to affect policy debates, as well as to those they adopt in their research papers. This point, like economics itself, is of more than academic significance. The success of the economics discipline in places like the modern United States is difficult to understand except in terms of a peculiar symbiosis of pure mathematical theory and applied economic studies.[12] Were it not for the applications, economists would not be in demand in banking, government, and business. Undergraduate students would not flock to introductory economics classes. Academic economics would lose much of the support that makes it the most powerful field in the modern social sciences. Conversely, the credibility of economic measurement and forecasting, cost-benefit analysis, and various budgeting systems depends at least in part on their presumed relationship to a recondite mathematical theory. And in general, as Mirowski notes, the usual ways of discussing the relationship between pure and applied economics have the undoubted advantage of protecting neoclassical theory from its critics.[13] The connection needs to be examined more carefully. This would not necessarily be a debunking exercise. We would, I am convinced, learn a lesson closely related to the ones sociologists have brought back from their encounters with laboratory life, namely that in these more practical affairs skill is of paramount importance. What has been the role of theory in maintaining and perpetuating the skills of economists? How do those skills relate to the prevailing language of economic objectivity in public and disciplinary rhetoric? Asking these questions could make history of economics a worthy part of history of science, and of political and social history as well.

References

Alchon, Guy. 1985. *The Invisible Hand of Planning: Capitalism, Social Science, and the State in the 1920s.* Princeton.

---

12. On this point see John Maloney's remarks on Pigou (Maloney 1985, 182).
13. Mirowski 1987, 24. Maloney 1985 shows how successfully this defense of neoclassical orthodoxy was used by Marshall himself.

Ashmore, Malcolm, Michael Mulkay, and Trevor Pinch. 1989. *Health and Efficiency: A Sociology of Health Economics*. Milton Keynes.
Barber, William J. 1985. *Herbert Hoover, the Economists, and American Economic Policy, 1921–1933*. Cambridge.
Biagioli, Mario. 1990. Galileo's System of Patronage. *History of Science* 28:1–62.
Cartwright, Nancy. 1989. *Nature's Capacities and Their Measurement*. New York.
Coats, A. W. 1967. Sociological Aspects of British Economic Thought, 1880–1930. *Journal of Political Economy* 175:706–29.
——— , ed. 1981. *Economists in Government: An International Comparative Study*. Durham, N.C.
Danziger, Kurt. 1990. *Constructing the Subject: Historical Origins of Psychological Research*. Cambridge.
Dumez, Hervé. 1985. *L'économiste, la science, et le pouvoir: le cas Walras*. Paris.
Etner, François. 1987. *Histoire du calcul économique en France*. Paris.
Fourquet, François. 1980. *Les comptes de la puissance*. Paris.
Furner, Mary. 1975. *Advocacy and Objectivity: A Crisis in the Professionalization of American Social Science, 1865–1905*. Lexington, Ky.
Furner, Mary, and Barry Supple, eds. 1990. *The State and Economic Knowledge*. Cambridge.
Gigerenzer, Gerd, et al. 1989. *The Empire of Chance: How Probability Changed Science and Everyday Life*. Cambridge.
Goodwin, Craufurd D. W., ed. 1981. *Energy Policy in Perspective*. Washington, D.C.
Heilbron, John L. 1982. *Fin-de-siècle* Physics. In *Science, Technology and Society in the Time of Alfred Nobel*, edited by C. G. Bernhard et al., 51–73. Oxford.
Ingrao, Bruna, and Giorgio Israel. 1990. *The Invisible Hand: Economic Equilibrium in the History of Science*. Translated by Ian McGilvray. Cambridge, Mass.
Kula, Witold. 1986. *Measures and Men*. Translated by Richard Szreter. Princeton.
McCloskey, Donald. 1985. *The Rhetoric of Economics*. Madison, Wis.
Maloney, John. 1985. *Marshall, Orthodoxy, and the Professionalisation of Economics*. Cambridge.
Mirowski, Philip. 1987. Shall I Compare Thee to a Minkowski-Ricardo-Leontief-Metzler Matrix of the Mosak-Hicks Type? *Economics and Philosophy* 3:67–95.
——— . 1989. *More Heat than Light*. Cambridge. [Citations are abbreviated *MHL*.]
Mirowski, Philip, and Pamela Cook. 1990. Walras' "Economics and Mechanics": Translation, Commentary, Context. In *Economics as Discourse: An Analysis of the Language of Economists*, edited by Warren Samuels, 189–215. Boston.
Mirowski, Philip, and Steven Sklivas. 1991. Why Economists Don't Replicate (Although They Do Reproduce). *Review of Political Economy* 3:146–63.
Mohring, Herbert. 1968. Urban Highway Investments. In *Measuring Benefits of Government Investments*, edited by Robert Dorfman. Washington, D.C.
Morgan, Mary. 1990. *The History of Econometric Ideas*. Cambridge.
Porter, Theodore M. 1992a. Objectivity as Standardization: The Rhetoric of Im-

personality in Measurement, Statistics, and Cost-Benefit Analysis. *Annals of Scholarship* 9:19–59.

———. 1992b. Quantification and the Accounting Ideal in Science. *Social Studies of Science* 22:633–51.

Ross, Dorothy, ed. Forthcoming. *Modernist Impulses in the Human Sciences.* Baltimore.

Schabas, Margaret. 1990. *A World Ruled by Number: William Stanley Jevons and the Rise of Mathematical Economics.* Princeton.

Shapin, Steven, and Simon Schaffer. 1985. *Leviathan and the Air-Pump.* Princeton.

Stigler, George. 1973. The Adoption of the Marginal Utility Theory. In *The Marginal Revolution in Economics*, edited by R. D. Collison Black, A. W. Coats, and Craufurd D. W. Goodwin, 305–20. Durham, N.C.

Weintraub, E. Roy. 1991. *Stabilizing Dynamics: Constructing Economic Knowledge.* Cambridge.

———, ed. 1992. *Toward a History of Game Theory.* Annual supplement, *HOPE* volume 24.

Winch, Donald. 1969. *Economics and Policy: A Historical Study.* New York.

Wise, M. Norton, with the collaboration of Crosbie Smith. 1989–90. Work and Waste: Political Economy and Natural Philosophy in Nineteenth-Century Britain. *History of Science* 27:263–301, 391–449; 28:221–61.

———. 1991. Uses and Abuses of Interdisciplinary History. Paper presented at the Duke Economic Thought Workshop Symposium "Rethinking the History of Economics in the Light of *More Heat*," Durham, 1–3 March.

A Method to Mirowski's Mad Use of Metaphor

Steve Fuller

The attraction of Mirowski's *More Heat than Light* (1989a) to a philosopher such as myself, a "social epistemologist" (Fuller 1988, 1989, 1992a), is quite clear. Mirowski revives the lost art of "synthetic" or "universal" history, that is, history *with a point*. The historiography that informed the philosophy of science throughout most of the nineteenth and twentieth centuries was of this type. For all their disagreements about which direction science was heading, Comte, Whewell, Mill, Mach, Duhem, and Meyerson all agreed that a direction could be discerned, in terms of which various events could be judged as "progressive" or not. The normative force of these histories lay in their ability to persuade the reader of science's "natural" trajectory, the next stage in which would be a particular project on the research front that the synthetic historian favored. This genre nearly died at the hands of Thomas Kuhn, whose *Structure of Scientific Revolutions* (1962) showed, perhaps unwittingly, that the history of science could be portrayed as passing through a developmental sequence that did not lead in any particular direction, except to another cycle of the sequence. Attempts by Lakatos (1979) and Laudan (1977) to revive the genre failed, largely because their defenses of scientific progress were not connected to substantive ends that science might be presently pursuing. The proof of synthetic history is not in the ingredients it mixes from the past, but in the pudding it serves up as policy for the future. The mere logical possibility of such pudding is very thin gruel indeed!

In reinventing the genre of synthetic history Mirowski finds himself in an awkward position. Unlike his distinguished predecessors he is the practitioner of a science that he believes has headed in the wrong direction. Consequently, error does not appear in his narrative as temporary interference in the course of overall progress. Rather, ever-deepening error turns out to define Mirowski's plot structure. One false turn in thinking about value in terms of utility, and then utility in terms of potential energy, and the history of economics was doomed to more than a century of dialectical frustration. To his credit, Mirowski realizes that his story cannot be quite so simple. For every turning point in history, even a false one, there must be a mechanism that enables the chosen trajectory to be followed. And so, if Mirowski's is a tale of error, it must be of *systematic* error, a proposition that he goes on to defend in terms of an intriguing, albeit largely implicit, theory of metaphoric transfer. Thus we are provided with an ideal opportunity for taking another stab at answering the question that the philosopher of science Richard Boyd posed in 1977: *What is "metaphor" a metaphor for?*

Mirowski argues that many of the central conceptual problems of modern economics are traceable to a faulty metaphoric transfer from the mid-nineteenth-century physical theory known as "proto-energetics" to the utility theory of value that continues to inform neoclassical economics. The faultiest transfer seems to have occurred between conservation principles of energy and conservation principles of . . . what? Utility? Income? Economists have since constructed elaborate attempts at formally circumventing this problem. However, when Mirowski traces the intuitive appeal of proto-energetics to the engineering backgrounds of distinguished economists, he is not simply describing or even explaining the limits of the theoretical imagination of economics. More importantly, he is *criticizing* this development, largely on the basis of a less than fully articulated *normative* theory of metaphoric usage.

After all, even granting Mirowski his version of the history of economics, it does not follow that the field deserves criticism. It has been quite common in the history of science for new disciplines to emerge by elaborating on some notions or techniques that another discipline has abandoned or superseded. In that case the lack of correspondence between the properties of objects in the two domains might signal the presence of two distinct ontologies, one irreducible to the other, but each governed by its own set of principles. Given Norton Wise's (1991) point, that during the period 1750–1850 economists and physicists were often one and the same people trying to understand both domains in terms of the same images, one might suppose that, contrary to its original packaging, proto-energetics really functioned better as a model of the economy than as a model of the physical universe, which is perhaps why physicists abandoned it while economists stuck with it. Moreover, as Margaret Schabas (1993) suggests, even if economists were trying to emulate physics as self-consciously, and as perversely, as Mirowski sometimes claims, their failure to make the metaphor fit should not necessarily count against them—especially if one takes seriously the idea (as philosophers have until quite recently) that physics is the methodological model for all the sciences. And so, on what basis can Mirowski's implicit theory of metaphor be used to criticize modern economic practice?

A good place to begin answering this question is by considering the tension that Michael Hobbs (1991) detects in Mirowski's use of metaphor in *More Heat than Light*. Hobbs attempts to situate Mirowski's usage in the context of the recent turn to rhetoric in economic theory, but he notices that Mirowski does not talk about metaphor in quite the same way as, say, Donald McCloskey (1985) does. McCloskey is primarily concerned with the deliberate use of metaphor in economic writing, especially the ways in which metaphors illuminate or obscure the message of that writing to a larger audience. Often he finds economists rhetorically inept, fostering expectations on which they are ill prepared to deliver. But he does not typically diagnose economists' mishandling of metaphor in terms of deep conceptual problems in the foundations of economic science itself. In fact McCloskey, himself a distinguished applier of the neoclassical tradition to British economic history (e.g., McCloskey 1973, 1981), clearly believes that metaphor is sufficiently detached from the field's conceptual foundations that greater attention to metaphorical expression will only serve to focus an already forceful message. While Mirowski too is not averse to citing the inept use of physics metaphors in economic writing, his rhetorical posture is quite opposed to McCloskey's and his target ultimately quite different.

Where Hobbs sees a tension, and perhaps even a contradiction, in Mirowski's use of metaphor, I would prefer to see an inchoate attempt at reconciling the two major roles for rhetoric in the classical tradition. McCloskey speaks for a *rhetorica utens*, rhetoric as an art for making the client's speech more effective. As a practicing economist Mirowski is not without this aspect, but he speaks more often for a *rhetorica docens*, rhetoric as an art for interpreting and critiquing speech from a standpoint that transcends the particular ends of clients and attests to values inherent in the very act of speaking. This side of Mirowski emerged in response to McCloskey's *Rhetoric of Economics* (1985). At that time, Mirowski (1989b) expressed discomfort at McCloskey's tendency to ignore the historical baggage that mathematical modeling brings to economics. This "baggage" is a deep, largely unconscious sense of metaphor that makes successive generations of economists think like mid-nineteenth-century physicists. More than a set of relatively useful formalisms, the mathematics carries with it some rather specific subliminal instructions for its use, which serve to limit both the range of mathematical tools that have subsequently been imported by economists and the ways in which the imported tools have been applied. Indeed Mirowski goes so far as to claim that these strictures have managed systematically to disadvantage the two leading rivals to the neoclassical paradigm, Marxism and institutionalism.

However, Hobbs wonders whether Mirowski is fair in criticizing economists so severely, if their captivity to physics metaphors is so deep. Or, is Mirowski really only charging economists with failing to take their own metaphorical commitments seriously, which would require that they change their conception of value as physicists changed their conception of energy and its measurement (Mirowski 1986)? Whatever answers are given to these questions, we shall need to go beyond most philosophical theories of metaphors, *especially* those put forth by analytic philosophers of science, whom we might have expected to be the most helpful under the circumstances. In particular, none of the standard theories captures metaphoric transfer as a *historic process* with consequences for objects in *both* of the domains brought into correspondence by the metaphor. Indeed, using Mirowski's history as a guide, we might imagine this process to unfold much as a Freudian neurosis would, thus adding some well-placed concreteness to Mirowski's own "physics envy" metaphor (*MHL*, ch. 7): After a fairly specific, perhaps even traumatic episode (such as the "Marginalist Revolution" in economics), in which properties of objects in one domain are explicitly transferred to properties of objects in another, the transfer is routinized to such an extent that its metaphorical character becomes repressed—that is, except for those occasions when an unforeseen anomaly forces a partial remembrance of the original transfer. Thus the major twentieth-century controversies concerning the formalization of economics that follow upon this transfer operate as "parapraxes," slips of the tongue collectively made by the economics community, which are remedied, not by clearer speech—as McCloskey might suggest—but by what? Therapy? Mirowski's preferred answer seems to be a new economic practice, one that brings to the center of the discipline traditions that had been shunted aside by the Marginalist Revolution, much as a therapist might advise developing aspects of a patient's life that lay dormant because of an overemphasis on the areas that now lead the patient to seek treatment.

The difference between this hint of an account and the ones that philosophers have developed could not be more striking. For example, the answer that Boyd gave to his own question was that metaphors were modes of epistemic access, a "positive heuristic" in Lakatos's sense, whereby hypotheses about the unknown features of objects in one domain are generated on the basis of known features of objects in another domain. Boyd (1979) considered the case of "information processing" as a metaphor for human cognition. He argued that this was a "mere" metaphor because of the failure of psychologists to provide what philosophers call a "type-type" correspondence between properties of computers and of humans. That is, no single property of the computer could be consistently mapped onto, say, the human property of "having beliefs," thereby rendering the metaphor problematic even for reasonably known properties of human cognition. However, the mereness of the metaphor does not detract from the overall significance of the finding, since, for Boyd, it implies an ontological difference between humans and computers. Against this view, the cognitive scientist Zenon Pylyshyn (1979) argued that the disanalogy identified by Boyd should not be taken as a refutation of the information-processing hypothesis, but as an incentive to question our ordinary assignment of properties to human cognition. Perhaps it signals an inconsistency in our conception of belief that can be clarified and resolved in terms of the information-processing metaphor.

In terms of subsequent developments in artificial-intelligence research, Pylyshyn's sense of the metaphoric transfer has been the better prognosticator. For better or worse, both "knowledge scientists" and ordinary folks are increasingly interpreting their thought processes in terms of computers (Collins 1990). Yet despite the level of interpretive interaction between the computer and the human, both Boyd and Pylyshyn envisage that the two domains will remain distinct. In the model of metaphoric transfer proposed below, I challenge this assumption in a way that starts to make sense of Mirowski's vacillation between criticizing deliberate ("living") and unconscious ("dead") metaphoric appropriations of physics in economic writing. To answer Boyd, "metaphor" is a metaphor for communication between representatives of two domains, the long-term consequence of which is that they exchange properties, such that it becomes difficult to distinguish the "known" from the "unknown" side of the original metaphor. In the case of Mirowski's thesis, this situation is complicated by an additional factor that Mirowski himself pays scarce notice to, namely, the implications that the (mis)perceived success of the physics transfer had on subsequent conceptions of the methodology of science, which itself became seen as an economic process, which, in turn, became a model for appropriate directions in which physics could develop.

The sense of communication that I wish to invoke is an ancient one that ties in nicely with the etymological root of "metaphor," namely, to "transport." To regain this sense, let us consider the scholastic conception of formal causation, that is, the "communication" of a form from one material object to another. Depending on the nature of the material, one object may be a better exemplar of the form than the other, just as—in a more ordinary sense of "communication"—one interlocutor may grasp or convey a message better than another. But the matter that conveys the form is itself "passive" in the sense of leaving the form unchanged, even if not well conveyed. Jumping ahead nearly a millennium, much of this sensibility is preserved in the model of communication associated with Shannon and Weaver's (1949) information theory. Here too one speaks of a medium as a better or worse conveyor of certain messages, according to the level of "noise" in the channel. However, the medium itself is not thought to alter the probability that messages of a certain sort will be sent and received. Those probabilities are affected only by changes in the beliefs and desires of the interlocutors, which are presumed to occur outside the communicative context. Those familiar with debates over the extent to which language can shape thought will find this separation of the properties of the medium from those of the message artificial.

Economists have their own way of thinking about this matter. A "medium"—in the broad sense of a mode of communication or transport—incurs costs of its own which are often borne by "third parties" that subsequently constrain how the medium will be used. It is easiest to think about this in terms of a transport medium like a road system. The wear and tear that roads undergo through repeated use can, in the long run, work to benefit certain users at the expense of others, and even to advantage people, without any personal interest in transporting goods on the roads, who may nevertheless be instrumental in seeing that the goods get through. Thus users of the roads may be required to pay taxes for road maintenance.

At this point let me introduce the figure who explicitly uses the economist's sense of "medium" to produce a generalized understanding of metaphor as embodied communication: Harold Innis, who is arguably Canada's leading economic historian (cf. Patterson 1990, ch. 1). As Innis's spiritual godson, the media critic Marshall McLuhan, tells it (1962, esp. 164), Innis was the first to take the metaphor of "metaphor" literally. Innis converted the literary maxim "all language is metaphorical" into the idea that all media are forms of transportation. The middle term in this conversion is the concrete sense of "communication" highlighted above, one more familiar to rhetoricians than to philosophers. Thus communication does not passively reproduce the form it communicates, but alters both the form and the communicative medium. Indeed a message is transmitted in a medium precisely by leaving (unconscious) marks on the interlocutors that alter the messages they are then inclined to transmit through that medium. In short, Innis drove home the idea that communication was a form of *causation* (Patterson 1990, ch. 5; cf. Reichenbach 1956).

Innis's innovation was to think of the economist's third parties as psychosocial "biases" that a medium imposes on its users (Innis 1951). For example, the fact that fur was the first staple to be transported down the waterways surrounding the St. Lawrence River biased the way in which the early Canadian settlers conceptualized, and ultimately utilized, the economic and political potential of the waterways. The later staples—lumber, wheat, paper pulp, and minerals—succeeded by introducing new biases into the system (Innis 1956, esp. 62–77). For example, whereas the fur trade favored the efficiency of upstream traffic on smaller rivers, the lumber trade, given its considerably heavier and bulkier products, emphasized the efficiency of downstream traffic on the large rivers. However, the intensity of the lumber trade spurred the growth of settlements, most of which were founded on the original fur route. In this way, steamboats were introduced to facilitate upstream traffic.

This turn of events can be portrayed as a pattern of metaphoric inference. In the first instance, fur was favored as a staple by virtue of its easy conveyance down the St. Lawrence. It thereby became a metaphor for the river trade in general. That is, the river trade was the background against which the figure of fur was understood, or the standard in terms of which fur was evaluated—depending on whether one takes metaphors to perform a descriptive or prescriptive function. Here our intuitions may be primed by I. A. Richards's (1936) distinction between the foregrounded "tenor" of the metaphor (cf. fur), which was understood in light of a background "vehicle" (cf. river trade). In keeping with Innis's concrete sensibilities, the metaphor also performed some long-term, unintended functions. In particular, the fur trade gradually became *identified* with river trade, and hence became the implicit standard against which other possible staples were judged. Thus a new staple could not become the dominant figure in the river trade unless it accommodated to, or compensated for, the bias that fur introduced. Compensation is the more radical course, as it typically requires the introduction of new media, such as the steamboat in the case of the lumber trade. Focusing on the media of trade specifically, McLuhan would say that the fur trade's birch-bark canoe is the "content" of the lumber trade's steamboat, in that the steamboat developed as it did because it was preceded by the canoe, which then set the terms in which the steamboat was understood and evaluated (cf. Patterson 1990, ch. 2).

What all this suggests is that an archaeology of metaphoric inference would uncover a sequence of technologies, each sublimating—that is, both incorporating and overcoming—its predecessor. A more familiar version of this point is McLuhan's thesis (1964, esp. ch. 1) that thought is the content of speech, which is in turn the content of writing, which is then the content of print. However, given the etymological roots of "content" in "container," it is easy to get the impression that the archaeology of metaphoric inference involves penetrating a set of nested spheres, each "containing" a hollow essence (cf. Ong 1958). Although this view of media has received new life from constructivist sociologists keen on opening the "black boxes" of technology (cf. Bijker et al. 1987), there is a more classical way of capturing the relevant relation here. It involves focusing on the implicit standard of evaluation between the two terms of the metaphor, or their Platonic *ratio*. Thought is the content of speech because the adequacy of speech is judged in relation to thought, specifically whether what one said captures what one remembers as having thought. Speech is the content of writing, in that the adequacy of the written text is typically judged as a transcription of what one said. This thesis, whose implications have been most thoroughly followed up by Derrida's "grammatology" (1976) is reinforced every time one reads to oneself what one has written to determine whether it "sounds" right.

Finally, writing is the content of print insofar as the ability of a book, say, to convey its message is judged against errors in spelling and grammar, which serve as effective standards when people are more practiced in the visual than in the aural presentation of language (cf. Ong 1986). Thus, as Richards emphasized, to evaluate the tenor of a metaphor by its vehicle is to judge immediate perception by distant memory.

By casting the archaeology of metaphoric inference in this light, I have exaggerated the degree of deliberation involved in the inference. This amounts to stressing the prescriptive function of metaphor—as measuring up to a standard—over its descriptive function, which would be normally performed without a second thought. Phenomenologically, the distinction that I intend to draw here is the one that Mirowski himself struggles with, namely, between explicitly evaluating a piece of writing against what was spoken and simply ignoring those aspects of the writing—perhaps even the actual wording—that do not capture what was said. To raise a subconscious (or "subliminal") perception of the latter sort to an explicit comparison of the former is to acknowledge that metaphor is the vehicle by which understanding takes place, the artifice that enables us to see the world as "natural." Both cognitive psychologists and literary critics have their own ways of, so to speak, "metaphor-consciousness-raising." Psychologists have identified "prototypes" that account for the ease or difficulty with which individuals are classified as being of a given kind. For example, it is easier to spot a blue jay than an ostrich as a bird because we tend to perceive candidate-birds through the prototype—the metaphor, if you will—of the robin (Lakoff 1987, esp. part 1). For their part, starting with the Russian Formalists, critics have defined as "literary" that quality of writing which draws attention to itself and, in so doing, transcends its status as surrogate speech, or what Merleau-Ponty called "the prose of the world" (Lemon and Reis 1965). The same writing can, of course, be read "prosaically," as when one fails to notice typos and malapropisms in the course of determining what the text means. Attending to the words on the page, and not simply to their meanings, is like attending to the features of the ostrich that make it difficult to classify it as just another robin-like bird. In both cognitive situations, once the metaphor is made explicit, the ways in which the case at hand resists the metaphor's strictures become evident, and the artifice is thus revealed. In such circumstances it would be fair to say that the metaphor is being tested, much like a scientific theory, for its "descriptive adequacy."

But metaphor-consciousness-raising is the exception rather than the rule. Because metaphors ordinarily remain subliminal, or "dead," the foregrounded figures can imperceptibly alter a background metaphor. For example, encountering enough ostriches in one's visual field will eventually render the viewer's bird-prototype more ostrich-like, and hence successive sightings of ostriches will appear increasingly natural. The point here is that there is a cognitive tradeoff in backgrounding the evaluative character of metaphor. On the one hand, when we no longer need to bring to mind that the robin is the standard against which birds are judged, we forget the locality of the standard and the questions that it raises: What are the prescribed places for observing birds such that a robin turns out to be the "typical" bird? Who has access to such places, and who does not? What sorts of creatures or shapes consequently drop out of sight or are demoted to a lower status because they are not sufficiently robin-like? By ignoring these questions, the locality of a particular species is leavened to the status of omnipresent universal: geography pumped up to ontology. On the other hand, while the status of robin as the bird-prototype is not uniquely in the eye of any given beholder, it is contingently so. In other words, unless disciplined otherwise, particular viewers will unwittingly make the prototype bend to fit the available experience, if only to reduce the cognitive dissonance produced by untreated disanalogies. Thus as the universal is reproduced in locale after locale, it is unlikely that it will remain the same—though these subtle shifts may be masked by the linguistic invariance that remains as people continue to use the word "bird" to describe an array of winged creatures and shapes that are seen through an assortment of prototypes (cf. Fuller 1988, esp. part 2).

Innis's vivid way of expressing the above tradeoff would be to say that the transmission of a prototype exhibits a "spatial bias," or what the sociologist of science Bruno Latour (1987) would call "mobility": that is, an ease of transmission that may require some loss of fidelity to the original message. Again thinking in terms of more concrete media, Innis took paper to display a spatial bias: it is easily portable, yet malleable to both the physical elements (it tears and burns easily) and the interpretive context. By contrast, clay tablets feature a temporal bias, in that they cannot roam so freely, but as a result their use and interpretation can be regulated more systematically. Temporally biased items are thus "immutable" in Latour's terms. But according to Latour, scientists aim to produce artifacts (by which he means to include both the specimens and canonical texts that serve as models for subsequent scholars) whose circulation patterns prove them to be "immutable mobiles," that is, at once spatially and temporally biased. And from Latour's *Science in Action* (1987) alone, one gets the impression that scientists sometimes succeed at what Innis and I would regard as an impossible task, since an item's being spatially biased would seem to preclude its being temporally biased as well. However, Latour's mobiles seem to be immutable only because he buys into a Pirandellian brand of social constructivism, whereby "It is so, if you say so." That is, a mobile is immutable if the bearers of the motion in question—the relevant scientific community—regard it as such. That Innis perceives a tradeoff in biases where Latour sees none reflects Innis's material, specifically economic, grounding of metaphoric inference in transportation, where the medium of conveyance exacts a toll independent of the good conveyed.

Perhaps Mirowski is also guilty of Latour's sin. As Wise (1991) has observed, one disturbingly idealistic element in Mirowski's synthetic history is that he treats the physical concepts imported into economics as, in effect, immutable mobiles which continue to act on the minds of today's economists, often two or three centuries after the concepts originally appeared in physics. This problem is not unique to Mirowski but is endemic to any historical narrative that relies on a "turning point" from which the rest of the story can be purportedly deduced (cf. Shapin and Schaffer 1985, on the long-term significance of the debates over experimental knowledge in the seventeenth century). As Jon Elster (1979) astutely puts it, such a narrative indulges in the species of action-at-a-distance known as "hysteresis": that is, the story fails to take into account mediating factors that, over the course of time, can serve to enhance or diminish the effects of an initial cause. Symptomatic of this problem is that while Mirowski focuses on physics as a vehicle for understanding economics, he neglects the role that this metaphoric transfer itself played as a vehicle for understanding the nature of science. Instead he holds constant the conception of science that legitimated the importation of proto-energetics, presuming that its (mis)perceived success by economists and some philosophical onlookers did not affect the way in which both physicists and economists (not to mention philosophers) subsequently thought about the common features of their inquiries. To extend Mirowski's metaphoric critique into this neglected terrain would mean examining the ways in which regarding science as a knowledge-production system closed under economic principles—however faultily grounded in physics—has influenced the standards by which an inquiry is evaluated as a science. As the following targets of opportunity suggest, this would involve nothing less than a deconstruction of modern philosophy of science (cf. Fuller 1992b):

1. Inspired by Comte, and codified by Pareto, philosophy of science is typically portrayed as aiming for a closed set of methodological principles that will enable us to understand the historical trajectory by which we have come to understand that the physical universe is itself governed by a closed set of principles. This is the so-called internal history of science, championed by Lakatos (1979) and, most recently, Shapere (1984; cf. Fuller 1989, ch. 1). But why must methodology itself reproduce the economy of physics in order to explain it?
2. Corresponding to the futile search for a generative but inexhaustible source of economic value, the nineteenth century also witnessed (often by the same people: Whewell, Mill, Jevons, Peirce) an equally futile search for a generative but incorrigible form of valid inference. The problems of both scarcity and induction, in turn, drew sustenance from the ultimate of futile quests, namely, that for a perpetual-motion machine (cf. Mirowski, *MHL*, chs. 2–3; Rescher 1978; Laudan 1981).
3. Veblen and Schumpeter developed the idea of the entrepreneur as the lifeblood of capitalism. The entrepreneur regularly looked to technological innovation as the source of new markets. Interestingly, Popper portrays the ideal scientist as likewise continually enterprising, namely, by taking calculated risks on hypotheses that may incur short-term losses (i.e., overturning standing presumptions) but promise long-term gains (i.e., a more comprehensive explanatory theory). Do entrepreneurship and good science apply the same thought processes in different domains (cf. Fuller 1985)? Or are they alternative descriptions of the same activity (say, "rational economizing": cf. Radnitzky 1987)? Or are they two distinct activities that stand in some determinate causal relation to one another? Or, is it all a "mere" metaphor?

References

Bijker, Wiebe, et al., eds. 1987. *The Social Construction of Technological Systems*. Cambridge: MIT Press.

Boyd, Richard. 1979. Metaphor and Theory Change. In Ortony 1979, 356–408.
Collins, Harry. 1990. *Artificial Experts*. Cambridge: MIT Press.
Derrida, Jacques. 1976. *Of Grammatology*. Baltimore: The Johns Hopkins University Press.
Elster, Jon. 1979. *Logic and Society*. Chichester: John Wiley & Sons.
Fuller, Steve. 1985. Bounded Rationality in Law and Science. Ph.D. dissertation, Department of History and Philosophy of Science, University of Pittsburgh.
———. 1988. *Social Epistemology*. Bloomington: Indiana University Press.
———. 1989. *Philosophy of Science and Its Discontents*. Boulder, Colo.: Westview Press. Paperback edition, New York: Guilford Press, 1992.
———. 1992a. *Philosophy, Rhetoric, and the End of Knowledge*. Madison: University of Wisconsin Press.
———. 1992b. What Price Creativity? The Hidden Costs of Psychoeconomics. *New Ideas in Psychology* 10:3.
Hobbs, P. Michael. 1991. On the Criticism of Economic Metaphors: Mirowski and the Neoclassicals. Paper presented at the Duke Economic Thought Workshop Symposium "Rethinking the History of Economics in the Light of *More Heat*," Durham, 1–3 March.
Innis, Harold. 1951. *The Bias of Communication*. Toronto: University of Toronto Press.
———. 1956. *Essays in Canadian Economic History*. Toronto: University of Toronto Press.
Kuhn, Thomas. 1962. *The Structure of Scientific Revolutions*. Chicago: University of Chicago Press. 2d ed., 1970.
Lakatos, Imre. 1979. *Methodology of Scientific Research Programmes*. Cambridge: Cambridge University Press.
Lakoff, George. 1987. *Women, Fire, and Dangerous Things*. Chicago: University of Chicago Press.
Latour, Bruno. 1987. *Science in Action*. Milton Keynes: Open University Press.
Laudan, Larry. 1977. *Progress and Its Problems*. Berkeley and Los Angeles: University of California Press.
———. 1981. *Science and Hypothesis*. Dordrecht: Reidel.
Lemon, L., and M. Reis, eds. 1965. *Russian Formalist Criticism*. Lincoln: University of Nebraska Press.
McCloskey, Donald. 1973. *Economic Maturity and Entrepreneurial Decline*. Cambridge: Harvard University Press.
———. 1981. *Enterprise and Trade in Victorian Britain*. London: Allen & Unwin.
———. 1985. *The Rhetoric of Economics*. Madison: University of Wisconsin Press.
McLuhan, Marshall. 1962. *The Gutenberg Galaxy*. Toronto: University of Toronto Press.
———. 1964. *Understanding Media: The Extensions of Man*. New York: McGraw-Hill.
Mirowski, Philip. 1989a. *More Heat than Light*. Cambridge: Cambridge University Press.

———. 1989b. Shall I Compare Thee . . . ? Or, Rhetoric, Mathematics, and the Nature of Neoclassical Economic Theory. In *The Consequences of Economic Rhetoric*, edited by A. Klamer et al. Cambridge: Cambridge University Press.

———, ed. 1986. *The Reconstruction of Economic Theory*. Boston: Kluwer.

Ong, Walter. 1958. *Ramus, Method, and the Decay of Dialogue*. Cambridge: Harvard University Press.

———. 1986. *Orality and Literacy*. London: Methuen.

Ortony, Andrew, ed. 1979. *Metaphor and Thought*. Cambridge: Cambridge University Press.

Patterson, Graeme. 1990. *History and Communications: Harold Innis, Marshall McLuhan, and the Interpretation of History*. Toronto: University of Toronto Press.

Pylyshyn, Zenon. 1979. Metaphorical Imprecision and the "Top-Down" Research Strategy. In Ortony 1979, 420–37.

Radnitzky, Gerard. 1987. Cost-benefit Thinking in the Methodology of Research. In *Economic Imperialism*, edited by G. Radnitzky and P. Bernholz, 283–331. New York: Paragon House.

Reichenbach, Hans. 1956. *The Direction of Time*. Berkeley and Los Angeles: University of California Press.

Rescher, Nicholas. 1978. *Peirce's Philosophy of Science*. South Bend: Notre Dame University Press.

Richards, I. A. 1936. *The Philosophy of Rhetoric*. Oxford: Oxford University Press.

Schabas, Margaret. 1993. What's So Wrong with Physics Envy? [In this special issue of *HOPE*.]

Shannon, Claude, and Warren Weaver. 1949. *The Mathematical Theory of Communication*. Urbana: University of Illinois Press.

Shapere, Dudley. 1984. *Reason and the Search for Knowledge*. Dordrecht: Reidel.

Shapin, Steven, and Simon Schaffer. 1985. *Leviathan and the Air-Pump*. Princeton: Princeton University Press.

Wise, M. Norton. 1991. Uses and Abuses of Interdisciplinary History. Paper presented at the Duke Economic Thought Workshop Symposium "Rethinking the History of Economics in the Light of *More Heat*," Durham, 1–3 March.

Part 2 Economic Problems and Mathematical Formalism

Neoclassical Economics as Mathematical Metaphysics

Jack Birner

Scholars disagree about the origin of the name of Aristotle's book *Metaphysics*. Does it refer to the content of the book, "that which goes beyond physics"? Or is it "that which follows *Physics*"? As a characterization of what Philip Mirowski's *More Heat than Light* argues neoclassical economics is, metaphysics in the first sense is certainly not adequate; metaphysics in the second sense comes much closer. According to Mirowski, neoclassical economics follows physics slavishly. Not slavishly enough, however, because it does not imitate the whole of physics, but only its mathematical superstructure. The consequence is that neoclassical economists get bogged down in problems that they unwittingly imported when taking over their mathematics from physics. This central thesis derives from another, more general thesis, which says that scientific disciplines are all part of the gradual unfolding of a complex of three metaphors. Mirowski links both theses by arguing that each discipline or group of disciplines that is defined by one metaphor develops by taking over either of the other metaphors, which belong to the domain of different disciplines. These are intriguing ideas, and Mirowski works them out in a provocative way. The speed of his argument tends to leave the reader gasping for breath, and wondering both where it all came from and where it is supposed to lead. I intend to provide some resuscitation and orientation by concentrating on the background of these ideas and, more particularly, on the role that mathematics plays in Mirowski's tale.

Mirowski on Metaphors

One of the reasons often cited for the loss of interest in the traditional Popper-Lakatos-Kuhn troika as a vehicle of methodological analysis in economics is the uneasy relationship that is argued to exist between these philosophies, which were developed for natural science, and their forensic application to the domain of economics. A recurrent criticism is that economics is not physics and therefore the philosophy of natural science is not applicable to economics. *More Heat than Light* deals with this head-on by making a strong case for the idea that neoclassical economics is very much like physics. Indeed Mirowski argues that on examination of the historical parallels between physics and neoclassical economics, "one rapidly discovers that the resemblances of the theories are uncanny, and one reason they are uncanny is because the progenitors of neoclassical economic theory boldly copied the reigning physical theories in the 1870s. The further one digs, the greater the realization that those neoclassicals did not imitate physics in a desultory or superficial manner; no, they copied their models mostly term for term and symbol for symbol, and said so" (*MHL*, 3). But instead of being led back to offering another application of Lakatos (or Kuhn, or Popper) to economics, Mirowski seeks comfort in the hermeneutic tradition: "I would wish that the following account might be regarded as a contribution to this tradition [of modern post-Heideggerian hermeneutics]" (406 n. 4).

What interests Mirowski is the transfer mechanism between physics and economics: Was physics merely used as a quarry of metaphors for a neoclassical economics that was in full control of its own theory, or was its influence less neutral and more profound? The study of the history of science has taught Mirowski that conservation principles have played a central role in its development. They involved, or gave rise to, the concept of energy. But energy is not merely a basic concept of physics. Energy is "a primal metaphor of Western thought, a vein winding through both physical theory and social theory. . . . Although it was ultimately called 'energy' in physics and 'utility' in economics, it was fundamentally the same metaphor, performing many of the same explanatory functions in the respective contexts, evoking many of the same images and emotional responses, not to mention many of the same mathematical formalisms" (4).

Even more basic than the energy metaphor are the metaphors of body, motion, and value. Mirowski places these four metaphors at the vertices of a conceptual triangular pyramid. The metaphors of body, motion, and value form the "metaphorical simplex" to which all scientific disciplines are reducible. To each metaphor corresponds a discipline: to motion, physics; to body, anthropomorphics (it remains entirely unclear what sort of discipline this is); to value, economics. Where does all this come from?

Mirowski's declared intellectual hero is the French historian and philosopher of science Emil Meyerson. Meyerson follows an empirical approach to the study of Reason with the objective of extracting the a priori principles that direct human thinking from the history of the cognitive endeavor par excellence: science.[1] The history of science is the history of the progress of human reason. The lessons Meyerson draws from the history of science are that science is not merely descriptive or predictive, but that it endeavors to find explanations. It does so by looking for one single constant and substantial reality underlying the variety of nature as it is given to our perception. A phenomenon has been explained when its diversity has been reduced to uniformity. Reality is rational to the extent that it can be reduced to identity.[2] To explain is to identify, and reality can be explained because it is, in part at least, rational.

In Meyerson's philosophy of science theories are not just collections of noncausal laws, but they seek causes. Causality is a form of identity too, and a fundamental understanding of change involves seeing that nothing has changed, that the effect was already present in the cause. Reason is never at rest as long as it has not succeeded in reducing all diversity to uniformity (or, what is the same, in identifying all diversity with uniformity), and ultimately to homogeneous space. Hence the importance of conservation principles and the attempts to eliminate time. They are part of the heuristics of science, that is, the principles regulating the progress of human understanding. However, the world resists these attempts to identify. There always remains a qualitative diversity, and to the extent that this remains, reality is irrational. This diversity or irrationality is the stimulus to further attempts at identification.

Mirowski follows Meyerson both in his concern and in his method. He is interested in the development of neoclassical economics, its origins, its methods, and its heuristical ploys, which he wants to discover by means of historical empirical research. He stresses the role of conservation principles and the identification of diversity with a limited number of basic concepts. Does this mean that Mirowski is simply fitting

---

1. "Nous avons voulu . . . , en suivant un programme tracé, mais non réalisé par Auguste Comte, parvenir *a posteriori* à connaître les principes aprioriques qui dirigent notre pensée dans son effort vers la réalité. Dans ce but nous analysons la science" (Meyerson 1926, viii).

2. "Ce qui, dans les choses, est rationel, c'est-à-dire se prête à être, par un certain côté, réduit à l'identique" (Meyerson 1931, 440).

Meyerson to economics? Let us look a bit closer at some parallels and differences.

Hermeneutics

Mirowski shares Meyerson's concern with the understanding of all human reasoning, not just science. But when he says that the metaphors of body, motion, and value are fictions "necessary for the organization of human discourse" (*MHL*, 140), he transcends Meyerson's philosophy into the domain of hermeneutics. This explains his stress on metaphors, which in Meyerson's work have a very minor role to play.

Meyerson studies natural science, Mirowski the interaction between different disciplines. Mirowski employs his basic metaphors to sketch the relations between physics and economics. He relates the three basic metaphors to one another in ways that are Meyersonian in spirit but go beyond Meyerson in the details of the mechanism. How does it operate? According to Mirowski, each discipline is associated with one basic metaphor. A discipline that is defined by one metaphor develops by incorporating (borrowing or imitating) one or both of the remaining metaphors. "The research program situated at each vertex derives legitimacy for its radically unjustifiable conservation principles from the homeomorphisms with the structures of explanation at the other vertexes" (116, italics omitted). The basic ideas are Meyersonian: conservation principles embody, or are the instruments of, identification, and that which drives the development of knowledge is something outside itself: "Tout raisonnement, pour avancer, a besoin d'un divers" (Meyerson 1934, 155). Mirowski goes beyond Meyerson in locating the *divers* in the metaphors that do not belong to the discipline whose development is the object of study.

Mirowski further embellishes Meyerson's theory of science by adding a theory borrowed from Kula, that measurement develops in three stages: the anthropomorphic, where man is literally the measure of all things and the metaphors of body, motion, and value are intertwined; the lineamentric, where natural numbers are introduced and the metaphors become distinct but still overlap; and the syndetic, in which the three metaphors remain distinct yet are unified in one measure, the energy metaphor (cf. 109–14). This helps Mirowski to construct a picture of science developing in a sort of spiraling motion when one discipline uses the metaphors of different domains in subsequent phases: "As the metaphors constitute a pyramid, the buck may continue to be passed ad infinitum" (117).

On my first reading of this passage, I thought it was meant as a joke. As I read on and saw the pyramid in operation, it became clear to me that Mirowski takes his own metaphor very seriously—so seriously, that one would have expected more by way of argument as to why these are the basic metaphors, and why they are related as Mirowski sketches them. We are told that the metaphors are "fiction[s] *necessary* for the organization of human discourse" (137, emphasis added). This is a strong statement. But it is also ambiguous, for it does not tell us whether these are the only possible fictions, or whether there could have been a different set of metaphors performing the same function.

Apart from a general reference to Meyerson, Mirowski does not tell us where he got his metaphorical simplex. In part its origin can be traced to Meyerson's emphasis on mechanism and atomism as the regulative ideas of natural science, where mechanism is the tendency to explain in terms of motion, and atomism the tendency to explain in corpuscular terms, which might be the background of the body metaphor.[3] Mirowski's third metaphor, value, seems to have its counterpart in Meyerson's argument (1926, xi) that all science, ancient and modern (but with the exception of medieval science) is dominated by the concept of quantity, the object of mathematics.

---

3. "La science tend véritablement à réduire tous les phénomènes à un mécanisme ou un atomisme universel. . . . Non pas que cette réduction soit réellement possible, ni que nous puissions croire que cet atomisme constitue l'essence des choses, ni qu'il soit capable d'offrir un système exempt de contradictions; mais parce qu'il est, parmis toutes les images que notre intellect est capable de concevoir, la seule qui, satisfaisant au moins jusqu'à un certain point, notre tendance à l'identité, offre en même temps de réelles et quelquefois de surprenantes concordances avec les phénomènes. C'est donc en suivant cette image, en la rendant de plus en plus adéquate aux faits que nous avons le plus de chance de connaître mieux ces derniers. En d'autres termes, la réduction au mécanisme et à l'atomisme n'est pas en elle-même un but, mais un moyen. C'est une règle qui guide la marche de la science" (Science truly tends to reduce all phenomena to a universal mechanism or atomism. . . . Not because this reduction is really possible, nor because we may believe that this atomism constitutes the essence of things, nor because it can give us a system that is exempt of contradictions; but because it is the only image among all those that our understanding is capable of forming that offers correspondences with reality that are both real and sometimes surprising. This is because atomism satisfies, at least to a certain degree, our tendency to identify. In following this image, in making it more and more adequate to the facts, we have the best chance of knowing these facts. In other words, the reduction to mechanism and atomism is no goal in itself, but a means. It is a rule [or regulating principle] which guides the course of science) (Meyerson 1926, 474).

Mathematics as the Mover of Metaphors

A widely held view on the role of mathematics in the sciences is that it is a neutral instrument that can be employed at will for proving theorems, settling disputes, reducing complexity, conducting quantitative analysis, or the systematic organization of theories. This idea has been able to survive mostly because of neglect. Mirowski rightly remarks that the study of the use of mathematics in economics (and other disciplines) has been sadly neglected (*MHL*, 195). Closer study of the way in which economists employ mathematics reveals that mathematics is not always so neutral; it often acts as a heuristics that exerts a strong guiding influence on the development of theories.[4]

According to Mirowski, mathematics is a superior method of thinking in metaphors, and thinking in metaphors is an integral part of science (cf. Mirowski 1987). Following Meyerson (as we shall see below), he sees the success of the application of mathematics as the result of the interaction between science and mathematics: "mathematics does not come to us written indelibly on Nature's Tablets, but rather is the product of a controlled search governed by metaphorical considerations, the premier instance being the heuristics of the conservation principle" (*MHL*, 7).

At least, this is how it works in physics. In neoclassical economics it is different: "Physicists have in the past displayed a dynamism and flexibility with regard to the meaning of the metaphors [of the pyramid] for which they can rightfully be proud. But with economics it is a different story. Economists have consistently lagged behind physicists in developing and elaborating their metaphors; they have freeloaded off of physicists for their inspiration, and appropriated it in a shoddy and slipshod manner" (108).

Neoclassical economists displayed the behavior of upstart nouveaux riches who are under the illusion that they may gain respectability by imitating the outward appearance of the ancient nobility. That is how the pursuit of mathematical goals could become an end in itself, unchecked by economic or empirical constraints.[5] This is a degeneration

---

4. Cf. the work of Meyerson, and Mirowski 1986a, 1987, 1989; Zahar 1980; Birner (forthcoming).

5. "[O]nce mathematical expertise has come to be the badge of the theorist in any science, then theory becomes isolated from that subset of the discipline responsible for empirical implementation and experiment. The mathematical theorist is given carte blanche by her prestige and her separation from the nitty-gritty of everyday observation to prosecute any mathematical

which amounts to a forgetting of the original—economic—problems. The mathematical models that were originally imported from physics as metaphors lost this status and were eventually taken for the literal, economic truth. The phenomena that did not fit into these models were ignored. The mathematics ran out of control and took over from the economics. But the neoclassical economists weren't even any good at imitating physics. They committed the blunder of failing to take over "the most important part of the formalism [of physics,] not to mention the very heart of the metaphor, namely, the conservation of energy. . . . [This] rendered the neoclassical heuristic essentially incoherent" (9). However, neoclassical economics made one contribution of its own: the law of one price. This law was the economic interpretation of a mathematical lemma which was implied by the mathematical concern with constrained maximization (Mirowski 1987, 197). But it was precisely this original addition of neoclassical economics to the physics metaphor that barred it from making progress, because it obscured the relevant conservation principles and for a long time kept the road closed to the formalism of Hamiltonian dynamics, which was needed to describe movements from one equilibrium to another (*MHL*, 227).

The story is a sad one for neoclassical economics, indeed. First, economists were wrong to follow the physics metaphors. Then they did not stick to the demands of these metaphors. And finally, the only element they added of their own made things even worse. But neoclassical economics could not keep avoiding the issue of conservation principles. The formalism which it took over from physics had an inner logic that compelled theorists to impose a conservation principle in the guise of Walras's law (cf. 326). The physical metaphors could be ignored for a while. But as they were an integral part of the vehicle of the mathematical formalism, the substance, so to speak, out of which the supporting structure was made, they acted as an automatic pilot, eventually steering the way back into the central body of neoclassical economics. "[M]ost neoclassical economists had no idea where the original utility framework had come from and were genuinely curious as to the minimum assumptions needed to preserve their well-behaved results. But since the 'nice' results had earlier been defined by the proto-energetics metaphor, is it

---

analogy and metaphor which captures her fancy. The negative component of any of these metaphors . . . can be effortlessly set aside for the time being, or dismissed as irrelevant, impounded in ceteris paribus conditions or otherwise neutralized, because for the theorist, it is only the mathematics that matters" (Mirowski 1987, 80).

any wonder that the neoclassicals eventually converged on just that right set of assumptions that—mirabile dictu—were necessary and sufficient to formalize the metaphor of a field of potential energy?" (366).

The picture we are presented with is at the same time optimistic and pessimistic. The optimism resides in the idea that in the end Reason outwits even the brightest of economists in a kind of autonomous, Hegelian process. In the long run the consequences of working with particular metaphors always come to the surface; in the end the Cunning of Reason always wins. The pessimism lies in the incapacity of individual theorists to make the formalism do what they want. Is this picture correct? True, if some formalism is to act as a heuristic, it has to impose some constraints. On the other hand, if the constraints are too strong, the use of the formalism may not be productive of useful results. What does the formalism take with it when it migrates from one discipline to another?

Mathematical Customs: Anything to Declare?

Metaphors cross boundaries riding on the back of mathematical formalisms. Can the formalism stand on its own feet after the metaphors have been removed? Are its restrictions as strong as Mirowski alleges? Or do they leave more room for maneuver? Two arguments are intertwined in Mirowski's book, one that concentrates on the specific use that neoclassical economists make of mathematics, the other related to the more general question whether mathematics is necessarily metaphorical.

Let us first look at the case of neoclassical economics. There is a marked asymmetry in Mirowski's tale. Economics has a trade deficit with physics. Physics has creative mathematical habits. It makes progress by means of the dialectical process of reasoning back and forth between physical metaphors and mathematical devices. Neoclassical economics merely imitates the outward, formal manners and garb of physics, and does not even succeed in tying the knots (or knotting the ties) correctly. I agree with Mirowski that in economics, especially (though not exclusively) of the neoclassical variety, attempts to solve economic problems are often replaced by attempts to solve mathematical problems, and that subsequently either no retranslation to the economic context takes place at all, or the translation is dictated and constrained only by the mathematical results. But that is not always or necessarily the case. Nor is it necessarily so that the Cunning of Reason operates in the form of the requirements of the metaphors embodied in the formalism.[6]

In Mirowski's treatment of the use of mathematics by neoclassical economists, the general argument about the nature of mathematics and the argument about the specific use of a specific piece of mathematics by neoclassical economists occur side by side. His discussion seems to presuppose the general argument that a mathematical formalism always embodies actual or metaphorical content, and on top of this the neoclassicals are blamed for their choice and handling of their mathematics, which is not as befits a responsible scientific community (cf. 278–79). He says that "mathematical formalization in physics and economics has by and large consisted of the passing back and forth from the social to the physical world of a very few key metaphors" (367–68). But what is to be gained by this? Can the metaphors be transported wholly intact, or is that not necessary for them to fulfill a useful role "abroad"? Mirowski spells out several aspects of the logic of scientific discovery in a way that justifies quotation at length:

> It is certainly true that one need not be obsessed with the exact duplication of all aspects of a metaphor when it is transported from one area of inquiry to another. However, one of the most attractive aspects of analogical reasoning is the prefabricated nature of an interlocked set of explanatory structures and constructs, allowing quickened evaluation of logical coherence. . . . The error of Pareto and every other historically sophisticated neoclassical theorist is to think that every aspect of the physics metaphor is equally expendable. . . . The essence of neoclassical economics is the appropriation of the physical concept of the field and its elevation to pride of place in the theory of value. While the notion of the field is a very flexible concept, it does possess a modicum of structural regularity that, if absent, undermines its logical integrity. The history of physics teaches that one indispensable element of a field theory is the imposition of some set of conservation principles. . . . The epistemological imperative of conservation principles in field theories is mirrored in their mathematics. (272)

Once the metaphors have migrated to a different discipline, they begin working on their own: "Scientific metaphors should set in motion re-

---

6. A number of cases both of economics leading the mathematical argument and mathematics leading the economic argument are discussed in Birner (forthcoming).

search programs that strive to render explicit the totality of the attendant submetaphors. They should provoke inquiry as to whether the implications are consistent one with another, as well as consistent with the tacit background knowledge" (278–79).

So, the logic of discovery according to Mirowski consists of transporting from one discipline to another parts of metaphors that are embodied in a mathematical formalism. The formalism is then put to work in explicating submetaphors. One cannot get any submetaphor one wants out of this, as the imported formalism imposes constraints that reflect the original metaphor. The submetaphors are subsequently tested for their consistency with one another and with the background knowledge of the importing discipline.

Mirowski does not tell us what the purpose or function of the consistency tests is. It may be the conservative goal of obtaining a set of noncontradictory statements in order to avoid ending up with a theory from which anything follows. Or these tests may have the more revolutionary function of making possible a breakthrough in the way that Meyerson has in mind (see below, where Zahar's ideas of the function of mathematics are discussed).

What Mirowski also fails to make clear is what the metaphors in their new homeland really do. Do they describe? Do they explain? Or do they remain metaphors? Buchdahl, who describes a very similar process of metaphorical transfer in the works of the great metaphysicians and scientists of Western thought, is clearer on this point. A metaphysical construct is endowed with some of the features of a concept in a different discipline. The construct may then be elaborated into a part of a descriptive theory. The characteristics of the construct as a metaphor, laid down in its "analogical grammar," are adapted and are taken literally so as to form an "ontological grammar."[7] In other words, what started as a metaphor is turned into a part of a descriptive and explanatory theory.

In Mirowski's tale the mathematical formalism taken over from physics keeps neoclassical economics in a stranglehold. Is it really as bad as that? I shall take this up later, when I discuss the use of mathe-

---

7. See Buchdahl 1969, 3–4, where Descartes's concept of God is given as an example: "God here serving as the metaphysical construct, whose analogical grammar is taken from the realm of theology." Such a metaphysical construct may act as an additional "center of gravity" in order to extend the original *partial* analogue so as to become the center of a new philosophical edifice, the ontological grammar, whose purpose is justificatory.

matics as a heuristic. By way of preparation I first discuss Meyerson's philosophy of mathematics.

Meyerson on Mathematics

Why are the calculi of logic and mathematics applicable to reality, Popper asked, and Wigner wanted to know the reason for "the unreasonable effectiveness of mathematics in the natural sciences."[8] They never gave the answer. This is because both saw the relation between science and mathematics as rather one-sided: science poses the problems, after which mathematics is called in for help.

Meyerson had addressed the problem earlier, and he did provide an answer. His solution is that as mathematics is undeniably applicable to reality, it must contain an empirical element; but as it is, or appears to be, purely formal and a priori, it must also have a foundation in the faculty of reason. The most basic concept of mathematics is that of identity, which is even more basic than the concept of relation. The application of identity is the essence of all reason (Meyerson 1934, 154), and "all mathematics . . . in the end resolves itself in equalities."[9] However, mathematical reasoning is never completely "pure"; it always contains empirical elements. This is because mathematical operations such as addition and subtraction can ultimately only be conceived of as operations on real objects (Meyerson 1934, 153). It could not even be otherwise, because, in order to make progress, thinking needs a *divers*. But then wherein does this *divers* reside in mathematics, from which all experience appears to be absent? The answer is, in the number system: "the number system is at the basis of all mathematical truth."[10] Numbers are abstractions, but these are subsequently transformed by us into something real. This is why we can subject them to operations, that is, real actions (cf. Meyerson 1931, para. 233). The fact that we are led to think that mathematical reasoning is devoid of empirical content hails from the powerful correspondence between the rational and the real which characterizes the number system and its properties. Analogously in geometry: the *divers* hails from the figure, that is, our spatial intuition.

---

8. See Popper 1963, Wigner 1960.
9. "Tout le mathématique . . . se résout en fin de compte en égalités" (Meyerson 1934, 162).
10. "La série des nombres se trouve au fond de toute vérité mathématique" (Meyerson 1934, 155).

The ultimate foundations of mathematics are numerical operations and geometrical axioms that embody human intuitions about space (cf. 1931, para. 241). In mathematical reasoning the a priori and experience are continuously involved, and their contributions become intermingled.[11]

Meyerson disagrees with Kant, for whom number and space are purely a priori. This, Meyerson observes, is not the view of modern mathematicians. The idea that mathematics involves free inventions of the mind does not come from mathematicians, but from philosophers of mathematics. Mathematicians feel they *discover* things. This is sufficient proof that mathematics is not a matter of free creation or invention, "[b]ecause discovery undoubtedly implies the intervention of a factor which comes from the outside, from sensory experience, the application of the intellect to something whose existence preceded its operation."[12] Meyerson does not consider fractional, negative, irrational, and imaginary numbers and non-Euclidean geometries to be counterexamples to his rejection of the possibility of free invention. Mathematicians treat irrational numbers and the concepts of non-Euclidean geometries as real numbers and objects. They subject them to the same categories as they do real objects, and they perform the same operations on them.[13]

So, mathematics always originates from something empirical, even when the original empirical domain from which a piece of mathematics arose, or for which a particular mathematical apparatus was developed, has been forgotten. This is a justificationist position: the success of mathematics in science is justified by an appeal to an ultimate empirical foundation. I shall call this Meyerson's *justificationist answer* to the question of the applicability of mathematics to empirical reality. We

---

11. "Pour nous, . . . *apriori* et expérience interviennent sans cesse l'un et l'autre ici et là et leurs interventions s'enchevêtrent" (Meyerson 1934, 165).

12. "Car la découverte, assurément, implique l'intervention d'un facteur venant du dehors, de la sensation, l'application de l'intellect à ce qui préexistait à son action" (Meyerson 1934, 158).

13. Cf., for example, Meyerson 1931, 381: "En créant ses concepts d'espaces non-euclidiens, le géomètre, par le fait même qu'il les déclare *espaces*, affirme que son intention de les traiter comme nous avons accoutumé de le faire à l'égard de celui de notre perception, sauf, bien entendu, en ce qui concerne les particularités où, en virtu de la définition même par laquelle ils ont créés, ils devront se comporter différemment" (When creating his concepts of non-Euclidean spaces, the geometer by the very fact that he declares them to be *spaces* affirms that he intends to treat them just like we are in the habit of doing with the space of our perception. Of course, he does not intend to treat non-Euclidean spaces in this way in as far as they have to behave differently by virtue of their special characteristics or the definitions by which they were created).

may add to Meyerson's answer that a standard strategy in mathematics is generalization. This means that the original, possibly empirical problem recedes into the background. Particular mathematical results that were obtained through generalization are applied to a different domain from the one that gave rise to it.

Meyerson also gives an answer to the question of the applicability of mathematics that I shall call his *heuristic answer,* as it explains the successful use of mathematics in the day-to-day work of physicists. Meyerson thinks that the effectiveness of mathematics in physics is the result of a process of mutual adaptation. Mathematics may serve as a heuristic, an instrument of scientific discovery. This idea has been elaborated by Elie Zahar, from whose work I shall quote to make the idea clear.[14]

> [T]he relationship between mathematics and physics is best described in dialectical terms as a to and fro movement between two poles. One moves from physical principles to idealising mathematical assumptions; then back to some more physics; then forward to fresh mathematical innovations with ever increasing surplus structure. The so-called harmony between physics and mathematics is not a miracle but the result of an arduous process of mutual adjustment. (Zahar 1980, 7)

The "surplus structure" to which he refers consists of the stronger physical assumptions which may result from translating a physical principle into a mathematical form. This may happen when the mathematical form imposes stronger restrictions than the principle as originally stated in physical terms. The physicist uses mathematical notions which are not abstracted directly from experience and "operates at the mathematical level, hoping that his operations mirror certain features of reality. However, he is not very clear as to how this mirroring takes place, so he lets himself be guided by the syntax, or by the symbolism, of some mathematical system" (Zahar 1980, 6–7).

Mathematics may have a second fundamental function in the discovery of physical theories: "through trying to find a *realistic* interpretation of certain mathematical entities which seem at first sight to be devoid of any physical meaning, the scientist may be led to a physical conjecture" (Zahar 1980, 7). According to Zahar, this may operate in two ways. The

---

14. Apparently Mirowski also follows Zahar when expounding Meyerson's mathematical heuristics (cf. *MHL*, 6–7).

first is that the empirical content of a theory may be increased by straightforwardly interpreting part of the "mathematical scaffolding" realistically. The second is to express a hypothesis in an equivalent mathematical form. Then progress may be made when the following is the case: the equivalent form involves a particular mathematical entity which is interpreted realistically by subsuming it under a philosophical category (such as substance) obeying general laws, but the equivalent formulation is then discovered to violate these laws. If this is the case, a breakthrough may come about when the equivalent formulation is modified in such a way as to be in accordance with these laws.

Mathematics without Metaphors

Mirowski's theory that mathematics is metaphorical is a hermeneutic version of what I have called Meyerson's justificationist answer: mathematics works because it is ultimately based on operations on numbers or space. This part of Meyerson's philosophy of mathematics is not only justificationist, it is also realist: where a particular mathematical tool does not work, this is because the domain to which it is applied is not (sufficiently) like numbers or space. Mirowski's theory of mathematics inherits Meyerson's justificationism: whether mathematics works depends on whether its metaphorical content is "appropriate" to the sphere to which it is applied.[15] This suggests that Mirowski is a realist too.[16] But this cannot be the case if he sticks to his hermeneutics seriously. If, as he says, the way in which metaphors work in a discipline is through the unfolding of their meaning,[17] this is certainly consistent with a justificationist view of science, but hardly with a realist one. For a realist what counts is truth, not meaning. I shall come back to this in the penultimate section.

Mirowski is a justificationist in his theory of science,[18] and the justi-

---

15. "Appropriate" seems to be Mirowski's translation of Meyerson's "adequate to the facts"; cf. the quotation in note 3 above.

16. This is also suggested by his discussion of Helmholtz (*MHL*, 46). But Mirowski expresses his uneasiness by enclosing the word "real" in quotes: "This habit of spying the 'real' unity hidden on phenomenal diversity is a preternatural trait of the mathematical mind."

17. Cf. 108: "Physicists have in the past displayed a dynamism and flexibility with regard to the *meaning of the metaphors* for which they can rightfully be proud" (emphasis added).

18. See, e.g., 117: "The fundamental justification of a conservation principle in any research programme . . . always comes to rest in the evocation of other conservation principles in other similarly structured disciplines."

ficationism of his theory of mathematics is consistent with this. Where mathematics works, it does so because it carries with it metaphors that are appropriate to a particular domain. Because mathematics is inherently metaphorical, for Mirowski there cannot be such a thing as a purely formal mathematics. Purely formal mathematics, an uninterpreted calculus, is a piece of mathematics that lacks a standard model. The requirement that a formal calculus always have a standard model is a justificationist demand. This is the message of Rosser and Wang, who discuss the position of logic as a formalization of mathematics, which in the present context is comparable to the status of mathematics as a formalization of aspects of reality: "We suspect that the idea that a logic must have a standard model if it is to be acceptable as a framework for mathematical reasoning is merely a vestige of the old idea that there is such a thing as absolute mathematical truth" (quoted in Lakatos 1978b, 39).

In the traditional philosophy of mathematics absolute mathematical truth has the same justificationist function as do metaphors in Mirowski's theory. Justificationism is not needed to explain how mathematics works in science. A piece of mathematics may impose constraints without carrying any metaphors. I will discuss the best-developed nonjustificationist philosophy of mathematics there is, that of Lakatos, below. But since I want to link this view of mathematics with the use of mathematics in economics, I first discuss the way in which economic models and theories develop.

Global Gloom versus Local Levity

Mirowski has a great deal to say about the "grand designers," the pioneers of neoclassical economics, those who wanted to unify all existing parts of economic theory into one encompassing scheme, such as Walras, Fisher, and Samuelson. This activity may be said to be located on the *global* level, the level of theories and research programmes.[19] Global analysis further deals with what we may call the characteristic propositions of a particular theory, that is, the propositions that enable us to distinguish one theory from another. The class of a theory's characteristic propositions consists of its premises (or "assumptions") and its

---

19. The distinction between global and local in the present context is related though not identical to that in Lakatos's *Proofs and Refutations* (1976).

most exemplary predictions. It is on this level that Mirowski paints the gloomy portrait of neoclassical economics clad in an ill-fitting mathematical garb.

However, most economists do not work on the grand problems of unification. They are engaged in solving humbler, isolated problems. They move on the *local* level. This is the level of (partial) models and their analysis. Locally, scientists are engaged in the solving of detailed and often technical (even highly technical) problems, or puzzles, that are posed by particular models or by a particular apparatus of analysis. Solutions to such problems may give rise to the need for adaptations of models. Scientists usually have a choice among different strategies of model development, a point that will be discussed just below. After that I shall try to show that the way in which mathematics operates locally in these strategies gives rise to a picture with more cheerful colors.

Making Models Move: Strategies of Model Development

The method of decreasing abstraction, as almost every introductory economics text tells the reader, is widely considered to be the typical method of economics. Basically, the method consists of starting with a highly idealized model to which subsequently more and more realistic assumptions are added. Until recently, idealizations and the method of decreasing abstraction have not been analyzed in any detail, but this has changed with the work of Krajewski (1977), Nowak (1980), and Musgrave (1981). I have discussed their work elsewhere (Birner 1990a and forthcoming), and I draw on that in what follows.

In this approach, which I call the Polish Idealization Model (PIM), a theory or a model[20] is defined as a set of lawlike statements, $(x)[C(x) \Rightarrow F(x)]$, where $C(x)$ and $F(x)$ are statements about properties of x. It will be assumed that the properties of x can be fully described by mathematical functions assigning some numerical value to characteristic parameters of x. The antecedent $C(x)$ states the initial conditions or "assumptions," the consequent $F(x)$ the predictions or "theorems." The antecedent may contain both factual and idealizing conditions. If it contains the latter, the model is an idealizing model. There is nothing in reality which corresponds to it; it is about ideal objects: "x is an ideal

---

20. As will become clear, the distinction between theory and model is relative, not absolute.

object . . . when it is an ideal limit of a sequence of real objects with diminishing value of some characteristic parameter p_i (usually there is a set of parameters). In other words, some of its parameters are equal to zero ($p_i = 0$), however we know that in all real objects they are positive ($p_i > 0$)" (Krajewski 1977, 23).

Four *strategies of theory development* may be distinguished:

(1) The strategy of *factualization or concretization*. This amounts to replacing the model's idealizing assumptions, $p_i(x) = 0$, one by one, by factual assumptions, $p_i(x) > 0$. The consequent may have to be adjusted as the idealizing assumptions are factualized. Thus, starting from a purely idealizing model M_I, we obtain a sequence of models with decreasing degrees of idealization which ends, in principle, with the purely factual model M_F.

M_I: $(x)\,[p_1(x) = 0\ \&\ p_2(x) = 0\ \&\ \ldots\ \&\ p_n(x) = 0$
        $\Rightarrow F(x) = 0]$

M_1: $(x)\,[p_1(x) > 0\ \&\ p_2(x) = 0\ \&\ \ldots\ \&\ p_n(x) = 0$
        $\Rightarrow F_1(x) = 0]$

M_{n-1}: $(x)\,[p_1(x) > 0\ \&\ \ldots\ \&\ p_{n-1}(x) > 0\ \&\ p_n(x) = 0$
        $\Rightarrow F_{n-1}(x) = 0]$

M_F: $(x)\,[p_1(x) > 0\ \&\ \ldots\ldots\ \&\ p_n(x) > 0$
        $\Rightarrow F(x) = 0]$.

The scheme shows the last step in the chain of factualizations to be a factual model that contains no idealizing assumptions at all. It is doubtful whether any model in any scientific discipline ever reaches this fully empirical status. The last step in the sequence may be an approximation.

(2) The second strategy is *idealization*, which operates usually in conjunction with *approximation*. This strategy works in the opposite direction of factualization, and can be shown in the above scheme as the transition from, for instance, M_F to M_{n-1}, where the prediction of $M_{n-1}, F_{n-1}(x) = 0$ may be an approximation of $F_n(x) = 0$, the prediction of M_F.

(3) The third strategy is the *revealing of idealizing conditions*: it may be discovered that the validity of a model which contains as a characteristic parameter F_1 and which was thought to be general is in fact conditional upon the assumption that a different factor, which was not included in the original model, influences the factor characterized by F_1. If we use F_2

for the characteristic parameter of this new factor, the discovery amounts to seeing that $F_1 = f(F_2)$, and that $F_2 = 0$ in the reconstruction of the existing model (cf. Krajewski 1977, para. 4.6).

If in addition to revealing idealizing conditions that previously had remained unnoticed a more general model is constructed or discovered that contains the previous model as a special case, then we are dealing with a different strategy of model development.

(4) This is the *correspondence strategy*. The discovery that a particular theory, which was thought to contain realistic assumptions, i.e., initial conditions that are true descriptions of reality, is in fact not an adequate description as it contains one or more false assumptions and is in fact an idealizing model, is sometimes followed by the construction of a new theory which contains, or encompasses, the old model as a special case. In such a case we will say that there is a correspondence relation between the two theories if:

1. The new theory is more general than the old one.
2. The new theory partly reconstructs the old one.
3. The new theory corrects the old one by replacing a parameter that was considered to be a constant by a variable.
4. The old theory is a limiting case of the new theory describing only what happens in a limited domain.
5. The new theory is logically incompatible with the old one.
6. The new theory explains why people holding the old theory thought their theory to be correct.
7. The new theory introduces a factor on which the value of the parameter that was considered a constant by the old theory depends.

In slightly more formal terms we can characterize the notion of correspondence as follows (I designate the old theory by T_i and the new one by T_j): T_j corresponds to T_i if

1. T_i contains a parameter F_1 which is a constant;
2. T_j contains F_1 as a variable;
3. F_1 is dependent on a variable F_2, which in T_i is not relevant for F_1;
4. if F_2 approaches a certain limit value, (e.g., 0 or ∞), F_1 in T_j approaches the constant value of F_1 in T_i.

If all of the above conditions are fulfilled, we will say, following Krajewski (1977, 41–42), that the two theories are related by the correspondence relation.[21] The old theory is called the corresponded theory, the new one the corresponding theory.

While PIM analyzes the syntactical structure of idealizing theories and models, Musgrave pays attention to the pragmatic or intentional aspects of idealizations and strategies of model development. Thus he is able to fill in important details, such as the role of criticism and the different functions which idealizing and factualizing assumptions may have in the development of a model. According to Musgrave, much of the confusion in discussions of false or unrealistic assumptions in economics is due to the fact that the analysis stays too much on the surface. Usually idealizations which are employed by economic theorists all have the same syntactical structure. But identical syntactical structures may conceal significant pragmatic differences. A feature that according to Musgrave further complicates the study of idealizations is that in the course of the life of a model they may change their meaning and function. And as different meanings and functions exert different influences on the model's further development, it is important to take this into account. I shall designate Musgrave's approach the Antipodean Idealization Model (AIM). Following Musgrave, we may distinguish three strategies of theory development.

(1) A *negligibility strategy* consists of introducing the assumption that particular factors G, which are present in reality and which are expected to exert an influence, may be omitted from the model's antecedent without altering its predictions at all, or without altering them in a way that is detectable.

(2) When a prediction by a model containing a negligibility assumption turns out to be false, one may decide to follow a *domain strategy:* to maintain the negligibility assumption but restrict the applicability of the model to just those cases in which the neglected factor is indeed negligible. The negligibility assumption is interpreted as a "domain assumption." Musgrave states that this transition may pass unnoticed, even though the status of the model undergoes a radical change; the transition "replaces a stronger or more testable model with a weaker or less test-

---

21. Weaker correspondence relations may exist than the one described in the text. It is not necessary for *all* the conditions to be fulfilled to still be able to employ the concept of correspondence.

able one. It is therefore an *ad hoc* modification in Popper's sense. But we cannot unreservedly condemn such modifications: we value strength but we also value truth, and the weaker theory might be true where its stronger ancestor was false" (1981, 381; "theory" has been replaced by "model").

(3) When on further examination it turns out that there is no empirical domain in which the factor G can be neglected, a *heuristic strategy* may be initiated. The assumption that G is negligible is turned into a "heuristic assumption" by examining what difference G makes to the prediction. Musgrave thinks the rationale for this strategy is that the structure of some theories is too complex to derive empirical predictions from them directly. Instead a method of successive approximation must be used.

The negligibility strategy may be shown as the transition from (1) to (1'):

$$(x)\,[p_1(x) > 0\,\&\,p_2(x) > 0\,\&\,\ldots\,\&\,p_n(x) = 0 \Rightarrow F(x) = 0] \tag{1}$$

$$(x)\,[p_1(x) > 0\,\&\,p_2(x) = 0\,\&\,\ldots\,\&\,p_n(x) = 0 \Rightarrow F'(x) = 0], \tag{1'}$$

where F' is an approximation of F. However, the syntactical analysis of PIM is incapable of capturing the distinction between a negligibility strategy and a domain strategy; both are described by the transition from (2) to (3).

$$(x)\,[p_1(x) > 0\,\&\,p_2(x) = 0\,\&\,\ldots\,\&\,p_n(x) = 0 \Rightarrow F_3(x) = 0], \tag{2}$$

$$(x)\,[p_1(x) = 0\,\&\,p_2(x) = 0\,\&\,\ldots\,\&\,p_n(x) = 0 \Rightarrow F_4(x) = 0]. \tag{3}$$

Their difference is pragmatic.

Musgrave stresses that the driving force behind the changing status of idealizations and the development of a model is criticism. He tacitly assumes that critics in discussions in economics have constructive purposes only. This oversight hails from an empiricist bias: he presupposes that the impulse for a transition to a different strategy is given by empirical criticism only. It is in that sense that we have to interpret Musgrave's observation: strength and truth are empirical (or factual) strength and empirical (or factual) truth. But very often in economics no empirical arguments are employed directly to criticize or refute predictions. What happens instead is that theorems are put forward, and the formal, mathematical conditions are stated from which they can be proved (the sufficient conditions), or that can be proved from them (the necessary conditions). The way in which mathematics is used on the local level of analysis fits very accurately into the above scheme of strategies of theory development (see just below). Another strategy of criticism, which Musgrave does not mention, is suggested by a comparison of his own model with the one of Krajewski and Nowak. This is the conscious search for hidden idealizations with the purpose of critizing a particular model for being valid under restricted conditions only. Not only is this a possible strategy of criticism, it is an important strategy of criticism in actual practice. This is also the case with the strategy which is often followed in response to this: the heuristic strategy, which attempts to demonstrate that the prediction continues to hold as the unrealistic assumptions are factualized.

The strategies of theory development as Musgrave sees them are *parts of immunizing stratagems*, that is, moves designed to decrease a theory's content under the force of criticism. But they can also be used in two other ways which Musgrave does not recognize. The domain strategy may serve as *an instrument of criticism*. And, finally, the strategies may be *vehicles of progress*, when models are replaced by corresponding models, or when it is shown that there is a correspondence relation between existing models. All three strategies are heuristic strategies. This can be seen most clearly when we translate them into the formalism of PIM, as was done above. Domain and negligibility strategies are special cases of the heuristic strategy. Their differences are not syntactical but pragmatic.

From the Science of Mathematics to the Mathematics of Science

Mirowski is correct that mathematics has a heuristic function, but we have found his metaphorical account wanting. How *does* mathematics operate in economics? To show this I now turn to a discussion of the work of Imre Lakatos.

The recent revival of interest in heuristics, or the logic of discovery, is in large part due to Lakatos. His *Proofs and Refutations (PR)* analyzes the logic of mathematical discovery, and the *Methodology of Scientific*

Research Programmes (*MSRP*) studies the logic of discovery in science. Unfortunately no substantial discussion of the role of mathematics in scientific discovery exists in Lakatos's work. I attempt to fill that gap.

Lakatos proposes to replace the idea that mathematics starts "from above," from indubitably true axioms from which theorems are derived, with the view that mathematics is organized around true theorems that are at the bottom of the deductive structure. The former position is called "Euclidean," the latter "quasi-empirical." According to the latter view mathematical theories are developed by a method of proofs and refutations in which formal mathematical theories are tested by means of the corresponding "informal" theories, that is, their intended applications. The informal theories act as "heuristic falsifiers," that is, as applications of the formal theories which, in case they are found unsatisfactory, may give rise to adaptations in the formal theories. *May,* not *do* as a matter of necessity: "testability in mathematics rests on the slippery concept of a heuristic falsifier. A heuristic falsifier after all is a falsifier only in a Pickwickian sense: it does not falsify the hypothesis, it only suggests a falsification—and suggestions can be ignored" (*MSRP*, 40). The suggestions can be ignored because formal mathematical theories are relatively autonomous. Regardless of the possibly empirical problem that may originally have given rise to them, mathematical theories postulate abstract structures, relations between variables that may be filled in in different ways. Man is free to invent such calculi, and he can freely import them, free from ontological or metaphorical charge, from other disciplines. Whether the formalism can be successfully applied cannot be determined in advance, but has to be discovered.

Proofs

The logic of mathematical discovery, or the method of proofs and refutations, has been so succinctly stated by Lakatos that it justifies quoting in full. The method, which is also called the method of proof analysis, consists of the following stages:

1. Primitive conjecture.
2. Proof (a rough thought-experiment or argument, decomposing the primitive conjecture into subconjectures or lemmas).
3. "Global" counterexamples (counterexamples to the primitive conjecture) emerge.

4. Proof re-examined: the "guilty lemma" to which the global counterexample is a "local" counterexample is spotted. This guilty lemma may have previously remained "hidden" or may have been misidentified. Now it is made explicit, and built into the primitive conjecture as a condition. The theorem—the improved conjecture—supersedes the primitive conjecture with the new proof-generated concept as its paramount new feature.

These four stages constitute the essential kernel of proof analysis. But there are some further stages which frequently occur:

5. Proofs of other theorems are examined to see if the newly found lemma or the new proof-generated concept occurs in them: this concept may be found lying at cross-roads of different proofs, and thus emerge as of basic importance.
6. The hitherto accepted consequences of the original and now refuted conjecture are checked.
7. Counterexamples are turned into new examples—new fields of inquiry open up. (*PR*, 127–28, italics not indicated)

The scheme reads like an accurate description of the structure of many articles in economics journals. Some examples can be taken from the Cambridge capital theory debate.[22] *Primitive conjectures* which were held to be true previous to the debate are the inverse relation between the rate of interest and capital intensity of production techniques, the nonrecurrence of the same technique of production at a different interest rate, and the inverse relation between the interest rate and the level of consumption. These conjectures were thought to be predicted by, and hence *provable, if not proved, from* the neoclassical production model. The *global counterexamples* to the primitive conjectures were found by Robinson, Garegnani, Pasinetti, Bruno, Burmeister and Sheshinski, and many others. This prompted a *reexamination of the proof,* or rather, as the conjectures had been believed to be so much in the spirit of neoclassical production theory that they had not been proved in any detail, an *examination of the proof*. The proof of the conjectures was discovered to be premised on *hidden lemmas,* one of which is that the ordering of production techniques as to capital intensity coincides with their inverse ordering according to the rate of interest at which they are eligible. In the

---

22. A detailed analysis is contained in Birner (forthcoming).

debate discovered lemmas or proof-generated concepts of the "crossroads" variety did not play any explicit role, though there have been some discussions whether the assumption of profit-maximizing behavior was unique to the neoclassical approach or whether it was something that was commonly held by authors working in different theoretical traditions. (cf. Kregel 1980). The ways in which in the capital theory debate *guilty lemmas are built into the primitive conjecture as conditions* coincide with the different strategies of theory development which were described above. Examples of the *checking of the hitherto accepted consequences* are Garegnani 1970, Pasinetti 1966, and Bruno, Burmeister, and Sheshinski 1966. There are also instances where *counterexamples were turned into examples which opened up new fields of inquiry:* Brown 1969, and Ferguson and Allen 1970.

Proofs and Programmes

If we look at the details of the proofs given in the capital theory debate, we can often observe that purely formal, mathematical steps are used in proving theorems. The primary reason why these steps are included seems to be purely mathematical: they are proof-generated. If we kept strictly to Lakatos's methodology in *PR*, all we could say about these proof-generated devices is that they help to prove the theorem. Successful proof-generated conditions are their own justification, and whether or not they are acceptable depends on the context of the proof: the proof is the only "problem-background" of proof-generated concepts (cf. *PR*, 147).

However, in the debate the problem-background of most authors is more complex than this. Proof-generated concepts are usually not judged by the formal requirements of the proofs only. When deciding whether or not particular proof-generated concepts are acceptable, participants also let themselves be guided by economic-theoretical considerations which are suggested by the economic research programme in which they are working.[23] Programmatic considerations of this kind constitute the major difference between the method of *PR* and the methods that are used in the capital theory debate. I refer to this influence as "programmatic guidance."

---

23. Whether a particular condition is originally, as a matter of historical fact, purely proof-generated can only be determined from a publication if the proof or its economic interpretation goes wrong, as is the case with Gallaway & Shukla (and perhaps Levhari).

The method of proofs and refutations offers an accurate general description of the way in which theoretical economists operate. They translate economic problems into mathematical theorems, which they then prove. To bring the proof to a successful conclusion it is often necessary to introduce formal conditions. Sometimes these are blindly proof-generated and remain formal. They may also be blindly proof-generated and interpreted in economic terms later. But where the choice is guided by considerations of consistency with a particular economic research programme, the analysis of *PR* has to be augmented by the idea of programmatic guidance which is taken from the *MSRP*. An economic research programme has a positive heuristic which provides global guidance for the choice and interpretation of lemmas that are needed to prove theorems. What lends thrust,[24] that is, drive and direction, to the debate are proofs and programmes. By incorporating this element from Lakatos's *MSRP* into the methodology of *PR* we obtain a programme-augmented proofs-and-refutations model of theory development. I refer to it as PR^+.

Proofs, Programmes, and Strategies: PR^+

Which among the various possible strategies of theory development one chooses depends both on local and global considerations: both the concrete problem situation and the research programme one belongs to. In a situation where a neoclassical production model is criticized, we are not surprised to find a neoclassical author defending the model by means of a heuristic strategy. Nor do we find it odd that an author who belongs to a rival research programme, such as the Sraffian programme, follows a domain strategy when criticizing a neoclassical model. For each local problem situation there is a strategy to follow, depending on whether one wants to criticize or immunize a particular hypothesis or model, or develop it in a progressive way.

In all strategies of theory development mathematics usually plays an important part. In a correspondence strategy, formulating both the corresponded and the corresponding model in mathematics makes it easier to compare their structures and find out which steps are needed to link them. In a domain strategy, mathematics may play exactly the same part. This is the case where there exists a standard model with a limited

---

24. I owe this term to Neil de Marchi.

domain of application. If one succeeds in showing that another model that has a claim to wider applicability can be reduced without residue to the limited model, one has successfully carried out a domain strategy, and mathematics has the same useful role as in the correspondence strategy. And mathematics may be used in heuristic strategies for suggesting, through proof-generated lemmas and devices, conditions that are relevant in economic terms but had been overlooked.

PR^+ in conjunction with the strategies described by PIM and AIM and with the distinction between global and local levels of analysis fully accounts for the interaction among economic research programmes, proofs of theorems, and mathematics.

Mathematics without Justification and the Practice of Economics

It may be objected that Mirowski's argument is completely consistent with PR^+ and that the programmatic guidance is provided by the physics metaphor. But that would not be satisfactory. It is hard to see how the physics metaphor can provide guidance in solving particular local problems in partial economic models. Mirowski's focus on the global level makes him overlook the details of the process on a local level, details which are described by PIM and the extended model of Musgrave.

Mirowski's uneven treatment of physics, which uses mathematics creatively, and neoclassical economics, the slavish and mindless imitator, can be discussed in terms of Meyerson's philosophy of mathematics. Mirowski applies Meyerson's heuristic answer only to physics. Mathematics is successful in physics because of the dialectical process of adapting the mathematics to the requirements of physical theory, and of physical theory to the constraints imposed by mathematics. For economics Mirowski follows a version of Meyerson's justificationist answer. According to Mirowski, the justification of the mathematics that neoclassical economics took over from physics lies in physics and nowhere else. For Mirowski, the *divers* of physics is much richer than the *divers* of economics. In neoclassical economics there is no room for programmatic guidance other than by the mathematical formalism and the physical metaphors incorporated in it, nor is there room for factual or empirical considerations. That is why the mathematics that was imported from physics is seen as inevitably leading to steps that are dictated by the metaphors embodied in the formalism.

However, if we look at economics, we see a diversity of programmatic ideas that owe nothing to physics, such as individualism, subjectivism, competition, evolution, and the idea of a spontaneous order.[25] Mirowski's conclusion that mathematics is not neutral is drawn from the justificationist idea that mathematics operates through its metaphorical meaning content. This illustrates the fact that true conclusions may follow from false premises. If Mirowski had taken the local level of analysis in economics more seriously, he would have had to give up this uneven treatment. If he had applied Meyerson's heuristic answer to economics, he would have had to recognize there is a richer *divers* of proofs, refutations, and programmatic guidance by economic theory, as well as factual and empirical influences. PR^+ can account for all of these factors.

PR^+ is based on Lakatos's work, which achieved a revolution in the philosophy of mathematics. By leaving justificationism behind, Lakatos does away with the distinction between what I have called Meyerson's justificationist and his heuristic answer. According to Lakatos, mathematics cannot and need not be justified, certainly not by an appeal to an empirical basis. It develops according to a particular logic of discovery that is set in motion by the wish to solve particular problems. There is no ultimate justification, there is only heuristics.

The Physics Envy: What Object?

The above criticism affects Mirowski's arguments insofar as it involves the role of mathematics. But that may still leave the thesis standing that neoclassical economics is nothing but imported physics and that if you take away the central physical metaphor of energy, the whole structure comes apart. The neoclassical physics metaphor "cannot seriously be repudiated or relinquished, because there is nothing else that can hold the neoclassical research program together. In the absence of the metaphor of utility as nineteenth-century potential energy, there is no alternative theory of value, no heuristic guide to research, no principle upon which to base mathematical formalism, no causal invariant in the Meyersonian sense, and most threatening, no basis for the claim that economics has finally become scientific" (*MHL*, 368, emphasis omitted).

Is the picture Mirowski paints of neoclassical economics as mockphysics correct? And if it is, what exactly did it imitate? Mirowski

---

25. The same point is made by Hands (1993, this volume).

presents case studies of Fisher, Samuelson, and others who took over the mathematical formalism of energy physics. But there is more to the relation between physics and classical economics. What economists took over, well before the marginal revolution, sometimes with and sometimes without the formalism, was what they took to be the *method* of physics. And there are methodological reasons other than the slavish imitation of a successful discipline that account for the fact that mathematics has come to be used so generally by economists.

Ricardo was one of the first economists to take the successful example of Newtonian physics to heart and to build up the system of economics as an abstract discipline. He constructed ideal models which are thought to represent some basic relations and mechanisms and examined to what extent reality conformed to these. This method of reasoning backwards from idealized models to more factual conditions, which we may call the conditional method, is mathematical in spirit.[26] It was seen to be successful in classical mechanics, and its success there led to its adoption in economics.

Carl Menger is an example of a later author who took this approach over from physics. He used it to structure his economic theory in the *Principles* and explained in his *Investigations on Method* that this was why he had succeeded in elevating economics to the same methodological level as physics and the other mature sciences. Clearly Menger and his followers have to be explained away by Mirowski, as their economics shares many features with neoclassical economics, notably the core of a logic of choice, but lacks many of its flaws. Austrian economics is emphatically dynamic, uses an intertemporal framework, and pays explicit attention to subjectivist features and temporal asymmetries and to evolution and order (culminating in the idea of a spontaneous order). This deserves a lengthier discussion, but there is no room for that here.[27]

Neither Ricardo nor Menger formulated theory in mathematical terms. But their conditional method, or the method of decreasing abstraction as

26. Mirowski (*MHL*, 198) calls it a proto-mathematical logic.

27. I will just give some brief comments on what Mirowski has to say about Menger. Menger does not fit Mirowski's statement that "there was little if any discussion of the reasons for the appropriateness of natural-science methodology in economic research; consensus on this point was simply taken for granted" (*MHL*, 199). It is also a plain falsehood that Menger's theory is severely Aristotelian (261). Menger is accused of the error of uncritically importing physical methods into economics: "How this is reconciled with his later jabs at the Historicists is a problem best left for someone else to figure out." Some of the figuring out is attempted in Birner 1990b.

it has come to be known since Wieser, almost naturally led to analysis in mathematical terms. The method preceded the mathematics.

Meaning versus Truth

Although Mirowski is inspired by Meyerson, he claims to be doing something different from Meyersonian metaphysics, namely hermeneutics. Consider the following list. On the left are the terms used by Mirowski, on the right I have put the terms that seem to be their closest realist correlates:

hermeneutics	metaphysics
metaphor	regulative principle, category
unfolding of meaning	description, explanation
concepts	theories
meaning	truth
fiction	real
discourse (unity of)	method (unity of)
language community	theory, research programme
communication	criticism
justification	testing

Mirowski is not consistent in his hermeneutics. Now and then he slips into more realist language—for instance, where he speaks of "structures of explanation" (*MHL*, 116) and the inappropriateness of metaphors. This seems to be an implicit admission that his hermeneutics is not adequate as a description of neoclassical economics. I suspect that Mirowski's Meyersonian background here asserts itself without Mirowski willing it, in very much the same way that Mirowski says the basic features of energy physics could not be suppressed by neoclassical economists. After all, Meyerson is a realist, both in his philosophy of science and in his philosophy of mathematics: when mathematics works it is because the structure of the domain of application *is* as the mathematics describes it. Mirowski's hermeneutic and metaphorical verbiage seem to hide a realist, traditional metaphysics of the Kantian variety. But there is one difference that transcends the substitution of "metaphor" for "category" or "a priori principle." Mirowski studies science as it evolves, whereas Kant studies science as a body of existing knowledge.

Mirowski shares this dynamic interest with another student of metaphysics, Collingwood. Collingwood (1940) conceives of science as an activity of questions and answers. He constructs his theory of metaphysics on the fact that, logically speaking, each question has a presupposition. Presuppositions in their turn are the answers to other questions. Collingwood thought that it was possible, through logical analysis, to work one's way backwards from questions to presuppositions and thence to arrive at presuppositions that are answers to no questions. These are the *absolute presuppositions of all science*. They are absolute in the sense that they are not questioned by a particular society at a particular epoch and that they are neither true nor false. They are just tacitly presupposed. I suggest that Mirowski's four basic metaphors have the same function as Collingwood's absolute presuppositions. But just as there is no logical reason why there should be absolute presuppositions in Collingwood's sense, as Watkins (1978) has demonstrated, there is no reason why there should be any basic metaphors, let alone the four metaphors Mirowski identifies.

This does not disprove the fact that science operates with general principles or metaphysical presuppositions. One cannot understand the development of science without a firm understanding of the role of metaphysics. If all that Mirowski claims were that for the development of a scientific discipline there is good metaphysics and bad metaphysics, that would be unobjectionable.[28] But I fail to see what Mirowski's metaphorical hermeneutics adds to this, nor where it improves upon the traditional philosophy of science of Meyerson and Popper, which takes metaphysics seriously.

To sum up my criticism of Mirowski:

1. He replaces a philosophy of science that analyzes the function of metaphysics in explanation by a philosophy that looks for the meaning of metaphors without adding to our understanding of science.
2. Though he is correct in arguing that mathematics is far from a neutral instrument in economics, he fails to give a satisfactory account of the way in which it operates as part of a logic of discovery. This is because he builds on the justificatory part of Meyerson's philosophy of mathematics.

---

28. This is an insight that is at least as old as the second edition of Whewell's *Philosophy of the Inductive Sciences* of 1847: "Physical discoverers have differed from barren speculators, not by having *no* metaphysics in their heads, but by having *good* metaphysics while their adversaries had bad; and by binding their metaphysics to their physics, instead of keeping the two asunder" (quoted in Watkins 1984, 224).

3. His description of the way in which neoclassical economics develops is incomplete, because he concentrates on the global level of economic analysis.
4. His *divers* is too poor to model the development of economics. Meyerson was more general in recognizing that the *divers* could also be located in empirical reality, whereas Mirowski depicts neoclassical economics as a purely sterile, formal and inward-looking occupation.

A Conspiracy of the Alphabet?

Mirowski has described neoclassical economists as being led by an invisible hand wielding a hidden agenda, and I have made the same observation about Mirowski's philosophy of mathematics. But it seems that I have fallen victim to a similar conspiracy. After I had finished the text for the oral presentation of this paper, I hit upon the title. Then I decided to look up metaphysics in *The Encyclopedia of Philosophy*. To my surprise I found that Metaphysics comes immediately after Metaphor. Meyerson is the next full entry, right after the reference to Methodology. And as if all this were not enough, the entry immediately preceding Metaphor is Metamathematics. I must confess to a feeling of being manipulated by the alphabet. I never believed in cabalism,[29] but perhaps it is time to change that.

References

Birner, J. 1990a. Idealizations and the Development of Capital Theory. *Poznan Studies* 16:127–49.
——— . 1990b. A Roundabout Solution to a Fundamental Problem in Menger's Methodology and Beyond. In Caldwell 1990.
——— . Forthcoming. *Strategies and Programmes in Capital Theory: A Contribution to the Methodology of Theory Development*. London: Routledge & Kegan Paul.
Brown, M. 1969. Substitution-Composition Effects, Capital-Intensity Uniqueness and Growth. *Economic Journal* 79:334–47.
Bruno, M., E. Burmeister, and E. Sheshinski. 1966. The Nature and Implications of the Reswitching of Techniques. *Quarterly Journal of Economics* 80:526–53.
Buchdahl, G. 1969. *Metaphysics and the Philosophy of Science*. Oxford: Basil Blackwell.

---

29. See Yates 1985, the index, under "Alphabet manipulation."

Caldwell, B., ed. 1990. *Carl Menger and His Legacy in Economics*. Annual supplement, *HOPE* volume 22.
Collingwood, R. G. 1940. *An Essay on Metaphysics*. Oxford: Clarendon Press. Reprinted 1979.
Ferguson, C. E., and R. F. Allen. 1970. Factor Prices, Commodity Prices, and Switches of Technique. *Western Economic Journal* 8:95–109.
Gallaway, L., and V. Shukla. 1974. The Neoclassical Production Function. *American Economic Review* 64:348–58.
Garegnani, P. 1970. Heterogeneous Capital, the Production Function and the Theory of Distribution. *Review of Economic Studies* 37:407–36.
Hands, D. Wade. 1993. More Light on Integrability, Symmetry, and Utility as Potential Energy in Mirowski's Critical History. [In this special issue of *HOPE*.]
Krajewski, W. 1977. *Correspondence Principle and Growth of Science*. Dordrecht: Reidel.
Kregel, J. 1980. The Theoretical Consequences of Economic Methodology: Samuelson's Foundations. *Metroeconomica* 32:25–38.
Lakatos, I. 1976. *Proofs and Refutations: The Logic of Mathematical Discovery*. Cambridge: Cambridge University Press. [Citations are abbreviated *PR*.]
———. 1978a. *Philosophical Papers*. Vol. 1, *The Methodology of Scientific Research Programmes*. Edited by J. Worrall and G. Currie. Cambridge: Cambridge University Press. [Citations are abbreviated *MSRP*.]
———. 1978b. *Philosophical Papers*. Vol. 2, *Mathematics, Science and Epistemology*. Edited by J. Worrall and G. Currie. Cambridge: Cambridge University Press.
Meyerson, E. 1926. *Identité et réalité*. 3d ed. Paris: Alcan.
———. 1931. *Du cheminement de la pensée*. Paris: Alcan.
———. 1934. Les mathématiques et le divers. In Meyerson 1936.
———. 1936. *Essays*. Paris: Vrin.
Mirowski, P. 1986a. Mathematical Formalism and Economic Explanation. In Mirowski 1986b.
———. 1987. Shall I Compare Thee to a Minkowski-Ricardo-Leontief-Metzler Matrix of the Mosack-Hicks Type? *Economics and Philosophy* 3:67–95.
———. 1989. *More Heat than Light: Economics as Social Physics, Physics as Nature's Economics*. Cambridge: Cambridge University Press. [Citations are abbreviated *MHL*.]
———, ed. 1986b. *The Reconstruction of Economic Theory*. Boston: Kluwer.
Musgrave, A. 1981. "Unreal Assumptions" in Economic Theory: The F-Twist Untwisted. *Kyklos* 34:377–87.
Nowak, L. 1980. *The Structure of Idealization: Towards a Systematic Interpretation of the Marxian Idea of Science*. Dordrecht: Reidel.
Pasinetti, L. L. 1966. Changes in the Rate of Profit and Switches of Techniques. *Quarterly Journal of Economics* 80:503–17.
Popper, K. R. 1963. *Conjectures and Refutations*. London: Routledge & Kegan Paul.
Watkins, J. W. N. 1978. Minimal Presuppositions and Maximal Metaphysics. *Mind* 87:195–209.

———. 1984. *Science and Scepticism*. London: Hutchinson.
Wigner, E. 1960. The Unreasonable Effectiveness of Mathematics in the Natural Sciences. *Communications in Pure and Applied Mathematics* 13:1–14.
Yates, F. A. 1985. *The Occult Philosophy in the Elizabethan Age*. London and Boston: Routledge & Kegan Paul.
Zahar, E. 1980. Einstein, Meyerson, and the Role of Mathematics in Physical Discovery. *British Journal for the Philosophy of Science* 31:1–43.

More Light on Integrability, Symmetry, and Utility as Potential Energy in Mirowski's Critical History

D. Wade Hands

In an earlier paper (Hands 1992) I argued that while there is much to be said in favor of Mirowski's central thesis in *More Heat than Light*, there are some questions raised by the technical part of his presentation. In particular, the standard Slutsky (or in inverse demand form–Antonelli) conditions that are sufficient for the "integrability" of demand do not seem to be sufficient to guarantee that prices form a conservative vector field as Mirowski argues (*MHL*, 223–27, 232–33, 250–53, 273–75). This means that the standard integrability conditions do not restrict prices (p) to be the gradient of the utility potential (∇U) as would be required for the complete translation of utility theory into the mathematics of energy physics. This criticism is not a trivial mathematical point; it is a criticism that has important implications for Mirowski's discussion of integrability. On the other hand, this technical criticism does not provide any indictment of Mirowski's general historical thesis. It seems clear that (at least some) early neoclassical economists were doing little more than translating energy into utility and that much of the development of modern neoclassical economics has been guided by the mandate of (old) physics envy. In fact, as I argued in the earlier paper, the criticism of Mirowski's technical comments on integrability can actually be used to lend additional empirical support to his general historical thesis.

This paper continues the investigation of integrability, symmetry, utility as potential, and related issues. The purpose, clearly consistent with Mirowski's central thesis, is to unpack these concepts and their influence on the development of neoclassical economics. In particular, the question of the symmetry of the Slutsky matrix and what it does and does not imply about utility as potential energy is carefully examined. Section 1 introduces the concept of prices as a conservative vector field.

1. Prices as a Conservative Vector Field

Suppose the prices of the three goods[1] are given by the vector field

$$p = (p_1, p_2, p_3),$$

where each p_i is a (differentiable) function of the quantities $x = (x_1, x_2, x_3)$ of the three goods: thus $p_i = p_i(x)$ for $i = 1, 2, 3$. Since price is the dependent, rather than the independent variable, these demand functions are the inverse of the standard Walrasian demand functions where $x_i = x_i(p)$.

If the vector field p is *conservative*, meaning that the line integral around any closed curve is equal to zero, then there exists a scalar potential function U such that

$$p = \nabla U = (\partial U/\partial x_1, \partial U/\partial x_2, \partial U/\partial x_3).$$

By calling this potential function $U(x)$, "utility," we have the "core physics metaphor of utility as potential energy" (*MHL*, 358). In this case, as Mirowski argues, prices represent "the vector field of gradients of utility in a commodity space" (232). For Mirowski this is the "key to understanding neoclassical economics . . . prices constitute a conservative vector field . . . such that given a scalar field of utility $U(x, y, z)$, the price vector field may be deduced from it" (223).

While I do not consider this "core physics metaphor" to be *as* fundamental to the development of neoclassical economics as Mirowski claims, I do agree that something like $p = \nabla U$ was in fact what certain early neoclassical economists had in mind and that attempting to work out (or circumvent) the difficulties associated with this metaphor has motivated a portion of modern microeconomic theory.[2] My disagreement is not really with this "core physics metaphor" but rather with the next step in Mirowski's argument, where he investigates the conditions that would guarantee that p does in fact constitute a conservative field.

If the vector field p is conservative, then it must be an exact differen-

---

1. To facilitate comparison with Mirowski's presentation and the relevant physical theory, discussion will be limited to the three-good case.
2. These points are argued more carefully in Hands 1992.

tial, which implies that its curl must be equal to zero (curl $p = 0$), where the curl is defined by

$$\text{curl } p = (\partial p_3/\partial x_2 - \partial p_2/\partial x_3, \partial p_1/\partial x_3 - \partial p_3/\partial x_1,$$
$$\partial p_2/\partial x_1 - \partial p_1/\partial x_2).$$

This vanishing curl condition is also equivalent to the symmetry of the Jacobian matrix of the inverse demand functions. Thus when p is a conservative vector field, the Jacobian matrix

$$[Jp] = \begin{bmatrix} p_{11} & p_{12} & p_{13} \\ p_{21} & p_{22} & p_{23} \\ p_{31} & p_{32} & p_{33} \end{bmatrix} \tag{1}$$

must be symmetric, that is $p_{ij} = p_{ji}$ for all $i \neq j$ where $p_{ij} = \partial p_i/\partial x_j$.

Mirowski repeatedly argues that these symmetry (or vanishing curl) conditions, conditions sufficient to guarantee that prices form a conservative vector field, are assumed as a matter of course in standard neoclassical theory. He claims that these symmetry conditions are nothing more than "the neglected and frequently misunderstood integrability conditions in neoclassical theory, which often appear under the rubrics of Antonelli conditions, Slutsky conditions, or the strong axiom of revealed preference" (232–33). According to this argument, the symmetry of the matrix of "substitution effects," or (when quantity is the independent variable) the "Antonelli conditions," is equivalent to curl $p = 0$ and thus guarantees that prices form a conservative vector field. Mirowski argues that since these conditions also have some additional, quite unreasonable implications—like "the sum of expenditure plus utility is conserved" (233)—they are treated as rather unimportant and esoteric mathematical properties in standard neoclassical theory. In other words, neoclassical economists always assume (via the symmetry of the Slutsky matrix) that prices form a conservative vector field, but because of the unreasonable implications of that assumption they are forced into a rather elaborate subterfuge (called "integrability") to avoid admitting what they are in fact assuming.

The difficulty with this story is that the symmetry of Jp is not implied by the symmetry of the Slutsky matrix or any of the other conditions Mirowski mentions in his discussion of integrability. Since $p = p(x)$ is the inverse demand function and since $[Jp] = [Jx]^{-1}$ when $x = x(p)$ is the corresponding Walrasian demand function, the symmetry of Jp does imply the symmetry of the Jacobian of the regular (Walrasian) demand functions. This symmetry of the Walrasian demands would mean that for any two goods, apples and oranges say, the impact of a change in the price of apples on the demand for oranges would need to be exactly the same (magnitude as well as sign) as the impact of a change in the price of oranges on the demand for apples (i.e., $\partial x_i/\partial p_j = \partial x_j/\partial p_i$ for all $i \neq j$). This is not very likely empirically, and more importantly for the discussion at hand, it is not an implication of the symmetry of the Slutsky (or Antonelli) terms or any of the other mathematical properties that pass for "integrability" conditions.[3] The condition Mirowski requires for prices to represent a conservative vector field is not the standard Slutsky condition or the equivalent condition for the integrability of demand, but rather the much stronger property of the symmetry of the Jacobian of Walrasian demands. Such symmetry is a very restrictive assumption that is empirically quite unreasonable. It is a property that would hold in certain special cases—such as vanishing income effects or homothetic preferences—but it is clearly not the standard property that Mirowski would have us believe.

In order more carefully to unpack these issues of integrability, symmetry, and prices being a conservative vector field, it is useful to differentiate clearly two separate aspects of neoclassical demand theory. The first will be, for want of a more appropriate term, the "utility first" approach. This utility-first approach is the demand theory of most neoclassical textbooks. It starts with a utility function, or ordinal preferences that can be "represented" by a utility function, and then deduces the properties of the demand functions generated by a consumer that maximize this utility function subject to a linear budget constraint with parametric prices and money income (or endowments in the pure exchange case). The second aspect of demand theory that needs to be considered is the "demand first" approach. This is the "integrability" question, the question of whether an (ostensibly) observable demand function could have been generated from a utility-maximizing consumer and the question of whether it is possible to "recover" the utility function from the demand function. Mirowski continuously fuses these two issues, but it seems more useful to keep them apart.

---

3. See Hurwicz 1971.

2. Demand Theory, Symmetry, and Related Issues

In the three-good case the standard consumer choice problem is given by

$$\max U(x)$$
$$\text{Subject to:} \quad \sum_{i=1}^{3} p_i x_i = M, \tag{2}$$

where $x \in R_+^3$, $U(x)$ is the utility function, and p_1, p_2, p_3, and M are strictly positive parameters. The utility function $U(x)$ is assumed to have sufficient structure to satisfy the first- and second-order conditions for an (interior) solution to the above problem. This solution is a set of consumer (Walrasian) demand functions given by

$$x_i^* = x_i^*(p_1, p_2, p_3) \quad \text{for all } i = 1, 2, 3.$$

The standard assumptions impose a number of restrictions on these consumer demand functions. Probably the most important of these restrictions is the symmetry and negative semidefiniteness of the "Slutsky matrix,"

$$S = \begin{bmatrix} S_{11} & S_{12} & S_{13} \\ S_{21} & S_{22} & S_{23} \\ S_{31} & S_{32} & S_{33} \end{bmatrix}, \tag{3}$$

where each S_{ij} term is given by

$$S_{ij} = \partial x_i^*/\partial p_j + x_j^* \partial x_i^*/\partial M. \tag{4}$$

The symmetry of this Slutsky matrix, $S_{ij} = S_{ji}$ for all $i \neq j$, thus implies

$$\partial x_i^*/\partial p_j + x_j^* \partial x_i^*/\partial M = \partial x_j^*/\partial p_i + x_i^* \partial x_j^*/\partial M$$

for all i and j,

but it *does not imply*, $\partial x_i^*/\partial p_j = \partial x_j^*/\partial p_i$, as would be required for the symmetry of the Jacobian in (1) and therefore the property of p forming a conservative vector field. The symmetry of the Slutsky *does* in fact imply the existence of a conservative vector field; it is just not the inverse (or Walrasian) demand functions that form it. The symmetry of the Slutsky matrix implies that the *compensated demand functions*, not $p(x)$, form a conservative vector field.

To demonstrate this last claim it is useful to recall another aspect of the standard consumer choice theory: the dual problem to the utility maximization problem in (2). The dual problem to (2) is the problem of minimizing the expenditure necessary to achieve any particular given level of utility ($\overline{U}$). This dual problem is written

$$\min \sum_{i=1}^{3} p_i x_i \qquad (5)$$

Subject to: $U(x) = \overline{U}.$

The solution to this dual expenditure minimization problem is a set of compensated demand functions,

$$x_i^c = S_i(p_1, p_2, p_3, \overline{U}) \quad \text{for } i = 1, 2, 3.$$

The derivatives of these compensated demand functions, $\partial x_i^c / \partial p_j$, are simply the S_{ij} terms in the Slutsky matrix (3). Thus the symmetry of the Slutsky matrix, while it does *not* imply $\partial x_i^* / \partial p_j = \partial x_j^* / \partial p_i$, does imply that $\partial x_i^c / \partial p_j = \partial x_j^c / \partial p_i$, and thus the compensated demand vector $x^c(p, \overline{U})$ has curl $x^c = 0$ and does form a conservative vector field. This implies that there exists a potential function $E(p, \overline{U})$ such that $x^c = \nabla E$.

Now this characterization of compensated demands as a conservative vector field is not the way the argument is usually presented in consumer choice theory. Even though it is not part of the standard presentation, $x^c = \nabla E$ is an implication of the standard theory. One well known implication of consumer choice theory is that compensated demand functions (x_i^c) are the price derivatives of the so-called *expenditure function* $E(p, \overline{U})$. Thus from standard consumer choice theory we have

$$x_i^c(p, \overline{U}) = \partial E(p, \overline{U}) / \partial p_i \quad \text{for all } i = 1, 2, \ldots n,$$

where the expenditure function $E(p, \overline{U})$ is defined by

$$E(p, \overline{U}) = \sum_{i=1}^{n} p_i x_i^c(p, \overline{U}).$$

But this is nothing other than saying $x^c = \nabla E$, which implies that compensated demand functions form a conservative vector field and that the expenditure function is the associated potential function.

Thus the Slutsky conditions do not imply that prices (inverse Walrasian demand functions) form a conservative vector field as Mirowski has argued. What we do find though, is that the Slutsky conditions imply that compensated demands, the solutions to the expenditure minimization problem, form a conservative vector field. Given this latter fact, it is actually possible to salvage a slightly modified version of Mirowski's original argument. If we define "prices" to be *compensated prices*, that is, the inverse of the compensated demand functions,[4] then it is possible to say, on this definition of prices, that "prices form a conservative vector field." The reasoning is as follows.

Since the standard compensated demand functions, $x_i^c(p, \overline{U})$ above, have quantity, not price, as the dependent variable, we might (following Hurwicz 1971, 175) define the Slutsky terms, the S_{ij}'s in (3), to be the *quantity*-substitution terms. Alternatively, the derivatives of the inverse compensated demand functions, with price as the dependent variable, should be called the *price*-substitution terms. But the symmetry of the standard Slutsky matrix (the matrix of the quantity-substitution terms) implies the symmetry of the price-substitution matrix, and this in turn implies that the inverse of the compensated demand functions, what might be called *compensated prices*, do form a conservative vector field. Thus while Mirowski's argument that Walrasian prices form a conservative vector field does not stand up to close analysis, it is possible to find support for a weaker version of his basic claim. Here, as many other places in neoclassical economics, the ultimate culprit is the income effect. Under the standard Slutsky conditions, compensated prices do form a conservative vector field while regular Walrasian prices do not, but the sole difference between the two is the income effect. Without income effects then $S_{ij} = \partial x_i^* / \partial p_j$ for all $i \neq j$, Walrasian prices would in fact form a conservative vector field, and the fundamental neoclassical metaphor could be fully exploited.

It is easy to find a bit of irony in the above results. Neoclassical economics is often, and I think rightly, characterized as an amalgam of two separate influences, the Marshallian/Chicago/pragmatic/partial-equilibrium view and the Walrasian/Samuelsonian/formal/general-equilibrium view.[5] Clearly Mirowski's thesis about the energy metaphor is aimed primarily at the latter (now dominant) aspect of the neoclassical tradition. The irony is that if one were intent on fully exploiting the energy metaphor, one would, on the basis of the above argument, focus

---

4. Since the Slutsky matrix is singular, these inverse demand functions should be discussed in the context of a normalized system.

5. There is of course a third, Austrian, tradition that has been present, but generally less influential than the Marshallian and Walrasian traditions.

exclusively on compensated demands and neglect income effects—a practice long associated with the Chicago tradition in microeconomics. Neglecting income effects and focusing on compensated demands was Milton Friedman's suggestion in his famous paper on "the Marshallian demand curve" (1949), and it has since become a standard part of the Chicago tradition. Of course the Chicago defense of this practice is always pragmatic, not formal. As Friedman argued, "the test of the theory is its value in explaining facts, in predicting the consequences of changes in explaining facts, in predicting the consequences of changes in the economic environment," issues such as "abstractness, generality, mathematical elegance—these are all secondary, themselves to be judged by the test of application" ([1949] 1953, 91). The point is that despite the rhetoric of practicality, this Chicago assumption actually solves the technical/Walrasian problem of exploiting the energy metaphor more effectively than the last half-century of work in the Walrasian tradition. Many of the problems that have proven recalcitrant to the Walrasian strategy of employing ever more sophisticated mathematical machinery, such as the stability and uniqueness of the general-equilibrium price vector, could quickly be solved by adopting this Chicago suggestion.[6]

Thus far the discussion in this section has focused exclusively on the "utility first" approach to demand theory; let us now briefly consider the alternative "demand first" approach and the concomitant question of integrability. The integrability problem is simply the reverse of the "utility first" problem discussed above. Instead of starting with utility and "generating" demand, the integrability problem starts with demand and "recovers" utility. The integrability question is: "What properties of the demand relations guarantee the *existence* of a '*generating*' utility function . . . , i.e., of a utility function that is maximized, subject to the budget, by these demand relations? Furthermore, if such a utility function exists, how can it be '*recovered*' (determined) from the knowledge of the demand relations?" (Hurwicz 1971, 176, italics his). Since the demands are obtained by the differentiation of utility, recovering the utility function from those demands is the question of "integrability."

The main integrability result for the kind of mathematically well-

---

6. In the pure exchange case, vanishing income effects would, for a normalized system, guarantee the negative definiteness of the excess demand Jacobian and therefore the uniqueness (Arrow and Hahn 1971, 235) and the global stability (Arrow and Hurwicz 1958, 536) of the Walrasian equilibrium. This result could easily be extended to a production economy since in production, as in exchange, the problem is primarily the income effect (see Mukherji 1974).

behaved problem considered above is Samuelson's. In his 1950 paper Samuelson proved that if the Slutsky conditions hold, that is, the symmetry and negative semidefiniteness of the Slutsky matrix given by (3) for $n = 3$, then the demand functions are "integrable." This result has been extended in various ways to demand systems with fewer mathematical restrictions,[7] but Samuelson's paper remains the major result for the standard model.

Notice that integrability is solely a "demand first" consideration: that is, given "observed" demands, how could we know they were generated by a utility-maximizing individual? Given the nature of neoclassical theorizing—that is, assume that agents are maximizing and deduce their behavior—integrability has played a relatively minor role in the overall evolution of the neoclassical program. The integrability conditions are, as Mirowski claims, equivalent to the Slutsky conditions; but as argued above, these are not equivalent to prices forming a conservative vector field unless "prices" are given a very special interpretation. Thus it is probably an overstatement to say, as Mirowski does, that the "befuddled treatment of the neoclassical integrability conditions should call into question the entire project of portraying utility as potential energy, in other words, they should undermine the entire neoclassical project of imitating physics" (*MHL*, 371).

3. Entrepreneurial Demand Functions

One episode in the history of neoclassical economics that Mirowski does not examine is the theory of "entrepreneurial" demand functions given by Hotelling (1932).[8] This episode is worth a careful examination, since it helps clarify the relationship between symmetry and utility as potential energy while providing some additional support for Mirowski's general historical thesis about the role of the energy metaphor in neoclassical economics.

Hotelling (1932) considered the demand function of an "entrepreneur," that is, someone purchasing goods in order to resell them. By focusing on such "entrepreneurial" demand Hotelling is "restricting attention to those cases in which money is spent, as the saying is, to

---

7. See Hurwicz 1971 for a discussion of these results.
8. Also see Court 1941 and Hotelling 1935.

make money" (1932, 592). The sales or total revenue function of the entrepreneur is given by

$$U(q) = U(q_1, q_2, \ldots, q_n),$$

where $q = (q_1, q_2, \ldots, q_n)$ is the vector of quantities of the n commodities.[9] With $U(q)$ as total revenue the net revenue or profit of the entrepreneur is given by

$$U(q) - \sum_{i=1}^{n} p_i q_i, \qquad (6)$$

where $p = (p_1, p_2, \ldots, p_n)$ is the vector of commodity prices.[10] The first-order conditions for this (unconstrained) maximization problem are given by Hotelling's equation (3) (1932, 590):

$$\partial U / \partial q_i = p_i \quad \text{for all } i = 1, 2, \ldots, n. \qquad (7)$$

Given the objective function in (6), the solutions to these n first-order conditions satisfy the following reciprocity (symmetry) conditions:

$$\partial p_i / \partial q_j = \partial p_j / \partial q_i \quad \text{for all } i \neq j. \qquad (8)$$

Hotelling remarks that since these symmetry conditions are necessary and sufficient for a function U satisfying (7), they are "known as 'integrability conditions'" (1932, 591). He goes on to admit that for the case where "the money expenditure is absolutely fixed"—that is, the standard consumer choice problem in (2)—the conditions in (7) and (8) "may not hold accurately" (1932, 592). For the strictly entrepreneurial case though, where (7) and (8) do hold, we have—by an argument identical to the argument used in sections 1 and 2 above—the following symmetry conditions for the case where price is the independent variable:

$$\partial q_i / \partial p_j = \partial q_j / \partial p_i \quad \text{for all } i \neq j. \qquad (9)$$

It is useful to quote at length from what Hotelling says about these symmetry conditions (equation 7 in his numbering scheme):

---

9. The vector q replaces the quantity vector x from the earlier discussion in order to be consistent with Hotelling's original paper.

10. If we let $U(q) = rf(q)$ where q is the factor input vector, $f(q)$ the production function, and r the price of output, then Hotelling's maximization problem in (6) reduces to the standard profit maximization problem for a perfectly competitive firm employing n inputs.

Just as we have a utility (or profit) function U of the quantities consumed whose derivatives are the prices, there is, dually, a function of the prices whose derivatives are the quantities consumed. The existence of such a function, which heretofore does not seem to have been noticed, is assured by (7). On the basis of physical analogies we may call this the "price potential." (1932, 594)

Thus we see that for Hotelling's case of entrepreneurial demands Mirowski's story about utility as potential is entirely correct. The "integrability" conditions are nothing more than the symmetry conditions which guarantee that there does exist a function $U(x)$ such that $p = \nabla U$. And in keeping with the fundamental neoclassical metaphor of treating utility as energy—as Hotelling says, "on the basis of physical analogies"—utility is the "price potential." The argument works here, and does not work for the standard consumer choice problem, because this is an unconstrained maximization problem. Since the problem is unconstrained, the first-order conditions are given by (7), the solutions have symmetric Jacobians [(8) and (9)], and the physics metaphor can be fully exploited.

Hotelling's paper is not only important because it demonstrates a special case where Mirowski's arguments about utility as potential would hold exactly, it also provides additional support to Mirowski's more general thesis that early neoclassical economists wanted—sometimes wanted desperately—to treat utility as potential energy. Notice how subtly Hotelling has defined the objective function in (6). Mirowski repeatedly argues (particularly in chapter 5) that the conservation of the sum of expenditure and utility—thus the addition of apples and oranges—is required to complete the neoclassical metaphor of utility as potential energy. Because $U(q)$ is defined to be "revenue" and not utility, Hotelling's argument is (technically) immune to this criticism. But also notice how subtly Hotelling lets "utility" creep back into the discussion. First he uses $U(q)$ for total revenue: not $TR(q)$, but $U(q)$. Certainly the reader is supposed to get the idea that what is really going on is the maximization of utility. Secondly, in the latter part of the paper (as quoted above), Hotelling explicitly says "a utility (or profit) function." Finally, Hotelling spends a portion of the paper (particularly 592–94) trying to convince the reader that entrepreneurial demand represents an empirically interesting case of consumer choice. One way this point is made is by the argument that the only difference between his case and that of maximizing utility subject to a budget constraint is the Giffen good "case of a rising demand curve for bread sometimes supposed to occur" (1932, 593). Thus while Hotelling's verbal ploy technically protects him from Mirowski's criticism about conserving the sum of utility and expenditure, Hotelling repeatedly confirms Mirowski's general argument that certain neoclassical economists were desperately trying to make utility into potential energy.

4. Conclusion

The above arguments provide both a criticism and an endorsement of Mirowski's *More Heat than Light*. Mirowski's technical arguments about the Slutsky conditions, integrability, and prices as a conservative field were criticized, and it was demonstrated that prices do not form a conservative vector field in exactly the way that Mirowski has argued. On the other hand, it was shown that a slightly weaker version of Mirowski's argument could be defended; in particular, if prices were redefined to be "compensated prices," his argument would in fact go through. The discussion of Hotelling (1932) provided some additional clarification of these technical issues while also providing some further support for Mirowski's general thesis about the relationship between neoclassical economics and energy physics.

None of the critical comments above are intended to undermine Mirowski's general historical thesis—no doubt the energy metaphor has been an active influence in the history of neoclassical economics. The real question about *More Heat than Light* is not whether the energy metaphor has played a role—it undoubtedly has. The real question is how *much* of a role it has played. As the discussion of Hotelling should make clear, I believe that for certain individual authors that role was quite substantial. However, I am not convinced that its overall role was nearly as great as Mirowski suggests.[11]

References

Arrow, K. J., and F. H. Hahn. 1971. *General Competitive Analysis*. San Francisco: Holden Day.

---

11. This argument is given further elaboration in Hands 1992.

Arrow, K. J., and L. Hurwicz. 1958. On the Stability of the Competitive Equilibrium, I. *Econometrica* 26:522–52.

Court, L. M. 1941. Invariable Classical Stability of Entrepreneurial Demand and Supply Functions. *Quarterly Journal of Economics* 56:134–44.

Friedman, M. [1949] 1953. The Marshallian Demand Curve. *Journal of Political Economy* 57:463–95. Reprinted in his *Essays in Positive Economics*, 47–99. Chicago: University of Chicago Press.

Hands, D. W. 1992. More Light and Less Heat: Mirowski on Economics and the Energy Metaphor. *Philosophy of the Social Sciences* 22:97–111.

Hotelling, H. 1932. Edgeworth's Taxation Paradox and the Nature of Demand and Supply Functions. *Journal of Political Economy* 40:577–616.

———. 1935. Demand Functions with Limited Budgets. *Econometrica* 3:66–78.

Hurwicz, L. 1971. On the Problem of Integrability of Demand Functions. In *Preferences, Utility and Demand*, edited by J. S. Chipman, L. Hurwicz, M. K. Richter, and H. F. Sonnenschein, 174–214. New York: Harcourt Brace Jovanovich.

Mirowski, P. 1989. *More Heat than Light: Economics as Social Physics, Physics as Nature's Economics*. Cambridge: Cambridge University Press. [Citations are abbreviated *MHL*.]

Mukherji, A. 1974. Stability in an Economy with Production. In *Trade, Stability and Macroeconomics: Essays in Honor of Lloyd Metzler*, edited by P. A. Samuelson, 243–58. New York: Academic Press.

Samuelson, P. A. 1950. The Problem of Integrability in Utility Theory. *Economica*, n.s. 17:355–85.

Paul Ehrenfest and Jan Tinbergen: A Case of Limited Physics Transfer

Marcel Boumans

More Heat than Light shows us a case of physics transfer around 1870. It expounds the history of those economists who appropriated the energy metaphor from physics but did not pay enough attention to the conservation principles needed to make this transfer. To make his history plausible Mirowski has to argue that the concept of energy permeated the whole of physics. But physics developed further: "modern physics has revised its approach to conservation principles and their significance, essentially leaving behind the nineteenth-century conception of energy" (*MHL*, 9–10). The state of physics sixty years later was most adequately described by Erwin Schrödinger in 1926: "The central conception in all modern theory in physics is 'the Hamiltonian' " (quoted in *MHL*, 35). In modern physics it is the time invariance of the Hamiltonian that implies the conservation of energy (*MHL*, 71). It is at that particular moment in the history of physics that I would like to take up the thread and show you a case of another physics transfer, the case of two physicists who got interested in economics and tried to use their background in physics to comprehend it. However, it was not the *energy metaphor* that guided them, but an *analogy in formalism*.

The first is Paul Ehrenfest (1880–1933), professor of theoretical physics at the University of Leiden. His notebooks kept from October 1917 until May 1918 contain numerous entries on *Öko-dynamik* (a contraction of *Ökonomie* and *Thermodynamik*). Ehrenfest was struck by the possibility of developing an analogy between thermodynamics and economics. He tried to formulate economic concepts as parallels of thermodynamic concepts, with the concept of equilibrium occupying the central position in both theories. He hoped to be able to use the highly developed formalism of thermodynamics to gain new insight into economic problems. Ehrenfest never published any of his work in economics but always maintained his interest in the subject (Klein 1970, 305–6).

The second physicist, the protagonist of this history, was Jan Tinbergen, a student of Ehrenfest. Tinbergen studied mathematics and physics at the University of Leiden from 1921 until 1925 and was Ehrenfest's assistant from 1923 until 1925. On 22 March 1929 he received his doctorate for the thesis "Minimumproblemen in de natuurkunde en economie" (Minimum problems in physics and economics). The doctoral thesis served to ease Tinbergen's transition to economics. He was interested in economics because of his concern for the unemployed. He was a member of the Socialist party and felt that he could be more useful as an economist than as a physicist (Magnus and Morgan 1987, 118–19).

As we shall see, Tinbergen used the formalism of Lagrange and Hamilton to deal with problems of dynamics. He was interested in dynamics because he aimed at a socialist economic policy. He succeeded by translating problems of economic policy into optimal control problems, and this enabled him to make use of Hamilton's formalism. Because of his background in physics he was familiar with this formalism. It shows exactly when one may speak of a dynamic system. A necessary condition for a dynamic system is that the total time derivative of one of the coordinates of the system also appears in the description of the system. In other words, a dynamic theory should include an intertemporal relation. In addition Hamilton's formalism shows the invariants of the system. Tinbergen defined endogenous motion as the motion due to the system itself, that is, motion by invariance of the system.

Discussion below considers only Tinbergen's early works, from the period of his first scientific publication in 1927 until his appointment as professor at the Rotterdam School of Economics in 1933, the year Ehrenfest died. The influence of Ehrenfest on this early work is detectable in Tinbergen's use of the adiabatic method. This method is based on Ehrenfest's adiabatic hypothesis (Ehrenfest 1916), a theorem on invariants of a system, which asserts that for any periodic system depending on certain parameters, the time integral of the kinetic energy taken over one period is invariant when the parameters are changed adiabatically (that is, sufficiently slowly). It enabled Tinbergen to make a distinction between fast and slowly changing influences on a system, to facilitate analysis. In the first instance the system is analyzed assuming that influences of the second kind are constant parameters; then the assumed constant parameters are replaced by slow changes. Tinbergen used this method in analyzing the shipbuilding cycle (Tinbergen 1931).

Ehrenfest also influenced Tinbergen in other ways. For instance, Tinbergen's dynamic scheme was developed during "inspired discussions" with Ehrenfest (Tinbergen 1930, 678n.). To develop this dynamic scheme Tinbergen made use of the findings of his doctoral thesis. Further, Ehrenfest was Tinbergen's first teacher in the realm of theoretical mathematical economics.

My object below is to specify the relation between Ehrenfest's physics and the dynamic scheme Tinbergen developed in the early 1930s. Section 1 goes further into the history of physics to clear up the shift in heuristics, the exploitation of analogies in the mathematical form. Section 2 gives an outline of Tinbergen's critique of economic science. Section 3 follows the course of work in which he developed and applied his dynamic market scheme, the basis of which was laid in his doctoral thesis. Section 4 gives a reconstruction of his ideas on economic policy. In the last section I consider whether Tinbergen took into account the rise of quantum mechanics.

1. Physical Analogies

Because of Mirowski's appealing history of the energy concept, one could forget that other fruitful methods of analogy than metaphors were put into play in theory construction (cf. *MHL*, 277–78).[1] An example is Maxwell's method for exploiting analogies of mathematical form. The result was a very fruitful development in electromagnetic theory. Maxwell adopted a new position with respect to the status of mechanics, and his new way of pursuing the mechanical ideal influenced many of his successors.

In his first paper on electromagnetism Maxwell carefully set forth the method he proposed to follow in his work. He would not begin by making "a purely mathematical formula," for then one would "entirely lose sight of the phenomena to be explained." Nor would he prematurely make "a physical hypothesis," that is, an assumption as to the real nature of the phenomena to be explained, for that would lead to "seeing the phenomena only through a medium," making one "liable to

---

1. This history and the quotations in this section can be found in Klein 1970, 53–74.

that blindness to facts and rashness in assumption which a partial explanation encourages." Instead Maxwell would exploit physical analogies. He meant something quite specific by a physical analogy: "that partial similarity between the laws of one science and those of another which makes each of them illustrate the other." In other words, to the extent that two physical systems obey laws whose mathematical form is the same, the behavior of one system may be understood by studying the behavior of the other, better-known, system. And this could be done without making any hypothesis about the real nature of the system under investigation. Maxwell stated clearly that a dynamic analogy, valuable as it might be, was not a substitute for "a mature theory, in which physical facts will be physically explained." His system of vortices and idle wheel particles constituted such an analogy, offered "not as a mode of connexion actually existing in nature" but only as "a mode of connexion which is mechanically conceivable and easily investigated." Nevertheless it was the analysis of this dynamic analogy that brought Maxwell to the first formulation of the electromagnetic theory of light.

In Maxwell's later theories the specific mechanical model disappeared. His vortex and particle model was replaced by a new and more schematic concept of dynamic analogy: "The former is built up to show that the phenomena (of electromagnetism) are such as can be explained by mechanism. The nature of the mechanism is to the true mechanism what an orrery is to the Solar System. The latter is built on Lagrange's Dynamical Equations and is not wise about vortices."

The only basic assumption he needed was that the system of charges and currents with its fields was a dynamic system. Lagrangian mechanics then allowed him to proceed without detailed knowledge of "the nature of the connexions of the parts of the system." Even this general dynamic treatment was far from a complete theory, however, because of the lack of evidence as to the true nature of electric current. Only when such questions were answered could a really explanatory theory be created.

Maxwell's success with a theory based on dynamic analogies stimulated a variety of reactions from his contemporaries. Some saw the dynamic analogy as only a mechanical model. To Lord Kelvin this was something to be admired: "It seems to me that the test of 'Do we or do we not understand a particular subject in physics?' is 'Can we make a mechanical model of it?'" But when Maxwell's analogy was only to the general structure of the dynamic equations, Kelvin was much less pleased and preferred trying to construct his own models. Others were distressed by Maxwell's models and lamented his failure to provide a proper deductive theory. The most outspoken of these was Pierre Duhem.

Other physicists recognized the value of the concept of physical analogy in trying to understand the essential features of the natural world. Hermann von Helmholtz was one of these. To understand the second law on the basis of mechanics he attempted a physical analogy, precisely in Maxwell's sense of the term. Helmholtz's analogy had its limitations and difficulties, but despite these it made a deep impression on Heinrich Hertz and was a major influence on Hertz's last work, *The Principles of Mechanics Presented in a New Form*. The most characteristic feature of Hertz's new axiomatic version of mechanics was his treatment of the concept of force. Hertz deprived force of its fundamental position and set up his mechanics without it, reintroducing it only later on as a useful but unnecessary auxiliary concept.

The whole Hertzian system is worked out in a closely reasoned analysis, presented in strict deductive style. Hertz's arguments demonstrated that his differential principle of least curvature provided an alternative starting point for mechanics, from which all the usual formulations—Newton's laws, Lagrange's equations, Hamilton's principle—could be deduced as theorems. The general reaction was that Hertz had offered only an "ideal program," to be achieved in the distant future, if at all. Quite apart from the question of its usefulness, Hertz's book is remarkable for its treatment of the role of mechanical explanation in theoretical physics. For Hertz mechanical explanation could only be understood in the sense of Maxwell's dynamic analogies.

He was quite explicit on this point in the section of his book entitled *Dynamical Models*. On the basis of a sharp definition of "dynamic model," Hertz proved that "in order to determine beforehand the course of the natural motion of a material system, it is sufficient to have a model of that system. The model may be much simpler than the system whose motion it represents." But he then went on to assert that the existence of concealed masses (essential to his mechanics) means that "it is impossible to carry out knowledge of the connections of material systems further than is involved in specifying models of the actual systems. We can then, in fact, have no knowledge as to whether the systems which we consider in mechanics agree in any other respect with the actual systems of nature which we intend to consider, than this alone—

that the one set of systems are models of the other." And, finally, Hertz saw "the relation of a dynamic model to the system of which it is regarded as the model" to be "precisely the same as the relation of the images which our mind forms of things to the things themselves."

These ideas on mechanics and the mechanical interpretation of nature found their most receptive audience in Ludwig Boltzmann, for whom mechanics was always the very core of physics. Throughout his career, Boltzmann admired, developed, and expounded Maxwell's ideas. He placed great importance on Maxwell's concept of analogies, describing Maxwell as having been "as much of a pioneer in the theory of knowledge as in theoretical physics" and as having clearly adumbrated all the various approaches to the nature of scientific theory that would be developed during the subsequent forty years.

Boltzmann himself found the concept of a scientific theory as an analogy or metaphor of reality a particularly liberating one. It allowed him to continue to develop mechanical explanations without having to assert, for example, that a gas "really" consists of molecules that "really" interact with one another according to a particular force law. If a scientific theory is only an image or picture of nature, one need not worry about developing "the only true theory," and one can be content to portray the phenomena as simply and clearly as possible. From this platform Boltzmann defended the mechanical theories against the claims of those who demanded their replacement by theories of some other, particular, kind. He devoted much time and effort during the 1890s to this defense, arguing that neither the believers in energetics nor the believers in purely phenomenological theories had a unique passkey to the domain of truth. No approach to physical theory should be excluded so long as it could provide insight, as mechanical theories had in the past and were likely to do in the future.

Boltzmann had mixed reactions to Hertz's *Mechanics*, as did most readers. He admired its structure, the simplicity of its premises, and the care with which they had been thought through, but still he considered it at best a program for the future. He deliberately chose to follow the traditional order of exposition, preferring forces to the more awkward and artificial-looking concealed masses.

In 1900 Boltzmann had occasion to deal with Hertz's mechanics in a very specific context. Hertz had always worked with a system of an arbitrary but finite number of discrete masses—a system of particles—although he evidently anticipated that there would be no difficulty in extending his methods to a continuous distribution of mass, such as a fluid.

Boltzmann was sure that the equations of motion of an incompressible fluid, and also of a rigid body submerged in such a fluid, could be derived from Hertz's principles. Instead of taking the Eulerian approach to hydrodynamics, where one works out the equations of motion of the fluid by considering what happens at a point fixed in space as the fluid flows by, one ought to adopt the Lagrangian method. Here one's attention is fixed on an element of the fluid as it moves through space, and this would be the natural approach to follow in generalizing a particle theory.

This suggestion of the proper method for generalizing Hertz's mechanics to fluids, endorsed by Boltzmann, was taken up by Paul Ehrenfest, at that time a student of Boltzmann. Ehrenfest decided to write his doctoral thesis on this problem and succeeded in solving it.

The kind of physics Tinbergen learned from Ehrenfest was that of Boltzmann: "Boltzmann initiated Ehrenfest into the substance and the spirit of theoretical physics, and Ehrenfest was to show Boltzmann's influence in his own research and teaching in years to come" (Klein 1970, 38). Ehrenfest's life had been tied to Boltzmann since he entered the university. Boltzmann, more than anyone else, by teaching and by example, helped set the direction of Ehrenfest's scientific interest and helped form his intellectual style (see Klein 1970, 76).

2. Critique of Economic Science

From the beginning, Tinbergen expressed his discontent with the economics of his day. Compared to the natural sciences, economics was "at a very primitive stage," certainly unsuitable for any policymaking. In a lecture held at the University of Amsterdam in February 1933 Tinbergen formulated his conception of the aim of economics: "the desire to know the implications of certain changes in the social mechanism or in the conditions under which that mechanism works" (1933a, 66–67).[2] He considered this to be the main point of any economic policy. Not only observation served this aim, but also forecast and explanation. Forecasts indicate the changes "that will appear without intervention from the outside," and explanation indicates the causes of a certain event (67).

---

2. Translations from Tinbergen's early works published in Dutch or German are all my own.

However, observation was not enough to gain the desired understanding. For that one should, in addition, make use of "reasoning." Tinbergen distinguished between deductive and inductive reasoning, comparing the first with "the economic part of reasoning" and the second with "statistical analysis" (69). He saw the "economic part of reasoning" as the deduction of propositions from one central principle: the economic motive, the pursuit of optimal satisfaction. Such propositions are subject to a number of given conditions. So all economic problems are constrained maximization problems. "Inductive reasoning" contributes to our knowledge about the connections behind the observations. Tinbergen believed in determined, "functional" connections (73–74).

2.1. Critique of the Scheme of Walras and Pareto

Tinbergen's introduction to economics was mainly through the works of mathematical economists, recommended to him by Ehrenfest. These works "you taught me" were those of Bowley, Wicksell, Pareto, Barone, and Roos (letter to Ehrenfest, 16 February 1930).[3] In particular, Tinbergen's introduction to the ideas of Pareto and Walras was mainly Bowley's *Mathematical Groundwork of Economics* (1924). This was a modernized version of the Walras-Pareto system. Starting with the simple case of two persons exchanging two commodities, Bowley deduced for each more general case equations describing static equilibrium.

Tinbergen noted that the "market scheme of Walras and Pareto" did not give an adequate description of modern society. This society was characterized by trustification and an increasing number of monopolies and did not show "the rest of equilibria, but a continuous movement around equilibria, which themselves change continuously" (Tinbergen 1928, 543). Because of ever-increasing concentration, "the theory of exchange under free competition will lose more and more significance compared with the theory of exchange with a monopoly or monopolies, either on one or on both sides of the market . . . besides, there is a general tendency to reduce the significance of exchange and to replace it in part by other economic transactions" (1929c, 529–30).

---

3. Paul Ehrenfest Archive, Museum Boerhaave, Leiden, The Netherlands.

2.2. Critique of Business-Cycle Research
and Theory

Besides his discontent with the static character of the scheme of Walras and Pareto, Tinbergen was also dissatisfied with the business-cycle research and theory he encountered at the Dutch Central Bureau of Statistics (CBS), which had borrowed its methods from the Harvard Economic Service and the Berlin Institut für Konjunkturforschung. Business-cycle research at these institutions consisted of the construction of economic barometers to forecast business cycles. That is, it investigated whether certain economic time series are correlated. If there is a lag between two correlated time series, it is possible to forecast the course of one time series with the aid of the course of the other.

The Harvard Economic Service, under the direction of Charles J. Bullock, Warren M. Persons, and William L. Crum, owed its international fame to the barometer based on three curves, the so called ABC curves. The construction and interpretation of this barometer was described in an article in the *Review of Economic Statistics* (Bullock, Persons, and Crum 1927). The authors emphasized the fact that their method was not based on any theory whatsoever; on the contrary, the curves "derived solely from observations of the facts." They added: "Causal relations have, indeed, received increasing attention from us; but no theory of causation or of time relation between cause and effect ever entered into the construction of the index" (79).

Tinbergen opposed the nontheoretical character of this kind of research. He believed there was a theory that could explain lags: "An economic dynamics could be constructed based on this [lagged] relation between economic quantities, that results in the derivation of perfect cyclic oscillations of an economic system" (1927, 715). However, he was also discontented with existing business-cycle theories. Business cycles were being explained by external cyclic phenomena, like sunspots, and not by the mechanism of society itself. With a numerical example Tinbergen demonstrated how a delayed adaptation of supply to the price generates fluctuations about equilibrium. This example could be extended by taking into consideration *expectations* based on observed movements in the past, or by attributing a delay to the demand: "All these assumptions lead to the same kind of results, of which the essence . . . consists in the explanation of cyclic motion by the economic mechanism itself" (1928,

546). A "very beautiful example of an isolated oscillating market" was the pork market (548n.). This market was studied by Hanau, who at that time was working at the Berlin Institut für Konjunkturforschung (Hanau 1928).

3. Dynamics

Tinbergen was in search of an economic dynamics, a dynamics that could explain cyclic motion by an economic mechanism. To solve this problem, Tinbergen had to answer two questions: When can one speak of an essentially dynamic system? What are the invariants of the system? Because of his background in physics he was familiar with a dynamic theory, namely physical dynamics. Motion in mechanics is traditionally described using Hamilton's equations of motion or their equivalent, Lagrange's equations. To assist Tinbergen's transition to economics, Ehrenfest proposed the following subject for his thesis: minimum problems in physics and economics. "The subject of this thesis was specially chosen because of the probable analogy between the physical problems treated and certain economic problems" (Tinbergen 1929a, 1). (Ehrenfest had been occupied with this ten years earlier.) "The general idea is to attempt to bring together in one survey the kind of problems that appear in different fields of physics, and to classify the different forms in which they appear from one point of view" (Tinbergen 1929a, 1). That "point of view" was formalizing the problem as a solution of a minimum problem. In fact this is what Hamilton's formalism manages so well for mechanics. Tinbergen elaborated a more general formalism and could thus classify different fields in physics. Economic problems were discussed in an appendix.

Only the economic part of the dissertation was published, in *Archiv für Sozialwissenschaft und Sozialpolitik* (1929b), and Tinbergen never returned to the subject again. The problems treated were determined by their mathematical analogy with physics and not by their economic relevance. Yet it can be shown that Tinbergen built on the findings of this research to conceptualize an economic dynamics.

3.1. Minimum Problems

To classify the different fields in physics, Tinbergen introduced an identity, I, an integral of a function F. F is a function of different independent and dependent variables. Because the economic problems treated are problems with one independent variable (namely the time) or none, this review of his thesis is confined to these kinds of problems.

$$I = \int_{t_0}^{t_1} F[q_i(t), \dot{q}_i(t), t] dt,$$

where t is the independent variable of the problem; and q_i ($i = 1, \ldots, n$) is a generalized coordinate of the system, which value specifies the configuration of the system. Between the q_i's there are no constraints. A dot denotes total time derivative.

The total differential of I is:

$$\Delta I = \int_{t_0}^{t_1} \sum_i (\frac{\partial F}{\partial q_i} \delta q_i + \frac{\partial F}{\partial \dot{q}_i} \delta \dot{q}_i) dt.$$

Integrating by parts, one obtains:

$$\Delta I = [\sum_i \frac{\partial F}{\partial \dot{q}_i} \delta q_i]\big|_{t_0}^{t_1} + \int_{t_0}^{t_1} \sum_i (\frac{\partial F}{\partial q_i} - \frac{d}{dt}\frac{\partial F}{\partial \dot{q}_i}) \delta q_i dt.$$

Now, it can be verified if a problem in physics (or economics) can be described as follows: to determine the functions $q_i(t)$ such that $\Delta I = 0$ for all admissible values of δq_i. This variational statement is known as Hamilton's principle when F is a Lagrangian function that describes a classical dynamic system and $q_i(t_0)$ and $q_i(t_1)$ are fixed.

Admissible are those values of δq_i which fulfill any limiting condition. Boundary conditions are expressed by the first term. For example, this term vanishes when $q_i(t_0)$ and $q_i(t_1)$ are fixed. There are no restrictions on the q_i's between t_0 and t_1. Hence the δq_i's are arbitrary in this interval, and the problem can only be solved when the q_i's in the interval fulfill the partial differential equations:

$$\frac{\partial F}{\partial q_i} - \frac{d}{dt}\frac{\partial F}{\partial \dot{q}_i} = 0 \quad i = 1, \ldots, n,$$

the so-called Euler equations (or Lagrange equations in the case of a classical mechanical system).

If there are no independent variables, one has only a description of an equilibrium, and the problem can be stated as follows: to determine the q_i's as functions of the constants left in F so that $\delta F(q_i) = 0$. This is a "normal" minimum problem, and the solution is given by

$$\frac{\partial F}{\partial q_i} = 0 \quad i = 1, \ldots, n.$$

The static equilibrium equations in mechanics are an example of this solution. This borderline case can be obtained from the Euler equations by putting all velocities equal to zero.

Tinbergen discussed alternative sorts of formalism too. For instance, Hamilton's equations are derived from Lagrange's equations by defining

$$p_i = \frac{\partial F}{\partial \dot{q}_i} \quad i = 1, \ldots, n,$$

and the Hamiltonian:

$$H(q_1, \ldots, q_n; p_1, \ldots, p_n, t) = -F(q_i, \dot{q}_i, t) + \sum_1^n p_i \dot{q}_i.$$

It follows that

$$\frac{\partial H}{\partial p_i} = \dot{q}_i \quad \frac{\partial H}{\partial q_i} = -\dot{p}_i \quad i = 1, \ldots, n,$$

which are the so-called Hamilton's canonical equations. It is now easy to see when the system is conservative:

$$\frac{dH}{dt} = \sum_1^n \dot{p}_i \frac{\partial H}{\partial p_i} + \sum_1^n \dot{q}_i \frac{\partial H}{\partial q_i} + \frac{\partial H}{\partial t} = \frac{\partial H}{\partial t}.$$

If H does not depend explicitly on the time, the system is a conservative system ($dH/dt = 0$).

The last part of the doctoral thesis is an attempt "to sketch in what way problems of the same structure appear in theoretical economics, hence, in what way use can be made of the conclusions derived in the physical problems" (Tinbergen 1929a, 47–48). Tinbergen did not pretend to be exhaustive. The economic problems served only for the purpose of illustration. He confined himself to problems in which only one ophelimity function appears. In these problems there is a striving to optimal ophelimity.

The first problems Tinbergen mentions are the most simple ones, the "normal" problems of the form $\partial F/\partial q_i = 0$, problems that are the concern of the "largest part of the existing mathematical economic literature."

The second kind of problems are the variational problems in which an independent variable appears, namely time. These are problems in which the extreme value of a singular integral is sought. In this connection the works of Charles F. Roos (1927) and G. C. Evans (1925) were exemplary. Both men insisted on the importance of building dynamic economic theories (Morgan 1990, 155). In his 1925 paper Evans stated that "the relation of economics to the calculus of variations is not accidental, nor the result of a generalization from previously found differential equations, since it is in the nature of an economic system that there should be a striving for a maximum of some sort" (94–95). Roos, influenced by Evans, aimed at a "dynamical generalization of the static theory of economic equilibrium of Walras and Pareto" (1927, 280). He showed that "the problem of equilibrium for a cooperative society is a problem for which it is desired to maximize a functional operator, and, also, that the problem for a competitive society is a problem for which it is desired to obtain partial maxima of several functional operators" (280).

Tinbergen formulated four conditions to translate an economic problem into a variational problem:

1. Only one ophelimity function occurs in the problem.
2. This ophelimity function can be represented by an integral.
3. The derivative of one of the coordinates occurs in the integrand.
4. This coordinate has fixed boundary values.

The first and second conditions are fulfilled when the ophelimity function signifies profit.

The third condition is worth noting, because one can also speak of variational problems when no derivatives occur in the integrand. Apparently Tinbergen wanted to maintain the second term of the Euler equation:

$$\frac{\partial F}{\partial q_i} - \frac{d}{dt}\frac{\partial F}{\partial \dot{q}_i} = 0.$$

The second term signifies change in time, which makes the equation dynamical. If F does not depend explicitly on any $\dot{q}$, this term disappears:

$$\frac{\partial F}{\partial q_i} = 0.$$

This is then a description of static equilibrium.

Tinbergen gave three examples of categories which fulfill the third condition:

1. *Inventory problems:* if a coordinate x denotes an inventory, $\dot{x}$ can be considered as the production surplus.
2. *Friction problems,* when one takes into account the costs of changes in production.

3. *Retardation problems*, when one takes into account the lags between different quantities: if one quantity is $x(t)$ and the other $f[x(t - \vartheta)]$, then the last one can be approximated by $f[x - \vartheta \dot{x}]$.

Cyclic problems and problems in which a new equilibrium is aimed at fulfill the fourth condition. Tinbergen was mainly interested in cyclic problems, because these problems refer to adaptation of the supply to seasonal cycles and business cycles. They could also serve as a basis for discussions about stabilization, namely, about the question "In which cases is stabilization the optimal business cycle policy?"

3.2. Stabilization of Business Cycles

> In their most simple form stabilization problems of business cycles are variational problems.—Tinbergen 1929a, thesis XIV

The part of his doctoral thesis in which Tinbergen discussed variational problems was also published in *Archiv für Sozialwissenschaft und Sozialpolitik* (1929b). In it he formulated the aim of business-cycle policy for an enterprise or a combined group of enterprises: "to determine for a time interval, $0 < t < T$, certain quantities (e.g., production) as functions of time, in such a way that the profit over this period T reaches a maximum value" (533). He supposed that the courses of all other quantities occurring in the problem are known.

He demonstrated this problem with a simple example. The profit of an enterprise (G) results from a monopolistic sale of a commodity. The price (p) of this commodity is a given function of the sold quantity (q) per unit of time. The cost price (a) does not depend on q. And $q(t)$ optimizes the profit:

$$G = \int_0^T (p - a)q \, dt. \tag{1}$$

The solution of this problem is obtained by the Euler equation:

$$(p - a) + q \frac{\partial p}{\partial q} = 0, \tag{2}$$

the "well-known monopoly equation."

Next Tinbergen distinguished two categories of causes of motion: (1) "natural" causes, for instance, the weather; (2) economic circumstances beyond the power of the considered enterprise. If equation (2) is considered as the business-cycle policy of a whole economy, then there are no economic circumstances outside the considered economy, and subsequently "stabilization of the endogenous business cycle is to be preferred" (535).

"Only if (2) depends explicitly on t, can equations of type (2) provide an oscillation, that is a time-dependent solution for q, as the optimal business-cycle policy. That is not the case for the endogenous business cycle" (535–36). This statement implicitly contains a definition of an endogenous motion. In his doctoral thesis Tinbergen formulated the problem of an endogenous motion as follows. If the integrand does not depend explicitly on time, "are cyclic solutions possible in this case? This would mean that stabilization of an endogenous business cycle of the considered production complex is not desirable" (1929a, 55). If the integrand does not depend explicitly on time, the system is conservative (see above):

$$\frac{dH}{dt} = \frac{d}{dt}(-F(q_i, \dot{q}_i, t) + \sum_i \frac{\partial F}{\partial \dot{q}_i} \dot{q}_i) = -\frac{\partial F}{\partial t}.$$

In other words, he defined an endogenous business cycle as the motion of a conservative system.

But he was not satisfied with this analysis, because it "does not express the important characteristics of the real facts": "This treatment neglects a kind of connection of the different points of time and their prices and sales, that plays an important role in reality" (1929b, 536). However, he added, the variational problems discussed in his doctoral thesis (the inventory, friction, and retardation problems) would show this connection: they demonstrate "in what way variational problems are suited to analyze certain economic problems; problems in which a direct adaptation to equilibrium is not possible because of a connection of the successive points of time. . . . Hence problems that are of an essentially *dynamic* nature, as emerges in the appearance of the differential quotient" (541).

To make a system essentially dynamic, an intertemporal connection is necessary. For example, if one describes profit in such a way that it only depends on momentary quantities, one describes only the static case. To describe dynamic cases, "velocities" must occur in the description of profit. An example is inventory problems. In each unit of time, an enterprise sells a quantity (q) of a commodity for a price $p(q, t)$. In addition, it holds an inventory, of which the cost per unit of time is $K(x, t)$. Hence production per unit of time is $y = q + \dot{x}$, and the costs of production are $k(y,t)$. The solution is given by those values of x and q which maximize

$$G = \int_0^T \{q \cdot p(q,t) - K(x,t) - k(q + \dot{x}, t)\}dt.$$

T is the period of a seasonal cycle or business cycle. The solution is given by the Euler equations:

$$-\frac{\partial K}{\partial x} + \frac{d}{dt}\frac{\partial k}{\partial y} = 0,$$

$$p + q\frac{\partial p}{\partial q} - \frac{\partial k}{\partial y} = 0.$$

Tinbergen distinguished the following cases:

(1) Where $K(x,t) = 0$, there are no inventory costs:

$$\frac{\partial k}{\partial y} = \text{constant} = c,$$

$$p + q\frac{\partial p}{\partial q} = c.$$

If p does not explicitly depend on the time, then q has a constant value.

(2) Where $x \equiv 0$, there are no inventories. The first equation disappears and the second converts into the monopoly equation:

$$p + q\frac{\partial p}{\partial q} = 0.$$

(3) The three terms of the integrand depend explicitly on time; in particular, they are cyclic functions of time. Then the following cases are possible: (1a) Only p depends on time, e.g., seasonal dependence of needs. (1b) Only k depends on time, e.g., seasonal dependence of the circumstances of production. (1c) Mixed cases. (2) Inventory is possible or not (cases 1 or 2 above).

(4) The integrand does not depend explicitly on time: endogenous movements. Note that a cyclic solution is still possible. Tinbergen gives the following example:

$$K(x) = A + Bx + \frac{1}{2}Cx^2 \qquad p = P - Qq$$

$$k(y) = a + by + \frac{1}{2}cy^2.$$

The solution of the Euler equations is $x = x_0 + z$, where

$$z = \frac{2cQ}{(2Q + c)C}\ddot{z}.$$

If $2cQ/(2Q + c)C < 0$, then z is cyclic.

Summarizing the findings of Tinbergen's doctoral thesis, a distinction can be made between endogenous motion and motion caused by changing the "energy" of the system. The first motion is due to the mechanism itself, that is, "change by invariance (of the system)," "change that does not appear to depend directly on the flow of time," change in Meyerson's sense of the term (cf. Mirowski, *MHL*, 6).

Besides this distinction, Tinbergen called a system dynamic when a time derivative occurs in the description of the system.

In his doctoral thesis Tinbergen translated a retardation between two quantities into "velocity": $f[x(t - \dot{\vartheta})]$ was approximated by $f[x - \dot{\vartheta}\dot{x}]$. Later he would not make this translation anymore and would define a dynamic theory as one where the "variables relating to different moments appear in one equation" (Tinbergen 1935, 241). In this later definition of a dynamic theory he no longer mentioned the maximizing of an ophelimity function. He gave the reason for this in the same paper:

> *The problem of the "optimal" policy.* .... we can now enunciate the "last" problem in this field, that is, which policy is the "best" one, the "optimal"? To answer this question, we should dispose of some general ophelimity function and calculate for which policy a course of events would occur giving a maximum to this general ophelimity function. Of course, at this moment any practical calculations of this sort are impossible. I shall not try to give them here.
>
> I shall only make some remarks on the frequent and, I think, justifiable assumption that stabilization of business cycles in employment is the optimum policy. (1935, 306)

3.3. Supply Regularization

The two papers I discuss next concern the results of Tinbergen's investigations into the structure of the supplying industry. He examined a number of different models. He was interested in the supply side of the market because of the influence of supply regularization on the price.

The first paper, "Bestimmung und Deutung von Angebotskurven" (1930), was an investigation of the market for potato flour, a product for which Holland was the main exporter in the 1920s (see also Morgan 1990, 154, 180–83). To test the separate models of supply, he had first to determine the demand curve. To do that he used a two-equation model and derived the reduced-form model to identify demand and supply parameters.

Most unusually for the period, Tinbergen made a clear distinction between the latent theoretical (virtual) economic variables and the observed data outcomes (Morgan 1990, 181). However, because of his background in physics he was used to working with virtual displacements. Hamilton's principle is based on it. According to this principle, the trajectory or path of the system between two configurations at two given times is that which makes the value of the integral of a Lagrangian function stationary relative to nearby paths between the same endpoints and taking the same time. A virtual displacement is the difference between the position of the particle in the nearby path and its position in the real path, taken at the same time.

After Tinbergen had determined the demand curve, he could test the separate models: static competition, static monopoly, limited competition under static conditions, dynamic competition, and dynamic monopoly. It turned out that Cournot's formula of limited competition provided the best explanation of the empirical data. In static monopoly, price is determined by maximizing the profit:

$$v(p) \cdot (p - k) - K,$$

where $v(p)$ is the demand function, k are the proportional costs, and K are the fixed costs. For limited competition Tinbergen used Cournot's formula "such as it was described by Chamberlin (1929)":

$$v(p) + \mu(p - k)\frac{\partial v(p)}{\partial p} = 0,$$

where μ is the number of competitors, and k the mean value of the proportional costs of all competitors.

Of all models, his dynamic model is here of most interest. It was first presented in this paper of 1930, and he formulated this specific model in only two other papers: "Ein Problem der Dynamik" (1932) and "The Notions of Horizon and Expectancy in Dynamic Economics" (1933b). I quote here from the last of these:

> In a theory of economic dynamics, the ophelimity function of individuals must be supposed to depend on the quantities of goods con-

sumed and the sacrifices brought, not only at the moment considered, but also at later moments. Their offer and demand schemes for each moment then depend not only on the prices governing at that moment, but also on the *price expectancies* the individuals have for the future.... As a first approximation it might be supposed that only the expectancies relating to a certain time period (the *"horizon"*) are of importance, and all of the same importance. That means that the subject is at every moment t making a definite plan for the period from t to $t + \tau$, and then realizes certain parts of that plan. Before other parts could be realized, the subject makes a "revision" at the moment $t + 1$, say, for the period from $t + 1$ to $t + \tau + 1$, etc. (1933b, 247)

(In his 1930 paper the time horizon was only two years.) Agents maximize

$$v_t(p_t) \cdot (p_t - k_t) + v_{t+1}(p_{t+1}) \cdot (p_{t+1} - k_{t+1}),$$

subject to

$$v_t(p_t) + v_{t+1}(p_{t+1}) = s_t + s_{t+1},$$

where s_t denotes supply of year t.

In the second of these papers (1932) Tinbergen gave a more systematic exposition of his dynamic scheme than in his potato-flour paper. The practicability of this scheme is demonstrated by the solution of some simple approximations of the problem to find out the relation between production and consumption of nonperishable agricultural products (see also 1933b, 247–48):

1. Demand has the form $v_t = f(p_t) + \alpha t$, with p_t being the average price during year t, α a constant;
2. Costs of carrying over may be neglected.
3. Expectations of further crops and demand may be "reasonable," which means that (A) crop expectations are supposed to be equal to the average crop produced on the acreage and to increase every year with α: $\bar{e}_t = \bar{e} + \alpha t$; (B) demand expectation is supposed to be in the same relation with price expectation as actual demand with actual price.

Then the problem can be formulated as follows. When demand, crop and carryover, u_t, of a year t are given, what will be the supply? There are only two possibilities:

1. A very short crop, p_t is supposed to be higher than $\mathbf{p_{t+1}}$:[4]
   $$\mathbf{p_{t+1}} < p_t \qquad v_t = E_t \equiv \bar{e} + u_t.$$
2. $\mathbf{p_{t+1}} = p_t \qquad v_t = \bar{e}_t + \frac{1}{\tau}(E_t - \bar{e}_t),$

τ being an average horizon of sellers. A third case in which p_t is lower than $\mathbf{p_{t+1}}$ is not possible, because the producers will retain their supplies, which leads automatically to an uplift of p_t.

The result is that consumption oscillations are smaller than production oscillations and that the proportion between them depends on the length of the "economic horizon."

An example of this dynamic scheme was the Brazilian coffee valorizations. In a study of the coffee market Tinbergen tried to answer the following question: "What can be deduced from the coffee valorization by the Brazilian government about the course of the price, consumption, and production of this commodity?" (Tinbergen and Luytelaer, 1932, 517). In this study he again tested the separate models of the structure of the supplying industry. He found that the dynamic model could explain best the policy of the Brazilian government.

4. Reconstruction of Tinbergen's Models of Supply

To verify that Tinbergen based his dynamic model on the dynamics of his doctoral thesis, it has to be proved that the dynamic scheme fulfills the criteria he formulated in his doctoral thesis. In particular, it has to be proved that the policy of an enterprise derived in his model equals the optimum of an ophelimity function that can be represented by an integral. Further, the derivative of one of the coordinates must occur in the integrand. This can be shown when the problem is stated as follows.

Producers optimize their profits over a period τ:

$$\delta \int_0^\tau v_t \cdot p_t \, dt = 0 \qquad p_t = p_t(v_t).$$

If there are no inventories, the static Euler equation has the form

$$\frac{\partial v \cdot p}{\partial v} = 0 \quad \leftrightarrow \quad p + v \frac{\partial p}{\partial v} = 0.$$

If producers build up inventories, the scheme becomes dynamic, be-

---

4. I have substituted boldface for Tinbergen's gothic letters.

Ehrenfest and Tinbergen: Limited Physics Transfer 151

cause a "velocity" appears in the model: only a part of the production is sold, the rest is retained as inventory (u_t):

$$v_t = e_t - \dot{u}_t \qquad e_t = f(t).$$

Now, u_t is the coordinate of the system, and the Euler equation has the form

$$\frac{d}{dt}\frac{\partial v \cdot p}{\partial \dot{u}} = 0 \rightarrow \frac{d}{dt}(p\frac{\partial v}{\partial \dot{u}} + v\frac{\partial p}{\partial v}\frac{\partial v}{\partial \dot{u}}) = 0$$

$$\rightarrow p + v\frac{\partial p}{\partial v} = C.$$

If one expects a constant price in this period, the optimal policy is a constant sale. Because Tinbergen assumed free competition, total demand and total supply in this period are equal:

$$\int_0^\tau v_t\,dt = \int_0^\tau e_t\,dt + u_0.$$

If the optimal policy is a constant sale, the sale in the first year will be

$$v_0 = \frac{1}{\tau}[\int_0^\tau e_t\,dt + u_0].$$

The first year crop is known: e_0. One expects a normal crop the next year: $\bar{e}$.

$$\int_0^\tau e_t\,dt = e_0 + (\tau - 1)\bar{e}.$$

The result is the same as in Tinbergen's 1932 paper:

$$v_{00} = \bar{e} + \frac{1}{\tau}[E_0 - \bar{e}] = v_{01} = v_{02} = \ldots = v_{0\tau}.$$

If there is *not* a normal crop the next year, the sale is adapted:

$$v_{11} = \bar{e} + \frac{1}{\tau}[E_1 - \bar{e}] = v_{12} = v_{13} = \ldots = v_{1\tau+1}.$$

Conclusions:

1. By including inventories, Tinbergen was able to make the model dynamic.
2. After every exogenous shock (overproduction) the sale is determined as if the system stays conservative.
3. There is no learning in the model. In spite of (regular recurrent) shocks producers assume that the crop next year will be normal.

4.1 Reconstruction of the Models of the Supplying Industries

Tinbergen was able to classify different fields both in physics and in economics with the aid of an "identity." It is possible to classify his models of the supply market in the same way. Consider the general case of μ producers in one particular market:

$$I = \int_0^T \sum_{i=1}^{\mu} \{q_i \cdot p(q,t) - k(q_i + \dot{x}_i, t)\} dt$$

$$y_i = q_i + \dot{x}_i \quad q = \sum_{i=1}^{\mu} q_i.$$

The coordinates of this general problem are x_i and q_i ($i = 1, \ldots, \mu$). If one optimizes profit ($\Delta I = 0$), then

$$x_i : \quad \frac{d}{dt}\frac{\partial k}{\partial y_i} = 0 \quad i = 1, \ldots, \mu$$

$$q_i : \quad p + q_i \frac{\partial p}{\partial q_i} - \frac{\partial k}{\partial y_i} = 0 \quad i = 1, \ldots, \mu.$$

4.2 Statics

At every moment, supply = demand. There are no inventories: $x_i \equiv 0$ ($i = 1, \ldots, \mu$).

(1) Supply regularization by production regularization: $y_i = q_i$. The coordinates that are left over are q_i ($i = 1, \ldots, \mu$). The Euler equations are

$$p + q_i \frac{\partial p}{\partial q_i} - \frac{\partial k}{\partial q_i} = 0 \quad i = 1, \ldots, \mu.$$

Tinbergen assumed that production costs have the form $k = k_0 + k_1 q_i$. Then the Euler equations are

$$p - k_1 + q_i \frac{\partial p}{\partial q_i} = 0 \quad i = 1, \ldots, \mu.$$

Where $1 \leq \mu < \infty$, the following deduction is valid:

$$\frac{\partial p}{\partial q_i} = \frac{\partial p}{\partial q}\frac{\partial q}{\partial q_i} = \frac{\partial p}{\partial q} \quad i = 1, \ldots, \mu.$$

So that Cournot's formula (Chamberlin 1929, 93–94) can be achieved:

$$\sum_{i=1}^{\mu} (p - k_1 + q_i \frac{\partial p}{\partial q}) = \mu(p - k_1) + q\frac{\partial p}{\partial q} = 0.$$

Where $\mu = 1$, we have a monopoly equation of a production without inventory:

$$p - k_1 + q\frac{\partial p}{\partial q} = 0.$$

Where $\mu \to \infty$, we have free competition:

$$p = k_1 \qquad (\frac{\partial p}{\partial q_i} = 0),$$

and q_i is indeterminate.

(2) Production is an exogenous variable: $q = y = f(t)$. There are no coordinates left over: $p = p[y(t)]$.

4.3 Dynamics

In a certain period (T), total demand = total supply. Production costs are not taken into account:

$$F = \sum_{i=1}^{\mu} q_i \cdot p = q \cdot p \qquad I = \int_0^T q \cdot p\, dt.$$

Inventory is possible: $q = y - \dot{x}$. Tinbergen considered the case in which production was determined exogenously: $y = f(t)$. In other words, supply regularization is realized by inventory regularization. This problem can be solved with the aid of the Hamiltonian:

$$\frac{\partial F}{\partial \dot{x}} = \lambda \qquad \frac{\partial F}{\partial \dot{q}} = 0$$

$$H = -F + \frac{\partial F}{\partial \dot{x}}\dot{x} = -q \cdot p + \lambda(y - q),$$

so that the Hamilton equations are

$$\frac{\partial H}{\partial q} = 0 \qquad \frac{\partial H}{\partial x} = -\frac{d}{dt}\lambda \qquad \frac{\partial H}{\partial \lambda} = \dot{x}.$$

From this it follows that

$$\frac{d}{dt}p = 0 \;\to\; \frac{\partial p}{\partial q}\dot{q} + \frac{\partial p}{\partial t} = 0.$$

In his doctoral thesis Tinbergen assumed that the paths of $p(q, t)$ and $y(t)$ were determined and known. Later he realized that agents could have only expectations about the future paths of p and y. He supposed that

$$E[y(t)] = \bar{y}.$$

In the next cases of the expected course of the price, "reasonable" entrepreneurs respond as follows:

$$E(\frac{\partial p}{\partial t}) = 0: \quad q = C \quad \rightarrow \quad q_0 = \bar{y} + \frac{1}{T}[y_0 - \bar{y} + x_0]$$

$$E(\frac{\partial p}{\partial t}) < 0: \quad q_0 = y_0 + x_0$$

$$E(\frac{\partial p}{\partial t}) > 0.$$

This last case is not possible.

5. Classical Dynamics

Tinbergen's work on dynamics must be considered in the realm of classical dynamics. When Tinbergen received his doctorate, Heisenberg's uncertainty principles had not yet been stated. Two years previously Ehrenfest had proved that "the averages of the quantum-mechanical variables satisfy the same equations of motion as the corresponding classical variables in the corresponding classical description" (Wichmann 1971, 348; see also Ehrenfest 1927, and Mirowski 1989b, 229). Moreover, Ehrenfest's adiabatic theorem was, in the first place, a rigorous theorem of classical mechanics. He had strong reasons for believing that adiabatically invariant quantities were the key to generalizing the statistical foundation of the second law of thermodynamics, so that it would withstand the undermining effect of the quantum theory. It was no accident that Planck had quantized the ratio of energy to frequency for his harmonic oscillations, since that ratio was the adiabatic invariant in this special case. And therefore, Ehrenfest conjectured, if one were to make a quantum theory for systems more general than Planck's oscillators, it would have to be done by quantizing the appropriate adiabatic invariants. The theorem Ehrenfest had found, that result in classical mechanics, was for him the clue to the generalization of the quantum theory.

I thank Arjo Klamer, Neil de Marchi, Philip Mirowski, and Geert Reuten for their comments and suggestions.

References

Bowley, A. L. 1924. *The Mathematical Groundwork of Economics*. Oxford: Clarendon Press.

Bullock, C. J., W. M. Persons, and W. L. Crum. 1927. The Construction and Interpretation of the Harvard Index of Business Conditions. *Review of Economic Statistics* 9:74–92.

Chamberlin, E. H. 1929. Duopoly: Value Where Sellers Are Few. *Quarterly Journal of Economics* 44:63–100.

Ehrenfest, P. 1916. Adiabatische Invarianten und Quantentheorie. *Annalen der Physik* 51:327–52.

———. 1927. Bemerkung über die angenäherte Gültigkeit der klassischen Mechanik innerhalb der Quantenmechanik. *Zeitschrift für Physik* 45:455–57.

Evans, G. C. 1925. Economics and the Calculus of Variations. *Proceedings of the National Academy of Sciences* 11:90–95.

Hanau, A. 1928. Die Prognose der Schweinepreise. *Vierteljahrshefte zur Konjunkturforschung*, Sonderheft 7.

Klein, Martin J. 1970. *Paul Ehrenfest: The Making of a Theoretical Physicist*. Amsterdam: North-Holland.

Magnus, Jan R., and Mary S. Morgan. 1987. The ET Interview: Professor J. Tinbergen. *Econometric Theory* 3:117–42.

Mirowski, Philip. 1989a. *More Heat than Light: Economics as Social Physics, Physics as Nature's Economics*. Cambridge: Cambridge University Press. [Citations are abbreviated *MHL*.]

———. 1989b. The Probabilistic Counterrevolution, or How Stochastic Concepts Came to Neoclassical Economic Theory. In *History and Methodology of Econometrics*, edited by Neil de Marchi and Christopher Gilbert. Oxford: Oxford University Press.

Morgan, Mary S. 1990. *The History of Econometric Ideas*. Cambridge: Cambridge University Press.

Roos, C. F. 1927. A Dynamical Theory of Economic Equilibrium. *Proceedings of the National Academy of Sciences* 13:280–85.

Tinbergen, Jan. 1927. Over de mathematies-statistiese methoden voor konjuntuuronderzoek. *De Economist* 76:711–23.

———. 1928. Opmerkingen over ruilteorie. *De Socialistische Gids* 13:431–45, 539–48.

———. 1929a. *Minimumproblemen in de natuurkunde en de ekonomie*. Amsterdam: H. J. Paris.

———. 1929b. Konjunturforschung und Variationsrechnung. *Archiv für Sozialwissenschaft und Sozialpolitik* 61:533–41.

———. 1929c. Vraagstukken van socialistiese ekonomie. *De Socialistische Gids* 14:528–40.

———. 1930. Bestimmung und Deutung von Angebotskurven: Ein Beispiel. *Zeitschrift für Nationalökonomie* 1:669–79; English summary, 798–99.

———. 1931. Ein Schiffbauzyklus? *Weltwirtschaftliches Archiv* 34:152–64.

———. 1932. Ein Problem der Dynamik. *Zeitschrift für Nationalökonomie* 3:169–84; English summary, 302.

———. 1933a. Het Waarnemen van Maatschappelike Verschijnselen. In *De Uitdrukkingswijze der Wetenschap*, 66–78. Groningen: Noordhoff.

———. 1933b. The Notions of Horizon and Expectancy in Dynamic Economics. *Econometrica* 1:247–64.

———. 1935. Annual Survey: Suggestions on Quantitative Business Cycle Theory. *Econometrica* 3:241–308.

Tinbergen, Jan, and Th. van Luytelaer. 1932. De Koffievalorisaties: Geschiedenis en Resultaten. *De Economist* 81:517–38.

Wichmann, Eyvind H. 1967. *Quantum Physics*. New York: McGraw-Hill.

**Part 3 The Mirowski Thesis and
Three Generations of Neoclassicals**

"Procrustean Beds and All That": The Irrelevance of Walras for a Mirowski Thesis

Albert Jolink

The Mirowski Theses: Ariadne's Thread or Gordian Knot?

I confess: Mirowski's *More Heat than Light* is provocative, intriguing, fascinating, tantalizing, seductive, paralyzing. Reading it is like entering the world you previously thought only Umberto Eco could describe, or maybe Lewis Caroll. From now on, the outside world is not what it seemed to be and may never be the same anymore. The reader cannot but feel that what appeared to be incompatible elements of a rather frustrating state of affairs can, in fact, be arranged into pure harmony. And since we refuse to believe that an unexpected harmony can be created by coincidence, we add to our Rubik's cube a Mirowski's pyramid.

Those acquainted with Mirowski's thesis will acknowledge that the non-non-Euclidian geometry presented by *More Heat than Light* explains, at least to some extent, the nagging question that has haunted the history of economics for some time now: How to explain this continual reference in economics to alien sciences such as physics? I admit, my interpretation of the Mirowski thesis is not quite as far-reaching as the inventor would prefer: according to Mirowski, there is no way of understanding economics without first understanding its relation with physics. In essence, the Mirowski thesis builds on the idea that scientific metaphors provide guidance and structure to the process of inquiry; as such, developments in physics have determined the evolution of economics. Whether developments in physics were the only influences, or whether they were the ultimate explanation, remains undiscussed in Mirowski's book, though that shouldn't detain us here.

A serious consequence of the Mirowski thesis is that once the lines set out by the metaphor are fixed, the itinerary for the scientific journey will prove to be a restrictive factor. Unfortunately, at least for neoclassical economists, the transplant of the so called "proto-energetics" metaphor into economics in the early days will eventually rebuff neoclassical plans today; or so we are told. If only the twentieth-century neoclassical economists had listened to their colleagues in the physics department, they would have noticed some of the problems attached to the energetics—but alas!

Venturing through the labyrinth of *More Heat than Light*, the reader may be subjected to an excess of proliferation called economics overrun with physics. The Mirowski compass, however, points to all directions at the same time, and the guide is never there when you need him. The considerable amount of speculation that follows creates a problem because it becomes impossible to speak of *the* Mirowski thesis: one can distinguish at least two theses, though I'm sure an intelligent critic might come up with a dozen. Preferring simplicity to multiplicity, I describe the two distinguishable theses that follow from *More Heat than Light*:

> Mirowski thesis 1 (MT1): Physics has been the purveyor to the Royal Economic Household within living memory.

> Mirowski thesis 2 (MT2): The continuity in neoclassical economics from 1870 until 1991 can be attributed to a common energetics metaphor.

The "problem," however, is not that there are two distinct, though related, theses, but rather that what should have been Ariadne's thread out of the economics labyrinth is starting to look like a Gordian knot. To prove the second thesis Mirowski takes great pains to prove the first. But to prove MT1, the reasoning assumes MT2 to be a fact. Let me put it differently. By stating that the physics metaphor adopted by, say, Walras is inherited by, say, Samuelson, one assumes that there was some sort of physics spell in the first place. Alternatively, by stressing the influence of physics on the work of Walras and the influence of physics on the work of Samuelson, as Mirowski does, one must assume that Samuelson followed in Walras's tracks. Although both theses may prove to be of importance in their own right, the combination of theses may well be more than one can chew.

In what appears to have become a tradition in dealing with Gordian knots, I would like to cut the evidence in two. Here I shall restrict discussion to neoclassical economics, in which two different "waves" of neoclassicism are distinguished, the first period ranging from 1870 to 1920 (give or take a decade) and the second ranging from 1920 to the present. Although this incision is bound to give an artificial representation of historical events, it is entirely in the "Mirowskian spirit," as the following citation confirms: "There was not just one Marginal Revolution, there were two. The second wave of scientific neoclassicism had to await fresh recruits from the physical sciences in the second quarter of the twentieth century" (*MHL*, 271).

The main thing here is to filter out the contaminating influence of MT2 on MT1 with respect to neoclassical economics. The relief of not needing to assume continuity in neoclassicism might then give an idea of the relevance of the metaphor in "first wave" or "second wave" neoclassical economics. In the following pages I elaborate my point by narrowing the discussion of argument and counterargument to a specific case. In the final section I reformulate what could have been *a* Mirowski thesis.

Substantial Evidence or Physical Attraction?

In the Mirowskian chronicle, neoclassicism comes in waves. During the second half of the nineteenth century a polyphonic choir of economists swelled in volume, giving voice to neoclassical economics. In general the developments in economic theory during "the 1870s" are considered a separate stage in the history of economic thought. In that respect *More Heat than Light* seems to link up with this general belief; so far so good. In addition it has often been discussed whether the works of these progenitors of neoclassical economics, such as the "fabulous four" (Jevons, Marshall, Menger, and Walras), should be regarded as close harmony or a cacophony. The most recent decades have shown that several pros and cons can be formulated in favor of either position, and Mirowski adds just one more argument: "the successful penetration of mathematical discourse into economic theory." It is worth mentioning that this extra argument not only expels Menger from the ranks of "official" progenitors of neoclassicism but also neatly separates neo-Austrians from modern neoclassical economists.[1]

The second wave of neoclassicism arose in the 1920s or 1930s and still seems to be resonating. Although some quite authoritative scientists

---

1. Similar arguments are brought forward for Marshall; for a critical review of these arguments see Coats 1993 (this volume).

may be mentioned to represent this second generation, only Samuelson appears to have deserved a spotlight in *More Heat than Light*. Whether this second wave is an echo of the first is clearly an important question for Mirowski and will depend on numerous circumstances (acoustics, etc.), but it remains unanswered for the time being.

Concentrating instead on the first wave, the question is what it took to be a neoclassical economist in the year 1870, as in the case of "the fabulous four minus one" above. The general feature of the answer to this question is, according to Mirowski, some sort of physics connection, given the evidence of the works of each separate economist. Hence, to answer the question: a nineteenth-century neoclassical economist may be expected to have adopted some version of a field theory of value. This implies that value is no longer an intrinsic, embodied substance but the outcome of a cognitive process of evaluation: "the mind is portrayed as a field of forces in an independently constituted commodity space." This field theory of value is, in a way, connected to the energetics metaphor that originated in the physics of the 1840s. Thus, to adopt the field theory of value, the nineteenth-century neoclassical economist must have some understanding of energetics, possibly obtained by some training as an engineer. Essential in the understanding of energetics is the conservation principle, that is, the conservation of energy, which should analogously be included in the economic theory. Finally, as stressed by Mirowski, a nineteenth-century neoclassical economist's appeal to the energetics metaphor should become apparent when his work is considered as a whole.[2]

Mirowski's position at this point is both interesting and puzzling. As if to contribute to the general confusion, the above description seems to apply only to neoclassical *economic theory*, but not to neoclassical *economists*. This may be illustrated by the following sequence of citations:

> It is no accident that, however otherwise diverse the cultural and social influences upon the various European progenitors of neoclassical theory, they all received training in natural sciences. (*MHL*, 217)

> The fact was that all the progenitors of neoclassical economics had

---

2. See, e.g., *MHL*, 258, with respect to Jevons's work.

> been trained as engineers, but their grasp of physics was shallow and superficial. (250)

> The first generation of neoclassical economists never completely explored their structural metaphor, largely because their understanding of it was so deficient. (269)

> Indeed, none of the conventional triumvirate of Jevons, Walras, and Menger understood the energy concept with any degree of subtlety or depth. (222)

Hence neoclassical economics in the 1870s had adopted the energetics metaphor although its masters did not know nor understand what they were dealing with.

Although I am convinced that the reader of *More Heat than Light* might be willing to believe in such schizophrenia, a twentieth-century economist is allowed to be skeptical and wonder whether there is any substantial evidence to support this rather innovative picture of neoclassicism. As this same economist might have expected, the answer is yes. This evidence can be found, according to Mirowski, in the way in which "production" is dealt with in neoclassical theory. Production was, in terms of a field metaphor, a bit of a problem because utility, prices, exchange, and a "conservation principle" really told the story. Hence neoclassical economists felt uneasy when production needed to be squeezed in. The very facts that (1) "*every* neoclassical discussion of production postdated the specification of the model of exchange" (*MHL*, 281) and (2) neoclassical production theory is characterized by "repeated citation of the law of the conservation of matter" (290) should serve as evidence that, indeed, the proto-energetics model had served as leading indicator for developments in neoclassical economics. Q.E.D.!

Q.E.D.?? I must admit that this evidence must come as a shock to the newcomer to the Mirowskian world. For one thing, how could these progenitors of neoclassicism do all those marvelous things described by (1) and (2) above, when they did not understand the metaphor in the first place? For another, the energetics metaphor may be an effective vehicle for introducing a production theory into economics, but that still leaves moot the question of whether even the economics of exchange was in fact driven by the energetics metaphor. And what, for that matter, does it prove that all these people talk about physics, if that is what they are really talking about? Mirowski's explanation is quite speculative and still remains to be proved; for the time being it may be referred to as "physical attraction," in particular "attracting" the author himself.[3] The following section reevaluates the evidence by giving it a more "down-to-earth" treatment via a closer look at the theory of Léon Walras.

Mirowski on Walras, Walras on Mirowski

Let me state an assumption first: that the Mirowski thesis, concerning the influence of physics on economics, with respect to neoclassical economics in general, is retraceable in the specific theories of a particular neoclassical progenitor. Keeping this in mind, and at the risk of being classified in the conservative field of orthodoxy sometimes referred to as "geriatronomics," I deny strenuously that Walras's theory "slavishly imitates physics." As one might have guessed, there are several layers to this question, which may be peeled off one by one.

In the first place, there is Mirowski's word. In *More Heat than Light* Walras is put forward as one of the whipping boys of early neoclassical economics: the odd case of someone who wanted to imitate rational mechanics from the very beginning of his career, but never understood it well enough to pursue the analogies on his own. Trained as an engineer, or at least surrounded by engineers, Walras is most likely to have been highly influenced in the conceptualization of value by metaphors of motion in physics at the time. A thus-introduced conception of a conservative field, however, would appear highly contradictory to Walras's production theory.

Somehow this position just rings false to me. Mirowski knows, as well as others do, that Walras's training as an engineer was not very successful. Walras failed the entrance exams for the prestigious Ecole Polytechnique twice and dropped out of the Ecole des Mines, where he was a student in name only. When he arrived at Lausanne he was surrounded by representatives of all sorts of disciplines, including those in his own law department. Although the engineers may have been more sympathetic to Walras's mathematical endeavors than his colleagues in law, there is little evidence that their possible contributions surpassed the borders of mathematical formalism (see, e.g., Walras 1965, letter 212).

The conceptualization of exchange value more resembled a "sub-

---

3. For a specific treatment of this trait see Schabas 1993 (this volume).

stance" theory than a field. Value in exchange, in that respect, was considered "a *property,* which certain *things* possess" (Walras 1984, section 41; emphasis added),[4] based on the utility and available quantity of things, or *social wealth*. Similarly, utility was "found in the *capacity* of the particular kind of social wealth under consideration to fill wants" (sections 71–72), either in potential (virtual utility) or effectively (effective utility). Although the "satisfaction of human wants" could be regarded as a "field" context, this falls beyond the *nature* of exchange in Walras's theory. Hence a rather peculiar situation arises in which value in exchange is regarded by Walras as a natural phenomenon and, as such, just one of many points of view from which to study social wealth.

Likewise, "production" is regarded as a point of view from which to study social wealth. Hence in Walras's theory value is not produced; instead social wealth is produced, which for Walras is quite a different matter. Although production changes the available quantity of social wealth, it does not necessarily influence the exchange value of social wealth. In relating Walras's theory to the mathematical model of exchange, as Mirowski does, one can hardly speak of a production theory: Walras's production equations only express that the quantities of productive services offered are effectively used in production. Even Mirowski's generous description of a Walrasian production theory gives too much credit to Walras. Hence, since there is no actual production theory, I do not quite see what problems Mirowski might have with respect to the conservation of energy, or whatever, in the case of Walras's theory.

But even with respect to (proto-)energetics, hardly anything can be found in Walras's work that indicates a deep understanding of physics. At least until 1906 Walras's impression of physics was shaped by a very rigid selection of classical mechanics, as is illustrated fairly by his 1876 article "Une branche nouvelle de la mathématique" (Walras 1987, 291–329) and by the mathematical introduction to the second (1889) and third (1896) editions of his *Eléments d'économie politique pure*, entitled "Des fonctions et de leur représentation géométrique: théorie mathématique de la chute des corps." Presumably his first acquaintance with what was going on in physics at the time was made through Poincaré's *La science et l'hypothèse* (1902) and Picard's *La science moderne et son état actuel* (1905), which Walras read around 1906.

---

4. This property is "that of being exchangeable against any other scarce thing in such and such a determinate ratio" (section 24).

In an unfinished, unpublished review (see appendix 1) of Poincaré's *La science et l'hypothèse* Walras did not reveal any sensitivity toward Poincaré's critical attitude with respect to energetics. He completely misunderstood what appeared to be a coquetry by Poincaré in the direction of probability and stochastic processes:

> I refer to Mr. Poincaré for what has been named [the law of] the property of the conservation of energy: "To sum up, and to use ordinary language, the law of the conservation of energy can have only one significance, because there is in it a property common to all properties; but in the determinist hypothesis there is only one possible, and then the law has no meaning. In the indeterminist hypothesis, on the other hand, it would have a meaning even if we wished it in an absolute sense. It would appear as a limitation imposed upon freedom" [Poincaré 1902, 133–34, also quoted by Mirowski, *MHL*, 75] (upon human freedom or the freedom of the Creator?). But Mr. Poincaré realizes that he "digresses" and that he "will leave the mathematical and physical domain." These scruples do not stop me. My metaphysics does not prohibit me from believing that the Universe has a certain relation with reason and that human freedom has the right and even the duty to inquire into these relations to his own profit. I will use freely these rights and perform this duty.

All in all, there is very little evidence after 1906 that Walras had any understanding at all of a proto-energetic metaphor. It is therefore questionable whether this metaphor, in his case, could have served "to provide guidance and structure in the process of inquiry." The suspicion arises that Mirowski is highly misled by the references to physics in Walras's work.

Passing on to a second layer, we still find ourselves left with the question whether an alternative hypothesis may be formulated, in the case of Walras, to replace the Mirowski thesis. In other words, could there be another reason why Walras insisted on possible analogies between physics and economics, in particular toward the end of his career, as illustrated in his article "Economique et mécanique" (1909)? I believe this may be the case, although it does require a brief introductory story.

When Walras arrived in Lausanne, his prime intention was to render to economics a scientific status. This implied that the formulations of "economic truths" and their applications in the determination of "economic conditions for society" would create the possibility for thinking about improvements in society. The formulation of "economic truths" would have to be based on a "scientific method" and would have to be irrefutable in terms of logic. In essence this implied that when social wealth was studied from the point of view of exchange, the resulting *pure* economics would require a *mathematical* method of inquiry (Jolink and van Daal 1989).

From the very start the mathematization of Walras's economic theory met hostility from each and every one he turned to. The initial sympathy from engineers and mathematicians was confined to minor mathematical problems, but even this support lost luster along the way, turning to resistance. The "Walrasian dream" of a mathematical economics was revived at the turn of the century by Henry L. Moore. This young American economist offered Walras openings for a market in the New World and, in turn, was presumably partly responsible for the confusion about the relation between physics and economics in Walras's work. Although Moore's contribution was restricted to transmitting the news that two French mathematicians had extolled the mathematical economics of the School of Lausanne at the World Fair at St. Louis, Missouri in 1904 (see appendix 2), it triggered Walras's desire to start a final offensive. These French mathematicians, Henri Poincaré and Emile Picard, had unwittingly supported the use of the mathematical method in economics by the simple fact that at the exhibition "economics was neatly placed side by side with mechanics and mathematical physics" (Walras to Moore, 25 December 1906; see appendix 2). Walras's article "Economique et mécanique" (1909) tried to elaborate the analogies in mathematics between Walras's pure economics and rational mechanics, naively assuming that it would finally convince the mathematical home front—alas! "Economique et mécanique" thus offers no contribution whatsoever to Walras's theory other than an ill-founded justification of a mathematical method in pure economics.

To sum up, my hypothesis would be that Walras was not at all interested in physics but that the reference to physics was an illustration of and justification for a mathematical method. This would also explain why Walras did not understand physics in the first place.

A final layer that may be uncovered is the question whether the very choice of the mathematics of constrained extrema (if it was the math that Walras was after) does not tie his economics to physics: whether, in other words, if it were not for the mathematical developments in physics, economics might not have existed. Although the question clearly embraces a very complex matter, a tentative answer would contain at least the following elements.

In the first place, there is nothing in Walras's work to suggest that physics is the paragon of mathematics. In terms of hierarchy, the order is reversed into one in which a sort of universal mathematics comes first. According to Walras, pure mathematics, which appears to be synonymous with geometry and algebra, could be applied to any science dealing with "appreciable," though not necessarily measurable, magnitudes. Hence, just as mechanics and astronomy were considered branches of mathematics, pure economics was suggested to represent a new branch of mathematics ("une branche nouvelle de la mathématique") on a level with other natural sciences though dealing with different phenomena. This is clearly elaborated in his "Economique et mécanique," distinguishing physico-mathematical sciences (mechanics, etc.) from *psy*chico-mathematical sciences (pure economics).

In the second place, Walras took great pains to explain that his economics had already existed, before the application of mathematics, in the works of his father. The use of a mathematical method was motivated only by the necessity of a deeper analysis where ordinary logic failed. In other words, the application would be seen as a very theoretical and abstract method of inquiry.

In the third place, Walras's mathematical handbooks did not figure at the frontiers of scientific advancement. Such books as Poinsot's *Eléments de statique* (1842), Haton de la Goupillière's *Eléments du calcul infinitésimal* (1860) or Duhamel's *Des méthodes dans les sciences de raisonnement* (1868) are occasionally quoted, though they primarily seem to reflect his childhood reminiscences, in which life was simple. On the other hand, the amount of mathematics in Walras's work did not require a great deal of sophistication.

So, as far as Walras was concerned, the continual references to *pure* mathematics ruled out the influence of *applied* mathematics as exemplified in physics. His main object—and also Mirowski's initial argument to distinguish neoclassicals from classicals—namely "the successful penetration of mathematical discourse into economic theory," finds itself eventually brushed under the carpet.

But *More Heat than Light* does offer a new opportunity to consider mathematical formalism as the Trojan Horse which smuggled in the energetics: "There can be no such thing as a mathematics of constrained extrema without some corresponding conserved entities or structures"

(*MHL*, 272–73).⁵ In Walras's case mathematical formalism was acquired from Paul Piccard, an engineer and professor of industrial mechanics at the Academy of Lausanne. It is not at all clear under what circumstances Piccard's contribution came about.⁶ The crucial two-page note signed by Piccard appears among several notes and suggestions by other colleagues, but only Piccard's idea of applying differential and integral calculus to the problem of maximization of wants was eventually selected by Walras. Hence if there ever was a Trojan Horse, at least it was towed in by Walras himself.

The question is whether the adoption of variational principles included a conception of conservation of a particular entity. The answer is quite simple: neither Piccard's note nor any of Walras's works mentions anything of the kind. In fact the entire discussion is not about the conservation of, say, utility, but about the expansion of "utility" through exchange. The simple mathematics could hardly be considered as being patented by a specific brand of physics and, as such, represents a general formalism "in that it makes no difference whether it be numbers, figures, stars, sounds, or any other object" (R. Descartes, *Regulae ad Directionem Ingenii*, quoted in Gaukroger 1980, 43).

Evaluating Mirowski on Walras and Walras on Mirowski, I find it all adds up to an image which does not quite live up to the reputation of *More Heat than Light*. In my view, the manner in which Walras enters into Mirowski's mise-en-scène is a bit of a farce which the book might be better off without.

A Mirowski Thesis: A "Procrustean Single"

Procrustean beds come in pairs, and so do Mirowski theses (MT1 and MT2). In the previous pages I have attempted to discuss MT1 for just a small period in history, say 1870 to 1910, and for just one person. Clearly this could hardly be very impressive. In that respect *More Heat than*

---

5. On the abuse of implanting ideas in mathematical formulations see Wise 1991.

6. The particulars of this have been partly reconstructed (see Jaffé's remarks in Walras 1965, letter 211 [4]), but the facts of the case remain speculative. The fact is that the concept of maximization of the satisfaction of wants as the underlying cause of exchange was included in Walras's theory only after the note by Piccard on want-curves ("courbes de besoins"). As can be inferred from an unpublished manuscript entitled "Application des mathématiques analytiques à l'économie politique (1871) 3e tentative" (postmarked 11 September 1872), Walras defined the key notion *rareté* as "absolute value"; possibly owing to Piccard's note it was later changed into the definite concept of "intensity of the last want satisfied."

Light has demonstrated that "elements that are incompatible at first sight place themselves in an unexpected order and form a harmonic unity; and we refuse to believe that an unexpected harmony is purely the result of coincidence. It seems we appreciate our conquest even more the more it has required some effort, or, we are more certain to have elicited the true secret of nature the more it has been guarded in jealousy" (Poincaré 1902, my translation). So Walras is not an apt exemplar within the Mirowski theses: so what? Does that mean that the Mirowski theses will fall to pieces? As I see it, that clearly depends on what the actual theses may be.

Suppose, for the sake of argument, that *More Heat than Light* is not about classical economics. (Clearly the thought that the physiocratic doctrine of a single tax was a projection of Quesnay's single incision during bloodletting is charming but never convincing.) Instead let us say that the book is about early and modern neoclassical economics.

Question: what is the problem and how is it solved? Answer: the problem is to find a common denominator that gives neoclassical economics a look of coherent unity for the past 120 years. This common denominator has to represent a specific circumstance which existed in the 1870s and has managed to survive. "Our" Mirowski thesis may thus provide the solution: physics envy! In this particular thesis, neoclassical economic theory can be directly traced, through the mathematical formalism used, to the developments in nineteenth century physics. In this same thesis, the mathematical-physical link binds all past and present-day neoclassicals together.

The funny thing about history is that although it can look both forward and backward, when explaining matters it is asymmetric: one finds it much easier to explain an event when the cause precedes the effect than when it is the other way round. Mirowski also seems to come to this conclusion: the "cause" is represented by the energetics metaphor, and the "effect" is the specific type of formalism adopted in neoclassical economics. His problem in *More Heat than Light* is that one does know the "effect," but not the "cause." So, in fact, one would always have to look back to find the "cause" of the present state. The drawbacks of this "economic theory in retrospect" are, firstly, that one is more or less committed to the successor's interpretation of the precursor's intentions; and, secondly, that the progenitor's work is evaluated only on one specific subject, namely what appears to be of interest at a later stage.[7]

---

7. The denunciation of this "whiggish" type of history of physics can be found in Wise 1991.

The case of Walras, as I have insisted in the previous pages, may serve as an example. I have argued that Walras did not understand physics nor did he have to. If any "energetics" can be interpreted from Walras's work, this is entirely due to the interpreter himself. Secondly, as I have argued elsewhere (Jolink 1991), the nature of Walras's theory changes once his entire work is considered as a whole. Although one may study Walras's work with respect to the subject of physics, one must also be aware that what is left out may be of more importance in a historical account than what is included.[8]

So if we suppose, again, that Walras is an odd case in this entire Mirowskian chronicle, that Menger is passé anyway, and that Jevons would not be able to carry all the weight by himself, it amounts to saying that the first generation of neoclassicals is to be excluded, thereby shortening the historical line introduced by the Mirowski thesis. If we repeat the above reasoning for other precursors, however, it may well be that this line becomes shorter and shorter, finally reeling in what may be the actual Mirowski thesis: the insufficiency of modern neoclassical economics and its inappropriate flirting with outdated physics. Between the lines, this even seems to be Mirowski's intention: "Failures of communication became endemic to twentieth-century economics. In one corner were the orthodox neoclassicals, unwittingly intent upon the reinvention of energetics from scratch" (*MHL*, 355). What started off as a universal history may thus end up as a plethora of irrelevant stories, either enlarged or shortened on the procrustean beds. Although the remaining story is worth pursuing as *a* Mirowski thesis, *More Heat than Light* on the whole only muddies the water.

Even if universal history may be the story of different intonations given to a handful of metaphors, one should nevertheless keep in mind that it is the content that counts. Once histories themselves are chained by metaphors they merely "follow the yellow brick road." It seems that *More Heat than Light* has relied on imagery once too often.

Appendix 1: Review by Léon Walras of H. Poincaré's *La science et l'hypothèse*

[The review is part of the Fonds Walras at Lausanne. Angle brackets in the transcription indicate material crossed out or written over by Walras. Square brackets indicate my own editorial elisions, supplements, or paraphrases.]

---

8. See also Coats 1993 (this volume).

Je viens de lire attentivement trois volumes extrêmement interessante de la *Bibliothèque de la Philosophie Scientifique* dirigée par le Dr. Gustave Le Bon (éditeur E. Flammarion), H. Poincaré, *La Science et l'Hypothèse*, *La Valeur de la Science*; E. Picard, *La Science Moderne et son état actuel*. Ces volumes, et les autres déjà parus au nombres d'une dizaine, traitent principalement de sciences physique ou physiologique; mais parmi les volumes en préparation annoncés figurent des travaux relatifs à la science morale: Ed. Perrier, *Les Procédés de raisonnement dans les sciences naturelles et sociales*; Emile Boutroux, *Science et Religion*. Et cette circonstance m'engage à formuler quelques réflexions que m'a inspirées la lecture des trois précédants.

Tout d'abord, j'ai été heureux de constater que je ne m'avancais pas trop ici même (*Gazette de Lausanne*, 18 juillet 1898) en parlant des "jours des grande fête scientifique" où tombaient entre les faits physiques, chimiques, végétatifs et vitaux "quelqu'une de ces [. . .] empiriques et provisoires comme ont tombée celles qui séparait la physique de l'astronomie, comme sont en train de tomber celle qui séparent les diverses parties de la physique elle-même."

Des volumes des MM. Poincaré et Picard il y résulterait, par exemple que, par suite de la constitution de la thermodynamique, la physique mathématique semblerait constitué (sinon définitivement au moins pour un certain temps) et cela par ce fait [. . .] que "Les rapports de l'électricité et de la lumière sont maintenant connus; les trois domaines de la lumière, de l'électricité, du magnetisme ⟨et de la chaleur?⟩, autrefois séparés n'en forment plus qu'un; et cette annexion semble définitive" [Poincaré 1902, 204]—"progrès éminente" accompli par les efforts successifs de Maxwell, de Helmholtz, de Rowland, de Lorenz [275–81]—et fondé sur les deux principes de la *conservation de l'énergie* et de la *moindre action* [148, 149ff.].

Je renvoi à M. Poincaré pour ce qui est dénommé ⟨la loi⟩ la propriété de la conservation de l'énergie — "En résumé . . . mais dans l'hypothèse déterministe . . . Dans l'hypothèse indéterministe limite imposée à la liberté" (à la liberté de l'homme ou à la liberté du Créateur?) — Mais M. Poincaré s'aperçoit ici qu'il "s'égare" et qu'il "va sortir du domain de mathématique et de la physique."

Ce scrupules ne m'arrête pas. Ma métaphysique ne m'interdit pas de croire que l'Univers a quelque rapport avec la raison et que la liberté humaine à le droit et même le devoir de chercher ces rapports et d'en faire son profit. J'use de ces droits et remplis ce devoir. Mais il est certain qu'ici l'homme de science mathématique et physique et l'homme de science moral sont dans un position opposante.

Le premier doit pénétrer les secrets de la nature.

Appendix 2: Two Letters of Léon Walras to Henry L. Moore

[Both are part of the Fonds Walras in Lausanne. As with appendix 1, angle brackets indicate changes in Walras's hand, square brackets my own.]

No. 1. Sometime between 14 November and 27 November 1905.

Mon cher collègue,

Suivant votre désir, je vous envoie ⟨aujourd'hui⟩ la brochure contenant mon "cours élémentaire," revu et corrigé avec le plus grand soin et tout prêt pour la traduction. Je crois que cette traduction avancerait beaucoup nos affaires et nous ferait arriver au but dans le délai fixé par le calcul ⟨la formule⟩ de Laplace.

Vous en jugerez en examinant vous même le cours en question. Je vous donne 2 ou 3 moins pour cela ⟨jusqu'à Pâques⟩. Si vous ne voyez pas moyen d'en tirer parti, vous me le renverrez alors avant le manuscrit de mon autobiographie, vu que je pourrais l'utiliser autrement. Si, au contraire, vous êtes tenté d'entreprendre la tâche, vous me le ferez savoir le plus tôt possible, et nous prendrons des ⟨autres⟩ arrangements en conséquence.

J'ai vu ces jours-ci, en parcourant le numero d'août des *Publications of the American Economic Association* que je reçois en qualité de membre honoraire, que votre "Columbia University" (qui parait être au premier rang pour les soutenances de dissertations de Doctorat en économie politique) publiait des "Studies in Economics" en volumes de 500 à 700 pages du prix de $3 à 4. Il me semble que notre volume trouverait assez bien sa place dans cette collection. J'ai vu en outre que le Prof. Edwin R. A. Seligman participait à la direction de ces publications. Comme nous entretenons nous lui et moi depuis un certain temps déjà, des rapports d'estime réciproques, je serais bien aise si vous [crussier?] pouvoir le mettre ⟨n'y voyez pas d'un convenient que vous le missiez⟩ au courant de notre affaire.

Cordialement

Tout à vous,

Léon Walras

P.S. Je n'ai toujours pas reçu l'article "The Personality of A. A. Cournot" (Harvard – May 1905) et les Programmes de vos cours.

No. 2. Clarens, 25 December 1906.

Mon cher collègue,

Merci de votre joli cadeau ⟨de votre bon et fidèl souvenir⟩ et de vos bons vœux. Recevez vous même pour Mrs. Moore et pour vous nos souhaits les plus effectueux à ma fille et à moi. Nous avons pris note de le promesse que vous nous avez faite de Brighton "de ne manquer aucune occasion dans l'avenir de nous faire une autre visite." Mais nous exprimons tous deux le désir que vous vous arrangerez pour la faire moins précipitée. Dans les premiers jours d'octobre ⟨Quelques semaines après⟩, ayant appris l'existence d'un volume de M. le Prof. Emile Picard de Paris: *La Science Moderne et son état actuel* (Paris. Flammarion eds. 26 rue Racine, 3 fr 50). J'en fait ⟨me suis empressé de le faire⟩ venir et j'ai eu le plaisir d'y trouver un chapitre

Sur les développements de l'analyse mathématique et ses rapports avec les autres sciences resumant "un conférence faite à l'Exposition Universelle de St. Louis" et à la fin duquel notre économique était nettement placée à côté de la mécanique et de la physique mathématique. J'ai écrit à l'auteur en lui offrant mes ouvrages qu'il a accepté en m'envoyant les siens. C'est là une relation que pourrait bien être très profitable et que je devrai à l'indication que vous m'avez fournie.

Bonne santé donc encore une fois et bon courage mon cher ami. Je commence à croire qu'il s'écoulera moins de 17 ans avant que notre révolution scientifique soit assuré. Cordialement

Tout à vous,
Léon Walras

References

Coats, A. W. 1993. What Mirowski's History Leaves Out. [In this special issue of *HOPE*.]

Gaukroger, S., ed. 1980. *Descartes: Philosophy, Mathematics and Physics*. Brighton: Harvester Press.

Jolink, A. 1991. "Liberté, Egalité, Rareté: The Evolutionary Economics of Léon Walras." Thesis, University of Rotterdam.

Jolink, A., and J. van Daal. 1989. Léon Walras's Mathematical Economics and the Mechanical Analogies. *History of Economics Society Bulletin* 11:25–33.

Mirowski, P. 1989. *More Heat than Light: Economics as Social Physics, Physics as Nature's Economics*. Cambridge: Cambridge University Press. [Citations are abbreviated *MHL*.]

Picard, E. 1905. *La science moderne et son état actuel*. Paris: Flammarion.

Poincaré, H. 1902. *La science et l'hypothèse*. Paris: Flammarion.

Schabas, Margaret. 1993. What's So Wrong with Physics Envy? [In this special issue of *HOPE*.]

Walras, L. 1909. Economique et mécanique. *Bulletin de la Société Vaudoise des Sciences Naturelles*, ser. 5, 166:313–27. Reprinted in *Metroeconomica* 12 (1966) and in Walras 1987.

———. 1965. *Correspondence of Léon Walras and Related Papers*. Edited by W. Jaffé. Amsterdam: North-Holland.

———. 1984. *Elements of Pure Economics*. Translated by W. Jaffé. Philadelphia: Orion.

———. 1987. *Mélanges d'économie politique et sociale*. Paris: Economica.

Wise, M. Norton. 1991. Uses and Abuses of Interdisciplinary History. Paper presented at the Duke Economic Thought Workshop Symposium "Rethinking the History of Economics in the Light of *More Heat*," Durham, 1–3 March.

Remaking the Mathematician as an Economist: Knut Wicksell and the Mittag-Leffler Circle

Clifford G. Gaddy

For more than one hundred years economists have felt compelled to defend themselves and their profession against a perception—from within and outside the profession—that there has been "too much" mathematics in economics. The defensiveness on this issue is curious, given the avowed attempts of the pioneers of neoclassicism, Jevons and Walras, to make economics rigorous precisely through the use of mathematics. Mathematics, they argued, would guarantee that economics became accepted as a science.

This ambiguous attitude in the relationship between economics and mathematics has been addressed in a series of works by Philip Mirowski (1984, 1986, 1989), broadly dealing with the origins of marginalism. There Mirowski argues that the adoption of mathematics by economists after 1872 was a historical accident, due initially to ignorance of mathematics on the part of the first marginalists and perpetuated by the ignorance of following generations. The consequences of this accident have been ominous. Not only has an overemphasis on mathematics in general been bad for the field (Mirowski 1986, 192ff.), but the problem has been compounded by the fact that the neoclassicals adopted a particularly narrow brand of mathematics—the calculus of constrained maxima.

> As previously observed, mathematics was integrated into economic theory simultaneously with the marginalist revolution, which appropriated a specific model from nineteenth-century physics and merely changed the names of the variables. An unintended consequence of this event was that a very narrow subset of mathematics came to be identified with neoclassical theory: that is, the mathematics de-

veloped specifically within the context of the physical theory of the late eighteenth and nineteenth centuries, the calculus of constrained extrema. . . .

One of the great misperceptions in the history of the discipline of economics is that which credits neoclassical theory with the wide-ranging appreciation and appropriation of mathematical tools. On the contrary, the neoclassical "box of tools" is very small: a purse, or a pouch. Neoclassicism has become little more than constrained optimization in ever-more baroque guises. (Mirowski 1986, 202–3)

In particular Mirowski faults the first neoclassicals for their ignorance of the major revolutionary developments occurring in mathematics at the time they worked. The implication apparently is that if they had been truly aware of what was happening in mathematics, they might at a minimum have adopted some other (and presumably less pernicious) brand of mathematics.

The physics model appropriated by the progenitors of neoclassicism was generated around the middle of the nineteenth century, just before the spread of the furore over the significance of the non-Euclidean geometries. The first generation of neoclassicals were contemporaries of [Felix] Klein's Erlanger Program . . . , which became the group theoretic manifesto, but the economists remained unacquainted with it. (Mirowski 1986, 203–4)

The Erlanger Program, which was based on the idea that any species of geometry is simply the study of invariants associated with a particular group of transformations, revolutionized the field of geometry and became one of the theoretical underpinnings of the theory of relativity in physics. But 1872 was not only the date of the Erlanger Program; it was also the year in which Richard Dedekind published his famous memoir on continuity and the infinite, *Stetigkeit und irrationale Zahlen*, and the year in which Georg Cantor published the article which marked his discovery of the theory of transfinite numbers.[1]

Felix Klein and Sophus Lie's Erlanger Program and Dedekind and Cantor's work on continuity and the infinite represent two main trends

---

1. Cantor's "Über die Ausdehnung eines Satzes aus der Theorie der trigonometrischen Reihen" was the third of three papers he published in 1870–72, ostensibly on a theorem relating to trigonometric series. For the significance of those papers in the history of mathematics see Dauben 1979, ch. 2, "The Origins of Cantorian Set Theory."

in mathematics, geometry and analysis, that had developed in the nineteenth century. The year 1872 thus marked a breakthrough of sorts for both directions, which had developed from many common roots and would intertwine again over the decades, both with important connections to physics.

Mirowski is undoubtedly right in stating that in 1872 the first generation of neoclassicals did not know of the Erlanger Program. They probably did not know of Cantor and Dedekind, either. But could they really be expected to? By 1872 the economists' works had already been published. (I am speaking here of Walras and Jevons; the third of the progenitor trio of the 1870s, Menger, never claimed to use mathematics.) In this sense it seems more relevant to ask not about the first generation marginalists—the literal contemporaries of the mathematical revolutionaries—but about the succeeding generation of economists, the so-called consolidators of the 1890s. They were the first economists who would conceivably have had the opportunity to know of the new directions in mathematics launched in the 1870s and their potential applications to physics. For this generation the choice of mathematical methods can be expected to have been a much more conscious choice. In many ways, then, it was they, not Jevons and Walras, who really shaped the future of neoclassicism.

I concentrate here on one such second-generation figure, the Swedish economist Knut Wicksell. For several reasons Wicksell is an interesting case study for Mirowski's thesis. First, Wicksell was an important pioneer in the development of neoclassical thinking. He played a key role in extending the doctrine of marginalism to new and fruitful areas of economics: capital theory, monetary theory, and business cycle theory in particular. Second, before he ever read any neoclassical economics at all, Wicksell had been trained as a mathematician and physicist. Fragmentary evidence indicates that he was conversant with some of the most sophisticated theories of late nineteenth-century mathematics. He therefore should have been as prepared as anyone to look at this new economics with a critical eye. Finally, from his very earliest works to his last, Wicksell showed an awareness of the issue of the role of mathematics in economics and commented explicitly on it.

My goal is to begin an investigation of the connection between mathematics and economics in the life and work of Wicksell. The primary focus here will be to ask *how much* and *what kind of* mathematics and mathematical physics Wicksell knew. The approach is biographical, using some previously unpublished information about this aspect of his life. I begin with his mathematical training and then examine the circumstances of his conversion to economics. In doing so I delve into his connections with a fascinating international circle of mathematicians based in Sweden in the 1880s. As it turned out, it was this circle that directly encouraged, and provided the funding for, Wicksell to embark upon his career in economics.

Having discussed the case of Wicksell, I shall return to Mirowski's thesis on the relationship between marginalism and mathematics. An appendix includes English translations of some of Wicksell's previously unpublished correspondence relating to mathematics.

Wicksell's Mathematical Training

Knut Wicksell (1851–1926) graduated from secondary school in Stockholm in the spring of 1869. With high recommendations from his mathematics teacher, he enrolled that autumn in Sweden's leading university, the University of Uppsala. According to an autobiographical sketch he wrote in 1890, he entered Uppsala "with a view to becoming a Doctor of Philosophy and university lecturer and perhaps even a professor of mathematics."[2] At this time, the general level of mathematics in Sweden appears to have been fairly modest.[3]

In the spring of 1872—that is, after only five semesters rather than the normal eight—Wicksell had earned his first degree, the *filosofie kandidat* [B.S.] *cum laude,* with majors in mathematics and astronomy. He proceeded immediately into his graduate studies, the next goal being the *licentiat* degree.[4]

---

2. *Fritänkaren*, 15 November 1890, cited in Gårdlund 1958, 29. For convenience, I cite the page numbers of the 1958 English-language edition for all quotations from Gårdlund's biography of Wicksell. However, it should be noted that the English edition has no footnotes on original sources. Hence whenever I cite original Swedish-language sources in connection with a reference from Gårdlund, the information comes from his original (1956) Swedish edition.

3. Elfving (1981, 71) writes that this was the case four years earlier, in 1865, when Gösta Mittag-Leffler, who will play an important role later in these pages, entered the Uppsala University mathematics program. Elfving states that Sweden's mathematical training at that time was generally on a par with Finland's, which he describes as ten years behind the leading centers in Europe.

4. The *licentiat,* which existed in Sweden until 1969, is an intermediate level between the bachelor's level *kandidat* and the doctorate and thus might be compared to an American master's degree. In fact, the late nineteenth-century Swedish system and present-day American system differ substantially. The level of training required, and the dissertation requirements, probably make the *licentiat* more comparable to an American Ph.D. today.

Wicksell devoted himself wholeheartedly to his studies, although he had to teach for a while in private school to support himself. While at Uppsala, he was active in the Physics and Mathematics Society. As the society's reporter in physics, it was his duty at the fortnightly meetings to present to his fellow members synopses of recent journal articles in the field of physics.[5] In 1874 Wicksell published a minor article, "On Checking Root Equations," in the journal *Tidskrift för matematik och fysik* (Journal of mathematics and physics).

At that time the *licentiat* degree at Swedish universities required about two and one-half to three years of coursework in three fields of specialization, plus a written dissertation. By the summer of 1875 Wicksell had completed all his coursework and taken initial examinations in mathematics and physics. This was, however, to be the last formal academic work he would do for nearly six years.

With financial needs pressing, Wicksell took the 1875–76 academic year off to work as a private tutor for the son of an ironmaster. By the fall of 1876, according to his 1890 autobiographical sketch (see above), he had begun to doubt whether he had "the perseverance and all-absorbing interest" that would be required to achieve anything of genuine worth in the field of mathematics. Moreover, he wrote,

> to be an independent scientist nowadays one must renounce almost everything else and be content to remain ignorant of almost every sphere of knowledge except the most relevant, a child in political and social life. This was beyond my resolution; on the contrary I became actively engaged in literary and social questions and, even more deeply, in religious ones. (Gårdlund 1958, 36)

He did indeed engage himself both in literary matters, publishing poetry and plays, and in social issues. In 1878 a strongly profeminist poem delivered at a ceremony in Uppsala earned him national prominence. The poem was first reprinted in newspapers in Uppsala, Kalmar, and Gothenburg, and later in national weeklies. Praise for his bold views was mixed with searing criticism. The result was the beginning of a national reputation for Wicksell, not as a scientist, but as a social *débatteur*.

That same year Wicksell began studies of neo-Malthusianism that culminated in February 1880, when he delivered a speech that was to shape

---

5. F. W. Hultman in *Tidskrift för matematik och fysik* (1969):39, reported in Gårdlund 1958, 29.

his future life. Addressing a temperance lodge in Uppsala, he linked the problems of alcoholism, poverty, prostitution, and other social ills to overpopulation. And the solution to overpopulation, he hinted, was birth control. This speech was quickly followed by a second in which he developed the solution—birth control and its methods—even more explicitly.

These lectures of early 1880 gained him national fame (and notoriety). Letters poured in from old and new friends and enemies. One such correspondent was a professor of mathematics at the University of Helsinki, Gösta Mittag-Leffler. A Swede, Mittag-Leffler had been head of the mathematics department in Helsinki since 1877. Five years older than Wicksell, he had also been trained at Uppsala, where he had received his Ph.D. in 1872, the same year Wicksell received his B.S. Mittag-Leffler must certainly have known Wicksell in Uppsala and may even have taught him. Mittag-Leffler had been an instructor of undergraduate mathematics in 1871–72, and after receiving his degree in 1872 he served for a year as an assistant professor (*docent*) in what undoubtedly was a very small mathematics department at Uppsala (Elfving 1981, 72).

Mittag-Leffler's letter of 19 May 1880 expressed support for Wicksell's social views, but, interestingly, his primary concern was for Wicksell's career as a mathematician. For the sake of his future in the field, Mittag-Leffler advised Wicksell to travel abroad for a couple of years and let the furor over his lectures subside. Then he could continue with mathematics. "If you have any plans for giving up mathematical science and taking up social sciences instead," he added, "in the interest of mathematics I should regret such a decision." In conclusion, Mittag-Leffler invited Wicksell to study with him in Helsinki.[6]

This letter is quite remarkable. From its content and tenor it is clear that Mittag-Leffler is more interested in Wicksell's potential as a mathematician than in his social and political activities. As will be shown below, at the same time that Mittag-Leffler was making this effort to keep Wicksell in mathematics, he was also engaged in a parallel endeavor

6. This 1880 letter (cited in Gårdlund 1958, 70) is the first previously documented contact between Wicksell and Mittag-Leffler. Evidence of their contact at Uppsala between 1869 and 1873, as referred to in the text here, is only circumstantial. However, examination of the correspondence between the two men in the archives of the Institut Mittag-Leffler reveals at least one letter that predates 1880. On 7 November 1877 Wicksell wrote to Mittag-Leffler in Helsinki (the latter had just assumed his position there earlier that year), thanking him for sending his papers on the theory of functions (see appendix, no. 1).

to rescue the Russian mathematician Sonya (or Sofia) Kovalevskaya for the field. Shortly thereafter he would return to Stockholm to head the mathematics department of the newly founded Stockholm University.

There is no evidence of a written reply by Wicksell to Mittag-Leffler's offer to come and start studying under him in Helsinki. Not until 27 January 1882 did he write to Mittag-Leffler, acknowledging the receipt of some of Mittag-Leffler's papers on the theory of functions and confirming that he would devote the spring semester to mathematics.[7] Apparently he did in fact do as promised, since at the end of that same year he again wrote to Mittag-Leffler that he was now nearly prepared for his final examination for the *licentiat* degree. However, he added that he had given up all plans for pursuing a serious academic career as a mathematician, saying that he lacked "both energy and, to be honest, sufficient interest in the matter." The tone of his letter indicates, however, that it may not have been mathematics per se that was his problem, but a lack of direction in his life in general: "The worst of it is that I am opposed, either by nature or habit, to toil in any shape or form and, as you know, that is not usually a characteristic of the men who really achieve anything in the world."[8]

But even though Wicksell says in this letter that he is almost ready for his final examinations, it would not be until the summer of 1885 that he finished the degree. He apparently had more examinations to take, in physics, and then to prepare and defend the required *licentiat* dissertation. There is no further evidence for the progress of his academic work in the intervening period (1883–84).[9] We have to assume that the dissertation was a project he undertook only after having finished his study of the theory of functions referred to during 1882.[10]

Whatever work Wicksell may have done on his dissertation in 1883–

---

7. Appendix, no. 2. The statement concerning absence of any correspondence until January 1882 refers only to materials in the archives of the Institut Mittag-Leffler. There may be earlier exchanges among the letters kept at the Wicksell archives in Lund, which I could not consult for this report. See my note on sources in the reference list.

Apart from the incomplete sources, however, there is another reason why there may have been no letters between Wicksell and Mittag-Leffler during 1881. Once Mittag-Leffler returned to Stockholm in 1881, the two were undoubtedly in personal contact and hence had less need of written correspondence. Uppsala is only 60 kilometers (40 miles) from Stockholm.

8. Appendix, no. 5, 19 December 1882. The passage quoted is also in Gårdlund 1958, 71.

9. Gårdlund has nothing on this period. The correspondence in the Mittag-Leffler archives (see appendix) jumps from 18 January 1883 (no. 6) to 19 October 1885 (no. 7).

10. An examination of the dissertation itself (now in the Uppsala University archives) might answer the question of how much, if any, effort Wicksell devoted to it in 1883–84.

84, that he was in the interim also preoccupied with questions far from mathematics is without doubt. His list of activities in these two years makes one wonder how he possibly could have had time for any academic work at all. In 1882 the author August Strindberg had conducted intensive negotiations with leading Swedish publishers regarding a project for a new radical literary magazine to be co-edited by Strindberg himself and Wicksell. Although the project never got off the ground in its original form, by 1883 it had emerged in the form of a new radical daily newspaper, *Tiden*, which claimed as correspondents and contributors some of the leading figures of the Swedish "'80s Generation" (*Åttiotalisterna*). Wicksell was a founder, part-owner, and editorial board member of *Tiden* (Gårdlund 1958, 74).

At the end of 1883 Wicksell became involved in another, related project, which would prove to be of relevance to his future career as an economist. In October he helped found the Uppsala branch of a new Swedish social and political organization, the Workers' Ring Movement. The national Ring Movement had shortly before been founded in Stockholm. With ideas adapted from the so-called *Kathedersozialisten* in Germany in the 1870s, the movement was based on the ideas of temperance, consumer cooperatives for workers, and worker-owned share banks (which would also be a source of finance for the movement). It also envisaged the establishment of labor exchanges and an annual "workers' parliament" to exercise its political influence (Gårdlund 1958, 75–76).

Despite these ventures into journalism and social activism, by May 1885 Wicksell did finally complete his final field examination, in physics, and shortly thereafter presented his dissertation in his principal field of mathematics: "On Proving the Existence of a Root of a Polynomial Equation." He was awarded the *licentiat* degree in September 1885 (Gårdlund 1958, 79).

Introduction to Marginalism, 1885–1886

Wicksell was now nearly thirty-four years old. He had a graduate degree in mathematics. At the same time, he was nationally known for his social and political views. But with the exception of Mill's *On Liberty* and a few neo-Malthusian tracts, he had no familiarity with economics whatever. It was only now, after an intensive period of refreshing his mathematics and physics knowledge, that he plunged into a serious study of economics, beginning directly with the latest work in the field, the writers we now call the neoclassicals.

As soon as he had completed the successful defense of his dissertation and received his degree in September 1885, Wicksell left for an eight-month stay in London. There he devoted himself to nearly full-time study of the works of Jevons (*Theory of Political Economy*, 1871) and Walras (a German translation of excerpts from *Théorie mathématique des richesses sociales*, 1883; the French original of *Théorie mathématique, Elements d'économie politique pure*, 1874), as well as the main works of the classical economists (Smith, Ricardo, Malthus, and John Stuart Mill), plus writings of Cournot and Gossen and others (Gårdlund 1958, 105).

The notes Wicksell took on his reading during the London trip have been preserved and are now in the Wicksell archives in the Lund University Library.[11] One can easily imagine that a great deal of these notes must have concerned his opinions of the use of mathematics among those economists, especially Jevons and Walras. Wicksell had, after all, just completed an intense period of graduate work in mathematics, including a dissertation. Unfortunately, however, his biographer, Torsten Gårdlund, offers only a few scattered remarks on this aspect of the evolution of Wicksell's thought. He dispenses with these "three thick books with notes and commentaries" from the 1885–86 study period in just a page and a half. The little that Gårdlund does say in this regard is disappointing and somewhat frustrating. For instance, his statements that Wicksell "struggled" with the mathematics of Jevons and Walras (105) and that "Walras' differential equations caused him the most trouble" (106) are ambiguous at the least. Given Wicksell's mathematical training, it seems unlikely that the mathematics used by the mathematically much less proficient Jevons and Walras could have given him trouble. It is just as likely that he may have been profoundly confused by their misuse of mathematics. These, however, are the questions that cannot be answered until after a close inspection of the notebooks.[12]

Pending such an examination, the only other evidence that reflects Wicksell's continued link to mathematics, at least psychologically, during his London stay is a pair of letters he wrote back to Sweden. Sig-

---

11. These notes are a potentially important piece of evidence that could not be used for this report. See my note on sources in the reference list.

12. Gårdlund's only direct quotation from the notebooks relating to the use of mathematics concerns Mill's wage fund theory. Wicksell stated that this theory—according to which increased wages lead to a decrease in capitalists' savings, which in turn results in decreased wages—is nonsense and adds: "Only a mathematical approach to economics can free it from this sort of stupidity" (Gårdlund 1958, 105).

nificantly, one of the first people to whom Wicksell wrote after arriving in London was Mittag-Leffler. The topic, though, is rather mysterious. Wicksell assured Mittag-Leffler that he had arranged for a copy of his dissertation to be sent to Mittag-Leffler, since Mittag-Leffler had promised to "take a look at" it. It is certainly curious why he would be sending a copy to Mittag-Leffler, if Wicksell had decided to drop mathematics forever. Moreover, the letter suggests that there may be some further plans for the dissertation, as he assures Mittag-Leffler that "there is no rush at all to finish reading it, since it's unlikely that anything can be done about this matter before spring." [13]

Wicksell also mentioned mathematics in a letter written from London to his friend Theodor Frölander in November 1885. He remarks that he had met Karl Kautsky in London and ended up in a dispute with him regarding socialism and Malthusianism. The trouble with Kautsky, writes Wicksell, is that "he has gone to the subject [Malthusianism, presumably] in a historical way only, whereas I think you must be accustomed with mathematics before, at the least so much as to be fully at home in the axioms of algebra" (Gårdlund 1958, 79–80).[14]

Wicksell returned to Sweden in the middle of June 1886. The 1885–86 research period in London had been financed with his own funds. His second encounter with modern economics, which this time included not only library research but also personal discussions with and lectures by leading economists, began in August 1887. Full funding to pursue this research for three years came from an institution known as the Lorén Foundation for Social Research (Gårdlund 1958, 103).

The Lorén Foundation

Before Wicksell had left for his first London trip in October 1885, he had been approached by a young man named Viktor Lorén regarding the possibility of Wicksell's serving as a director of a soon to be established foundation for social science research. The original board was to consist of five people, of whom all but one, the economist David David-

---

13. Appendix, no. 7, 19 October 1885. I have taken it for granted that the document to which Wicksell is referring in this letter is his *licentiat* dissertation, as he had just completed that work. The Swedish word he uses—*afhandling*—can (less commonly) refer to other types of academic papers, but there is no evidence that Wicksell had produced any other major work before the autumn of 1885.

14. Wicksell wrote this letter in English.

son, were in the orbit of Mittag-Leffler (as was Lorén himself). The other four in addition to Davidson were Mittag-Leffler's sister, the radical author Anne Charlotte Edgren-Leffler; Mittag-Leffler's protégé and fellow Weierstrass student, Sonya Kovalevskaya; Mittag-Leffler's cousin and business associate, the economist Johan Leffler; and Wicksell.

As it turned out, Wicksell decided not to join the board of the Lorén Foundation, but only because that would have disqualified him from becoming the first recipient of its funds. He applied for, and received, a grant to finance his serious studies in economics, up to and including the publication of his first work, *Über Wert, Kapital und Rente*. The key persons involved in the Lorén project thus deserve our attention.

Viktor Lorén (1857–1885)

The son of a wealthy brewer, Lorén had grown up in the Leffler home (that is, the parents of Gösta and Anne Charlotte) after his father's death. Following a period at Uppsala University beginning in 1876, he had studied in Leipzig under one of the leading exponents of the historical school in economics, Wilhelm Roscher.[15] Lorén was forced to interrupt his own education owing to incurable illness. As early as 1882 he decided to donate his substantial fortune to the promotion of social science research.

Only days before his death on 1 December 1885, he drew up a will establishing the Lorén Foundation with a donation of around 150,000 kronor.[16]

---

15. Lorén may have been following in his "step-cousin" Johan Leffler's footsteps. Leffler had received his Ph.D. at Leipzig under Roscher in 1876.

16. Manasse (1949, 73) gives 1 December 1885 as the date of Lorén's death. Gårdlund (1958, 102) states that he died on 1 November 1885.

Since the role of the Lorén Foundation in linking Wicksell to mathematics after his degree is the centerpiece of this report and its main addition to the previous biographical information on Wicksell, it is worth noting how the foundation has been portrayed in previous literature. That the Lorén Foundation funded Wicksell's research is noted in most accounts of Wicksell's life—e.g., Gårdlund (1956, 1958), Lindahl (1958), and Uhr (1987). Of these, only Gårdlund lists the members of the foundation's board, but even he fails to note either the crucial connections of Lorén himself to the Leffler family or the links of four of the five proposed board members to Gösta Mittag-Leffler. He states only that Lorén's choices for the board, in addition to Wicksell, "included two economists, David Davidson and Johan Leffler, and two women radicals, the Russian-born mathematician Sonja Kovalevsky and the authoress Anne Charlotte Edgren" (Gårdlund 1958, 102).

Apparently no detailed history of the Lorén Foundation exists, even in Swedish. According to notes on sources in the Swedish edition of Gårdlund (1956, 386), the bulk of the archives

Johan Leffler (1845–1912)

Johan Leffler was the first cousin of Gösta Mittag-Leffler. In a career that reminds one of Wicksell's, Leffler had begun studies in the natural sciences at Uppsala but then abandoned them for a time before switching over entirely to a new track in economics and finance. Leffler received his Ph.D. in 1876 under Wilhelm Roscher in Leipzig.

While in Leipzig he had established contacts with the newly founded *Verein für Sozialpolitik*, or *Kathedersozialisten*, a group which advocated radical social and economic reforms, supported by the active intervention of the state. In contrast to the socialists, however, the *Kathedersozialisten* stood firmly on the foundation of private property.

After returning to Sweden, Leffler attempted to put these reformist ideas into practice by helping to found the Ring Movement, which Wicksell was quickly to join. Leffler shared his expertise in the areas of worker-owned consumer cooperatives, banks, and insurance companies, and was the director of the Ring Movement's own bank from 1883 to 1886. In addition he taught economics at Stockholm University off and on from the academic years 1888–89 to 1901–2 and served during 1885–88 as a member of the Lower House of Swedish Parliament.

Leffler's insurance expertise led him in 1882 to collaborate with his cousin Gösta Mittag-Leffler in founding Sweden's first life insurance company, Victoria.[17]

Anne Charlotte Edgren-Leffler (1849–1892)

The younger sister of Gösta Mittag-Leffler, Anne Charlotte Leffler began writing plays and novels in the 1870s. By 1880 she had become an acknowledged literary figure, "mentioned in one breath with Ibsen and Strindberg" (Koblitz 1983, 181). Her home was one of the centers of the

---

of the Lorén Foundation are reported to have been destroyed. Gårdlund adds, however, that "it is possible that some archival materials may still exist in the unorganized parts of the archives of the Institut Mittag-Leffler in Stockholm." Wicksell was required by the terms of his stipend to send quarterly progress reports to Anne Charlotte Edgren-Leffler. However, in a letter to me, Institut director Dan Laksov states that the archives contain no correspondence between Wicksell and either Anne Charlotte Edgren-Leffler or Sonya Kovalevskaya.

17. This successful company later became Skandia, Sweden's largest insurance company. The third partner in this enterprise was J. H. Palme, a member of another leading liberal bourgeois family in Stockholm and grandfather of the late Swedish premier Olof Palme. Facts in this section on Johan Leffler are from encyclopedia articles by Hölcke (1948, 1979).

"'80s Generation" in Sweden. If she did not know Knut Wicksell from before (possibly through her brother at Uppsala in the early 1870s), she—like the rest of Sweden—could not have escaped noticing his activities after his 1878 poem on women's rights and his scandalous 1880 lecture series on birth control. In her own 1883 novel, *I krig med samhället* (At war with society), she chose Knut Wicksell as the model, at least in part, for one of her main characters, the radical author and Malthusian, Berndtson (Lindström 1979, 436).

Sonya Kovalevskaya (1850–1891)

At the time of her appointment to the Lorén Foundation board Sonya Kovalevskaya could rightly be called the leading female scientist in Europe. She had left her native Russia at the age of eighteen to seek higher education abroad, since the Russian universities, like most in the rest of Europe, were closed to women. She began studies in Heidelberg, where the university administration permitted her to sit in on classes but not officially register for them. She was then advised to go to Berlin to study under the great mathematician Karl Weierstrass. Although the University of Berlin prohibited her from even auditing public classes, Weierstrass agreed to take her on as a private pupil. Through the graces of Weierstrass, who called Kovalevskaya his "most talented disciple," she was granted a Ph.D. in absentia from Göttingen in 1874 (Koblitz 1987). She was the first woman in Europe ever to receive a doctorate in mathematics.[18]

Unable to find work at any level in either Germany or Russia, Kovalevskaya left mathematics entirely. During the late 1870s Weierstrass made repeated attempts to rescue her for the profession. In 1876 he had commissioned another former pupil of his, Mittag-Leffler, to urge Kovalevskaya to return to Germany. But with no guarantee of work there, this attempt was doomed to failure. By 1880 Mittag-Leffler had become the head of the mathematics department at Helsinki University and was

---

18. Fearing that every excuse would be used by those who opposed awarding a Ph.D. to a woman, Weierstrass required Kovalevskaya to write not one but three doctoral dissertations. The topics illustrate the breadth of her interests and expertise: (1) partial differential equations; (2) degenerate Abelian integrals and applications to the equations of motion of a rigid body about a fixed point; and (3) the shape of Saturn's rings (Cooke 1984, 20). More facts on Kovalevskaya which are peripherally relevant to the Wicksell case are contained in Gaddy 1990.

personally in a position to offer her a job. Despite his efforts, however, it proved impossible to have Kovalevskaya accepted for the Helsinki faculty—not, interestingly, because of prejudice against her gender, but because of her purported revolutionary leanings and contacts (Finland was of course a Russian province until 1918).[19]

Mittag-Leffler had more freedom when he himself moved from Helsinki to Stockholm in 1881. He finally got her a position in 1883 at Stockholm University. The Lefflers became her "substitute family" as soon as she arrived in November 1883 (Koblitz 1983, 179). She also ended up as a professional colleague not only of Gösta, but of Anne Charlotte as well: Sonya and Anne Charlotte co-authored two plays.

By October 1885, when Viktor Lorén announced his selection of the members of the board of his new foundation, Kovalevskaya was not only a tenure-track assistant professor at the University of Stockholm (the first female professor in Europe since the Middle Ages) but also an editor of Mittag-Leffler's influential new journal, *Acta Mathematica*. In the latter capacity her chief responsibilities were as liason with the leading mathematicians of Paris, Berlin, and Russia (Koblitz 1984, 23).

Thus all of these individuals on the Lorén Foundation board (with the exception of David Davidson) were part of the network of Gösta Mittag-Leffler. Not only were all of them heavily influenced by Mittag-Leffler, but they all in varying ways were dependent upon him. Although he was not himself on the board of the Lorén Foundation, there seems to be little doubt that Mittag-Leffler was the controlling force behind the project.[20] A good deal of biographical information about Mittag-Leffler has already appeared throughout the preceding pages. But it might be worthwhile to look more closely at his activities during the 1880s, that is, in the years between his offer to Knut Wicksell to study mathematics under him at Helsinki (in 1880) and Wicksell's completion in 1893 of his second Lorén Fellowship project, the writing of *Value, Capital, and Rent*.

19. The Tsarist government's suspicions were not without ground. Throughout her life Kovalevskaya maintained the contacts she had established with Russian nihilist circles in her adolescence. During her university years in Germany she took time off to live and work as a nurse in the Paris Commune in 1871 (Koblitz 1983, 106).

20. Indeed, to judge by Wicksell's own attitude toward him, Mittag-Leffler directly controlled the foundation's pursestrings. See his letters to Mittag-Leffler of 22 September 1893 (no. 9 in the appendix), 29 August 1895 (no. 12), and 25 and 28 October 1899 (nos. 17 and 18).

Gösta Mittag-Leffler (1846–1927)

Mittag-Leffler is perhaps best known in the history of mathematics as the founder and editor of the journal *Acta Mathematica*. Founded in 1882, *Acta* quickly became the premier journal in Europe, and Mittag-Leffler himself a leading organizer of the Continent's mathematical community. He was the key figure in international cooperation among mathematicians, particularly in helping reconcile the German and French mathematics establishments in the decade or two following the Franco-Prussian War. These efforts culminated in the first international mathematics congress in Zurich in 1897, which he organized. His person and his journal most directly linked two of the main schools of mathematics in late nineteenth-century Europe: those of Karl Weierstrass in Berlin (including Weierstrass's pupils and close friends Alfred Hurwitz, Lazarus Fuchs, Vito Volterra, and Sonya Kovalevskaya, as well as Mittag-Leffler himself) and Charles Hermite in Paris (whose pupils included Hermite's son-in-law Emile Picard, Pierre Appell, and Henri Poincaré). Mainly through Sonya Kovalevskaya, the circle also extended beyond France and Germany to Russia and the school of P. L. Chebyshev (whose students included A. A. Markov and A. M. Lyapunov).

In late 1880, the same year that he was corresponding with Wicksell regarding the latter's future as a mathematician, Mittag-Leffler was just beginning to take the first steps to establish this network. At that time he was preparing his return from Helsinki to Stockholm to head the mathematics department of the newly founded Stockholm University (*Stockholms Högskola*). He came with the ambitious goal in mind of making Stockholm an international center of mathematics. Part of that grand design would be the founding of a new international journal.

The concrete proposal to start a new mathematics journal in Scandinavia came from the Norwegian Sophus Lie (the founder, together with Felix Klein, of the Erlanger Program). Lie and Mittag-Leffler met in Stockholm in the late spring of 1881 to discuss the project. Over the next few months Mittag-Leffler called upon his international networks at all levels, up to and including the king of Sweden, Oscar II, to support the project (Domar 1982).

Although Lie had originally conceived the idea of the new journal, and Karl Weierstrass, among other eminent figures, assisted Mittag-Leffler in organizing support for it, the key role was played by Henri Poincaré.

Mittag-Leffler is reputed to have been one of the foremost champions of Weierstrass and his ideas, and their relations were in general close and trustful. But judging from their correspondence, there was little contact in this period [1881–82] and perhaps also slight strains in those relations. . . .

Mathematically and personally, Mittag-Leffler had at that time far more intimate contacts with Hermite, with whom he maintained a steady exchange of notes and letters. Through Hermite, he obtained detailed information on the mathematical life in Paris, and very early he had become aware of the trio of exceptionally gifted young students of Hermite: Appell, Picard and Poincaré. Hermite had written about Poincaré's marvelous talents, and Mittag-Leffler had taken up a regular correspondence with the young genius. In March 1882, Mittag-Leffler suddenly realized how he could use Poincaré in order to give a Scandinavian journal a brilliant start and that this had to outweigh the possible complications with Weierstrass. In a letter to [Carl Johan] Malmsten [a former mathematics professor and Swedish cabinet minister] some days later, he writes: "According to my firm belief, we now find ourselves in a period quite similar to that of the discovery of elliptic functions. Then Abel made the success of Crelle's *German* journal. In the same way Poincaré will make the success of our *Swedish* journal." (Domar 1982, 4–5)

Mittag-Leffler wrote to Poincaré on 29 March 1882 and explained both the project and the key role he projected for him. Mittag-Leffler wanted an important manuscript for the first issue. He ended up with an abundance: Poincaré's *Theorie des groupes fuchsiens*, his *Mémoire sur les fonctions fuchsiennes*, and pieces by Appell, Picard, and Hermite all appeared in the first issue of the journal in December 1882.

Ironically, although *Acta Mathematica* was to become in effect the house organ of the Mittag-Leffler–Poincaré group, the journal's initial fame was probably due not to Poincaré's work but to that of Georg Cantor. Beginning with the second issue, *Acta* published a series of French translations of Cantor's groundbreaking works on transfinite set theory (some previously published in German, others unpublished).[21] These publications in the journal reflected yet another important link between

---

21. Even this was with Poincaré's assistance: he and Picard supervised the translation of Cantor's works into French (Grattan-Guiness 1971, 355).

Mittag-Leffler and the pioneers of mathematics in the late nineteenth century. In 1879, the year that Cantor had broken with Dedekind, Mittag-Leffler stepped in to provide Cantor with both the stable intellectual friendship and the publishing outlet he needed to complete his revolutionary work. Mittag-Leffler wrote Cantor almost monthly through 1884 and then less intensively through about 1887 (Dauben 1979).[22]

This description of Mittag-Leffler's activities in the 1880s could be continued. However, the examples above should suffice to demonstrate that he not merely maintained contact with every leading mathematician in Europe during this decade; he was at the center of some of the most revolutionary developments in mathematics of his age. Cantor's theory of transfinite numbers has already been mentioned. The 1880s were also the decade of Poincaré's work on partial differential equations, the three-body problem, and hydrodynamics.[23] Mittag-Leffler's daily activity during the 1880s was to ensure that these works came to the attention of the mathematics profession and thereby push the field in new directions. And yet—to return to Wicksell—it was during these same years that he also exerted substantial efforts on behalf of one member of his circle to go far beyond mathematics.

Wicksell returned from London in the summer of 1886, having read the works of the neoclassical economists for the first time. He then applied for funds from Mittag-Leffler's circle to pursue this research in economics further and to write a book that would extend marginalism into the new domain of capital theory. That book, *Über Wert, Kapital und Rente nach den neueren nationalökonomischen Theorien* (Value, capital and rent), was published in the early autumn of 1893. Wicksell

---

22. Although the intensive period of correspondence between Cantor and Mittag-Leffler regarding Cantor's new discoveries of transfinite numbers ended around 1887, their contact continued. At the end of September 1888 Cantor, Mittag-Leffler, Sonya Kovalevskaya, and Weierstrass all met in Germany (Grattan-Guiness 1971, 358). As a curiosity—since there is no further evidence of contact at this time—note that Wicksell was residing in Berlin on his Lorén Foundation fellowship from the fall of 1888 to the spring of 1889 (Gårdlund 1958, 111–18).

23. In addition to Cantor's early articles (1870–72), translated and republished in *Acta Mathematica* in 1883–85, his famous *Grundlagen einer allgemeinen Mannigfaltigkeitslehre* was published in 1883. Poincaré's *Mémoire sur les courbes définies par une équation différentielle* was published in 1881–86; his *Sur le problème des trois corps et les équations de la dynamique* was published in 1890. One might also add Lyapunov to this list (see Gaddy 1990). Lyapunov's dissertation, "Obshchaya zadacha ob ustoychivosti dvizheniya," was presented in 1892. Henry (1987) notes that in the twelve years from 1881 to 1892, "the qualitative theory of differential equations emerged from scratch to become the core of a new field of mathematics."

immediately mailed copies to distinguished scholars, including Eugen Böhm-Bawerk and Léon Walras. He delivered Gösta Mittag-Leffler's copy in person.[24]

With this picture in mind of the circles in which Wicksell was moving, let us now return to Mirowski's thesis on the relationship between the early neoclassical economists and mathematics.

Mirowski on Mathematics and Marginalism

Mirowski's most explicit explanation of the history of relations between neoclassical economics and mathematics is in his "Mathematical Formalism and Economic Explanation" (1986). According to that article, in the early 1870s the marginalist fathers looked to the mathematics of physics to legitimize their discipline as a "hard science." They adopted calculus and constrained optimization, and then came up with an economic rationale to justify the use of this particular brand of mathematics. Mirowski's train of logic, then, is as follows:

1. The neoclassicals wanted to make economics a science.
2. The only science they knew was (engineering-style) physics.
3. The characteristic feature of that—the thing that, to them, made it *science*—was the mathematics.
4. The type of mathematical techniques associated with the physics they knew was the mathematics of constrained optimization, or calculus.
5. Having adopted the calculus, they needed to justify its use. So they adopted the physics metaphor with which it was associated.
6. As a last step, they made their economics fit the metaphor. As Mirowski says, "The mathematics . . . came first and the economics second" (1986, 197).[25]

---

24. See appendix, no. 9, 22 September 1893.

25. This version of history seems to me to differ somewhat from the one Mirowski presents elsewhere, both before and after the 1986 article, "Mathematical Formalism . . ." In "Physics and the Marginalist Revolution" (1984) and again in *More Heat than Light* (1989), Mirowski says that even before the marginalist revolution, economics had already wedded itself to the physics metaphor. Then physics changed, and so economics just had to follow, or else lose all credibility. But the main points remain the same: (1) the marginalists were trying to hitch a free ride on the physics train, and (2) they were so ignorant of real physics and real mathematics that they could not themselves see where the metaphor broke down.

Equally important as what happened when this mathematics was adopted is what happened—or did not happen—later. Once the physics metaphor was adopted, it was never abandoned.

> The most curious aspect of this program to make economics more rigorous and more scientific is that *not one* neoclassical economist in over one hundred years has seen fit to discuss the appropriateness or inappropriateness of the adoption of the mathematical metaphor of energy in a prerelativistic gravitational field in order to discuss the preferences and price formation of transactors in the marketplace. (Mirowski 1986, 187, emphasis his)

But while no *economist* ever questioned what was going on, there were individuals in other fields who did. In *More Heat than Light* (241–49) Mirowski gives examples of "real" mathematicians and scientists at the turn of the century who recognized what the economists were up to and tried to call their bluff. They included men such as Hermann Laurent and Vito Volterra. Mirowski sums up their efforts:

> What happened around the turn of the century was really quite simple. A number of mathematicians and scientists stumbled upon some of the writings of the early neoclassicals and immediately apprehended what was going on: These economists were calling energy "utility." Their reaction was to try to see if these economists were merely using the physical mathematics to browbeat and hoodwink their colleagues, or if there actually were legitimate parallels in the two traditions. (*MHL*, 249)

Not surprisingly, the scientists' verdict, according to Mirowski, was the same as his own: the economists were indeed browbeaters and hoodwinkers. But luckily for the neoclassicals, the attack of the prying scientists was somehow warded off. The economists were smart enough to play dumb—or they simply *were* dumb. In any event, because of lots of "defensiveness, incomprehension, and farrago" from the economists' side, the scientists eventually just gave up trying to argue their point (*MHL*, 249). Then, after this close call, the marginalists managed to "forget" the physics metaphor (270). They obscured it so no one could recognize it anymore.

Who was complicit in this scam? While Walras, Jevons, Edgeworth, and Pareto are the main culprits, Mirowski also indicts nearly every other member of the first and second generation of marginalists. Only two economists escape being immediately lumped together with the "Gang of Four": Menger and Marshall. Mirowski exonerates Menger by simply declaring that he "cannot be considered a neoclassical economist" (261). Marshall, however, turns out to be the worst villain of all. Whereas Jevons, Walras, and the rest could invoke ignorance and incompetence in their defense—what they did, they did unknowingly—Marshall could not. He did know mathematics and physics.[26] But rather than use his knowledge to expose the abuses of the marginalists, Marshall actually helped conceal them, by "soft-pedaling" the mathematics and by "controlling, masking, or perhaps altering some of [the] more objectionable aspects" of the energetics metaphor (263).

Where, then, does Mirowski place Knut Wicksell? He does not mention him, so we will have to try to figure out ourselves where he would fit in. This paper has shown that Wicksell knew a great deal of mathematics and physics. So he cannot be classed with the naive Jevons and Walras. He used mathematical formalism in his own work and considered it important to do so.[27] Hence he is not a Menger. Is he then in the same category as Marshall, that "soft-pedaller and masker" of the energetics metaphor? Was he a person who, while completely aware of the abuse of physics and mathematics which Mirowski imputes to the other neoclassicals, nevertheless concealed it from those around him?

The biographical facts, old and new, presented in this paper, provide no conclusive answer whether or not Knut Wicksell's name should be added to the list of villains in *More Heat than Light*. The facts do, however, show that from the very beginnings of his study of economics and even before, Wicksell was surrounded by the very same kind of people who appear as *heroes* in *More Heat than Light*—the Laurents and Volterras, the "true mathematicians and scientists" who tried to expose the marginalists' scam. And not only did such people surround Wicksell; they *paid* him to learn and to develop neoclassical economics. Why didn't *they* protest at least? Mittag-Leffler read Wicksell's book, and then proceeded to give him more money to do more of the same.

26. "No other economists understood enough physics to discuss its [the energetics metaphor's] implications and flaws" (Mirowski 1984, 373).
27. The use of mathematics in economics is a recurring theme in Wicksell's own writings. For key statements at three different periods of his career—1893, 1911, and 1925—see Wicksell 1954, 52–53; 1934, xxii–xxiii; 1958, 103–7.

Appendix: Selected Correspondence between Knut Wicksell and Gösta Mittag-Leffler, 1877–1924

Letters from the archives of the Institut Mittag-Leffler, Djursholm, Sweden. Twenty-three items are filed under the Wicksell–Mittag-Leffler correspondence in the archives. The first twenty-one are reported below. Nos. 22 and 23 are notes from the Wicksell family after his death. The translations from the Swedish below are my own.

No. 1. Letter, 7 November 1877, from Wicksell in Uppsala to Mittag-Leffler in Helsinki, where he had just begun his position as head of the mathematics department at the University of Helsinki. Excerpt.

Dear Colleague,

I don't know how to thank you for being so kind as to send me your papers in the theory of functions, which I had already had a chance to read in the Academy of Science "Review," and will now have the pleasure of incorporating into my little library. . . .

No. 2. Letter, 27 January 1882, from Wicksell in Uppsala to Mittag-Leffler in Djursholm, outside Stockholm. Mittag-Leffler had now started at the University of Stockholm. This letter is mentioned in Gårdlund, but only in reference to Wicksell's plans to study mathematics the next semester. Complete text.

Dear Colleague,

Warmest thanks for being so very kind as to send me your many papers on the theory of functions. I will plunge into them immediately, since I plan to study mathematics this semester. I can't say that the theory of functions has appealed to me so far—I audited a seminar by Söderblom last semester, and I almost got the impression that it was a large crate containing a few small jewels of value surrounded by a huge amount of wood shavings and other packaging. I'd rather see the jewels and the wood shavings dealt with separately, unless the latter could just be assumed to be obvious. This may be due to my incomplete understanding. Still, it doesn't make much of an impression when you hear a lecturer, just returned from Berlin, say something like the following: The proof which I will now present is admittedly much more complicated than I actually think is necessary, but I don't dare change a line of what the great Berlin mathematician said in his lectures. Those in the audience, who have yet had reason to develop any great enthusiasm for Professor W. [Weierstrass], would feel more satisfied if the lecturer declared that he himself were more persuaded of the necessity of the theorems he was presenting. To turn oneself into a semi-unconscious echo of someone else's thoughts—no matter how genial—is hardly worthy of a scientist.—Please excuse my chatter and let me once again thank you sincerely for your longstanding friendship of which I am so little deserving.

Knut Wicksell

No. 3. Letter, 4 December 1882, from Wicksell in Uppsala to Mittag-Leffler in Djursholm. December 1882 was the date of the first issue of *Acta Mathematica*. The "assignment" referred to in the letter is to write a journalistic review of the new journal. Complete text.

Dear Colleague,

Thanks for your kind letter. I accept your assignment with pleasure, and in a couple of days I will send you what you want; I just hope you'll be happy with it. I had in any event been planning to write a modest announcement which I would have submitted somewhere, for instance, to the local Uppsala newspaper.

What I mainly had wanted to emphasize there were the numerous inconveniences that arise from the manner in which Swedish mathematicians (and those in the rest of Scandinavia and Finland) have hitherto been compelled to publish their work, namely either in foreign journals or in the proceedings of academic societies. The former are not read by Swedes; the latter not by anyone, with the exception of those few who have access to public libraries and take advantage of them. That it is entirely your energy and self-sacrifice which we can thank for this grand enterprise is obvious to anyone who is the least bit familiar with the circumstances. I am just surprised that it is not stated more clearly in the prospectus that you alone are the actual editor of the journal and the other editors merely assistants. I am, however, delighted to hear that you have perfectly free reins; I only hope that you won't be overwhelmed by this burden. There can be no doubt that it will be a heavy one, even if it is glorious. But I can't imagine anyone disputing that this enterprise will be fruitful for the field of mathematics in Scandinavia. Just don't let the journal become *too* learned, at least not in the beginning. Historical overviews such as your own excellent submission for the professorial chair in Helsinki should not, in my opinion, be entirely ruled out. The price of the journal is so low (400 pages with an elegant layout for 10 kronor!) that if each reader finds at least something in each issue that he can understand without great difficulty, he should be quite content. Will you only be accepting academic papers, and no reviews? I doubt that such a principle would be entirely correct. Things are different in Germany, where there already are three or more mathematics journals, as well as special literature journals. It is unquestionably best if you can satisfy as many needs as possible, although I admit that you can easily end up without pleasing anyone. But I imagine you have more important things to do than to listen to my chatter. Farewell, dear colleague! If my best wishes could contribute to the success of your enterprise, it would have a great future.

Your loyal friend,
Knut Wicksell

No. 4. Postcard, 15 December 1882, from Wicksell in Uppsala to Mittag-Leffler in Djursholm. Wicksell assures Mittag-Leffler that the requested review is forthcoming.

No. 5. Letter, 19 December 1882, from Wicksell in Uppsala to Mittag-Leffler in Djursholm. (A passage from this letter is quoted in Gårdlund 1958, 70–71. I have kept the translation of that part of the text below.) Wicksell sends the promised review of *Acta Mathematica* and tells Mittag-Leffler he can use it as he sees fit. Wicksell apologizes for taking so long.

> [. . .]
> —In case you are interested in hearing about my modest person, I can mention that I have been fairly diligent in studying math this semester, and I hope to soon be ready for my exams, albeit with modest pretensions. I have long ago abandoned all illusions about my future as a man of science. It's not that I don't still enjoy the subject, but I think, as Lagrange is reputed to have said long ago, that the "mine is too deep." Anyone who wants to work it nowadays, with the slightest hope of success, must, like other miners, give up all intercourse with men above ground and well-nigh all participation in their occupations for the greater part of his life. For such a decision I lack both energy and, to be honest, sufficient interest in the matter. The worst of it is that I am opposed, either by nature or habit, to toil in any shape or form and, as you know, that is not usually a characteristic of the men who really achieve anything in the world.—But enough of that. As regards the review, I had earlier planned to accompany it with a little sketch of currently ongoing trends in mathematics, as I understand them, but for several reasons I have omitted that outline. Farewell dear colleague.
> K. Wicksell

A postscript praises Anne Charlotte Leffler's new novel, *Ur Lifvet* (From life).

No. 6. Postcard, 18 January 1883, from Wicksell in Uppsala to Mittag-Leffler in Stockholm. Wicksell has received a gift copy of *Acta* from Mittag-Leffler. He thanks him, but says he has already taken out a subscription on his own, and wonders if he could donate the extra copies to a library in Uppsala.

No. 7. Letter, 19 October 1885, from Wicksell in London to Mittag-Leffler in Djursholm. Wicksell has just arrived in London on what would be an eight-month visit to study classical and neoclassical economics for the first time. Complete text.

> Dear colleague Leffler,
> Following up on your gracious promise to take a look at my opus, I've sent a letter to T. Mall in Uppsala, asking him to make a copy of my dissertation. It will then be delivered to you through my friend Öhrvall in Stockholm.

There's no rush at all to finish reading it, since it's unlikely that anything can be done about this matter before spring.

I've only been here in London since Saturday but hope to soon learn my way around, since I have managed to meet some particularly friendly people who have been willing to help me in every way.

I would of course appreciate it if your sister could give me a recommendation to anyone whom she thinks it might be useful for me to meet. At present, I am only worried about how I will ever find time to get around to all the people I have decided to visit here. As you know London is *a very large city* [italics written in English in the original].

In friendship and gratitude
Knut Wicksell

No. 8. Postcard, 21 January 1891, from Wicksell in Stockholm to Mittag-Leffler in Djursholm.

No. 9. Letter, 22 September 1893, from Wicksell in Stockholm to Mittag-Leffler in Djursholm. Wicksell's first book, *Value, Capital and Rent*, had just been published. (With reference to Wicksell's request to be able to teach at the University of Stockholm, note that Mittag-Leffler had previously served two terms as president of the university, in 1885–86 and 1891–92, but did not have that post at the time of this letter.) Complete text.

Dear Mittag-Leffler,

When I came by your house to deliver a copy of my book, I had something else I wanted to discuss with you, which time did not allow. Let me therefore present it in writing.

As I think you well understand, the object of all my endeavors right now is to be able to devote myself to scientific activity in the field in which I have primarily been engaged for the past eight years. Thanks to the great kindness that you have of old shown me, I want to ask you to give me your frank assessment of whether I have any prospects in this respect, and in particular, with regard to the following two questions:

(1) Would it be possible for me to hold a series of lectures at the university [University of Stockholm] this spring? As far as I know, there are funds available (or they could be made available) for the subject of economics in addition to Johan Leffler's salary, and since the subject is included in the university curriculum, I would think that instruction in that area should be made as multifaceted and rich as possible. I would not require much money, but I cannot give lectures for free. My topic would be: "The modern theory of value with applications to the theory of capital interest and *finance theory*"—the latter problem, which has been treated by the German Sax and the Italians Ricca-Salerno, Mazzola, et al., is of major interest and to some extent highly topical for us right now.

(2) In the event my just-published book should be favorably received abroad, do you think that the Lorén Foundation would be willing to support me in the writing of a new work, which would deal mainly or exclusively with finance theory? I don't want to submit a formal application until I see how things go with my present book, but it would be good to know in advance what I can expect in this direction.

I would appreciate it if you would give me an answer to these questions as soon as possible. If all prospects are closed to me in the aforementioned areas, then it looks like I will have to leave Stockholm and try to find work as a newspaperman in a smaller town, and if that's the case then the sooner I get moving in that direction the better.

Hoping that you won't be offended by these lines, I remain your friend,

Knut Wicksell

Nos. 10, 11. Date unclear. From Wicksell in Stockholm to Mittag-Leffler in Djursholm. Wicksell encloses a copy of a letter in German to him from Eugen Böhm-Bawerk on his book, *Value, Capital and Rent*. Böhm-Bawerk calls Wicksell "ein echter Theoretiker." Accompanied by a little note to Mittag-Leffler written on a calling card.

No. 12. Letter, 29 August 1895, from Wicksell's wife in Djursholm to Mittag-Leffler in Djursholm, asking for advice on how much Wicksell should request from the Lorén Foundation for his next book.

No. 13. Letter, 6 May 1897, from Wicksell in Djursholm to Mittag-Leffler in Montreux about renting a house which Mittag-Leffler owns.

Nos. 14–16. Letters, 30 October 1898, 30 January 1899, 2 February 1899, from Wicksell in Uppsala to Mittag-Leffler in Djursholm asking Mittag-Leffler for help and advice on how to get an Academy of Science prize for the best published scientific work during the year.

Nos. 17, 18. Letters, 25 and 28 October 1899, from Wicksell in Uppsala to Mittag-Leffler in Djursholm. Wicksell is applying to the Lorén Foundation for a grant for several years to write a comprehensive economics textbook "on modern foundations." Another applicant is a G. Steffen. Wicksell thinks him quite capable, and if a choice has to be made between the two, Wicksell says, go ahead and give it to Steffen.

Nos. 19–21. Letters, 17 November, 15 December, and 21 December 1924, from Wicksell in Stocksund to Mittag-Leffler in Djursholm. Mittag-Leffler apparently wants Wicksell to return some old notes of Weierstrass's lectures that he had lent to him. Wicksell is now seventy-three years old, Mittag-Leffler seventy-eight; the handwriting is difficult to decipher. The notes in question must have been lent forty or fifty years earlier. Wicksell can't find them.

References

In addition to the sources listed below, this report is based on archival materials from the Institut Mittag-Leffler of the Swedish Royal Academy of Sciences in Djursholm, Sweden. The Institut provided me with photocopies of the twenty-three letters in their files of correspondence between Gösta Mittag-Leffler and Knut Wicksell. Excerpts from the letters are translated in appendix 1.

Other archival materials exist of which I am aware but which I could not use for this report: (1) The Knut Wicksell archives in Lund have the notebooks Wicksell kept during his London visit of 1885–86. (2) Uppsala University has a copy of Wicksell's *licentiat* dissertation and probably also other materials (e.g., transcripts) from his studies there. (3) Kungliga Biblioteket, the Royal Library of Stockholm, has material concerning Anne Charlotte Edgren-Leffler.

Cooke, Roger. 1984. *The Mathematics of Sonya Kovalevskaya*. New York: Springer.

Dauben, Joseph Warren. 1979. *Georg Cantor: His Mathematics and Philosophy of the Infinite*. Cambridge: Harvard University Press.

Domar, Yngve. 1982. On the Foundation of Acta Mathematica. *Acta Mathematica* 148:9–13.

Elfving, Gustav. 1981. *The History of Mathematics in Finland, 1828–1918*. Helsinki: Societas Scientiarum Fennica.

Gaddy, Clifford. 1990. A Note on the Links between the Mittag-Leffler Circle, Poincaré, and Lyapunov. Manuscript. February.

Gårdlund, Torsten. 1956. *Knut Wicksell: Rebell i net nya riket*. Stockholm: Bonniers.

———. 1958. *The Life of Knut Wicksell*. Translated by Nancy Adler. Stockholm: Almqvist & Wiksell.

Grattan Guiness, Ivor. 1971. Towards a Biography of Georg Cantor. *Annals of Science* 27:345–91.

Henry, C. 1987. Lyapunov Functions. In *The New Palgrave: A Dictionary of Economics*, edited by John Eatwell et al., 4:256–58. London: Macmillan.

Hölcke, Olov. 1948. Leffler, Johan Anders. In *Svenska män och kvinnor*, edited by Torsten Dahl, 4:505–6. Stockholm: Bonniers.

———. 1979. Leffler, Johan Anders. In *Svenskt biografiskt Lexikon*, edited by Erik Grill and Birgitta Lager-Kromnow, 22:428–31. Stockholm: Norstedts Tryckeri.

Koblitz, Ann Hibner. 1983. *A Convergence of Lives: Sofia Kovalevskaia: Scientist, Writer, Revolutionary*. Boston: Birkhaeuser.

———. 1984. Sofia Kovalevskaia and the Mathematical Community. *Mathematical Intelligencer* 6.1:20–29.

———. 1987. Sofia Vasilevna Kovalevskaia (1850–1891). In *Women of Mathe-*

matics: A Bibliographic Sourcebook, edited by Louise S. Grinstein and Paul J. Campbell. New York: Greenwood Press.

Lindahl, Erik. 1958. Introduction: Wicksell's Life and Work. In Wicksell 1958b.

Lindström, Gösta. 1979. Leffler, Anna Charlotta (Anne Charlotte) Gustava. In *Svenskt biografiskt Lexikon*, 22:434–39. Stockholm: Norstedts Tryckeri.

Manasse, Georg. 1949. Loren, Viktor Edvard. In *Svenska män och kvinnor*, edited by Torsten Dahl, 5:73. Stockholm: Bonniers.

Mirowski, Philip. 1984. Physics and the "Marginalist Revolution." *Cambridge Journal of Economics* 8:361–79.

———. 1986. Mathematical Formalism and Economic Explanation. In *The Reconstruction of Economic Theory*, edited by Philip Mirowski, 179–240. Boston: Kluwer.

———. 1989. *More Heat than Light: Economics as Social Physics, Physics as Nature's Economics.* Cambridge: Cambridge University Press. [Citations are abbreviated *MHL*.]

Uhr, Carl G. 1987. Wicksell, Johan Gustav Knut (1851–1926). In *The New Palgrave: A Dictionary of Economics*, edited by John Eatwell et al., 4:908–10. London: Macmillan.

Wicksell, Knut. 1925. Matematisk Nationalekonomi. *Economisk Tidskrift* 27.4–5:103–25.

———. 1934. *Lectures on Political Economy*. Vol. 1, *General Theory*. Translated from the Swedish by E. Classen. London: Routledge & Kegan Paul.

———. 1954. *Value, Capital and Rent*. Translated by S. H. Frowein. New York: Rinehart.

———. 1958a. Mathematical Economics. In Wicksell 1958b.

———. 1958b. *Selected Papers on Economic Theory*. Edited by Erik Lindahl. Cambridge: Harvard University Press.

What Was Abandoned Following the Cambridge Capital Controversies? Samuelson, Substance, Scarcity, and Value

Avi J. Cohen

> [T]he true nature of Samuelson's [surrogate production function] project . . . was to reconcile classical substance theories of value with the neoclassical field theory of production.
>
> [The Cambridge U.K. critics' unrecognized] mandate was to explore all of the ways in which a substance theory of value was inconsistent with a field theory of value.
>
> [The] suppressed conservation principle . . . is the Achilles heel of all neoclassical economic theory.
> —Mirowski, *More Heat than Light*

In his brilliant, wide-ranging, and revolutionary book Philip Mirowski makes numerous provocative claims. This paper examines two of his claims, referred to in the epigraphs above. The first is that a major determinant of the outcome of the Cambridge capital controversies was the conflict between two economic value theories, each appropriated from a different physics theory—the classical substance theory and the neoclassical field theory. In evaluating whether or not Mirowski's claim provides new insight into this exhaustively discussed episode in the history of economic thought, I focus (as does Mirowski) on Samuelson's surrogate production function, which was an attempt to integrate production into the neoclassical scarcity theory of value. The results of this focused examination may then be used to evaluate a second, much larger claim that is part of the "Mirowski thesis": Does the lack of a coherent conservation principle in the appropriation of mid-nineteenth-century physics by the neoclassical scarcity/field theory of value fatally flaw all neoclassical economic theory and justify its abandonment?

I argue that while Mirowski's first claim of physics-based insight into the Cambridge capital controversies is well substantiated, his second claim is greatly overstated. However, by distinguishing between value theory and price theory, I show that his insights into the Cambridge controversies do substantiate the existence of fatal flaws in neoclassical *value* theory, which has subsequently been abandoned.

Value Theory and Natural Explanation

The most general form of the Mirowski thesis is the claim that, for classical political economy and neoclassical economics, "the theory of value, *the very core of the explanatory structure,* has been dictated by the evolution of physical theory" (*MHL*, 396, emphasis added). In addition, the dominance of these two schools of economic thought during their respective historical periods "is due to their emulation of physical explanation and their resonance with the primal metaphors of body/motion/value." Before we can evaluate this thesis in the small or in the large, we must articulate the distinctive *explanatory role* of value theory in the discipline of economics. Although economists now use the terms "value theory" and "price theory" interchangeably, they are distinguishable.

Both classical and neoclassical economic theories use simultaneous equations models to determine relative prices (Walsh and Gram 1980). For a given output, classical "prices of production" depend on the technical conditions of production and the real wage. Neoclassical prices are the outcomes of the interdependent optimizing decisions of economic agents, assuming as given endowments, preferences, and the technology. Price theory stresses simultaneous determination and interdependence, and makes no unequivocal claims about how changes in underlying parameters will affect relative prices.

Value theory attempts to go beyond interdependence to identify a price-independent parameter which is the source of price. According to Meek (1977, 151), value theory involves "the postulation of some kind of (relatively) independent 'determining constant' from which one proceeds to the final conclusion by means of a simple one-directional *catena* of causes." Value theory recognizes simultaneous determination but attempts to expose an underlying or ultimate determinant of price. One-directional causal *catenae* make *unequivocal* claims about how changes in parameters cause changes in price. Following in the Meekian tradition, Mirowski views a theory of value as an attempt to identify an underlying determinant of price, to ground the explanation of price in something permanent, objective, and law-governed.

The two major value theories in the history of economic thought use either labor or utility as the ultimate determinant of price. For the classical labor theory of value, the relative price of a commodity reflects its difficulty of production, which is determined by its price-independent quantity of embodied labor. All increases (decreases) in relative price are ultimately caused by increases (decreases) in the quantity of embodied labor. For the neoclassical scarcity theory of value, the relative price of a commodity reflects its relative scarcity, which is determined by its utility and its quantity, both of which are price-independent. All increases (decreases) in relative price are ultimately caused by increases (decreases) in utility or scarcity.

Mirowski ties these simple one-directional *catenae* of causes to earlier physical theories: the labor theory of value to the substance theory of energy, and the scarcity theory to the field theory of "proto-energetics" physics.[1] As a result of these ties, the underlying determinants of economic and social phenomena become natural and physical. "The natural law of society [is] reduced to physical law in form and in content" (*MHL*, 158).

Mirowski (141) establishes these ties by defining a value theory in economics as the combined responses to three questions which combine Marx's value theory questions about the qualitative and quantitative equivalence of commodities with Emile Meyerson's (1962) principles of invariance and change:

1. What is it that renders commodities commensurable in a market system, hence justifying their value?
2. What are the conservation principles that formalize the responses to (1), permitting quantitative and causal analysis in a Meyersonian sense?
3. How are the conservation principles in (2) united with the larger

---

1. Mirowski (*MHL*, 63) defines proto-energetics as "physical theory that includes the law of the conservation of energy and the bulk of rational mechanics, but excludes the entropy concept and most post-1860 developments in physics." The exclusion of irreversible thermodynamic processes is important; in proto-energetics time is reversible, so that no physical laws are violated if the system runs backwards or forwards. This timelessness, where outcomes are independent of processes, is an important characteristic of neoclassical equilibrium theory which was shown to be violated in the Cambridge controversies. The role of irreversibility in the neoclassical field theory of value is discussed below.

metaphorical simplex of body/motion/value . . . , which provides the principles with their justification?

These questions provide a useful structure for describing the classical substance theory of value and the neoclassical field theory of value that came into conflict in the Cambridge capital controversies.

Classical Substance Theory of Value

According to classical substance theory of value, a commodity's value derives from the labor embodied in it. This value is created in production and resides in the commodity itself. Commodities are commensurable because they embody a homogeneous value substance. Differences in value reflect differences in the quantity of embodied value substance, which correspond to differences in the difficulty of production.

Value is created in production, destroyed in consumption, but conserved in exchange. This requires that the quantity of embodied value substance be price-independent. The conservation principle provides a structural stability to price and a guarantee that all trades (of inputs and outputs) are a zero-sum game, the exchange of equivalents.

The resonance with the body/motion/value simplex stems from the conception of value as embodied human labor (body) and a value substance like the Cartesian energy substance that accounts for motion. In effect, "the triumvirate of physical substance, physical production, and physical science summed up for the classical economist all that was objective and lawlike in the determinants of social behavior" (*MHL*, 286-87).

Neoclassical Field Theory of Value

For the neoclassical field theory of value, a commodity's value derives from the utility which consumers obtain from its consumption. Because a commodity derives its value from the field of consumer preferences in which it is located, value is located in the field, not in the commodity. Commodities are commensurable because they provide utility. The law of one price ensures that the same commodity provides the same (marginal) utility to every consumer. Differences in value reflect differences in utility (preferences in the field) or differences in scarcity (quantity of commodities in the field).

Value is conserved in production and increases through exchange, the opposite configuration from the classical substance theory. With the assumption of constant returns to scale, production is a zero-sum game where the value of inputs equals the value of outputs. This allows the theoretical isolation of increases in value through exchange alone.

The theory requires the conservation of total utility plus total expenditure.[2] This conservation principle implies reversibility for the activities of consumers and producers—outcomes must be independent of the processes that generate them. Trade must not alter either the consumer or the commodity, and utility and the measurement of endowments must both be price-independent. The principle also implies that there can be no endogenous changes in preferences and no divergence between the anticipation and realization of utility. The equivalent production conservation principle is the existence of a conservative technology field. Production must not alter either the available technology or the factors of production, and the technology *and* the measurement of factor inputs *must both be price-independent*. Prices persist over time only when endowments and preferences (and technology) are conserved. If endowments vary due to prior trades or due to production, prices have no temporal integrity.

The resonance with the body/motion/value simplex stems from the wholesale appropriation of the mathematical variational principles and the physics formalisms of energy and motion. "The neoclassical appropriation of nineteenth-century energetics hinged upon a comparison between mass points coming to rest in a space permeated by a field of force and commodities coming to rest in a configuration of fields of utility" (*MHL*, 280). Additional resonance comes from the fact that "both energy and utility were based on large-scale prohibitions of 'something for nothing': perpetual motion was banished in physics; natural scarcity was reified in economics" (218).

These two economic value theories, each appropriated from a physical theory of energy, were at the root of the conflict in the Cambridge capital controversies and are the object of reconciliation in Samuelson's surrogate production function.

---

2. This conservation principle is the source of the integrability problem discussed by Hands (1993, this volume).

Surrogate Production Function: Substance Theory of Production and Field Theory of Value in Conflict

What It Attempts

Samuelson's surrogate production function attempts two forms of reconciliation. First, it attempts to consistently integrate production and the pricing of factors of production into the scarcity/field theory of value. Second, it attempts to further a Marshallian combination of classical conceptions of production/substance/capital with neoclassical conceptions of exchange/field/utility. Let us examine each of these attempts in turn.

The early neoclassical presentations of the scarcity/field theory occur in pure exchange models. Preferences and resource endowments (commodities) are given exogenously, and prices reflect the utility and scarcity of commodities.[3] Malinvaud's pure exchange model (1985, ch. 5), which makes the strong assumption that all commodities are gross substitutes, is useful for illustrating the key propositions of the scarcity theory of value. (1) As a commodity becomes scarcer, its price increases. (2) If the utility of a commodity increases, its price increases. Although this value theory is most often referred to as the utility theory, the term "scarcity theory" is equally appropriate and provides a sharper focus on the production issues which were the subject of debate in the Cambridge controversies.

These two propositions are *value theory* propositions in that changes in price are explained causally by changes in underlying (price-independent) determinants.[4] The corresponding modern *price theory* proposi-

---

3. According to Walras (1954, 69): "Thus any value in exchange . . . partakes of the character of a natural phenomenon. . . . If [commodities] have *any value at all*, it is because they are scarce, that is, useful and limited in quantity—both of these conditions being natural."

4. These value theory propositions are a modern restatement of Walras's claims (1954, 148) about his pure exchange model: "Given two commodities in a market in a state of equilibrium, if, all other things being equal, the utility of one of these two commodities increases or decreases for one or more parties, the value of this commodity in relation to the value of the other commodity, i.e. its price, will increase or decrease. If, all other things being equal, the quantity of one of the two commodities in the hands of one or more holders increases or decreases, the price of this commodity will decrease or increase."

This passage from Walras (as well as that in note 3 above) makes it clear why I believe that Jolink (1993, this volume) is mistaken in claiming that Walras held a substance theory of

tions would be much weaker, stating only that in models with less restrictive assumptions, prices are *determined* by preferences and endowments (and technology in models with production). Price theory makes no (unequivocal) claims about unambiguously signed price effects of underlying parameter changes.

Samuelson's surrogate production function attempts to extend the *value theory* propositions of the pure exchange model to a model with capital and production. The legitimacy of this extension is not immediately obvious, since in what sense are commodities scarce if they can be produced?[5] The value theory propositions of price as a scarcity index can be sustained, however, as long as commodities are produced from exogenously given resources under conditions of constant returns to scale and diminishing marginal productivity. These conditions allow the scarcity theory to be extended to obtain a positive relation between relative factor scarcity and factor price. In particular, capital services are treated as a factor of production the price of which—the rate of interest—is determined by the relative scarcity of capital. With this extension, the distribution of income to factors of production becomes merely a subset of general price determination.[6]

The second attempt of Samuelson's surrogate production function is to advance the Marshallian combination of classical conceptions of production/substance/capital with neoclassical conceptions of exchange/field/utility. All classical production conceptions are substance-based.

---

value. Walras's allowance for a change in the value of a commodity caused by factors *external* to the commodity (changes in preferences—utility—or quantities), is the hallmark of a field theory of value. It is inconsistent with a substance theory, where the value substance must be *embedded in* the commodity and independent of external changes.

5. Mirowski (*MHL*, 293) raises the same issue, but in the context of the physics metaphor: "There is a good reason why the Marginalist Revolution made its first beachhead in the area of exchange rather than production. The metaphor of utility as potential energy was predicated upon a Weltanschauung of a closed, bounded system that exemplified the natural state of mankind as enduring ineluctable scarcity. If and when production was to be introduced into this morality play, it had to be done in such a way as to prevent the contravention of the scarcity principle, all the while maintaining the field theory of value. After all, in the Laplacian dream, can you really get something for nothing?"

6. Böhm-Bawerk (1959, 2:347) makes the earliest explicit statement of this principle: "The exchange . . . which constitutes the source of the phenomenon of interest, is merely one special case under the rubric of the exchange of goods in general. And so it follows as a matter of course that determination of price in this field cannot proceed under any laws other than those which govern determination of price in all economic exchange." And the general laws which determine price or exchange value stem from the fact that goods "are *useful* and . . . they are *scarce*" (1:91).

Production is the embodiment of the value substance and is therefore the locus of value creation. Similarly, in the production function, capital is a value-creating substance, creating a return for the use of productive capital services. The reconciliation of these conceptions with neoclassical conceptions of exchange/field/utility is obviously problematic. The conception of production as value-creating violates the field theory principle that value must be conserved in production. Production also alters the commodities in the preference field, violating the utility field theory principle that endowments must be conserved during exchange. Furthermore, production has the potential to affect factor prices, violating the technology field theory principle that factor inputs must be conserved during production.

Despite these problems, reconciliation was highly prized because it would mean (1) preserving and extending the explanatory structure of the scarcity theory of value to models with production and (2) preserving the appealing explanatory features of classical substance theory, rooting explanations of value in the physical productivity of the production technology. There was an apparent compatibility between the neoclassical field and classical substance theories of value in that both grounded their explanations of value in underlying determinants that were physical and natural, and exogenous to society: utility and technology. It is worthwhile exploring how and why Samuelson's reconciliation attempts succeed in the one-commodity case but fail in the more general heterogeneous commodity case.

The Successful One-Commodity
Surrogate Production Function

Samuelson's surrogate production function attempts to treat aggregate capital as a resource whose price is determined by its relative scarcity.[7] His one-commodity model (1962) has a well-behaved, constant returns-to-scale production function. In competitive equilibrium, the price of labor (the wage rate) is determined by the relative scarcity and marginal productivity of labor. The marginal product of labor, $\partial Y/\partial L$, is a ratio of two physical magnitudes that are independent of prices. Analogously, the price of capital services (the rate of interest) is determined by the relative scarcity and marginal productivity of aggregate capital.

---

7. This section and the next draw extensively on Cohen 1989.

Since capital and output are the same commodity, the marginal product of capital, $\partial Y/\partial K$, is a technological datum also measurable in strictly physical quantities. The explanations of the wage rate and the interest rate do not depend on prices. *Resources are physical substances measurable independently of distribution* that can explain distribution. Because the production function is well behaved, as a resource becomes scarcer, its price increases. There is a unique inverse relation between factor intensity and relative factor price. Even with production, (factor) prices in the one-commodity model (in the form of physical returns to factors of production) reflect relative scarcities (Pasinetti 1969, 519).

The key to Samuelson's success in integrating production into the scarcity theory of value is the *price invariance* of the one-commodity model, which allows all resources, including capital, to be defined in exogenously given physical quantities. In turn the rate of interest is determined by the physical marginal product of capital, depending solely on the technology and the scarcity of capital relative to consumption demand. All prices, including the price of capital services, reflect the relative scarcity of the exogenously given resources.

The reasons for the success are made much more apparent when described in terms of Mirowski's emphasis on conservation principles. First, the price invariance of the model ensures the conservation of the technology field. The quantity and measurement of the factors of production are conserved in production. Second, the assumption of constant returns to scale means that the value of inputs is equal to the value of outputs, so that value is conserved in production. This is a substance-like notion; the value of inputs is transferred exactly to the output. Production does not create value. Instead value emanates from the scarcity (relative to consumption demand) of the original factors of production. Diminishing returns and constant returns to scale guarantee the preservation of "natural" scarcity even with the existence of production.

Samuelson's one-commodity surrogate production function thus successfully reconciles (1) production and the pricing of factors of production with the scarcity/field theory of value and (2) classical conceptions of production/substance/capital with neoclassical conceptions of exchange/field/utility. It succeeds because it meets the requisite conservation principles for both theories of value. The invariance of the conservation principles allows Samuelson to sustain strong causal claims about change (in a Meyersonian sense), extending the key propositions of the scarcity theory of value from a pure exchange model to a model incorporating production. Those key propositions both articulate unambiguously signed price effects of changes in underlying parameters, and ground explanations of value in underlying, price-independent determinants that are physical and natural, and exogenous to society: utility and technology.

The Failed Heterogeneous Commodity Production Function

The results of the one-commodity model do not hold in heterogeneous commodity models. The unique inverse relation between capital intensity and the rate of interest as well as the key propositions of the scarcity theory of value are both violated by the possibilities of reswitching and capital reversing.

In aggregate models with truly heterogeneous commodities, the interest rate is no longer determined by a purely physically defined marginal product of capital. Changes in the relative scarcity of a capital good no longer affect just the technical productivity of capital but also the relative prices of consumption and capital goods. Once relative prices can vary, the marginal product of capital becomes ∂ value output / ∂ value capital. Scarcity, the technical productivity of capital, *and prices* now determine the interest rate. Distribution depends not only on independent physical magnitudes but also on prices which, in turn, depend on distribution.

It is this complication of price changes, resulting from the differing factor proportions underlying the production of heterogeneous commodities, that allows for reswitching and capital reversing. Reswitching violates the uniqueness of the relation between capital intensity and the rate of interest. The inverse nature of that relation is violated by capital reversing. With capital reversing, a "lower capital/labor ratio" is associated with a lower interest rate. In comparing two equilibrium positions it is as though capital services have a *lower* price in the position where capital is "more scarce." Malinvaud's proposition 1 of the scarcity theory of value is violated.

The reasons for the differences from the results of the one-commodity model are again made much more apparent when described in terms of Mirowski's emphasis on conservation principles. Because prices vary with changes in distribution in heterogeneous commodity models, the technology field is no longer conserved. With the integration of production into the model, the quantity and measurement of the factors of production are no longer conserved; the measurement and value of capital become price-dependent.[8]

Without the requisite conservation principles Samuelson *cannot* sustain the strong causal claims about change (in a Meyersonian sense) embedded in the key propositions of the scarcity theory of value. The explanations of value in terms of underlying, price-independent determinants that are physical and natural, and exogenous to society—utility and technology—no longer obtain.

What Was Abandoned?

Following the failure of Samuelson's surrogate production function, neoclassicals admitted the logical inconsistencies revealed by the Cambridge controversies and abandoned aggregate production function analysis.[9] This analysis, which contained classical substance theories of capital and production, was seen as expendable because it was not integral to the coherence of the fundamental neoclassical theoretical project. Disaggregated general equilibrium analysis, as the neoclassicals correctly claimed, remained logically consistent and unscathed by the controversies (Ferguson 1972, 164; Hahn 1982, 373).[10]

In Mirowski's terms the failed reconciliation of substance and field theories of value led to a retreat to a pure field theory of value in general equilibrium analysis. But within general equilibrium analysis, value theory claims about unambiguously signed relations between underlying parameter changes and prices are not sustainable, and these too were abandoned. Bliss (1975, 85) puts it clearly and baldly:

> Even people who have made no study of economic theory are familiar with the idea that when something is more plentiful its price will be lower, and introductory courses on economic theory reinforce this

---

8. The feedback effects of price changes on the value of capital are analogous to the income effects discussed by Hands (1993, this volume), where price changes have complicating feedback effects on the value of income (endowments), violating the requisite conservation of endowments.

9. This section draws on Cohen 1992.

10. In Mirowski's words (*MHL*, 341): "Samuelson's attempted reconciliation of the metaphor of technology as a field and a homogeneous capital substance was mathematically incoherent. Nevertheless, Cambridge, Massachusetts, quickly recovered from what their opponents felt was a coup de grace, because the classical substance theory of production was perceived to be expendable within the neoclassical scheme of things."

common presumption with various examples. However, there is no support from the theory of general equilibrium for the proposition that an input to production will be cheaper in an economy where more of it is available.

This is an abandonment of the scarcity theory of value. Samuelson's surrogate production function was an attempt to provide one-directional causal explanations in the value theory tradition. His attempt "to provide *some* rationalization for the validity of the simple J. B. Clark parables" (Samuelson 1962, 194), can be linked to Clark's straightforward causal explanations: "as capital increases, while other things remained unchanged, interest falls, and, as the labor force increases, if other things remain the same, wages fall" (1891, 312). Changes in relative factor prices are explained by corresponding changes in the underlying factor scarcities.[11] The demise of the scarcity theory of value in aggregate production function analysis prompted a neoclassical retreat to general equilibrium analysis, which has no logical problems. But the switch to general equilibrium, rather than saving the scarcity theory of value, abandoned it.

The significance of the vitiation of the scarcity theory of value has not been emphasized sufficiently. Given the general indeterminacy of comparative static results in general equilibrium analysis, aggregate production function analysis had provided the only economy-wide or macroeconomic context where the scarcity theory of value (it was thought) could be extended beyond pure exchange to encompass production and distribution. When this extension was shown to be impossible, the move to general equilibrium marked the final abandonment of the scarcity theory of value. The Cambridge controversies demonstrated that—outside of one-commodity models, which all sides recognize as too restrictive and where, in any case, the labor substance theory of value is equally valid—there is no general neoclassical model where the scarcity theory of value can explain the set of all relative prices, including factor prices. Neo-

---

11. All participants in the debate tried to be careful in their use of language and to make statements like "more capital *will be associated with* a lower rate of interest" rather than "an increase in capital will *cause* a fall in the rate of interest." Samuelson (1975, 45) writes "that when a mathematician says, 'y rises as x falls,' he is implying nothing about temporal sequences or anything different from 'when x is low, y is high.'" He uses this careful language not because of a lack of belief in causal explanations, but to avoid Joan Robinson's criticism about deducing causation from comparisons of equilibrium states. (See Cohen 1984 on the role of Robinson's methodological criticism in the Cambridge controversies.)

classical theory, as Hahn puts it (1981, 128), "is not committed to a relative scarcity theory of distribution."

Thus both aggregate production function and general equilibrium analyses fail to meet the criteria for a "useful" theory that Samuelson himself put forward, criteria that describe the purpose of *value theory* explanations:

> It is the task of comparative statics to show the determination of the equilibrium values of given variables (unknowns) under postulated conditions (functional relationships) with various data (parameters) being specified. Thus, in the simplest case of a partial-equilibrium market for a single commodity, the two independent relations of supply and demand, each drawn up with other prices and institutional data being taken as given, determine by their intersection the equilibrium quantities of the unknown price and quantity sold. If no more than this could be said, the economist would be truly vulnerable to the gibe that he is only a parrot taught to say "supply and demand." Simply to know that there are efficacious "laws" determining equilibrium tells us nothing of the character of these laws. In order for the analysis to be useful it must provide information concerning the way in which our equilibrium quantities will change as a result of changes in the parameters taken as independent data. (1947, 257)

With the causal claims abandoned, what remains of neoclassical distribution theory are, using Samuelson's terms, "parrot"-like specifications of simultaneous equation systems, and (correct) statements about how factor returns are *equal to* or *measured by* disaggregated marginal productivities (Blaug 1975, 7; Bliss 1975, 110; Hahn 1972, 2–4). Gone are the "useful" claims about unambiguously signed changes in the interest rate resulting from changes in the quantity of capital.

The value theory perspective that Mirowski emphasizes also provides insight into the fruitless interchanges during the Cambridge controversies about simultaneous equations.[12] Neoclassicals often complained that Cambridge U.K. economists did not understand that the equilibrium solution to a set of simultaneous equations does not entail causal relationships. Von Weizsäcker (quoted in Harcourt 1982, 249) provides a typical example:

---

12. This argument is taken largely from Harcourt (1982, 249–51). For an alternative argument using Schumpeter's concept of vision to distinguish between simultaneous equations and causal explanations in general equilibrium theories, see Cohen and Cohen 1983.

I really fear that Joan Robinson . . . has not really understood the basic principle of a system of simultaneously solvable equations and therefore worries about the derivation of the rate of interest from the capital stock, while the definition of the capital stock presumes the knowledge of the interest rate. Where does the puzzle come in all this if one has really understood what a system of interdependent variables is all about?

While this characterization of simultaneous equations is correct, it ignores the fact that the neoclassical parable was an attempt to go beyond simultaneous interdependence and provide one-directional causal explanations. When that attempt failed conclusively, neoclassicals retreated to a defense of simultaneous equations and general equilibrium. The Cambridge U.K. critics continued to press the causal point that had been at issue in the neoclassical parable, but the neoclassicals had sidestepped the point by abandoning the scarcity theory of value and retreating to *price theory* statements about interdependence and simultaneous equations.

What Remains of Neoclassical Theory?

The Cambridge capital controversies led to the neoclassical abandonment of substance theories of capital and value as well as scarcity-theory-of-value explanations of price. Causal claims about unambiguously signed price effects of changes in underlying parameters, like the propositions in Malinvaud's pure exchange model, were abandoned. But do these results substantiate Mirowski's second, larger claim that the lack of a coherent conservation principle in the appropriation of mid-nineteenth-century physics by the neoclassical scarcity/field theory of value fatally flaws all neoclassical economic theory and justifies its abandonment? This second claim can be substantiated only if neoclassical *value theory* and *all neoclassical economic theory* are isomorphic, and I would argue that they are not.

A limited version of Mirowski's second claim, however, can be substantiated: the lack of an economically coherent conservation principle vitiates neoclassical *value theory*. The missing conservation principle leaves the second of Mirowski's three questions on value theory unanswered and justifies the abandonment of neoclassical value theory. Without the invariance provided by a conservation principle, there can be no causal explanations of change which are the distinctive hallmark of value theory. The retreat from Samuelson's attempts at causal value theory explanations in the surrogate production function to disaggregated general equilibrium and temporary equilibrium analysis is a direct consequence of problems with conservation principles (*MHL*, 349). Subsequent dissatisfaction with the lack of results in these models has led to a further shift away from general equilibrium and toward more limited models and game-theoretic analysis. All of these developments can, I believe, be integrated into the Mirowski hypothesis, even though their treatment in *More Heat* is sketchy and needs elaboration regarding the physics metaphor connections.

But even with the value-theoretic shortcoming stemming from the lack of an economically coherent conservation principle, much remains of neoclassical economic theory. General and temporary equilibrium analysis are logically consistent and provide respectable and coherent *price theory* explanations. Other, partial equilibrium versions of neoclassical price theory, such as the Chicago approach, also remain intact and provide predictions that are consistent with empirical data.[13]

The persistence of price theory despite the abandonment of value theory is also consistent with Mirowski's argument, because he admits that even without an *economically* coherent conservation principle, neoclassical theory smuggles in a *mathematically* coherent conservation principle, usually in the guise of "convenient" assumptions for "mathematical tractability," such as the Antonelli or Slutsky conditions.[14] The mathematically coherent conservation principle allows for the mathematical determinacy of outcomes, but no causal economic analysis is possible because of the lack of an economically coherent conservation principle.

What also remains of neoclassical theory is the resonance with the metaphors of body/motion/value and the idea of natural law—an appeal to causal explanations in terms of underlying natural determinants

---

13. Hands (1993, this volume) also points to the Chicago tradition of pragmatic, partial equilibrium analysis, which, by focusing on compensated demand functions and ignoring income effects, sidesteps the conservation problems associated with the Walrasian general equilibrium approach. Schabas (1993, this volume) also sees the consistency with empirical data as a potential defense against Mirowski's claim of a fatal flaw in all neoclassical economics.

14. Hands (1993, this volume) points out that Mirowski's claim that these assumptions guarantee that prices form a conservative vector field is not quite right. The correct claim is that *compensated* prices (the inverse of the compensated demand functions) form a conservative vector field. Even with this correction, Hands still accepts a "slightly modified version" of Mirowski's thesis about the relationship between energy physics and neoclassical economics.

of economic phenomena. Mirowski makes this very point: "In both economics and physics, the three metaphors of body, motion, and value mutually reinforce the validity of conservation principles, even in the face of disconfirming evidence" (*MHL*, 8). The idea of utility maximization as human nature, independent of social organization, appeals to the metaphors of body and natural law. When the assumption of nonsatiation is coupled with finite resources, scarcity becomes an unavoidable natural condition and resonates with the impossibility of perpetual motion. Self-interest and competition also provide causal explanatory mechanisms that are genuine strengths of neoclassical economics—the inevitable exploitation of all unexploited opportunities for gain, and the competitive enforcement of objective outcomes.

Thus Mirowski's own arguments (*MHL*, 396) about the dominance of neoclassical theory due to its "emulation of physical explanation and . . . resonance with the primal metaphors of body/motion/value" tell us that the lack of an adequate conservation principle will not justify the abandonment of neoclassical theory. Thus his claim of a fatal flaw in neoclassical economics cannot be substantiated. His incisive analysis of the physics underpinnings of economic theories does, however, provide significant insight into the Cambridge capital controversies and the neoclassical abandonment of value theory. And his emphasis on conservation principles, causal analysis, and value theory serves as a welcome stimulus to focus on the crucial but inadequately addressed question of what constitutes an adequate explanation in economics as a social rather than natural science.[15]

References

Blaug, Mark. 1975. *The Cambridge Revolution: Success or Failure?* Rev. ed. London: Institute of Economic Affairs.
Bliss, Christopher J. 1975. *Capital Theory and the Distribution of Income*. Amsterdam: North-Holland.
Böhm-Bawerk, Eugen von. 1959. *Capital and Interest*. Vols. 1–3. Translated by George D. Huncke. South Holland, Ill.: Libertarian Press.

---

15. De Marchi (1993, this volume) addresses directly the question of what distinguishes a *social* theory of value from the natural theories of value (labor/substance and utility/field) which have dominated economics and rooted explanations in underlying (natural) determinants exogenous to society. See also Cohen 1989, 244–49.

Clark, John Bates. 1891. Distribution as Determined by a Law of Rent. *Quarterly Journal of Economics* 5:289–318.
Cohen, Avi J. 1984. The Methodological Resolution of the Cambridge Controversies. *Journal of Post-Keynesian Economics* 6:614–29.
———. 1989. Prices, Capital, and the One-Commodity Model in Neoclassical and Classical Theories. *HOPE* 21:231–51.
———. 1992. Samuelson and the 93% Scarcity Theory of Value. In *Festschrift in Honour of Luigi Pasinetti*, edited by M. Baranzini and G. Harcourt. London: Macmillan.
Cohen, Avi J., and Jon S. Cohen. 1983. Classical and Neoclassical Theories of General Equilibrium. *Australian Economic Papers* 22:180–200.
de Marchi, Neil. 1993. History through the Lens of "Social" Value Theory. [In this special issue of *HOPE*.]
Ferguson, Charles E. 1972. The Current State of Capital Theory: A Tale of Two Paradigms. *Southern Economic Journal* 39:160–76.
Hahn, Frank H. 1972. *The Share of Wages in the National Income*. London: Weidenfeld & Nicholson.
———. 1981. General Equilibrium Theory. In *The Crisis in Economic Theory*, edited by Daniel Bell and Irving Kristol, 123–38. New York: Basic Books.
———. 1982. The Neo-Ricardians. *Cambridge Journal of Economics* 6:353–74.
Hands, D. Wade. 1993. More Light on Integrability, Symmetry, and Utility as Potential Energy in Mirowski's Critical History. [In this special issue of *HOPE*.]
Harcourt, Geoffrey C. 1982. The Cambridge Controversies: Old Ways and New Horizons—or Dead End? In *The Social Science Imperialists*, edited by Prue Kerr, 239–78. London: Routledge & Kegan Paul.
Jolink, Albert. 1993. "Procrustean Beds and All That": The Irrelevance of Walras for a Mirowski Thesis. [In this special issue of *HOPE*.]
Malinvaud, Edmond. 1985. *Lectures on Microeconomic Theory*. Rev. ed. Amsterdam: North-Holland.
Meek, Ronald L. 1977. Value in the History of Economic Thought. In *Smith, Marx and After*, 149–64. London: Chapman & Hall.
Meyerson, Emile. 1962. *Identity and Reality*. New York: Dover.
Mirowski, Philip. 1989. *More Heat than Light: Economics as Social Physics, Physics as Nature's Economics*. Cambridge: Cambridge University Press. [Citations are abbreviated *MHL*.]
Pasinetti, Luigi. 1969. Switches of Technique and the "Rate of Return" in Capital Theory. *Economic Journal* 79:508–31.
Samuelson, Paul A. 1947. *Foundations of Economic Analysis*. Cambridge: Harvard University Press.
———. 1962. Parable and Realism in Capital Theory: The Surrogate Production Function. *Review of Economic Studies* 29:193–206.
———. 1975. Steady-State and Transient Relations: A Reply on Reswitching. *Quarterly Journal of Economics* 89:40–47.

Schabas, Margaret. 1993. What's So Wrong with Physics Envy? [In this special issue of *HOPE*.]

Walras, Léon. 1954. *Elements of Pure Economics*. Translated by William Jaffé. Homewood, Ill.: Richard D. Irwin.

Walsh, Vivian, and Harvey Gram. 1980. *Classical and Neoclassical Theories of General Equilibrium*. New York: Oxford University Press.

Part 4 Perspectives on Constructivist History

Modernism in Economics:
An Interpretation beyond Physics

Arjo Klamer

> The cultivated man of today is gradually turning away from natural things, and life is becoming more and more abstract.—Piet Mondrian, 1919
>
> Yes, 1932 was a great time to be born as an economist. The sleeping beauty of political economy was waiting for the enlivening kiss of new methods, new paradigms, new hired hands, and new problems.—Paul Samuelson, 1986

Economics is an odd discipline. For one, it looks odd. Just consider the most celebrated economic picture of all (figure 1). Anyone who has had a brush with academic economics will instantly recognize a demand/supply diagram; everybody else will be mystified. Colleagues in the humanities, for example, tend to be bewildered when told that in economics the picture is for real and could represent virtually any market—from the market for clams to the market for spouses. "Where are the people?" is the standard question. Economists can suppress the doubts of their students with a little arm-twisting ("it will be on the exam!"). Humanists are left with their disbelief.

And then the picture covers only the facade. Odder still is the sight of the intricate mathematics in the pages of academic journals, as well as the mechanistic models that the mathematics articulate. "That is not me," the businessman exclaims when confronted with his theoretical counterpart in those models—provided he cares to pay attention.

If the unrealism of modern economics strikes the uninitiated as odd, the unimpressive predictive record of economists and their passionate disagreements must seem an embarrassment. After all, those who don

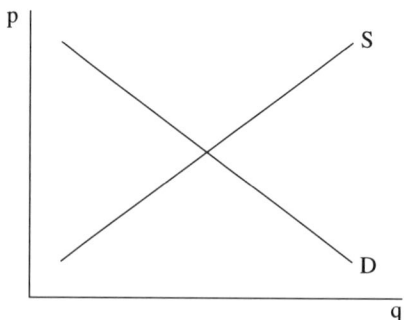

Figure 1

the mantle of science purport to have a grip on reality, including its future.

The oddities and the frustrated expectations demand a story. It has to be a story that accounts for the values and strategies that produce the abstract pictures and models and generate expectations that cannot be met. Preferably, it would also be a story, if not with a denouement, then with a sense of the direction in which the discipline of economics is heading.

Via Rhetoric and Physics to Modernism

One possible account for the oddness of economics is McCloskey's. In a barrage of articles and books this pioneer in cliometrics has pierced the scientistic justification of economists' diagrams and mathematical equations, exposing them as rhetorical devices (McCloskey 1987, 1990). In his rhetorical perspective economists are participants in a conversation or, to use a more topical term, a discursive practice (see Klamer 1984, 1988; Samuels 1990). To be credible, participants must employ the right rhetorical devices, which nowadays include diagrams and mathematical equations.

McCloskey's account, however, is more a characterization of economics than a story, and a limited characterization at that. It exposes the diagrams and models as metaphorical or analogical ways of reasoning,[1]

---

1. For the distinction between metaphors and analogies, as well as a categorization of types of metaphors as they function in economics, see Klamer and Leonard 1993.

but does not tell us how they came to dominate economic discourse or why they are persuasive. Furthermore, uncovering and identifying the metaphors and stories in economics is only a first step. The next step is more challenging: how to characterize the metaphors and stories. By alerting economists to their rhetoric McCloskey hopes for a change in their attitude, that is, for less sneering, less methodological arrogance, less scientism, and a willingness to rejoin the human conversation.[2] The question is then: Why are economists so unwilling to implement these perfectly sensible proposals? And why, for that matter, does the economics profession greet the rhetorical perspective with suspicion and irritation? (See Klamer 1988.) McCloskey's account does not tell.[3]

When historians of thought address the onset of mathematical rhetoric in economics, they habitually point to nineteenth-century figures such as Léon Walras, William Jevons, and Augustin Cournot. The suggestion is that economics gradually and naturally evolved into a mature science, and that means math with statistics. Yet that story of continuity gives more credit to the pioneers than they deserve and does not account for the sudden eruption of enthusiasm for abstract and mathematical reasoning in the 1930s.[4] It also does not explain why after World War II, for example, the center of gravity in economics shifted across the Atlantic Ocean from the United Kingdom to the United States. Finally, is it reasonable to expect that economics will continue to evolve and become ever more scientific, that is, more verifiable, more mathematical, more predictive, more realistic, more abstract . . . indeed, more what?

The most convincing story thus far is that told by Philip Mirowski in *More Heat than Light* (1989) and other publications. Superficially it is a story about the ghost of nineteenth-century physics in the machine of modern economics. In a deeper sense it is about the belief of economists that the Social is identical to, or isomorphic with, the Natural, and about the quest for the invariant deep structure in economic processes that such a belief inspires. His narrative exposes the foibles of neoclassical economics, glorifies the few economists who were not blinded by the desire

---

2. The latter plea is most explicit in the introduction to Klamer, McCloskey, and Solow 1988.
3. In McCloskey (forthcoming) and Klamer and McCloskey 1992, however, McCloskey appears to be willing to further the argument.
4. That the 1930s and 1940s were a revolutionary period in economics shows in the personal accounts of the then maturing economists. See, e.g., Breiter and Spencer 1986.

to imitate protoenergetics and hence were marginalized, and makes one long for an economics that is uniquely itself, and hence different from what it is now.

Mirowski's account is not unique: C. Y. Hsieh and M.-H. Ye have constructed a similar story in *Economics, Philosophy, and the Physics* (1991). When scholars come independently to the same story line, it apparently was waiting to be told. As good stories go, this one has several morals. One is that those neoclassicals are sneaky fellows. Another is that we need to know physics if we want to understand what happened to twentieth-century economics.

But although Mirowski, and Hsieh and Ye, have made the comparison with physics work well for economics, I do not think that we all have to flock to the physics and engineering libraries. Surely, doing so will enrich our historiography; the vein that these writers have struck is deep and asks for further exploration. But the story does not end there. I suggest the humanities library as a promising extension. By situating economics in its wider intellectual context we are able to relate another, more comprehensive story which accounts for the physics envy of modern economists, and for a great deal more. That story is, as I see it, the one that connects economics with "modernism," that is, the cultural moment that has characterized Western intellectual and artistic life during most of the twentieth century. (A list of characteristics of modernism appears near the end of this essay.)

A warning: what follows is not a causal story. The painter Piet Mondrian did not prompt Paul Samuelson to formalize economics. Samuelson's affinity for modernist art would bolster the story, but his dislike or indifference would not make a difference. Apart from, or, better, because of the virtual impossibility of sorting out intellectual influences— am I writing this story because I ran into an interesting artist some years ago, or did I run into the artist because I wanted to write this story?— the story is about discursive practices. Where individuals appear, they do so to motivate the characterization. The question is not why Samuelson did what he did, but why what he did could become an exemplar for mainstream economics. The answer involves more than the story of one person, or two, or three. Forget a heroics history for the time being. Discourse comes about; individuals are participants.

With the focus on discursive practice, this project follows the projects of Thomas Kuhn, Michel Foucault, Hayden White, and so many others, Mirowski included. The purpose is the characterization of the "constitutive" (see Klamer and Leonard 1993), "paradigmatic" (cf. Kuhn 1970), or "formative" or "epistemic" (cf. Foucault, and Amariglio 1988) elements that constrain but also facilitate discourse. The conceptualizing of distinctive discursive practices amounts to a rejection of stories that impart continuity and evolution to the history of economic thought. A story as I want to tell it makes sense only where differences and discontinuities matter. Accordingly it intends to highlight the distinctive characteristics of the discourse in, say, Oxbridge during the 1930s vis-à-vis the discourse in the American Cambridge during and immediately after World War II, or that discourse vis-à-vis classical discourse.

The following story is only a beginning. Intellectual and artistic life is multifaceted and immensely rich, too much so to do it justice in a few pages. This is also not the occasion to emulate Mirowski's assiduous grubbing in the past of economics. References to economics are for now limited because the main objective is the construction of the modernist story as such. Completeness is not the intent, nor is originality. Many others have been telling the story of modernism in greater depth and with more breadth than I will ever be able to do. (For the grand narratives see, for instance, Harvey 1989, Lyotard 1984, Jameson 1991, Toulmin 1990, Jencks 1986, Schorske 1981, Kern 1983, and Berman 1982.) This is a version by an economist for economists who are willing to read beyond their own domain, or that of physics and engineering.[5]

Narrating the "Naturalization" of Economics

The story of modern life usually begins with "a room heated by an enclosed stove," where René Descartes "had complete leisure to meditate on [his] own thoughts" (Descartes [1637] 1968, 32). There he sat, around the year 1619, pondering the intellectual baggage he had accumulated in his years at Jesuit schools. He decided to expunge any received knowledge of which he could not be sure. And now the whole world knows: the single piece of knowledge that was left after his exercise of destruction was *Cogito ergo sum*. He decided that its truth was "so cer-

---

5. There are other accounts of the connection between modernism and economics. See in particular Amariglio (1990), who stresses the role of uncertainty in economics. For quite different accounts see Dow 1990 and Ruccio 1991. Mirowski 1991 is more a presentation of his theory of social value than an account of (post)modernism in economics. Most interesting is Szostak (1992), who, as I do here, raids the world of arts in order to learn something about economics; the art on which he focuses, is, however, different.

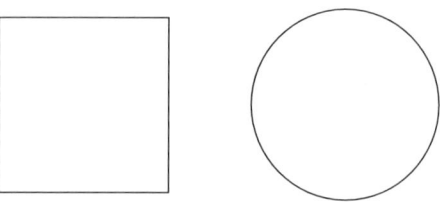

Figure 2 The Cartesian worldview

tain and so evident" that he "could accept it without scruple as the first principle of the philosophy I was seeking" (1968, 54).

The system that Descartes built upon his first principle never caught on, as it was quickly overtaken by Newton's ordering of the universe. But his idea to found knowledge on principles that are "certain and evident" did strike the imagination of his contemporaries. Timing also helped Descartes. Surrounded by the products of scientific and technological inventions, the intelligentsia of the time had to be receptive to the view that, given the possibility of certain knowledge, man could control nature (cf. Toulmin 1990). Or maybe they came to crave for certainty and control because of the political and spiritual turmoil at the time. Whatever, the Quest for Certainty, as John Dewey named it three centuries later, was on.

At the root of Cartesianism, as the epistemological legacy of Descartes came to be known, is the metaphorical representation of the world in twos: mind and body, the mental and the material, subject and object, thought and reality, value and fact, free will and necessity, the Social and the Natural, and so on. I offer the square and the circle as the constitutive metaphors for this way of viewing the world (figure 2; see also Klamer 1990). The square contains "square" elements such as the objective, the material, the body, fact, the Natural. The circle is the realm of the subjective, the mind, thought, value, the Social. Cartesianism tells us that we humans can probe, grasp, and control reality from within the square with logical analysis as our guide. Being square we are our rational self. Divorced from this rational self is the nonrational self with its emotions, prejudices, and morals. To find this self we are advised to move from the domain of the square into the circle. The square and the circle frame the story that follows.

The Enlightenment philosophes threw themselves into the square and, *pace* Newton, expected to unlock the secrets of nature by means of methodical analysis of the facts. The knowledge that they were looking for was the knowledge of universal laws which would order and rule the Natural. That knowledge was expected to be universal, unaffected by the personal and social circumstances of its progenitors. It furthermore would not be knowledge for knowledge's sake. Confronted with a world enveloped in religious wars, the Enlightenment philosophes sought for the means to overcome the differences among humans and control nature. Progress, unification, and civil liberty were their political objectives, which they expected to attain through education, clarification, and demystification.

If these aspirations seem similar to the aspirations that have come to define the twentieth-century mindset, an important difference looms when we shift our attention to the circle. In the view of the positivist twentieth-century mind the circle is drawn small. Economists, for example, ignore the subjective by assuming a structure of constant preferences; positivist epistemologists downplay the subjective as an inconvenient and potentially distracting presence. In the eighteenth-century mind, on the contrary, the circle is drawn large. In Cassirer's characterization, the eighteenth century "looks upon the affects not as a mere obstacle, but seeks to show that they are the original and indispensable impulse of all the operations of the mind. . . . Far from ruling the 'lower' faculties of the mind, reason is constantly dependent on their aid; without the cooperation of sensibility and the imagination reason cannot take a single step forward. . . . Voltaire says in his *Treatise on Metaphysics* that without the passions, without the desire for fame, without ambition and vanity, no progress of humanity, no refinement of taste and no improvement of the arts and sciences is thinkable" (Cassirer [1951] 1979, 106–7). Cassirer cites Voltaire's declaration that "the passions are the wheels which make all these machines go." Hume concurs, with his maxim that "Reason is, and ought to be, a slave of passions." Imagine a contemporary philosopher making such a statement![6]

The square was gradually expanded to include elements that first were identified as "circular" phenomena. Kant did the job for morality by in-

---

6. Michael Polanyi (1962) is the exception that proves the rule.

sisting that the road to moral life is paved by reason, not emotion as David Hume had argued at the time. Hugo Grotius, the Dutch legal scholar, had already hinted in 1625 at the possibility of capturing the Social in the square (see Toulmin 1990, 107), but it was not until late in the seventeenth century that the Social came to be conceived as a machinelike phenomenon, just as the Natural was, thus becoming the subject of systematic inquiry. The Social comprised the economy. Breaking away from moral thinking about commercial transactions—as, for example, Thomas Aquinas did in the thirteenth century with questions such as "whether a man may lawfully sell a thing for more than it is worth"— eighteenth-century philosophers, pamphleteers, physicians, and bankers were now able to conceive of the economy as a "thing," or an independent entity that could serve as a subject of study. Because the body and the machine had already been conceived as such, it made sense to study "the economy" in bodily and machinelike terms, that is, to conceptualize the Economic in analogy with the Natural. And that is what budding economists such as the French Physiocrats and Scottish moral philosophers did at the time.[7]

At this point the reader might want to pick up Mirowski's *More Heat than Light* and watch the plot thicken. For Mirowski tells us all about the play that the Natural got in the formative stages of modern economics, showing in particular how nineteenth-century conceptualizations of energy shaped the modern theory of (economic) value.

We now see, however, how Mirowski's narrative might be situated in a more comprehensive narrative. By starting the story with Descartes in his room—thinking the world from the foundations up, imagining the Natural as distinct from the Social, and conceiving the machine as the constitutive metaphor for the study of the Natural—and by tracing his line of thought through the eighteenth century, we come to acknowledge that eighteenth- and nineteenth-century economists were in step with the modern tradition when they sought to shape their subject after the image of the Natural. Sir William Petty (1623–87), Daniel Bernoulli (1700–1782), David Ricardo (1772–1823), Johann Heinrich von Thunen (1783–1850), Augustin Cournot (1801–77), Herman Heinrich Gossen (1810–58), William Stanley Jevons (1835–82), and Léon Walras (1834–1910) all proved themselves to be worthy disciples of the doctrines of

---

7. For an elaboration of the analogy with the body see Foucault (1973), and his interpreter for economics, Amariglio (1988).

Descartes, Newton, and the philosophes. They made (for their time) a modern move by suppressing the moral overtone of political economy in favor of the impersonal tone of the diagram, the statistic, and the mathematical equation. Their objectives appeared to be those of the Enlightenment philosophes: clarification, demystification, and improvement of (economic) reality.

The sketch provided here would profit from additional development and elaboration. But the point is made: economists picked up the Cartesian world view and fit their subject into the square of "scientific," "objective" analysis.

A Change around the Turn of the Century: A First Foray into Art

The narrative gets into trouble, however, when it has to negotiate the turn of the century. Mirowski's narrative takes this hurdle as if it did not exist; it moves continuously and smoothly from the last into the current century, telling us in great and lively detail how Irving Fisher continued to pursue the physics analogy. The twist in his narrative arrives with the ascendancy of Paul Samuelson and his alleged coverup of the physics metaphor. There is neither a *fin-de-siècle* episode in the story nor an account of the advent of modernism, the characteristically twentieth-century mode of representation.

My claim is this: there is something different about the twentieth century. Virginia Woolf may have been facetious when she observed, in 1924, that "in or about December, 1910, human character changed." But her sentiment resonated across the intellectual and artistic playing fields. In literature, her own field, the novels of Marcel Proust and James Joyce—and those of Woolf herself—signified the change. Instead of stories they presented explorations of the structure of human experience. Woolf's novels, for example, represented that experience as a "stream of consciousness."

The interdisciplinary rupture—or should it be interruption?—is most visible in the visual arts. It shows in the reconstruction of their history in modern museums of art. Take the National Gallery in Washington, D.C., as an example. The Gallery happens to consist of two buildings. The West Building houses the art up to 1910 or thereabouts; its architecture is, quite appropriately, classical, complete with a dome and pillars. The tour in the West Building starts with ancient art, moves along to the icons of the Renaissance, a display of the seventeenth-century Dutch masters, the baroque of the seventeenth century, the romantics of the nineteenth century, including some "indigenous" American art, and ends with the Impressionism of Renoir, Monet, and Seurat, and the Expressionism of van Gogh. Then the rupture—or is it interruption?—occurs.

In order to move from the nineteenth century to the twentieth century the visitor must follow an underground walkway to reach the East Building, where modern art is exhibited. The change is dramatic. First there is the change in space. In contrast to the heavy, imposing classical space of the West Building, the immense space of the East Building generates an airy, light feeling. No domes and pillars here. The architecture, which was designed by the modernist I. M. Pei, is taut, formal, and angular. A sense of movement is created by a colorful mobile by Alexander Calder and by the flow of people across the bridges that crisscross the space and along the escalator that appears to be carved into the wall.

If this change in space does not strike the senses of a casual visitor, the change in art will. I cannot imagine how it could not. Even a perfunctory glance will discern that the art in the twentieth-century gallery of the East Building is altogether unlike anything that the West Building exhibits. At the entrance the visitor is greeted by a huge canvas by Morris Louis that is mostly white except for a few bands of color flowing down at each side. Adjacent hangs a colorful collage by Robert Rauschenberg. The sight of these paintings must be perplexing to anyone who has the imprint of the nineteenth century art on his mind. The inevitable questions are "What the hell is this?" or "What does it mean?" These two paintings are like nothing seen before.

The same applies to Rauschenberg's immense black-and-white collage that follows, the color paintings by Mark Rothko, the wild lines of de Kooning, the flags and assemblages by Jasper Johns, the silkscreens by Andy Warhol, the jittery lines and monochromatic planes of Barnet Newman, the three-dimensional paintings—or are they constructions?—by Frank Stella, and the imposing scorched-earth paintings by the German artist Anselm Kiefer. Human figures are rare in the exhibition. The figures in Warhol's work, or in Lichtenstein's blowups of cartoons, are ironic commentaries and disallow the musings and fantasies that the figurative paintings of Auguste Renoir, Titian, and Rembrandt evoke. In Giacometti's sculptures the human form is so emaciated and elongated that it seems to "melt into air."

At any rate, the first impression holds up: with apologies to the art historians who work hard to expose the richness of forms, subjects, colorings, and symbols shared throughout all eras, we have to conclude that twentieth-century art is radically different from any art that preceded it.

The rupture also occurs in architecture. Once again the National Gallery of Art is exemplary, with its classical nineteenth-century West Building and modern twentieth-century East Building. The break away from classical architecture is reported to have begun at the end of the nineteenth century. In *fin-de-siècle* Vienna, for example, the utilitarian approach to urban design displaced Greek and Baroque architecture. Otto Wagner was the responsible architect. His designs were intended to meet the "demands of efficiency, economy, and the facilitation of the pursuit of business" (Schorske 1981, 73). (Wagner, incidentally, won out over Camillo Sitte, who had envisaged a city that would evoke the past with cozy squares and celebrations of artisanship.) A major impulse for modernist architecture came from the Bauhaus movement in the 1920s, with its call for a minimalist, rationalistic style of architecture that is free from historical and cultural references and therefore apt for applications at any place at any time. Walter Gropius, who headed this movement and would later move to the United States, advocated the mass production of modular dwellings. In the spirit of Descartes, the French architect Le Corbusier proposed to flatten an entire *quartier* in Paris in order to build a modern city from the ground up, all for the sake of efficiency, rationalization of design, and equalization in the quality of dwelling for all. The Austrian Mies van der Rohe perfected the sense of pure form in rigorous and sparse constructions such as the Seagram Building in New York City. "Less is more," he was reputed to have said, a credo that also characterized the early work of Philip Johnson and other proponents of the "International Style." Nowadays the products of this modern imagination are all around us. I happen to be writing in one; the building is functional, with rectangular offices and white walls and without any distracting decorations, quite unlike the Gothic buildings that decorate—or should one say burden?—the Ivy League campuses.

For further contrasts consider the transformation that occurred in the conceptualization of labor around the turn of the century. Anson Rabinbach tells in *The Human Motor* (1990) how the moral appreciation of labor in centuries preceding the current one—with Calvin proclaiming labor as the conduit for salvation, Locke claiming it as the source of value, and Marx viewing it as essential to human species—lost force and made way for a mechanical conception of labor, in which labor became an instrument or a machine to be managed and designed for optimal efficiency. The complexities of human labor in a commercial society were reduced to (and conflated with) a concept belonging to classical mechanics: work was assigned to the realm of the square. The familiar names in this story are Max Weber, who observed the trend towards rationalization and bureaucratization of the workplace; F. W. Taylor, who published *The Principles of Scientific Management* (1911); and Henry Ford, who realized a form of enlightened labor control that came to be known as Fordism. Rabinbach reminds us, however, that these were only the tip of the iceberg, for many more were engaged in shaping the science of work and exploring the human motor in order to change the way we work and think about work.

This story about the human motor, incidentally, alerts us to a problem with the earlier narrative. Descartes, after all, had already written in 1639 about humans as machines. What happened with the machine metaphor in the interim? The answer is, a great deal in the form of running commentaries; but the experience of rupture around 1900 suggests that other, competing metaphorical conceptions of the world imposed themselves on pre-1900 discourse. The story on the transformation in the concept of work, for example, points at the nineteenth-century custom of thinking in moral terms. To make the economic connection, the moral and philosophical dimensions were prominent in the practice of political economy. At American colleges the shaping of moral character was the central objective. The curriculum typically culminated with a course in political economy, which was often taught by the college president, who was typically a minister.

To set the nineteenth century further apart, the thinking of the time was preoccupied with history; ahistorical accounts of social phenomena would have seemed hopelessly incomplete. Yes, Cartesian threads are woven throughout its tapestry; like Descartes, Walras and Jevons created a structure without reference to historical context. The ahistorical mode, however, was only a minor form of discourse in their time, as the cold reception of their work should have made clear. This was, after all, the century that produced Georg Wilhelm Friedrich Hegel, Karl Marx, Jacob Burckhardt, Leopold von Ranke, Alexis de Toqueville, and Benedetto Croce. Henry Adams, in *The Education of Henry Adams* (1918), lets us know how intensely historical the nineteenth century mindset was; any event or social phenomenon had to be understood as the outcome of a historical process. Even Darwin's *Origin of Species* (1859) is consistent with this historical mode. Though Darwin's subject is Nature, presumably outside the domain of history, his theory of evolution implied that not only the Social but also the Natural can be understood historically, that is, in the context of change through time.

Historical thinking also dominated the practice of political economy. We do not need to zero in on Marx and the German Historical School to see that: flipping through the pages of economic publications of the time will suffice. Those pages are filled with history, description, theory, and philosophy, and not with the mathematical notations and diagrams of modern economic journals. Economic history and the history of economic thought, now marginal disciplines within the economics curriculum, constituted the core of nineteenth-century economics.

Other nineteenth-century anti-Cartesian forces are apparent in the antiscientism propogated by the Romantics, the advocacy of artisanship by William Morris and his fellow Pre-Raphaelites, and, of course, in Friedrich Nietzsche's proposal to creatively destroy everything that was sacred. Nietzsche in particular targeted with a vitriolic pen all square constructions, including truth, rationality, and Kantian ethics, and posited himself squarely in the circle with the assertion that the will to power is the beginning and end of all.

All this goes to show that somewhere around 1900, or 1910 in Virginia Woolf's opinion, the world changed as artists, intellectuals, and also economists turned away from history, morality, tradition, Nietzsche, and the classics to embrace the Cartesian world view and its Quest for Certainty. Modernism appeared as Cartesianism reincarnated. All intellectual attention was drawn to the square at the expense of the circle. Just think of the Vienna circle and its version of logical positivism, the *Principia Mathematica* of Bertrand Russell and Alfred N. Whitehead, cubism, the geometric art of Piet Mondrian, the square buildings of the Bauhaus and Mies, the rationalization of business management, and, in the 1930s, the foundational analysis of mathematical economics.

The case seems clear: modernism appears to be a rationalistic or scientistic movement that was preoccupied with the square and left the circle, or the realm of human sensibilities, to the humanities. This rift between the sciences and the humanities was what, in 1959, C. P. Snow observed and lamented.

The Fleeting and the Invariant

Although I made the case earlier (Klamer 1987a), I now find the characterization of modernism as Cartesianism reincarnated wanting. The simple reason is that too many individuals in the first part of the twentieth century take exception to the Quest for Certainty. In the arts first Dada and surrealism and, later, abstract expressionism questioned that quest; in philosophy Henri Bergson, Ludwig Wittgenstein, and John Dewey did the same; and if James Joyce and Marcel Proust sought certainty in modern experience they surely did so with unsettling prose. In economics the institutionalists, John Maynard Keynes, Frank Knight, and so many others appeared to defy the "squaring" of the discipline (see Amariglio 1990). With so much resistance toward square reasoning a rethinking seemed in order.

Other writers weaken the claim for a rupture around 1900, or 1910 as Virginia Woolf wanted. Berman (1982) and Harvey (1989) do as much by weaving into their stories of modernism strands that go back to 1848 or thereabouts. Harvey perceives in those unsettling years, with their great political upheavals, economic instability, and technological change, the origin of the confusion and uncertainty that brought about modernism. Berman finds support in Marx and Engels when they characterize this "bourgeois episode" as one in which "all fixed, fast frozen relationships with their train of ancient and venerable prejudices and opinions, are swept away, all new-formed ones become antiquated before they can ossify."[8] The beginning of the next sentence, "All that is solid melts into air," is also the title of his book.

Henry Adams attests to the general confusion of the time, even if his penchant for self-deprecation overstates his case. At the close of the nineteenth century he mused (in the third person) that "satisfied that the sequence of men led to nothing and that the sequence of their society could lead no further, while the mere sequence of time was artificial, and the sequence of thought was chaos, he turned at last to the sequence of force; and thus it happened that, after ten years' pursuit, he found himself lying in the Gallery of Machines at the Great Exposition of 1900, his historical neck broken by the sudden eruptions of forces totally new" (Adams [1918] 1946, 382). Adams is referring here to new technologies such as the dynamo, the automobile ("a nightmare at a hundred kilometers an hour"), and the x-ray. Kern (1983) colors in the dramatic changes that affected the perception of time and space during the period 1880–1918. The perception of space changed with the arrival of speedy transportation (locomotive, automobile) and communication (telegraph

---

8. From *Manifesto of the Communist Party* as reprinted in Tucker 1972, 476.

and telephone). And so did the sense of time. Train schedules proved to be very cumbersome as long as each locality had its own time. Standardization of time was called for. But not long after time was brought under control in good Cartesian fashion and standard time zones were established, Albert Einstein came with the message that time cannot be fixed.

All is relative; all is changing. That was the message that the world appeared to give to those who were alive around the turn of the century. The message accounts for the epistemological sensitivity in the modernist works of Proust, Joyce, Dada, the Surrealists, Knight, and Keynes. For if the world is changing, the question is how we can know it and represent it on paper or canvas. And that is an epistemological question.

Visualizing the Outlines of Modernism's Story: A Second Foray into Art

If this is true and the epistemological question motivates modernism, we have a problem with the Cartesian connection of twentieth-century scholarship and art. How, for example, to account for the self-assuredness with which economists were wont to discuss a changing economy in terms of simple diagrams, axioms, and mathematical equations? I am not prepared to give a full account. For clues I briefly refer to the story of modern(ist) art, not because art has necessarily influenced economists—for all I know, it has not—but because art displays visible signs of modernist values and beliefs.

The story of modernist art typically begins with the essays of the French poet Charles Beaudelaire. "For us the natural painter, like the natural poet, is almost a monster," we read in *The Salon of 1859*, a famous series of essays of his on painting. "The exclusive taste for the True (so noble a thing when it is limited to its proper applications) oppresses and stifles the taste of the Beautiful" (as quoted in Frascina and Harrison 1982, 19). The preoccupation with being true to the picture of Nature, Beaudelaire warns his contemporaries, might disarm the artist in face of the emergence of photography. In another essay he urges liberation from history and tradition: "If a painstaking, scrupulous, but feebly imaginative artist has to paint a courtesan of today and takes his 'inspiration' . . . from a courtesan by Titian or Raphael, it is only too likely that he will produce a work which is false, ambiguous and obscure" (in Frascina and Harrison 1982, 24). He condemned the then prominent painter Ingres for his attempt to "impose upon every type of sitter a more or less complete, by which I mean a more or less despotic, form of perfection, borrowed from the repertory of classical ideals" (24).

Beaudelaire foresaw a new sensibility, with openness to change and an eagerness to find the eternal amidst the change. "By 'modernity,' " he wrote in *The Painter of Modern Life* (first published in 1863), "I mean the ephemeral, the fugitive, the contingent, the half of art whose other half is the eternal and the immutable" (in Frascina and Harrison 1982, 23). Here is, in one line, the epistemological challenge that drives modernism: the representation of the ephemeral and fleeting in immutable forms. One of the first painters who met this epistemological challenge was Edouard Manet (not to be confused with Monet).

In museums Manet can usually be found among the Impressionists. Yet in real life he preceded them. To the modern eye his paintings present recognizable though somewhat curious pictures of real life. I, at least, had to have pointed out to me the deliberate crudeness and flatness of his painting to recognize that Manet was not just an early and relatively uninteresting Impressionist. Today few will bat an eye when confronted with Manet's crude and flat painting of somewhat odd situations, but during his own time it shocked most viewers, though it delighted someone like Emile Zola, the French writer. Manet fulfilled Beaudelaire's conception of the modern as he broke away from Nature. Zola captures the modern movement in the following passage:

> Feeling that he was making no progress by copying the masters, or by painting Nature as seen through the eyes of individuals who differed in character from himself, he came to understand, quite naturally, one fine day, that it only remained to him to see Nature as it really is, without looking at the works or studying the opinions of others. From the moment he conceived this idea, he took some object, person or thing, placed it at the end of his studio and began to reproduce it on his canvas in accordance with his own outlook and understanding. He made an effort to forget everything he had learned in museums; he tried to forget all the advice that he had been given and all the paintings that he had ever seen. All that remained was a singular, gifted intelligence in the presence of Nature, translating it in its own manner. . . . From then onwards Manet found his direction; or to put it better, he had found himself. He was seeing things with his own eyes, and in each of his canvases he was able to give us a translation of Nature in that

original language which he had just found in himself. (In Frascina and Harrison 1982, 30)

In this interpretation Manet made the typically Cartesian move: he tried to forget everything he had learned and began anew, relying on his own insight. In the process he turned away from his subject and became interested in what was happening on his canvas.

The Impressionists made a similar move. Inspired by Manet's example, they too struggled to liberate themselves from the old doctrines. They sought to represent their world as they saw it themselves. That did not mean, however, that they indulged in purely subjective art. The intent was scientific: the blurred outlines and the dots represented scientific explorations of human perception. Impressionists wanted to represent the world as we really and truly see it.

Painting entered a new stage with Paul Cezanne. If any one collection of works is an exemplar for a modernist painter, Cezanne's studies of still lifes and Mont Sainte-Victoire are it. His works showed budding artists, such as Pablo Picasso, Henri Matisse, and Piet Mondrian, that painting occurs *on the canvas*. Cezanne "read" into his subjects the forms that make a consistent painting. Like Manet and the impressionists he stepped away from his subject and focused on the forms and colors that appeared on his canvas, but unlike them he also stepped away from his own subjectivity. Cezanne experimented in a "discourse" that was disciplined and formal.[9] He intentionally distorted "reality" to compose with pastel colors and the (for him) elementary forms: cylinder, cone, and sphere. As a critic noted at the time of Cezanne's death in 1906, "he never reaches the conception of the circle, the triangle, the parallelogram: those are abstractions which his eye and brain refuse to admit. *Forms* are for him *volumes*" (Maurice Denis in Frascina and Harrison 1982, 57). Form, abstraction: Cezanne changed the terms of the discourse.

After Cezanne's formal still lifes and landscapes came Picasso's *Demoiselles d'Avignon*. It has been designated as the first truly modernist painting, the precursor to Cubism. Picasso completed the painting in 1907 but kept it from the public eye for two years. Its distorted, flat female figures with their masklike faces violated everything that one would expect from a good painting. Even the impressionists had re-

---

9. Painting is as much about discourse as is economics—only the medium is different.

spected the classical human figure and one-point perspective. Picasso threw all that up in the air. All perspective is gone. Instead of drawing the eye of the viewer into its depth, as a classical painting does, Picasso's *Demoiselles* leaves the eye wandering across its surface. All parts of the canvas appear to be equally important. And instead of giving aesthetic pleasure, as the impressionist paintings do, this painting asks for intellectual effort.

Here we see modernist art at work. Like Descartes back in the seventeenth century, it seeks to shock in order to defamiliarize the familiar and point to the possibility of liberation and a new beginning. *Les Demoiselles d'Avignon* demystifies the female figure as it was represented in the classical art of a Rubens or an Ingres, abstracts from any female figure in particular, and poses the epistemological problem of representing the invariant, the immutable, the eternal of that figure. Taking clues from African masks, Picasso wanted to explore the formal aspect of the female figure. The prostitutes who apparently were his models, were only the excuse; whatever really happens, happens in the painting itself.

As in *Demoiselles*, the subject of the Cubist paintings that followed is painting itself. The medium is the issue. The Cubist paintings of Picasso and Braque are studies in form. In contrast to Cezanne's paintings, which are constructions after nature, cubist paintings "deconstruct" nature; they decompose a guitar, a still life, or a head, and rearrange its forms to construct a painting. A Cubist painting is a measured and rigorous distortion of reality as it appears to us.

The rhetoric of Cubism resembles scientific rhetoric. Like the Pointillism of Pisarro and Seurat, Cubism is a disciplined method for the scientific representation of reality. But whereas Pisarro and Seurat still sought to represent reality as we see it, Picasso and Braque sought for reality beyond the appearances. Thus they confronted the epistemological problem to which natural scientists had called attention and which had inspired the theories of Karl Marx and Sigmund Freud, namely that the essential structures of reality elude the naked eye and ear. Like science, modernist art represented the desire to cope with the fleeting and contingent world of appearances by searching for the invariant and immutable. The dominant strategy of modern artists was to *abstract* from reality as it seems, and construct it anew—just as Descartes had done:

> Roughly speaking, the history of painting from Manet through synthetic cubism and Matisse may be characterized in terms of the gradual

withdrawal of painting from the task of representing reality—or of reality from the power of painting to represent it—in favour of an increasing preoccupation with problems intrinsic to painting itself. (Michael Fried, in Frascina and Harrison, 1982, 115)

The Characteristics of Modernism

There is no point in pretending to know what "modernism" is. Like "market," "democracy," and "capitalism," it is a contested concept with multiple meanings. Yet just as "market" is an indispensable concept to an economist who seeks to discern patterns in economic life, modernism is an indispensable concept for anyone who seeks to cope with the intellectual complexities of the early twentieth century. The story of painting gives a few clues as to the main characteristics of modernism. But remember, these are guesses that have to be tested in other stories, including the story of "modernist" economics.

The central problem of modernist art appears to be an epistemological one: how to represent a reality that is in constant flux. Manet showed the way by stepping away from his subject and turning toward his canvas. Like Descartes, the modernists sought to liberate themselves from all that they had learned and to create the world anew. Le Corbusier's proposal to raze a Parisian neighborhood to make room for his ideal city is typical. The bulldozer is the characteristically modern machine.

After the bulldozing, modernists construct. Their constructions, however, vary widely. Cubism presents only a minor but influential variant. Wassily Kandinsky painted colorful abstractions of cosmic themes. Piet Mondrian sought to express his spiritual experience in geometric paintings which reduced everything that exists to lines, planes, and primary colors. Kazimir Malevitch and his fellow Russian constructivists developed the so-called suprematist style which culminated in the proto-modernist painting, the black square. The American abstract expressionists sought to express themselves in color (Mark Rothko), by dripping paint on the canvas (Jack Pollock), or by painting wildly (Willem de Kooning). Dada showed how art was something to play with. By placing a urinal in a gallery Marcel Duchamp claimed that art could be anything. Surrealists did something similar by playing with reality on the canvas.

The modernist turn was inward. According to the art critic Clement Greenberg, "the essence of Modernism lies . . . in the use of the characteristic methods of a discipline to criticize the discipline itself—not in order to subvert it, but to entrench it more firmly in its area of competence" (1965, 193). The medium is the issue, as could be expected if the central problem is epistemological.

For all I know the early modernists had lofty motives. The story that they would tell if they had to tell a story about their activity—Lyotard (1984) calls such a story metanarrative—was the Enlightenment story of emancipation and liberation. Malevitch believed that his art would serve the Russian revolution in that it would enable the masses to shed tradition and embrace the new. Mondrian wanted to express a cosmic truth, and so did Kandinsky. Fernand Leger painted machinelike workers to express his expectation of progress by means of technological development. All these modernists were revolutionaries in that they hoped to transform social, political, and spiritual life by transforming the expressions of that life.

Modernism, however, is not singleminded. Much of the confusion about what modernism actually signifies probably arises in that modernism operates both in the square and in the circle. Mondrian appeared to look in the square for answers; his was a rigorous, formal approach. (He never forgave his friend Van Doesburg for painting tilted planes at a slanted angle, because in those angles he saw a violation of the "objective" right angles.) Pollock's approach, on the other hand, belongs in the circle because of its spontaneity—Mondrian would have called it subjectivity.

Let me suggest—for I cannot do more than that here—that this tension between the square and the circle has been enacted in society at large. The rationalization and professionalization of public life define modern life in the square; the psychologization of personal life constitutes modern life in the circle.

Let me close by listing eight major characteristics of modernism that our foray into the world of the arts has suggested:

1. *Problematization of representation.* Appearances deceive: reality is not what it seems to be. Reality is not as it presents itself. When appearances deceive, the representation of reality becomes a problem. (Cf. physics, Marx, Freud.)
2. *Exploration of the invariant structure of reality while recognizing its ephemeral appearance.* To highlight the problem of representation some modernists wanted to express the "transient, the fleeting, the

contingent." Others were intent on exploring and determining the fundamental, invariant structure that underlies the appearances.
3. *Predilection for formal, reductionistic and axiomatic representations.* For those looking for the invariant, logic, geometry, and mathematics were the preferred languages; the dominant heuristic prescribes the development of formal systems from a minimal set of axioms, of which at least some concern the characteristics of the most basic units of the system (particles, individual decision makers).
4. *The machine as a dominant constitutive metaphor.* The machine suggests the possibility of perfection and control, of predictability and a means to overcome uncertainty. As such it answers the ideal of a better life.
5. *A break with history.* Commitment to the new called for a liberation from tradition. The future, and not the past, should determine the present. (Cf. the avant garde, the shock of the new, the bulldozer.)
6. *A turn inward.* The medium becomes the issue. The significant audience comprises the initiated, the insiders, that is, colleagues and knowledgeable critics. Much of modernist work is self-referential and reflexive. One implication is the distinction between highbrow and lowbrow, that is, academic art (or economics) from popular art (or economics). Another implication is the professionalization of the arts and sciences, and the departmentalization of their instruction in universities.
7. *The square versus the circle.* Modernism operates both in the square and the circle. The square is the domain of the scientific, the circle of the therapeutic. The sharp distinction between the square and the circle in modernist consciousness accounts for a basic tension within modernism. It is responsible for the gulf that separates the humanities and the sciences in modern academia, as well as professional and personal life in general.
8. *Endorsement of the Enlightenment metanarrative.* Modernists seek to overcome historical and cultural barriers in their search for universal truth, peace, or a better world, or all three.

Conclusion

As yet the story of modernism has no ending. But events of the last twenty years have indicated that the moment of modernism is disintegrating. Modernism's metanarrative—the promise of a better world by means of separate explorations in the square and the circle—has become incredible. In the arts Warhol assaulted the academization of art, in the business world managers were confronted with the role of the nonrational, in the sciences the conclusion was reached not only that the epistemological problem was unsolvable but also that attempts made to solve it might ultimately destroy whatever is human. The square constructions of the modernists were perceived to be too far removed from subjective experience, causing a sense of emptiness, loss, and purposelessness.

As a consequence we are currently experiencing all around us rebellions against modernism. The world is in flux again, only now artists and scientists appear to have given up the hope that they can halt the flux in some representation or another.[10] Art has become art for art's sake. To know where this reaction will end, we have to wait and see.

Whether economics fits the story line remains to be seen. Elsewhere I have undertaken preliminary explorations with encouraging results (Klamer 1987a, 1987b). If the story applies, the oddness of academic economic discourse makes sense for the same reasons that account for the abstract paintings of Cubism, suprematism, and Mondrian. The problem was epistemological, namely, how to represent a world in flux; the response consisted of a move toward abstract, that is, nonfigurative or nonrealistic representation. Like the Impressionists, the suprematists, and Mondrian, economists sought to emulate the example of physics; only they went further out on the limb—much too far, according to Mirowski.

Regarding the differences between the discourse of Oxbridge in the 1930s and the American Cambridge in the 1950s, I suggest that they mimic the differences between, say, the Impressionists and the formalists. Keynes and his followers still wanted to draw the human figure in their scientific interpretations of the economy. That is why Keynes's *General Theory* is filled with references to psychological factors such as confidence, temperament, optimism, and animal spirits. Samuelson expunges the subjective in an attempt to fit his discourse within the square only. He is like Mondrian, who got upset with the slightest curve or

---

10. Among the numerous discussions of postmodernism, as the general rebellion against modernism is called, are Gablik 1984, Foster 1983, Harvey 1989, Toulmin 1990, Jencks 1986, Jameson 1991, and Connor 1989.

slanted angle simply because he considered those subjective. Because modern economics followed his example, and not that of Keynes, "Keynesian" economists might more appropriately be said to walk under the banner of Samuelsonian economics.

How, then, does this way of telling the story of economists play out? First consider the alternatives.

The Samuelsons, the Lucases, and the Blaugs among economists present a romantic scenario. They tell us how economists have overcome numerous barriers and succeeded in constructing ever more sophisticated and better models of the economy which provide ever more resolute answers to policy questions. If their narrative is critical it is because of portrayal of economic characters who are fainthearted and compromise on the naturalization and scientification of economics. With their story they tell us that they want to steam ahead.

Mirowski's narrative has the theme of overcoming as well, only now the Samuelsons, Lucases, and Blaugs are the barriers to overcome. It characterizes physics metaphors as a straitjacket instead of a liberating device as conventional wisdom has it, and flags the more and less blatant flaws in the modern economic framework. The apparent intent is to generate a desire for change—which Mirowski finds in a social theory of value with a mathematics that is not borrowed from physics.

Incidentally, either version accounts for the oddness of modern economics for noneconomists: namely, that the mathematical and diagrammatic representations of economic reality express the value that the economist study the economy by stepping away from it and reflecting whatever he observes in the mirror of nature. Only the appreciations of the oddness differ, with the Samuelsons justifying it and Mirowski advocating an alternative but still odd theoretical form.

A story about modernism in economics, however, will lead to a confrontation with its unraveling. Accordingly, after the disappearance of the human subject, economics will lose its metanarrative, if it has not already lost it. Notice, for example, the loss of faith in economic management and the increasing conviction that economics is ineffective when it comes to improving the rationality of economic behavior. Doubts also increase with respect to the theoretical project of representing a changing world in mathematical models. When models are made more realistic, equilibrium solutions are harder to find, so it seems. In short, the story promises change without telling what that change will be.

If I had to make a guess, I would say that economics will become more modest in its design. Economics will be designed less to control reality than to understand it. Respect for history will return, as well as the desire to bring back the human subject—precisely what we observe in contemporary art. The result will be a more interpretive economics, that is, an economics that will take the richness of economic life to heart with thick descriptions informed by clear theoretical concepts. So you see, there is an overcoming in this story, too.

Thanks to Tim Leonard for his comments.

References

Adams, Henry. [1918] 1946. *The Education of Henry Adams*. Boston: Houghton Mifflin.
Amariglio, Jack. 1988. The Body, Economic Discourse, and Power: An Economist's Introduction to Foucault. *HOPE* 20.4:583–613.
―――. 1990. Economics as Postmodern Discourse. In Samuels 1990.
Berman, Marshall. 1982. *All That Is Solid Melts into the Air*. New York: Simon & Schuster.
Breiter, William, and Roger W. Spencer. 1986. *Lives of the Laureates*. Cambridge: MIT Press.
Cassirer, Ernst. [1951] 1979. *The Philosophy of the Enlightenment*. Princeton: Princeton University Press.
Connor, Steven. 1989. *Postmodernist Culture*. Oxford: Basil Blackwell.
Descartes, René. [1637] 1968. *Discourse on Method and The Meditations*. London: Penguin Classics.
Dow, Sheila C., 1990. Is There Such a Thing as Postmodern Economics? Unpublished paper.
Foster, Hal, ed. 1983. *The Anti-Aesthetic: Essays on Postmodern Culture*. Port Townsend, Wash.: Bay Press.
Foucault, M. 1972. *The Archaeology of Knowledge*. New York: Harper & Row.
―――. 1973. *The Order of Things*. New York: Vintage Press.
Frascina, Francis, and Charles Harrison, eds. 1982. *Modern Art and Modernism*. New York: Harper & Row.
Gablik, Suzi. 1984. *Has Modernism Failed?* New York: Thames & Hudson.
Greenberg, Clement. 1965. Modernist Painting. *Art and Literature* 4:193–201.
Harrod, Roy. 1939. An Essay in Dynamic Theory. *Economic Journal* 49:14–33, 377.
Harvey, David. 1989. *The Condition of Postmodernity*. Oxford: Basil Blackwell.
Hsieh, C. Y., and Ming-Hua Ye. 1991. *Economics, Philosophy, and the Physics*. Armonk: M. E. Sharpe.
Jameson, Fredric. 1991. *Postmodernism, or, The Cultural Logic of Late Capitalism*. Durham, N.C.: Duke University Press.

Jencks, Charles. 1973. *Modern Movements in Architecture.* New York: Anchor Books.
———. 1986. *What Is Post-Modernism?* New York: St. Martin's Press.
Kern, Stephen. 1983. *The Culture of Time and Space, 1880–1918.* Cambridge: Cambridge University Press.
Klamer, Arjo. 1984. *Conversations with Economists.* Totowa, N.J.: Rowman & Allanheld.
———. 1987a. The Advent of Modernism in Economics. Unpublished manuscript.
———. 1987b. New Classical Economics: A Manifestation of Late-Modernism. Unpublished manuscript.
———. 1988. Economics as Discourse. In *The Popperian Legacy in Economics,* edited by Neil de Marchi. New York: Cambridge University Press.
———. 1990. Towards the Native Point of View. In *Economics and Hermeneutics,* edited by Donald Lavoie. London: Routledge & Kegan Paul.
Klamer, Arjo, and Thomas Leonard. 1993. So What's an Economic Metaphor? In *Natural Images in Economics,* edited by Philip Mirowski. New York: Cambridge University Press.
Klamer, Arjo, and Donald N. McCloskey. 1992. The Market as Conversation. Unpublished manuscript.
Klamer, Arjo, Donald N. McCloskey, and Robert M. Solow. 1988. *The Consequences of Economic Rhetoric.* New York: Cambridge University Press.
Kuhn, Thomas S. 1970. *The Structure of Scientific Revolutions.* 2d ed. Chicago: University of Chicago Press.
Lyotard, J. F. 1984. *The Postmodern Condition: A Report on Knowledge.* Minneapolis: University of Minnesota Press.
McCloskey, Donald N. 1985. *The Rhetoric of Economics.* Madison: University of Wisconsin Press.
———. 1990. *If You're So Smart: The Narrative of Economic Expertise.* Chicago: University of Chicago Press.
———. Forthcoming. *Knowledge and Persuasion in Economics.* New York: Cambridge University Press.
Mirowski, Philip. 1989. *More Heat than Light: Economics as Social Physics, Physics as Nature's Economics.* Cambridge: Cambridge University Press.
———. 1991. Postmodernism and the Social Theory of Value. *Journal of Post-Keynesian Economics* 13:565–82.
Polanyi, Michael. [1958] 1962. *Personal Knowledge: Towards a Post-Critical Philosophy.* Chicago: University of Chicago Press.
Rabinbach, Anson. 1990. *The Human Motor.* New York: Basic Books.
Ruccio, David. 1991. Postmodernism and Economics. *Journal of Post-Keynesian Economics* 13:511–24.
Samuels, Warren J., ed. 1990. *Economics as Discourse.* Boston: Kluwer Academic.
Schorske, Carl E. 1981. *Fin-de-siècle Vienna.* New York: Vintage Press.
Skidelski, Robert. 1983. *John Maynard Keynes.* Vol. 1. New York: Viking/Penguin.

Snow, C. P. [1959] 1964. *The Two Cultures and A Second Look*. Cambridge: Cambridge University Press.

Szostak, Rick. 1992. The History of Art and the Art in Economics. *History of Economics Review*, 70–107.

Toulmin, Stephen. 1990. *Cosmopolis: The Hidden Agenda of Modernity*. New York: The Free Press.

Tucker, Robert T., ed. 1972. *The Marx-Engels Reader*. New York: Norton.

White, Hayden. 1973. *Metahistory: The Historical Imagination in Nineteenth-Century Europe*. Baltimore: The Johns Hopkins University Press.

Zola, Emile. [1867] 1982. Edouard Manet. Reprinted in Frascina and Harrison.

Chalk and Cheese:
Mirowski Meets Douglas and Bloor

Robert J. Leonard

> After this experience [of working with neoclassical economists] I could never join the anthropologists who profess to despise economic analysis. For me, an abiding sense of the practise of a highly disciplined band of scholars, deeply concerned about methodology, is the most awe-inspiring outcome of the whole exercise.—Mary Douglas, *The World of Goods*

> [Neoclassical] economic research has always met with the greatest difficulties in establishing the credibility of its results and in fending off charges of charlatanism and quackery.—Philip Mirowski, *More Heat than Light*

The culmination of more than six years' work, Mirowski's *More Heat than Light* is a combination of historiography and polemic, deftly interwoven and forcefully delivered. In what can only be described, by admirers and detractors alike, as a tour de force, the author offers a radical revision of the "standard" history of economic ideas. Admirably abandoning the conventional historiography of economic thought, Mirowski claims to have uncovered the deterministic thread which has shaped all our theoretical conceptions of economic life till now. The inevitable factor, he claims, has been the prevailing conception of the natural world, as revealed through theories in physics. Any economic theory that has gained a significant degree of credibility or influence, he suggests, has done so only by replicating in its basic structure the physical theory that happened to be dominant at the time. So, for example, classical political economy with its labor theory of value is a reflection of the physical conception of energy as a "substance," and neoclassical economics owes its existence to its crude appropriation, in the form of utility, of the late nineteenth-century conception of energy as a "field." Moreover, because neoclassical theory retained this appropriated metaphor in order to retain utility maximization, it has remained inextricably bound to what has since become an outdated physics: therefore it too is outdated, a dead end in social inquiry. However, for Mirowski—and this is his overriding message—salvation lies not in updating economics through the appropriation of a more recent physical metaphor, but in relinquishing, once and for all, the link between the two domains of inquiry: having been made conscious of the hand that has invisibly guided them until now, economists have been liberated and can concentrate on the construction of a physics-free, and therefore better, economics.

As part of the justification of his thesis, Mirowski claims to owe a great intellectual debt to a small group of predecessors and contemporaries in anthropology and the sociology of knowledge: in particular, Emile Durkheim, Marcel Mauss, Bruno Latour, Mary Douglas, and David Bloor: "The importance of Bloor, Latour and Douglas for the theses of this book, as well as those of the philosophical anthropology of Emile Durkheim and Marcel Mauss, are so extensive that they require a separate screed" (*MHL*, 404 n. 1, ch. 2). However, Mirowski sees himself as transcending the boundaries within which they generally remain. Referring to the work of, among others, Latour, Harry Collins, and Bloor's colleagues Barry Barnes and Steven Shapin, he says: "Much of this literature has been inspirational for what follows; and yet, there is a sense in which the subsequent text aspires to go a bit further than these predecessors" (107). What he means by this is that having ostensibly been guided by them in his approach to the historiography of economic thought, he then goes further, turning that history into a criticism of neoclassical theory: history, suitably interpreted, becomes a logical and rhetorical weapon with which to condemn current practice.[1] But despite his claim that he owes much to these predecessors, Mirowski makes very few references to them in the text and, beyond the cursory asides quoted above, gives no significant description of how they contribute to his thesis.[2] My object here is to show that his claim to the tradition of

---

1. To Mirowski, therefore, McCloskey's analysis of the rhetoric of neoclassical economics has been a failure, insofar as its effect on the practices of the economics profession "has been nil" (1990a, 243).

2. *More Heat than Light* makes five references to Bloor, seven to Douglas. None of these discusses their work in detail, and neither Durkheim nor Mauss makes it into the index.

Durkheim, Mauss, Douglas, and Bloor is at best tenuous.[3] In the absence of any extended treatment by these authors of the history of economics, against which Mirowski's might be simply compared, our task is not an easy one: there is no "smoking gun," no conclusive "proof." However, on examining the salient work of Douglas and Bloor and comparing their sociological stance with that of Mirowski, we can see that the latter's interpretation is particularly strained and scarcely congruent with their collective framework.

What are the consequences of this assertion for what may safely be called the "Mirowski thesis"? The story in *More Heat than Light* does not "succeed" or "fail" based on its supposed linkage with a particular interpretative sociological tradition: the author will likely remain as attached to his thesis as beforehand; neoclassical theorists, even if they read it, will likely remain unmoved by the energy or cogency of his argument; and skeptics of neoclassical theory will still find attractive his innovative criticism of the mainstream monolith. However, by properly denying Mirowski this particular rhetorical support, we can help keep his story in perspective: that is, we can view it as a highly individualistic, energetically argued historical interpretation, which stands nonetheless in greater intellectual isolation than the author would have us believe.[4]

Section 1 offers a brief view of the sociology of knowledge associated with Mary Douglas and David Bloor. Although in different stages of their careers, each features in the work of the other, their approaches are complementary, and they both explicitly draw on the ideas of Durkheim and Wittgenstein. In short, one can speak of a Douglas-Bloor framework. Section 2 outlines, in much abbreviated form, the primary argument of *More Heat than Light*, illustrating in particular the metaphorical dialectic central to the thesis. How Mirowski's interpretation departs in crucial ways from the analytic approach of Douglas, Bloor, and their mentors is the subject of section 3. Not only does the latter group's philosophical stance lend little to the critique launched by Mirowski, but their attention to structure and contextual variety is suggestive of a much richer and

---

3. The work of Latour is not explicitly considered here. Our thesis is unaffected, however, as, for our purposes, his style is in keeping with that of both Douglas and Bloor. See Latour and Woolgar 1979 and Latour 1987.

4. This essay should not be interpreted as either a "knee-jerk" defense of neoclassical economics or as a slight on Mirowski's scholarship. My respect for the latter is great, but does not extend to letting him "get away with murder"!

many-faceted view of neoclassical practice. The conclusion puts it all in a nutshell.

1. The Douglas-Bloor Framework

Mary Douglas's work on the sociology of knowledge stems from her anthropological work with the Lele tribe in the Belgian Congo in the 1950s. There she noted that everyday social rules were directly related to unstated assumptions about how the universe operates: the tribe's social self-conception and their rules about what constituted proper behavior were both reflected in and supported by their views of the natural world. The two formed a circle of influence, the social determining their perception of the natural, which in turn reinforced the social. For example, as a fishlike tree dweller the pangolin, or scaly anteater, symbolized the union of heaven and earth, a union also evoked in the choice of tribal leaders. Thus the pangolin was seen as chieflike and was revered in a cult: this centered on a ritual eating of the pangolin by selected male initiates, which endowed them with secret knowledge. The full significance of this group cult could only be understood, therefore, with reference to Lele cosmology, and the latter reinforced that social practice (see Douglas 1975, inter alia). While this archaeology of the circular interaction of the social and the natural was later to become a hallmark of Douglas's approach, she also found herself speculating: "If we can understand how the inarticulate, implicit areas of Lele consciousness are constituted, we should be able to apply the lesson to ourselves. If they use appeals to the a priori in nature as weapons of coercion or as fences around communal property, it is probable that we do likewise" (1975, xi).

Douglas relates the development of her thought to the earlier work of Durkheim and Mauss. In his *Rules of Sociological Method* (1895), Durkheim reflected on the generation of beliefs in traditional societies, that is, societies not dependent on the exchange of goods and services. There, he claimed, similarity of beliefs results from individuals' internalizing and sacralizing the social order. The sacred was both dangerous, inspiring awe, and endangered, requiring vigilance on the part of society. The ideas were developed further in an essay with Marcel Mauss in 1903: "What had already been a long-term conviction (that true solidarity is based on shared classifications), started to become a method. . . . Durkheim and Mauss proposed to analyze the extent to which the mundane classifications we use are projections of the social structure partaking in the area of sacredness" (Douglas 1986, 97). Again, in 1912, Durkheim's *Elementary Forms of Religious Life* located the entrenchment of individual belief in commitment to the social group: a priori commitment to beliefs is something which is transmitted socially and not the result of personal, detached reflection. Needless to say, this view evoked strong objections; Durkheim was branded a rationalist for downgrading the individual and a conservative for his apparent reification of "society" (see Douglas 1986, 10). Durkheim, however, did not in fact push his suggested program to the logical limit and apply it to knowledge creation in modern industrial society, a feature about which Douglas speculates. Beyond being deterred by the broader philosophical opposition just mentioned, Durkheim, she suggests, really believed primitive societies to be different from our own: they were homogeneous and their simple worldly existences lent tremendous scope to the organizing function of the mind. We, on the other hand, became possessed of objective scientific knowledge, knowledge of an entirely different kind, and Durkheim balked at the idea of subjecting this to the type of analysis he proposed for primitives. In this respect, she regards him as having shown excessive anthropological restraint, and her work may be seen as bridging this chasm that blocked Durkheim: "To me . . . the details of tribal organisation do not seem intrinsically more tedious than those of the history of medicine" (Douglas 1986, 43).

So, moving from the study of tribal behavior in the Congo, Douglas has steadily applied this method to belief systems and conventions in all types of society, industrial and nonindustrial. Knowledge is treated like any other convention: as something which springs from a particular social configuration and, in turn, serves as a reaffirmation of that social pattern. As an organizing principle by which to explore the cultural and cosmological characteristics of diverse social groupings, Douglas has devised grid-group analysis, a scheme which organizes the conceivably infinite array of social arrangements into a few types.[5] On the horizontal axis, we place the "group" characteristic: the extent to which the social activity in question (be it that of a tribe, a committee, a church, or an academic discipline) has group solidarity. Social activities which are low on this scale lack the cohesion and group differentiation attached to those

---

5. This first appeared in *Natural Symbols* (1970), was refined in *Cultural Bias* (1978), and formed the basis for an edited volume, *Essays in the Sociology of Perception* (1982), discussed below.

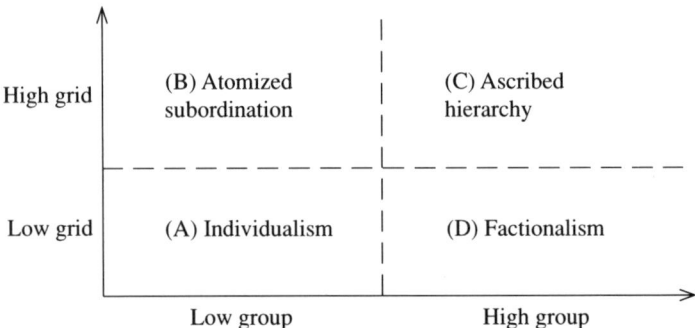

Figure 1
Source: Douglas 1982a, 4.

further along the continuum. The further along this axis one moves, the less likely the group is to disintegrate, the more sharply the group boundary is drawn. The vertical axis features the "grid" variable: this reflects the degree to which the individual, in interaction with others, is subject to a system of rules. At the low end, the rules governing interaction between individuals are minimal, and intercourse is relatively unconstrained. As one moves up the grid spectrum, rules and social hierarchies constrain relational possibilities: faculty and janitorial staff do not dine together; economic theorists steer clear of history conferences. The two axes together form a quadrant on which social activities may be arrayed, producing four broad types of social context (see figure 1).

Douglas's strong claim is that these four types are permanently present, "inexorably drawing individuals into their ambit, delivering to their recruits the choice of thinking alike or suffering the penalties of failure and ostracism" (1982a, 4). Having created this crude typology, one may ask how it can shed light on particular forms of social organization, beyond simply slotting them into one of the above fields. Douglas uses this scheme as a point at which to enter the circle of influence which runs from the social (how the group works, functions or organizes itself) to the natural or cosmological (how the group sees its natural environment or universe). The social context, as determined by the activity's position in the grid-group array, will constrain the belief systems and values used to make sense of the environment, and the cosmology thus constructed echoes back to reinforce the social organization as it is constituted. The influence is entirely simultaneous and circular: as a structural anthropologist, Douglas is concerned to reveal these binding links, rather than engage in deterministic explanation.[6]

Douglas deftly "predicts" how each of the four types will deal with such concepts as nature, time, human nature, and social behavior. The attitude to death, for example, as part of human nature, will be an important part of each type's cosmology. In low group, death has little social place, will be rarely discussed, and should ideally happen quickly, drawing as little attention as possible. With strong group definition, however, death is hugely important, receiving prolonged social attention, and funerals are significant social affairs. The weaker the grid, the more private is one's passage from this world, but the freedom with which one can choose to have an abortion, commit suicide, or sanction euthanasia will diminish with increased group strength (1982a, 183–254). Douglas's applications of this method of social archaeology have been confined to anthropological explorations of particular social groups. She has not explored the place of different modes of academic inquiry in the cosmology of such societies. However, in *The World of Goods* (Douglas and Isherwood 1979), she confronts at length the practice of neoclassical economists in their work on consumption behavior. Her interest is to embellish the strictly economic interpretation of consumption by recognizing the anthropological significance of goods as a form of communication in society. This is not the place to comment on the economic anthropology she constructs in that work. However, it should be noted that she comes away with a distinctly favorable impression of neoclassical practice—as the epigraph at the beginning of this paper will indicate.

In a laudatory review of Douglas's *Implicit Meanings* (1975) Barry Barnes and Steven Shapin offer four distinct, but not mutually exclusive, variants of her main thesis, all of which are worth quoting:

1. Knowledge is to be distinguished from belief by its acceptance as convention. There is no logical necessity, no "logic of justification." Communal authority sustains knowledge; justifications of knowledge can be justifications only because and so long as that communal authority exists: justifications are institutions. Here

---

6. Structuralist approaches are criticized by determinists, such as Marxists, for their lack of a predictable dynamic, that is, their inability to account for change.

Douglas follows Wittgenstein and her original inspiration, Durkheim.

2. Knowledge is constitutively practical. It is never generated solely by the contemplation of the world from some disembodied external vantage point. It is generated in the course of activity, in the "hurly-burly of political life"—"the known cosmos is constructed for helping arguments of a practical kind" [Douglas, xix].
3. The structure of social relationships between men in a society may be reflected as homologies and isomorphisms in systems of natural classification. Our sense of sameness and difference in nature is not fixed and may be mediated by the social structure. In particular, "fundamental" distinctions and "logical" divisions of natural kinds are generally conventional distinctions of particular social significance.
4. Knowledge, at every level from its general structure and organization to its detailed content, is liable to be generated with a view to the legitimation of institutions and social relationships. It is not simply that knowledge may be used in this way, but that an interest in this kind of use perpetually bears upon the processes whereby knowledge is produced. Knowledge emerges out of the consciousness of men who collectively are always concerned with problems of social order and control; that concern influences the production, transmission, and acceptance of knowledge of all sorts, in all societies. (Barnes and Shapin, 1977, 64)

What emerges from Douglas, therefore, is a variegated web of ideas on knowledge creation, all anchored by the underlying premise that it is socially constituted. That these themes find a favorable audience in Barnes and Shapin will come as no surprise to anybody familiar with their work, for they, along with David Bloor, form the core of what has become known as the "strong programme in the sociology of science" (SPSS). This perspective, most cogently synthesized in Bloor's manifesto, *Knowledge and Social Imagery* (1976), is very similar to that of Douglas. In the strong view, the function of the sociology of science is to search for laws and theories which explain what comes to be construed or held as knowledge. Knowledge is not defined as true belief, but as "whatever men take to be knowledge . . . those [collectively endorsed] beliefs which men confidently hold to and live by" (1976, 3). Here the strongest challenge to the progressivist vision of science is offered, and our attachment to traditional Cartesian logic is revealed as merely that: an attachment. Bloor uses Evans-Pritchard's *Witchcraft, Oracles and Magic among the Azande* (1937) to demonstrate the possibility of alternative systems of logic: thought worlds which are perfectly coherent, yet utterly different from that which we are accustomed to inhabiting.

In a later book, *Wittgenstein: A Social Theory of Knowledge* (1983), Bloor develops the link between the strong program and Wittgenstein's (post-*Tractatus*) views on language, particularly as expressed in *The Blue and Brown Books* (1933–35) and *Remarks on the Foundations of Mathematics* (1964). According to Bloor, Wittgenstein rebels against the notion of *finitism*, the idea that the meaning of words determines their usage. The opposite, he argues, is the case: usage determines meaning, and both are continually changing: "the established meaning of a word does not determine its future applications" (1983, 25). Similarly, he claims, Wittgenstein rejects *psychologism* and its attendant claim that outward expressions (thoughts, feelings, etc.) are the results of inward events: "The mental experiences which accompany the use of a sign undoubtedly are caused by the usage of the sign in a particular system of language" (19). The reason why, in practice, we accord so much significance to individual mental acts is that by some mysterious process of condensation our shared practices become concentrated in those acts. Thus, for example, the mental acts of pointing and naming reflect a condensation of the shared practices associated with these acts: naming becomes a "sacramental act," a "magic relation" (20). Bloor suggests that this style of thinking is essentially Durkheimian: just as the sacred is a symbol of the power of society over the individual, so "the real source of 'life' in a word or sentence is provided, not by the individual mind, but by society" (20).

From this conception of language as a fluid, social phenomenon stems the Wittgensteinian notion of a "language game." Shared social conventions, practices, and theories are simply manipulations of language: provisional agreements on what they mean for the collectivity. On the question of how such language games change, Wittgenstein was rather unclear: he spoke vaguely of "needs" giving rise to choice of one "grammar" versus another but never suggested what such needs might be or how they should arise. Bloor sees the strong program in sociology of science as an exploration of these "needs": they are social interests. Questions must be asked, he says, about how language games, or changes in them, serve particular institutions and parties. Without this, "the social dimension of the theory appears to be arbitrarily truncated" (49). A concrete link between Douglas and Bloor is forged in the latter's contribution to Douglas's edited volume *Essays in the Sociology of Perception* (1982b). Taking Lakatos's (1976) historical reconstruction of the debates on the Euler Theorem, Bloor uses grid-group analysis to organize the stances adopted by various mathematicians in dealing with mathematical anomalies. Just as the method is useful in uncovering how particular societies cope with anomalies in the classifications with which they make sense of their physical and spiritual worlds, so is it useful, Bloor claims, in discussing the practice of mathematicians, even though mathematics is commonly held to be somehow beyond social influence and, hence, sociological analysis. Bloor shows how particular parties to the debate can be placed in parts of Douglas's grid-group scheme. Thus (see figure 1 above) those who allow the coexistence of theorem and counterexample correspond to section B; those who engage in what Lakatos terms "monster-barring," where group restraints are more rigid, are associated with section D. He then relates these different theoretical responses to changes in the social conditions of the theorists in question.[7] His clear overview of what constitutes good sociology of science is particularly pertinent for our discussion of Mirowski:

> The final form in which a language-game is actually played can only be understood if one knows all of the factors that underlie each move. If we just look at the technical problems confronting a thinker we will not understand why this rather than that is counted as a solution. If we just look at the social circumstances (conceived in a broad and superficial way), we will not discern their connections with the rest of thought. *If we filter out certain patterns of relevance, and pick out only some of the contingencies that impinge on a particular piece of discourse or concept application, we will have failed in our descriptive enterprise. We will be lapsing into over-simplified models of language that it was Wittgenstein's aim to refute.*[8] (Bloor 1983, 111, emphasis added)

---

7. Douglas remarks: "This essay is admittedly tentative, but it is extremely suggestive for directions in which this kind of analysis can be tried" (1982b, 118).
8. The suggestion that one can know "all of the factors that underlie each move" is hardly to be taken literally. Bloor's remarks certainly suggest, however, that he would regard the attempt to explain the development of the language game of neoclassical economics in terms of a turn taken by physics a century ago as an "over-simplified [model] of language."

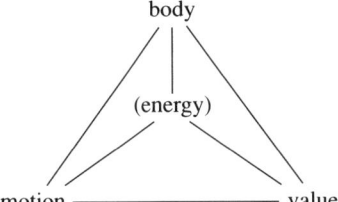

Figure 2

2. Mirowski Reviewed

Mirowski sets the stage for his account of the evolution of economic thought by positing what he calls a metaphoric triad (figure 2). This represents the way the uses of metaphor in various domains resound with their use in other spheres, the net effect being a certain coherence in the way the world is perceived at any given time. Joining up the three vertices of the outer triangle, we have three faces which represent the pairwise interaction of our biological (body), economic (value), and physical (motion) worldviews. The energy concept is something which is not present at the outset but appears later, adding a fourth vertex which binds the other three further together and forming a metaphoric pyramid of the whole. Borrowing a classification from Kula (1986), Mirowski represents the evolution of this metaphoric triad as one of expansion and consolidation in three stages: anthropometric, lineamentric, and syndetic. In the first of these, man is the "measure of all things" and the three vertices have not yet separated. In the lineamentric phase, we witness a "gradual estrangement" of the three metaphors and the emergence of three distinct systems of explanation. Finally, in the syndetic stage, the energy metaphor appears, linking the other three together. This fourth metaphor finds its reflection in the body as the gene, in motion as energy (*sic*), and in value as money abstracted from any commodity. The component systems of explanation "operate in the same cultural milieu, partake of much the same language and formalisms and most important, maintain a reciprocal metaphorical legitimation and support: they remain a pyramid" (*MHL*, 108). We have at the outset, therefore, a system that recognizes, in principle, the interconnectedness of things, the way that our conceptions of the social (value/economics) are both determined by and reflected in our prevailing views of the natural (motion/physics and body/biology).

Figure 3 links the key phases in economics and physics with the evolution of this triad. The anthropometric phase of the triad's evolution is appropriate for discussion of economic questions prior to the appearance of mercantilism. Here the three metaphors are bound up together, the conceptions of the body, motion, and value are entirely intertwined. Thus in the time of the ancients, Mirowski explains obliquely, "trade . . . represents Aristotelian motion, the resultant of violent displacements from the natural rest point of the body." For Thomas Aquinas, a "just price . . . draws upon all sorts of considerations beyond the object vended . . . [with] no need for a reified value index" (*MHL*, 146).

The appearance of mercantilist pamphleteering coincided with the "incipient meiosis of the body-motion-value metaphor" (*MHL*, 147), the transition into the lineamentric stage of value theory. What Mirowski terms "balance of trade" mercantilism, by viewing trade as a zero-sum game in a closed system, reified a "physicalist notion" of value conservation and thus marked the first appearance of a conservation principle in Western economic thought (see *MHL*, 148). The "free trade" branch, on the other hand, "did not comprehend" the need for some conservation principle, and hence "their program was a dead end" (151). Now solidly in the lineamentric stage, both physiocracy and classical political economy were based on the consolidation of the substance idea in physics. In particular, "the most basic practice of reification in classical political economy was the postulation of a metaphor of value as a discrete substance in motion, created in production, conserved in the exchange of equivalents and destroyed in consumption" (176).

Physiocracy was the economic equivalent of Cartesian rational mechanics, with its conservation of motion: its success was due to Quesnay's successful fusion of the metaphors of body (blood flow) and motion (circulation of the substance) with value, embodied in *blé* (wheat). In England this notion of value as substance was reflected in the economics of Smith, Ricardo, and Marx. The "name of the substance changed . . . but the general structure of explanation was the same" (192).

Smith initially faced several difficulties, Mirowski claims. First, he was partial to the Cartesian theories of motion, but these had been displaced in physics by Newton. Second, the extent to which he could borrow from physiocracy was limited by not only his "Scots wariness

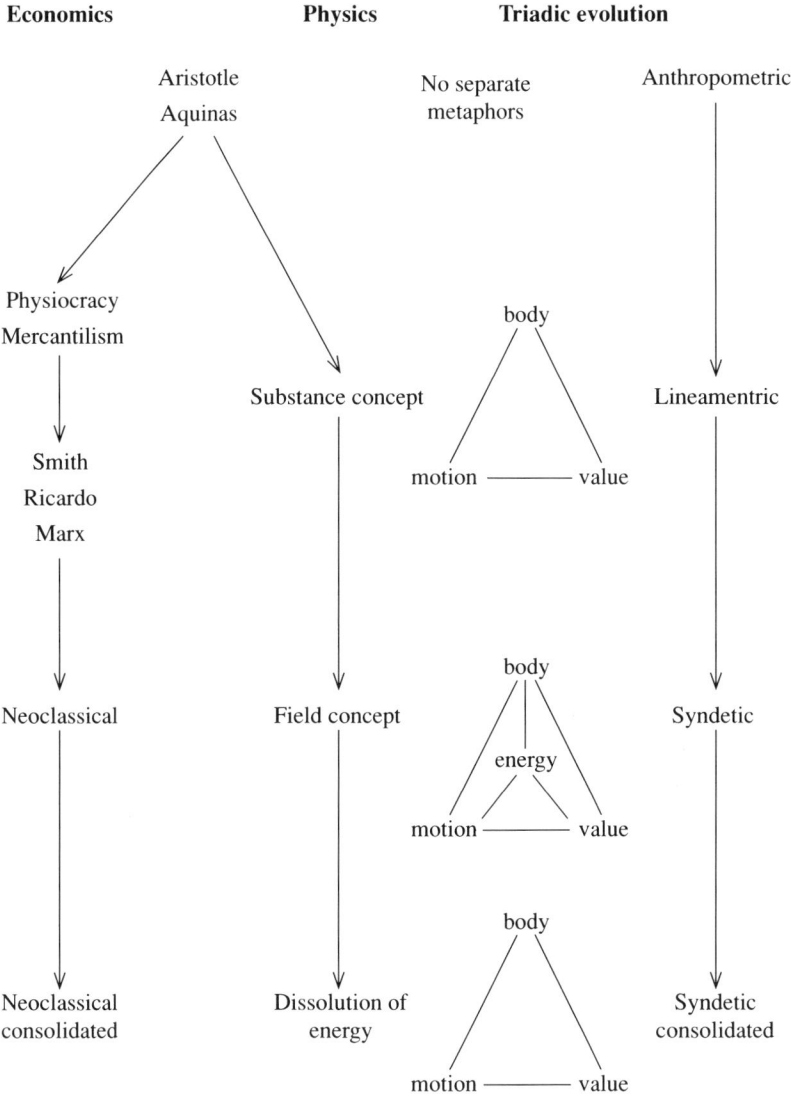

Figure 3

of the body" but by his broader conception of wealth and his desire to "paint a rosy picture of the natural development of market structures" (165). The result was a weakened form of physiocracy, with wealth as tangible, physical stock and all saving turned into new capital, a conservation principle which permitted the separation of the real and monetary sides of the economy.

Ricardo, on the other hand, is portrayed as "a zealot intent on raising the scientific status of political economy" (171), without the necessary scientific background. His first appropriation of a substance appeared in the form of the corn model. Then to illustrate better the falling rate of profit, he moved away from a one-good model to one with an embodied-labor theory of value. This was a return to the physically outdated Cartesian concept of substance in motion seen in Smith, with the metaphor of the body reincorporated through the notion of human labor. The difficulty lay in the reconciliation of the two: the stock concept yielded an equalized rate of profit, but the labor theory did not. For Mirowski, however, the true Ricardian vice was unfamiliarity with science, coupled with use of an outdated image of science taken from predecessors.

Even though Marx, alone among the three, warned against the "slavish imitation of the natural sciences" (*MHL*, 176), he himself apparently made liberal use of both organic and physical analogies. The transition of the substance metaphor to the field metaphor in science reflected itself in what Mirowski sees as essentially two Marxian labor theories of value: a crystalized labor (substance) approach and a real cost (field) version. In the first of these, only the labor process produces value, which becomes embodied in goods: in the second, value is made contingent on the production arrangement, so that, for example, a shortage of cotton could raise its embodied labor value. The problem for Marx was that the first of these was intractable, and that the second, tractable version violated the primacy of production, the exchange of equivalents, and the declining rate of profit. According to Mirowski, Marx deliberately fudged the issue by indiscriminately mixing both models as he saw fit, saving the publication of jury-rigged numerical examples until the posthumously published volume 3 of *Capital*. Summing up the schools of physiocracy and classical political economy, Mirowski says: "[It] is possible to regard the variegated theories of Quesnay, Smith, Ricardo and Marx as manifestations of a single class of value theory, associated with the lineamentric stage of metrology, rendered coherent by a particular conception of science" (143).

However, just as physics was experiencing a sea change in the form of the adoption of the field metaphor, classical political economy was condemned to lose its rhetorical relevance. The challenges to the Euclidean monolith which had begun in the late 1700s, followed by Samuel Bailey's attack on the analogies employed by Ricardo, were, Mirowski claims, all signs of what was to come. Classical political economy had made stronger the link between economics and science and was consequently at greater risk when science changed: "the solid earth was being spirited away out from under the feet of the classical political economists, and they, trusting souls, were not the least bit aware of it" (91).

By the 1860s, physics had evolved from a disparate array of disconnected mathematical models of celestial motion, heat flow, and electricity conduction to a fairly consolidated discipline "unified around variational principles and the conservation of energy" (*MHL*, 217). This energy physics was in some textbooks by the 1860s, and Mirowski claims that it was the imitation of this growing physics literature that shaped what became neoclassical economics. What would ultimately be coined the Marginalist Revolution was, more than anything else, a reflection of the metaphorical change that occurred in physics with the advent of energy as a field. The nascent neoclassicals thus "boldly copied the reigning physical theories in the 1870s . . . mostly term for term and symbol for symbol, and said so" (3). It is this assertion that has formed the basis of much of Mirowski's work in recent years, has given rise to his extensive exploration of metaphor in *More Heat than Light*, and underlies his campaign to replace the dominant neoclassical paradigm with an economics independent of physics (see Mirowski 1984, 1986, 1990a).

Mirowski points to the fact that Jevons, Walras, Edgeworth, and Pareto were all explicit about the need to make economics scientific and openly did so by molding it to the contemporary physics of energy, dubbed "protoenergetics," equating energy with utility. Jevons, although apparently inept at the mathematics of rational mechanics, was influenced by Faraday, Joule, and J. Clerk Maxwell, and in *The Theory of Political Economy* (1870) chose the physical analogy of the lever for the exchange process, without realizing the consequences in terms of potential and kinetic energy. Walras adopted both the lever and the relationship between celestial bodies as economic metaphors, and Edgeworth too compared the circulation of cosmic bodies to the movement of "souls," each maximizing pleasure. Pareto was perhaps the most energetic advocate of the physical analogy, but apparently neither he nor Walras was capable of mathematically defending the choice when challenged by contemporaries in physics such as Hermann Laurent (*MHL*, ch. 5). The most explicit linking of utility to a conservative vector energy field is that in Irving Fisher's *Mathematical Investigations* (1926), where he compares the individual to a particle, energy to utility, force to marginal utility, etc. The fact that neither Fisher nor any of his neoclassical predecessors carried the appropriated through to its full consequences is the reason Mirowski incriminates both them and their theoretical legacy.

In comparing utility with energy the neoclassicals adopted a variational principle but neglected the corresponding conservation principle. Had they pursued the matter, Mirowski claims, they would have discovered that this implied that the total of expenditure and utility remain constant. This confers an ontological equivalence on income and utility, something which makes no sense whatsoever. It is this implicit, incongruous conservation principle that, in Mirowski's mind, continues to dog economics to this day. Whenever faced with accounting for this, economists have essentially "fudged" the issue, imposing conservation of utility, or of income, or of their sum, "in higgledy-piggledy fashion . . . depending on their own idiosyncratic preferences" (*MHL*, 273). For example, utility conservation has been maintained through ruling out endogenous taste change; income conservation through the assumption of exogeneity; and conservation of the total through the integrability conditions or the Slutsky restrictions, or by assuming a constant marginal utility of money. As for production theory, neoclassical economics has had to try to reconcile this substance metaphor with the field metaphor in consumption theory, an impossible task given that the two are derived from distinctly different mathematical constructs in physics. Attempts at this reconciliation have motivated the profusion of forms of neoclassical production theory, including the Marshallian supply curve, the induction of new value substance in Keynesian national income, and, most commonly, technology as a field in commodity space. Mirowski sees the claim by late twentieth-century neoclassicals that capital could be abandoned in their system as the final supersession of the field—by the substance metaphor.

Difficulty with the underlying conservation principle notwithstanding, neoclassical economics has persisted with the use of utility maximization, even when the protoenergetics of the late nineteenth century has long since been replaced in physics by a string of theoretical innovations including thermodynamics, relativity theory, quantum theory, and chaos theory. This, says Mirowski, is a result of the "pincers movement" (358) in which neoclassical economics found itself: although the underlying metaphor grew obsolete as physics changed, substantial metaphorical adoption of any of these new developments would have signaled the end of the utility concept. This, Mirowski claims, is something the discipline could not countenance, for "there is nothing else that can hold the neoclassical research program together" (368).

The delicate and difficult task of maintaining an air of scientific rigor while remaining wedded to a nonsensical metaphor taken from an outdated physics has been handled in exemplary fashion, we are told, by Paul Samuelson. In a career characterized by legerdemain and subterfuge, Samuelson has devoted himself to "straining to evoke the parallels between neoclassical theory and twentieth-century physics, while simultaneously maintaining an assured cleared distance from the substantive content of modern physics. . . . It was a tough act to get past the critics, but Samuelson pulled it off time after time" (*MHL*, 380). First of all, in an effort to reduce dependence on utility, Samuelson attempted to derive the indifference mapping with Revealed Preference Theory. However, as Houthakker showed in 1950, the necessary conditions for this are nothing other than the integrability conditions, which represent the incongruous conservation principle discussed above. In an attempt to retain an air of rigorous science, Samuelson sought the superficial rhetorical benefit of Bohr's Correspondence Principle and Ehrenfest's Le Chatelier Principle, in neither case drawing on the underlying mathematics. Under Samuelson's influence, economic theory entered an "age of technique," where "many displaced engineers and previously unemployed mathematicians" (386) gained influence developing econometrics and manipulating Hamiltonians. This was done, says Mirowski, without realizing that it was all simply a continuation of the late nineteenth-century dream of rendering the world comprehensible through a set of deterministic equations: as such, the neoclassical program has "misled generations of students" (399).

3. "East is East and West is West and . . ."

In comparing the two views implicit in the writings of Douglas and Bloor, on the one hand, and Mirowski, on the other, we focus largely on the latter's treatment of neoclassical economics. Something can first be said, however, of the longer history which he has written. In particular, Mirowski moves freely between viewing the appropriation of physical metaphor as something *inevitable*, which must be done if one is to make sense, and as a task in which theorists have freedom of *choice*. With regard to the schoolmen, living in the anthropometric stage, they had little choice: value, motion, and body were not separate metaphorical areas. In the case of the mercantilists, however, the "balance of trade" school used natural philosophy metaphors, but the "free trade" school did not. With the classical school, we are told that Smith made the conscious choice of "old" Cartesian over "new" Newtonian metaphors and thus faced a rhetorical difficulty, to such an extent that he had to disguise all "in a great bed of digressions" (*MHL*, 165). Ricardo, the "zealot," ignorant of the history of the sciences, also opted for Cartesianism. Marx presents us with an enigma, for he both warned against mimicking physics and proceeded with the use of a substance metaphor. By the time we reach neoclassicism, its early proponents opted explicitly for what was then modern physics; but their successors, led by Samuelson, have retained those obsolete analogies and, beyond the borrowing of terminology, live in metaphorical ignorance of modern physics. By the twentieth century, in other words, there seems to be such leeway attached to the choice of metaphor that the notion of all being bound by the all-encompassing metaphoric triad seems lost. Not only did neoclassicals retain the protoenergetics metaphor but, to the extent that they invested in the substance metaphor implied in production theory at all, they were even more "outdated." As a framework describing the unspoken rules of resonance that any discipline must obey, the triad seems to have become inadequate. On this point Mirowski is again somewhat oblique: the dissolution of the energy concept, at the beginning of the twentieth century "is indicative of . . . the further consolidation of the syndetic metrological stage of discourse. Metaphors of the body, of motion, and of value are far more perfectly reconciled by means of the realization that each is fiction, but the same fiction, a fiction necessary for the organisation of human discourse" (137).

At the same time as portraying the appropriation of metaphors as a sequence of deliberate, conscious choices, Mirowski sees his exploration as falling in line with the work of Douglas on the interlocking of the natural and the social. But as we have seen (section 1 above), Douglas seems to be dealing with a much deeper level of influence where metaphorical resonance is felt but not seen: "the effort to build strength for fragile social institutions by grounding them in nature is defeated as soon as it is recognised as such. *That is why founding analogies have to be hidden and why the hold of the thought style upon the thought world has to be secret*" (1986, 53, emphasis added).

However, it is in his general discussion of neoclassical economics that I believe Mirowski both paints an unpersuasive picture and can least claim the support of Douglas or Bloor. His thesis, recall, is two-edged: first, economics today is simply outdated physics and therefore it too is obsolete; second, a better economics would abandon physics altogether. The second part of this claim is a means of making room for the Mirowskian Alternative, a new value theory, glimpses of which we have seen in his specific, if somewhat oblique, "Mathematical Formalism and Economic Explanation" (Mirowski 1986) and his more general "Social Theory of Value" (Mirowski 1990b). We leave history to judge the value of this work. The first part of his claim, however, is more provocative, both for defenders of neoclassical theory and for those historically minded agnostics, like myself, interested in uncovering the discipline's variegated social underpinnings. The claim by Mirowski that neoclassical economics is somehow faulty, inappropriate, or "less-than-true" is based on the fact that it ignores the ontological consequences of its implied conservation principle. The reason this has not been noticed before involves both Samuelsonian subterfuge and the "deployment of mathematical formalisms . . . and unfounded appeals to psychology and methodological individualism" (*MHL*, 398). In short, society has been hoodwinked into accepting a flawed theory that is scientific only in an obsolete sense. Such an observation, I suggest, would be regarded as trivial by both Douglas and Bloor. The latter reminds us that "knowledge for the sociologist is whatever men take to be knowledge. It consists of those beliefs which men confidently hold to and live by. In particular the sociologist will be concerned with beliefs which are taken for granted or institutionalized, or invested with authority by groups of men" (1976, 3). And, as if in the same voice, Douglas says, "The entrenching of an idea is a social process. . . . the burden of entrenching a theory is as much social as it is cognitive" (1986, 45).

In his description of neoclassical economics Mirowski has missed the point as Douglas or Bloor would surely see it: that four generations of a growing discipline have collectively endorsed the basic neoclassical framework. This is all the more pertinent in that it has eclipsed its rivals in economic theory and has had considerable imperial success within the social sciences: the rational choice framework has greatly influenced political science and, increasingly, sociology. Mirowski suggests that this is simply because rival economic theories have never been compared on a point-by-point basis (see *MHL*, 398). But what schools of thought, one might well ask, have ever been compared on such a basis? To suggest that groups choose among beliefs, or theories, in this "rational" manner is naive. For Douglas and Bloor, the relevant feature of neoclassical economics would likely be that it has lasted so long. What social purposes does an economics based on rational optimization serve? What is it in "mainstream" economic theory that finds resonance in other realms, social, political? If knowledge is constituted by society for practical purposes, our concerns must be for those considerations which make it coherent, both for its practitioners and for the extended intellectual and political community for whom it must somehow "make sense." The relevant factors would include, at the very minimum, questions of education and group loyalty, the role of economic theory or theorists in designing policy, and the response of theory to political change. As Douglas says, "Only one term sums up all the qualities that enable a speculation to become established and then to escape oblivion; that is the principle of coherence" (1986, 90).

If one accepts that neoclassical theory has indeed become established and thus far escaped oblivion, then Douglas would have us believe that it must somehow be coherent. No doubt Mirowski would respond that in cultivating his critique of neoclassical economics he has stepped beyond the limits respected by Douglas and Bloor. However, one can contend that not only is Mirowski's critique philosophically foreign to them, but that in his urge to dismantle he has written a one-dimensional, deterministic history devoid of the analysis of social influence for which they are known. As we are reminded by Douglas (1975, xiv), while it may lend tremendous energy to polemic, "hostility breeds the wrong atmosphere for philosophising."

Conclusion

In making the case for his interpretation of the history of economic theory, Mirowski claims to offer a sociology of science congruent with that of Mary Douglas and David Bloor. A closer examination of the work of these two sociologists reveals this claim to be a largely rhetorical, rather than substantive, one. In both spirit and method, Mirowski's approach deviates from the multi-faceted type of inquiry characteristic of

Douglas and Bloor. With regard to neoclassical economics, in particular, in his drive to illustrate its incoherence, Mirowski ignores a host of factors that a richer sociology of science would emphasize. The ironic aspect of this is that he ends up resembling the Samuelson he criticizes: just as the latter supposedly makes a shallow, rhetorical appeal to physics in order to lend authority to his theoretical work in economics, Mirowski buttresses his historiography of economics by appealing to sociology in parallel fashion.

I am grateful to the Comité d'Aide Financière aux Chercheurs, of the University of Québec at Montreal, for financially supporting part of this research. For their helpful comments I thank Bob Coats, Gilles Dostaler, Craufurd Goodwin, Neil de Marchi, and Urs Rellstab. Remaining errors are mine.

References

Barnes, Barry, and Steven Shapin. 1977. Where Is the Edge of Objectivity? *British Journal for the History of Science* 10:61–66.
Bloor, David. 1976. *Knowledge and Social Imagery*. London: Routledge & Kegan Paul.
———. 1983. *Wittgenstein: A Social Theory of Knowledge*. New York: Columbia University Press.
Douglas, Mary. 1970. *Natural Symbols*. London: Barrie & Jenkins.
———. 1975. *Implicit Meanings*. London: Routledge & Kegan Paul.
———. 1978. *Cultural Bias*. London: Royal Anthropological Institute.
———. 1982a. *In the Active Voice*. London: Routledge & Kegan Paul.
———. 1986. *How Institutions Think*. Syracuse: Syracuse University Press.
———, ed. 1982b. *Essays in the Sociology of Perception*. London: Routledge & Kegan Paul.
Douglas, Mary, and B. Isherwood. 1979. *The World of Goods*. New York: Basic Books.
Durkheim, Emile. [1895] 1938. *The Rules of Sociological Method*. Translated by S. Soloway and J. Mueller. New York: Free Press.
———. [1912] 1961. *The Elementary Forms of Religious Life*. Translated by J. Swain. New York: Collier.
Durkheim, Emile, and M. Mauss. 1963. *Primitive Classification*. Translated by R. Needham. London: Cohen & West.
Evans-Pritchard, Edward. 1937. *Witchcraft, Oracles and Magic among the Azande*. Oxford: Clarendon Press.
Fisher, Irving. 1926. *Mathematical Investigations into the Theory of Value and Prices*. New Haven: Yale University Press.
Jevons, William. [1870] 1970. *The Theory of Political Economy*. Edited by R. Black. Baltimore: Penguin Books.

Kula, Witold. 1986. *Measures and Men*. Princeton: Princeton University Press.
Lakatos, Imre. 1976. *Proofs and Refutations*. Cambridge and New York: Cambridge University Press.
Latour, Bruno. 1987. *Science in Action*. Cambridge: Harvard University Press.
Latour, Bruno, and S. Woolgar. 1979. *Laboratory Life: The Social Construction of Scientific Facts*. London and Beverly Hills: Sage.
Mirowski, Philip. 1984. Physics and the "Marginalist Revolution." *Cambridge Journal of Economics* 8:361–79.
———. 1986. Mathematical Formalism and Economic Explanation. In *The Reconstruction of Economic Theory*, edited by Philip Mirowski, 179–240. Boston: Kluwer.
———. 1989. *More Heat than Light: Economics as Social Physics, Physics as Nature's Economics*. Cambridge: Cambridge University Press. [Citations are abbreviated *MHL*.]
———. 1990a. The Rhetoric of Modern Economics. *History of the Human Sciences* 3.2:243–57.
———. 1990b. Learning the Meaning of a Dollar: Conservation Principles and the Social Theory of Value in Economic Theory. *Social Research* 57.3:689–717.
Wittgenstein, Ludwig. [1933–35] 1969. *The Blue and the Brown Books*. Oxford: Basil Blackwell.
———. 1964. *Remarks on the Foundations of Mathematics*. Edited by G. von Wright, R. Rhees, and G. Anscombe. Translated by G. Anscombe. Oxford: Basil Blackwell.

What Mirowski's History Leaves Out

A. W. Coats

> Economics is more metaphor than science, a way of imposing interpretative order on the buzz of transactions that make up a modern economy. Forecasting, in particular, is a narrative art form; there's no black box to grind up the numbers and produce a reliable prediction.—Charles R. Morris, *New York Times Magazine*, 27 January 1991

My brief is very broad—indeed, almost limitless—and I have no intention of taking it literally. I did not in fact choose my title; but in a sense I asked for it toward the end of my review (1991) of *More Heat than Light*, and our organizer was quick to hoist me with my own petard. On the face of it my task is easy enough, if interpreted loosely. All historical accounts are necessarily incomplete. Selection is unavoidable,[1] and as a historian of economics of uncertain vintage I am hardly likely to be completely taken in by Philip Mirowski's bold, brilliant, fascinating, and at times exasperating and outrageous attempt to wrap up my discipline in his slender Ariadne's thread.[2]

Unlike our author, who confidently straddles a vast domain, I am constrained by the limitations of my knowledge to concentrate on his

---

1. "There is no neutrally objective history of economic thought. There must always be some organizational principles of selection, since no work can adequately summarize all thought even within a narrow range of issues and controversies" (Mirowski 1985, 1). But cf. note 4 below.

2. "The adoption of the proto-energetics metaphor and framework of mid-nineteenth-century physics is the birthmark of neoclassical economics, the Ariadne's thread that binds the protagonists, and that can lead us to the fundamental meaning of the neoclassical research program" (*MHL*, 222). Whether there is in fact a single fundamental meaning to that program is, indeed, one of the "fundamental" points at issue.

treatment of "economics as social physics," leaving to others the task of unraveling the story of "physics as nature's economics." Even so, both facets of *More Heat* must be taken into account in considering Mirowski's calculated omissions. With respect to "physics as nature's economics" he deliberately excludes certain "rather tired and worn themes" such as "the prosaic fact that technological innovations may have provided inspiration for certain physical theories . . . the old Weberian chestnut about capitalist rationality writ large . . . [and] the perennial whipping boy of the history of science literature, the Marxist-inspired Hessen thesis" (*MHL*, 100; cf. 106). Further exclusions are enumerated in the concluding chapter, where he deftly deflects the charge that his account reduces to the historically unworthy portrayal of economics as merely the tail wagged by the physics dog. A more complete account, we are assured, to be incorporated in a future volume entitled *The Realms of the Natural*, will address "any number of other intellectual concerns" which have inspired "many concepts in the history of economic thought." There have, indeed, been

> entire schools of economic thought [which] have denounced and resisted the siren song of a social physics: the German Historicist school for one, and the first two generations of the American Institutionalists for another (Mirowski 1988). Nevertheless, I do assert that within the ambit of the dominant schools of Western economic thought—classical political economy, neoclassical economics, and Marxian economics—the theory of value, the very core of the explanatory structure, has been *dictated* by the evolution of physical theory. Indeed, this has necessarily been the case for the dominant schools in Western culture, for their dominance is due to their emulation of physical explanation, and their resonance with the primal metaphors of body/motion/value.[3] (396, emphasis added)

---

3. Presumably Mirowski's forthcoming study will identify the intellectual earplugs that enabled members of those schools to resist the "siren song." Why did they not succumb to the dominant influence of "physical explanation?"

It should be noted that Mirowski also excludes two other approaches in addition to the physics-dominated view: "the full-scale denial of value" associated with Barbon, Turgot, and Bailey (cf. 151, 163, 187–91, 399–400), and the "social theory of value" (400), a concept he does not explicate. (But see Mirowski 1990a.) The concept of "social value" has a long and intriguing career in economic writings, one that has not yet found its historian. See Lutz 1990, esp. the chapters by Thomas O. Nitsch and William R. Walters. (Perhaps Mirowski intends to fill this gap.) In general, *More Heat* has the curiously old-fashioned effect of restoring the theory of value to the central place it once occupied in the historiography of economics.

As my opening epigraph suggests, the concept of economics as metaphor now has wide currency; but for the present purpose it is vital to distinguish between literary and scientific metaphors. By contrast with literary metaphors, which often serve only ornamental purposes, according to Mirowski,

> much of normal scientific activity can be interpreted as an attempt to render unseemly aspects of metaphors intelligible and pedestrian. A hallmark of scientific metaphors is the fact that they are deemed failures if they can muster only temporary impact and do not manage to become the object of pedantic explication and elaboration. . . . Scientific metaphors should set in motion research programs . . . [because] they provide guidance and structure in the process of inquiry, which might otherwise be even more rife with rampant individualism and random research than is already the case. (278–79)

The basic similarity between Mirowski's scientific metaphors and Kuhn's paradigms is immediately obvious (cf. *MHL*, 301), at least for periods of "normal science"; yet there are also disquieting differences. For example, Mirowski claims that there is "free play inherent in metaphorical reasoning," as exemplified by the manner in which Adam Smith and J. B. Say developed "disparate theories" based on "essentially the same structural metaphors" (170), while the Cambridge Capital Controversies demonstrate that conflicting scientific metaphors can coexist within the same disciplinary matrix (338ff.). There is no unique way of interpreting a metaphor (or a paradigm?). Thus "the conservation of energy kept undergoing the figure-ground reversal central to Gestalt psychology: depending upon how you looked at it, it was either the most obvious and most important principle in science, or simultaneously the most metaphysical, convoluted, and implausible doctrine to have come down the pike in a long time" (58). How can such a metaphor provide the stability required for a coherent and ongoing program of scientific research?

Unstable, and difficult to interpret though they may be—according to Mirowski—metaphors can have extraordinary staying power and disturbing, unforeseen implications, both intellectual and sociological—although he considers the latter aspect only in passing. For instance, the "effort to reduce economic value to a conserved substance in motion" *dominated* economic thinking "from the mercantilists to the mid-nineteenth century" (185–86); but the explanation of this longevity is apparently sociological rather than purely intellectual, namely, the persistence of the desire "to elevate moral philosophy and political economy to the status of a natural science" (186). Sometimes a metaphor can take over, for once a research strategy has been adopted, a "powerful inertial guidance system" comes into operation (279); and the well-known "principle of tenacity" discourages the abandonment of a budding research program as soon as it encounters unexplained anomalies or seemingly disconfirmatory evidence. At a later stage, as the sorcerer's apprentice discovered, it may be too late to break away. On the other hand a metaphor can be a necessary "fiction" (137),[4] or a "lifeline" (162); and "the trick to metaphorical evaluation is an ability to sense when one has finally ventured beyond the pale, so that the coherence of the metaphor is strained to the point of dismemberment" (314).[5]

According to Mirowski, the economists' subservience to physics metaphors has been a sorry tale of ignorance, error, misappropriation, self-delusion, and resistance to change. In general, "economists have consistently lagged behind physicists in developing and elaborating metaphors; they have freeloaded off physicists for their inspiration, and appropriated it in a shoddy and slipshod manner" (108). Classical economics (note that Mirowski constantly reifies particular schools and phases in economic thought) backed the wrong horse, becoming "inextricably identified with the paradigm of substance theories in physics, and therefore its days were numbered" (201). The conventional triumvirate of marginalist revolutionaries neither understood the energy concept nor grasped its full implications (222), and when physics subsequently underwent fundamental changes

> the neoclassical research program was *forced* to regulate and prohibit the further substantive importation of novel physics metaphors, just as it had to discourage any other conception of value. Consequently, by the 1960's the neoclassical research program became helplessly

---

4. Earlier, in discussing the central metaphors of body, motion, and value, he emphasizes that "the central syndectic principle at the heart of each [vertex] is purely conventional and thus, . . . simply false" (116; cf. 397). This of course implies that there must be something "true" with which such principles can be compared.

5. "One of the most attractive aspects of analogical reasoning is the prefabricated nature of an interlocking set of explanatory structures and constructs, allowing quickened evaluation of logical coherence" (272). This suggests that the criterion by which the success or failure (truth or falsity?) of a research program must be judged is internal coherence, rather than, say, the capacity to survive thorough and repeated efforts at falsification.

locked into the physics of circa 1860, and persists in this predicament to the very present. (393–94, emphasis added)

Here we see little evidence of "the freeplay inherent in metaphorical reasoning" (170), scope for divergent and even incompatible interpretations, or opportunity to play the "trick" of "metaphorical evaluation" (cf. 314). Once harnessed to the obsolete physics metaphor, the neoclassical research program's fate was sealed. Coyness and ambivalence was of no avail. The physics metaphor

> cannot seriously be repudiated or relinquished, because *there is nothing else that can hold the neoclassical research program together*. In the absence of the metaphor of utility as nineteenth-century potential energy, there is no alternative theory of value, no heuristic guide to research, no principle upon which to base mathematical formalism, no causal invariant in the Meyersonian sense, and most threatening, no basis for the claim that economics has finally become scientific. (368, emphasis his)

So although the essential problems of neoclassical economics are intellectual—ontological, epistemological, and theoretical—the greatest threat is sociological, that is, the loss of scientific status. No wonder that when competent physicists pronounced the upstart proto-energetics wanting, the early neoclassical economists responded to their "slings and arrows . . . with hurt incomprehension, bluster, farrago, protests that the physics was irrelevant, and finally, a feeling of betrayal" (241). There were, of course, challenges from the underworld of economic theory, but they were uniformly unsuccessful, although their history has yet to be written.

How is the critic to respond to Mirowski's argument, after recovering from the initial shock of his breathtaking sweep and the boldness of his claims? Is it sufficient to concentrate on the level of "universal history," the handful of primal metaphors and the "higher plane of synthesis . . . that uncovers the unity of discourse behind the quotidian barriers of fields or disciplines, or indeed, between the social and the natural" (107)? To raise minor objections about specifics would surely be pedantic and petty-minded. (Nevertheless I touch on a few of his more striking deviations from conventionally accepted versions of the history of economics below.)

To judge by his breezy, witty, often throwaway style, a good deal of

Mirowski's text needs to be taken figuratively rather than literally. He too is presumably entitled to a "metaphoric license" that permits him "to slide effortlessly from economic connotations to those of quantitative measurement to those of general worth or virtue" (141). No wonder it is difficult to pin him down! Nevertheless, after his unqualified assertion of the physics metaphor's indispensability to the neoclassical program (quoted above), he adds, somewhat unexpectedly, that "the only proof of this statement can be historical, irredeemably inductive" (368). Unfortunately he makes little effort to provide the evidence required for such a proof.[6]

In his brief concluding chapter Mirowski explains that his critique of neoclassical economics—unquestionably the project's main driving force—proceeds simultaneously on three distinct levels which may, for convenience, be respectively described as internalist, polemical, and conceptual/sociological (or cultural) (398–401). None of this is intrinsically historical or inductive, and this is somewhat surprising, given his earlier work in economic history. In his first book, *The Birth of the Business Cycle*, Mirowski made a systematic effort to integrate the history of economic ideas on his topic with concurrent or earlier developments in economic history; but there is hardly a trace of this effort in *More Heat than Light*. Of course the two projects are very different. *Business Cycle* is not designed as "universal history," and the theory of value, one of the central strands in *More Heat*, is obviously less likely to be closely linked with the historical context than the theory of business cycles, whether as cause or effect. Indeed, in *Business Cycle* Mirowski describes value theory as "the underlying metaphysics of economics," adding that "because of this, it *rules* economic epistemology" (90, emphasis added). In support of this contention, he cites J. S. Mill (via Gunnar Myrdal) to the effect that "the smallest error on the subject infects with corresponding error all our conclusions; and anything vague or misty in our conception of it creates confusion and uncertainty in everything else" (90). This much, at least, is common to both projects. Whereas *Business Cycle* is a blend of conventional *Dogmengeschichte* and economic history, *More*

---

6. However, there is substantial warrant for his complaints that "economics has been the most rigidly doctrinaire of all the social sciences" and that whenever intellectual challenges have appeared, defenders of the mainstream have been remarkably successful in "either co-opting the rival metaphor or else amputating the new offending doctrines as unsound and unscientific" (368). One hopes he will elaborate this historical claim in one of his forthcoming works.

Heat is essentially metaphysical history, if that is not a contradiction in terms.

Oddly enough, by contrast with several of Mirowski's earlier publications, in *More Heat* it is the history of physics rather than economics that inspires his most intriguing, if somewhat offhand, references to the relationships between ideas and the historical context. For instance, after declaring that "an authentic genetic account of the energy concept must expand to encompass social and economic history" (108), he proceeds to examine Kula's suggestive theory of the various stages in "metrology," adding, a few pages later, that the "lineamentric" and "syndectic" stages in the history of physics "roughly coincide with, respectively, the rise of the world mercantile economy and the institution of the world industrial economy" (119).

How the connections between intellectual innovations and these extremely broad and ill-specified historical processes are to be established is not clear, although we are told that to do so "would demand an entire volume, and would be an immense undertaking in the history of science" (119)—if, one must add, it is possible at all. Still, nothing daunted, our author confidently refers to the "striking" hypothesis that "the major innovations in the theory of motion follow the changing center of gravity of the major trading axis of early modern Europe, stretching from northern Italy through the low countries and terminating in southeastern Britain" (119–20ff.). Most conventional economic historians would surely be reluctant to accept this as more than intriguing speculation; and much the same applies to his claim that "the dematerialization" (or "denaturalization") of the value concept was directly associated with the evolution of the economy, in which "Britain was being surpassed as a manufacturing power and moving towards an economy based on finance and trade . . . as manufacture gave way to finance, seeing conservation principles in nature gave way to seeing them more as contingencies, imposed by our accountants in order to keep confusion at bay" (134–35). (What about other countries?) By this time, unfortunately, it is difficult to repress the suspicion that it is Mirowski who "sees" the ubiquitous conservation principles, not his historical subjects. How could a historian go about checking (let alone testing) the evidence for such a claim? Is it a matter of chance correlation, or causation? Or is it, perhaps, not to be taken that seriously?

I can sympathize with Mirowski's impatience with the crudely materialistic idea that "the base controls the superstructure" on the grounds that "experience with evolving economic structures altered perceptions of the metaphor of value, and that in turn set off resonances with the attendant theory of motion" (119). But this, surely, is simply to accept a modified version of the materialist explanation, as it were, at one remove.

Perhaps my objections simply boil down to dissatisfaction with the task of bringing Mirowski's "higher plane of synthesis" down to the historian's mundane level. At least as far as the history of economics is concerned, he does not live up to his slogan that "the best way to talk about science is to examine how people have done it" (8). If economics is "what economists do," as the saying goes, then most of what economists do and have done is missing from *More Heat*. Economic theory in general, and the theory of value in particular, comprise only a part—albeit a fundamental part—of economics, which is, after all, primarily a policy science (8).[7] To study the development of the metaphysical underpinnings, or what Veblen called "the preconceptions of economic science," is a perfectly legitimate undertaking, one that can indeed be revealing; but it is certainly not the whole story—perhaps just the beginning of a new one.

Whatever may be said of Mirowski's universal history, his wide-ranging account of the history of economic thought is frequently defective. Three severely abbreviated examples must suffice for the present purpose. More could of course be cited.

(1) Mirowski correctly notes that "the essence of mercantilism is extremely elusive" (147). Nevertheless he confidently proceeds to subdivide the literature into two discrete categories: "the balance of trade school" and "the free trade school," each identified with a specific

---

7. One does not need to go as far as Leo Rogin, who focused too narrowly on the "uses" to which economic ideas have been put and the social issues that have invested them with "a public, hence objective character" (1956, 10). A distinguished economist's attempt to interpret the history of his discipline in Deweyite instrumentalist terms is Mitchell's (1967, 1: ch. 1). At the other extreme of the ideas–environment spectrum is Pribram (1983), who is concerned with "the conflicting currents of thought which have *determined* the development of methods of reasoning in *all* fields of intellectual, social, political and moral activities" (xlix, emphasis added). The collection of essays edited by Warren Samuels (1983) provides a useful introduction to the range of possible approaches to the subject.

Mirowski does not, in *More Heat*, follow his own earlier injunction that one way to introduce the requisite "principles of selection and organization" is "to first examine the parallel principles of other authors who have sought to outline the history of thought" (*Business Cycle* [1985], 1).

period (early to mid-seventeenth century, and 1660–1700). "The first appearance of a conservation principle in Western economic thought" supposedly occurred in the earlier phase, though he concedes that this is "not terribly explicit" (148).

Apart from the fact that Mirowski completely ignores the substantial peculiarities of British mercantilism, as compared with its counterparts elsewhere, there were no genuine "schools" of economic thought in that period, and his categorization and periodization grossly oversimplify a complex story.[8] In general his brief account exemplifies the dangers of "reading into" seventeenth- and eighteenth-century economic thought sophisticated twentieth-century ideas that were only dimly perceived, if at all, two or three centuries earlier.[9] The mercantilist conceptions of value, money, trade, employment, etc., were embedded in a large, complex, highly uneven literature that was neither wholly systematic nor yet incoherent or entirely preanalytic. Schumpeter's apt term "quasi-system" (1954, 194) draws attention to the evolution of mercantilist theory and policy recommendations in association with changing economic conditions; and Mirowski's practice of extracting out of the context bits and pieces designed to support his preconceived thesis does indeed "overly distort the pamphlet record" (147).

(2) Mirowski's discussion of Adam Smith, a notoriously difficult writer to interpret both consistently and sympathetically, contains a serious error in his analysis of the physiocratic influences on Smith's economics. Far from expressing "disdain for the country peasant and the agricultural economy" (165), Smith went to inordinate lengths in praising the rural husbandman by contrast with the stupid and ignorant factory worker. Moreover, he flatly asserted the priority of agriculture over manufacture, domestic trade, and foreign trade, with respect to the amount of employment generated by the investment of a given sum of money (Smith [1776] 1976, 360ff., 782–83), a contention that almost

---

8. For example, balance of trade ideas persisted throughout the pre-1776 period and beyond, though the evolution of doctrine and changing economic conditions led to an increasing emphasis on the balance of employment rather than, or in addition to, foreign trade in the narrower sense. Mirowski's quartet of free traders (150)—though Petty does not really belong in that company—constituted an intellectually interesting but wholly unrepresentative and uninfluential minority writing at a time when protectionist ideas were in the ascendant. These writers were largely forgotten, and disinterred by nineteenth-century free-trade enthusiasts, writing in an entirely different "liberal" intellectual context.

9. For an elaboration of this contention see Coats 1973, 485–95.

gave McCulloch apoplexy. Neither of these views can be even remotely characterized as disdainful, or evidence of Smith's "wariness of the body," whatever that means!

(3) Mirowski's treatment of Marshall (Mirowski 1990b), at least in part, is willfully perverse. To describe that dedicated, careful, painstakingly overcautious and defensive man as "slapdash" (*MHL*, 300, 301) is outrageous, and so is the effort to reduce him to the status of a mere popularizer (262) on a par with Jane Marcet, Harriet Martineau, and Henry Fawcett (83). This may be entertaining, knockabout stuff; but it is hardly serious doctrinal history, for it grossly undervalues Marshall's contribution as a major synthesizer and founder of a doctrinal tradition that dominated academic economics in the leading country of the time for several decades. As Marshall, like Menger, does not fit into Mirowski's general scheme, he is denied the status of a "major protagonist" in the emergence of neoclassical economics (194), although it was largely from his work that neoclassical economics derived its name. Second Wrangler though he was, Marshall was not, unlike Jevons and Walras, a mathematical theorist "first and foremost" (195), and Mirowski, like some earlier commentators, is irritated by Marshall's lack of interest in mathematical consistency (372). This was deliberate, however, stemming from Marshall's low personal and professional valuation of pure theorizing, rather than from any intellectual deficiency. In this sense Marshall's case illustrates the misrepresentation involved in characterizing neoclassical economics as "reprocessed physics" (251). Marshall's goals were primarily social (including professional) and ethical. Admittedly there are legitimate questions as to the precise nature and extent of Marshall's originality, doubts fostered by his uneven and sometimes ungenerous acknowledgment of his debts to his predecessors. But Mirowski is unwilling to grant Marshall any credit whatsoever on this account, and he also fails to acknowledge the work of another major independent founder of modern marginalism, John Bates Clark, who was certainly no physicist manqué.

These remarks have been distinctly more skeptical and critical of *More Heat than Light* than my review cited at the outset, partly because the latter was largely devoted to exposition, but also because a different overall judgment has emerged from a closer rereading with greater attention to specifics. Even now, the most general issue—whether *More Heat* is reliable and accurate, as well as brilliantly stimulating and insightful history—has not yet been squarely addressed.

Without an adequate knowledge of the history of physics, which I lack, it is impossible to justify my strong impression that the focus on metaphors and analogies employed in two such disparate disciplines as physics and economics does not constitute sufficient evidence of similarities and linkages between them.[10] So much of economics, in particular, is omitted from Mirowski's account that it remains highly suggestive, rather than persuasive. Perhaps this is an inescapable consequence of so-called universal history.

It may be appropriate to conclude with the dictum that historians complain if a work is underresearched, not that it is underanalyzed, whereas among economists almost exactly the reverse applies. In this sense my comments here represent a historian's still somewhat baffled reaction to *More Heat than Light*.

References

Coats, A. W. 1973. The Interpretation of Mercantilist Economics: Some Historiographical Problems. *HOPE* 5:485–95.

———. 1991. Review of *More Heat than Light*, by Philip Mirowski. *Kyklos* 44.1:131–35.

Lutz, Mark A., ed. 1990. *Social Economics: Retrospect and Prospect*. Boston: Kluwer.

Mirowski, Philip. 1985. *The Birth of the Business Cycle*. New York and London: Garland.

———. 1988. *Against Mechanism*. Totowa, N.J.: Rowman & Littlefield.

———. 1989. *More Heat than Light: Economics as Social Physics, Physics as Nature's Economics*. Cambridge: Cambridge University Press. [Citations are abbreviated *MHL*.]

———. 1990a. Learning the Meaning of a Dollar: Conservation Principles and the Social Theory of Value in Economic Theory. *Social Research* 57:689–717.

———. 1990b. Smooth Operator: How Marshall's Demand and Supply Curves Made Neoclassicism Safe for Public Consumption but Unfit for Science. In

---

10. This point has been made effectively by M. Norton Wise and Crosbie Smith (1989, 291, 193): "The *practice* of political economists was not the practice of natural philosophers, for they employed different conceptual and analytic tools even where they employed the same terms to describe natural systems. . . . There is no reason to suppose that political economists should have developed a conservation principle for economic value from their analogies with physical systems, where it had very limited utility" (emphasis added).

Alfred Marshall in Retrospect, edited by Rita McWilliams Tullberg. Aldershot: Edward Elgar.

Mitchell, Wesley. 1967. *Types of Economic Theory: From Mercantilism to Institutionalism*. Vol. 1. Edited by Joseph Dorfman. New York: Kelley.

Pribram, Karl. 1983. *A History of Economic Reasoning*. Baltimore: The Johns Hopkins University Press.

Rogin, Leo. 1956. *The Meaning and Validity of Economic Theory*. New York: Harper.

Samuels, Warren. 1983. *The Craft of the Historian of Economic Thought: Research in the History of Economic Thought and Methodology*. Vol. 1. Greenwich, Conn.: JAI Press.

Schumpeter, Joseph A. 1954. *History of Economic Analysis*. New York: Oxford University Press.

Smith, Adam. [1776] 1976. *An Inquiry into the Nature and Causes of the Wealth of Nations*. Edited by Andrew Skinner and Roy Campbell. Oxford: Oxford University Press.

Wise, M. Norton, with the collaboration of Crosbie Smith. 1989. Work and Waste: Political Economy and Natural Philosophy in Nineteenth-Century Britain. [Part 1.] *History of Science* 27:263–301, 391–449.

History through the Lens of "Social" Value Theory

Neil de Marchi

As a last morsel, at the very close of *More Heat than Light*, readers are offered the thought that cultural concerns "really must be central to any logical economic theory" (401). A clue as to what that might mean is to be found in the introductory chapter, where we are told that the book should be thought of as "prolegomenon to a social theory of value" (10); but that clue is clearly a marker within a larger project because it is left undeveloped in the book itself. So we have a work of four hundred pages whose true purpose is only hinted at in the end pages, as it were. We now know something more of what the larger project involves (see Mirowski's own contribution to this volume); moreover, it is possible to piece together from more recent publications of his what he had in mind when he alluded to cultural concerns and a social theory of value. I shall try to show what the theory is, in the process producing a small window opening onto *More Heat than Light* from the outside. My main concern, however, is not with *More Heat than Light* as such, but with the ways in which a social value perspective might open up new paths in the history of economic thought.

I spoke just now as if the social theory of value had been fully developed and could be *re*-presented as a rounded whole. That is not the case. Mirowski, to date, has been preoccupied with finding an alternative formalism to that used in neoclassical economics, for discussing some old questions—how is value preserved in exchange? (which turns out to be about the role of money)—and for formulating some new ones: why are prices additive? He has begun to talk about a radically stochastic value theory, in which opening bids and offers are truly arbitrary. And he has hinted at the need for economists to become participant-observers so that they might study at first hand how groups function in markets to determine the path toward the (moving) target of arbitrage-free prices. But all that we have on paper so far is the alternative formalism, to which I shall confine my attention. My sources, in addition to *More Heat than Light*, are Mirowski's "Lecture Notes on an Institutionalist Theory of Value" (1989a) and several of his essays: "Mathematical Formalism and Economic Explanation" (1986), "Learning the Meaning of a Dollar: Conservation Principles and the Social Theory of Value in Economic Theory" (1990), "Postmodernism and the Social Theory of Value" (1991a), and "Symmetries, Arbitrage and the Social Theory of Value" (1991b). Mirowski regards "Meaning of a Dollar" as a literary version of things stated more abstractly in "Postmodernism," but I find it useful to have all three recent statements at hand (including "Symmetries") in trying to fathom what is being said.

Valuation as Social

We have got out of the habit of thinking of valuation as social. Smith's "natural" rate of wages depends on accepted social conventions, as does Ricardo's "subsistence" minimum. And, of course, there is Marx's socially necessary labor time. But Mirowski's concern is not with these elements, each of which can be taken, for the purposes of market analysis, as a datum. Mirowski wants to stress the "social" in the very process of exchange, what we might call the sociality of catallactics. That, however, is something that even sounds odd, partly because it is agreed that valuation is personal and we cannot pry into that, and partly because mainstream developments in exchange theory have tended to find ways around that very problem, enabling us to leap right to the group outcome level, making catallactics into a study of system equilibrium properties in a way that subsumes both the individual and interactions between individuals. Thus the Jevons-Marshall-Samuelson tradition studies the equilibrium properties of anonymous-agent exchange at the level of the market, with the aid of well-behaved preferences and price-quantity information, hence regular demand curves, and the law of one price. And the more modern Arrow-Debreu tradition focuses on precoordinated market-level outcomes using the fiction of what Hicks called "Arrow Securities."

How might the social be reintroduced? One way, which in fact does not command Mirowski's attention, at least not at this stage, is simply to lower the level of abstraction and give real names and functions to markets and the sorts of individuals in them. In the interactions between these sorts of individuals we might then discover genuine social processes in the making. For an intriguing example of what this can yield, with the stock options market as a case to be studied, see Baker (1984). A particular variant of this approach, which I find attractive because it forces me to think about the economic problem confronting different types of market transactors, is to take as unit of analysis particular forms of contract and try to decompose these into their constituent elements.

To illustrate this approach I borrow a framework developed by Williams (1986) for futures markets, though I shall translate it for the art market since my own current work involves valuation and pricing in the Netherlandish art markets of the seventeenth century. Start by treating market transactions not as isolated sale or purchase operations but as a complex method of gaining temporary use of resources. Thus, though it is a bit farfetched, consider art transactions as a form of repurchase agreement, which is to say as a type of forward contract. Take an art dealer and a painter. A two-way deal may be struck between them regarding a particular painting. The painter, impecunious but unwilling to part permanently with this, a favorite piece, offers to place the painting with a dealer in return for a loan of money. The painter agrees to pay interest on this loan and perhaps a storage fee (as one would for grain "parked" with a grain elevator operator). The dealer finds it useful to enlarge his stock for viewing (even if not for sale) in this way, and agrees to lend the money at interest to the painter and to pay to the artist a use fee or rental to compensate for the loss of "use" of the painting.[1] On this way of looking at things we have an explicit spot market in art, and an explicit market in loans. There is also a third market, an implicit futures market. For should the painter come into some money, the initial transactions could be reversed in the future (the repurchase part of the spot agreements). It does not in fact matter that this end of things is left implicit. The obligations of the initial two transactors might even be passed on to others, without destroying the sense that we have to do here with what is in principle a two-way, reversible deal.

---

1. Netherlandish artists in the seventeenth century often sold directly from their studios, in which case being without a painting represented a loss of a part of their means of self-advertisement.

Already this strongly suggests a social element in valuation: here we have a network of markets associated with the (temporary) acquisition of a painting, replete with all sorts of roles and institutions. But we can make the social element even more plain by focusing on the dealer's economic problem. Since the money loaned is secured by a painting, but the same money could have been put into a safe bond, the dealer would like to be assured that the painting will appreciate by at least the bond rate of interest. The best way to have that assurance is to make sure that the painting (or the artist, or both) is in vogue. It is with vogue in art as with beauty: to paraphrase Keynes, what one finds beautiful is often no more than what one thinks the majority finds beautiful, so that winners are chosen based on some consensus notion. Of course, art dealers need not be passive; they can do what is in their power to shape the consensus in particular ways and thereby influence directly the exchange rate of the paintings they hold as security against other paintings, or against money. Either way, the valuation is strictly social. There is no need to search for something deeper in which value might be said to consist (the labor time or skill of the artist; the physical characteristics of the work; the subjective estimate of the aesthete).

That is the conclusion of J. B. Clark, and of Benjamin Anderson and others who might be said to stand in a social value tradition (see de Marchi 1992a). Mirowski refers explicitly to Anderson, Veblen, Myrdal, and Commons; but ultimately he does not borrow much from them beyond the basic premise that we choose and construct our notions of value. To see what this premise undergirds in Mirowski's particular version of social value theory we need more than the idea of market networks, which has emerged in the form of multiple linked markets in my illustration of art transactions as (implicit) repurchase agreements. We need a precise sense of how transactions within a single market are constrained to display certain properties that Mirowski thinks of as symmetry properties. The required precision comes from adopting some formalisms—in this instance, those of group theory and (directed) graph theory.

A New Set of Formalisms for Portraying Exchange

Why formalisms of any sort? And why new formalisms? Without knowing Mirowski's answer to the first question, I infer that it must have to do with what he sees as the formal incoherence of neoclassical economic theory. The charge of incoherence arises out of the neoclassicals' desire to adopt the formalisms of field physics without confronting directly the problem that there is an incomplete analogy between "energy" and "utility." There is no physics analogue to the law of one price (I am summarizing from Mirowski's most recent, and for me clearest, statement of the issues, in his contribution to this volume). To impose the conservation of energy required by the physics necessitates an economic fudge. The law of one price implies that every time there is a change in the quantity chosen of a commodity, the price of each unit of it must alter, thereby also altering remaining real income and all other prices. In the physics, that would suggest a change in all forces whenever there is a change in one of them. That won't do; so some artificial form of economic invariance must be used to supplement (in a sense, dominate) the law of one price. Economists have opted for the invariance of tastes and of total expenditure. But in doing this a switch has been effected from commodity space to "budget" space, and that has ruled out direct integration from commodity space back to a utility function. Therein lies the incoherence; that criticism runs like a scarlet thread through *More Heat than Light*.

Herein too is the answer to the second question. "In effect," Mirowski writes in *More Heat*, "the neoclassical theory of exchange was an offshoot of the metaphor of energy, *buttressed by the mathematics of rudimentary rational mechanics*" (196, emphasis added). As happened with field physics (30, 100), the mathematics and the economic theory have become so intertwined—the assertion is made quite directly in "Symmetries"—that a formal consideration of a *non*-neoclassical theory of value must also invoke a different mathematics.

So, in the presentations of a social theory of value alternative that we have so far, we are witnessing a direct extension of the battle joined in *More Heat*: the issues are the same, only new, unstained, weapons have been taken. The battle lines drawn in *More Heat*, recall, were determined by the issue of consistency in the deployment of conservation principles. Conservation is interpreted both broadly and narrowly by Mirowski. Broadly, as he sees it, deciding upon some form of invariance, against which change may be measured, is the touchstone of explanation, at least in the West. Compelling, and coherent, causal explanations require a proper attendance upon invariance (5–6). Narrowly, the history of physics (and of economics) offers concrete lessons in how difficult it is to attend properly to invariance. Mirowski's social theory of value alter-

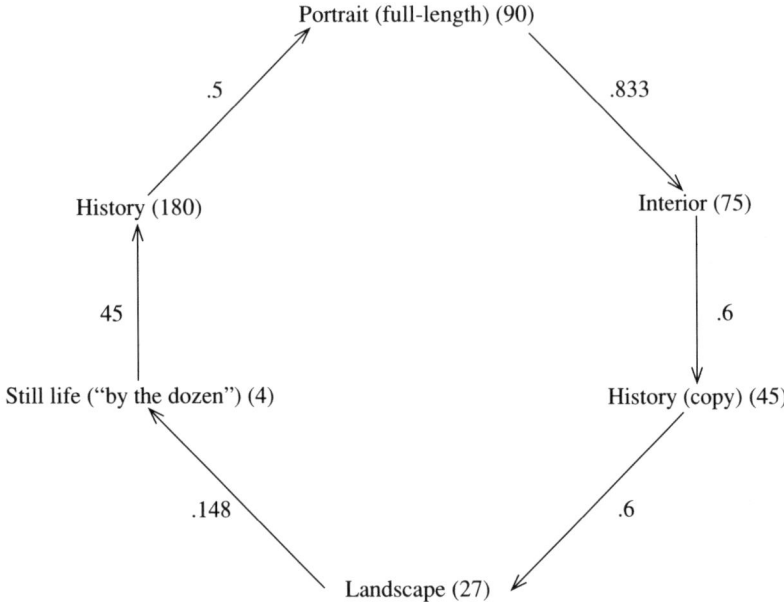

Figure 1 An illustrative closed-circuit exchange for art products

native, formally considered, is (almost) all about invariance, only in the form of symmetry.

I shall not reproduce Mirowski's formalisms but instead give an illustration, modeled on one of his, to show how they work themselves out in practice. I employ the language of invariance rather than symmetry, but nothing is lost thereby.

Take a functioning market for art—seventeenth-century, again.[2] For would-be collectors, or investors, there is a range of products, including in this example five types of painting, plus the option of a copy of one of them (see figure 1). These can all be thought of as substitutes, and they exchange at the rates indicated. The rates, shown alongside the arrows, can be taken as given, for the moment. In figure 1 the arrows

---

2. Mirowski acknowledges that his social theory of value applies only to well-developed markets, not those still emerging.

connecting each kind of substitute art commodity flow in one direction, making a closed circuit of exchange. Some of them could have gone in the other direction, preventing a complete circuit from forming; but even then, money could be used to enable us to imagine an exchange in the direction needed for a closed circuit. That is one function of money, to facilitate "virtual" exchanges. The other is to allow us to keep account of the exchanges as we go along. This "keeping track of" function identifies value in exchange, without our having to depend upon either the physical characteristics of some commodity or other, which is operationally impossible anyway, or on the (equally impossible) comparison of subjective valuations.

Notice that all of the rates of exchange, when multiplied together, equal 1, implying that in the circuit as a whole value is preserved (is invariant), no matter what our starting point. This invariance means too that there is no addition to total value merely through exchange.

We took the rates of exchange temporarily as given. But they are in fact created, by the very people who engage in exchanges and make up this particular market. Art dealers have a role, as suggested in my earlier illustration. So too do artists themselves (Rembrandt, though he rarely made prints after his own paintings, is known to have bought up copies of such prints as he did make, to reduce the supply). Studio entrepreneurs, who may be artists themselves (Rubens, for example), set up workshops employing apprentices or lesser artists to produce multiple copies of masterworks. In doing so they directly affect the supply and can control the price to some degree. Guilds (in the seventeenth-century Netherlands) tried to exercise control over the numbers of sales and those works that might be offered, thereby influencing relative supply, and prices. So too did those who commissioned specific works or sorts of work, as well as amateur art lovers/investors who offered board, lodging, and materials in exchange for the services of particular artists, which meant paintings of a particular sort. Mirowski hints that, given that would-be market participants may start with a wide range of bids and offers, institutions will develop to determine common rates quickly and effectively. Think of specialist market makers on the New York Stock Exchange, and price setters in the London gold market. In my example there is no official market maker, but there clearly are social groups—a limited number of them—who have price-influencing functions. Either way, there is a strong social component to how rates of exchange are determined.

In our market circuit, prices can be attached to each sort of product involved, consistent with the rates of exchange. In figure 1 they are shown in parentheses next to each product name.[3] These prices are the tags used to track transactions. They possess a feature consistent with value invariance. Let a forward exchange (in the direction of the arrow) between two adjacent products count as 1, and a backward exchange (a "virtual" exchange) with the product immediately preceding count as -1. Then take triples of products around the circuit in succession: a starting product, its forward substitute and its backward substitute, thus: portrait with (forward) interior and (backward) history; next, interior with (forward) history (copy) and (backward) portrait; and so on. In each triple, multiply forward the price of the starting product by the exchange rate times 1, and backwards by the inverse of the rate times -1. The algebraic sum of all these operations will be zero. Mirowski calls this the linearity of prices, and is greatly taken with the property. Symmetry conditions are notoriously difficult to interpret economically, and this one seems to be no exception. Intuitively, I think the property can most sensibly be taken as stating that in a closed circuit, if we work in money, and all transactions are properly recorded in a double-entry bookkeeping manner, there must be overall balance. The circuit of forward transactions exactly balances the (virtual) circuit of backward transactions, as in the more familiar circular flow diagrams of macroeconomics. The transactions sometimes look silly because they seem to involve fractions of indivisible products: it does not make practical sense for a holder of a history painting to offer 1/45th of the painting for the rights to a "by the dozen" still life. But that's what money is for; and the point is anyway that for the market as a whole debits and credits wash out.

Mirowski puts the point somewhat differently. In "Symmetries" he says: "The purpose of the market graph formalism is to explain the structure of interpretation and accounting in a market system." The association in this quotation of interpretation with accounting, and with market graph formalism, is very deliberate. Starting with the formalism, the point is that our formalisms are not given us by "the reality of the situation" ("Postmodernism," 1991a, 578); we choose them. At that most basic level, this is part of what having a "social" value alternative means: we select even our mathematics, as seems appropriate, rather

---

3. The prices used are taken from actual transactions in the seventeenth century. Since price varied with size, finish, artist, and so on, a single price is not very informative. These, therefore, should be treated as illustrative yet not wholly arbitrary.

than merely borrowing formalisms developed for another discipline. Accounting, even more obviously, is a construct, with its own contingent history. Applied to whole markets, or even to networks of markets, it is readily viewed as a way of giving social expression to value invariance.[4] In the end, with a selected (directed graph) formalism, the conventions of accounting, the device of money, and the social roles chosen by market participants (who affect exchange rates and interact to effect exchanges), we get a sense of how value is transferred in society without having to depend on the physical characteristics of any commodity, or on the particular deterministic formalism of optimization, inextricably intertwined as it is with the history of value as subjective. But it is after all only a sense, a sense of "what it is like to 'read' the economy without presuming there is a single fixed text to be read, or a single correct interpretation to be arrived at" (1991a, 579).

One final element needs to be explained before we can turn to the uses for history of the social value alternative. Mirowski accepts that individuals hold subjective valuations of commodities and come to the market with starting bids and offers that may not bear much resemblance to final, systemwide equilibrium prices. This is important to his approach: he wants to restore a sense of process—path dependence—to discussions of valuation. The law of one price nominally allows that starting prices may not be equilibrium prices (there may be "false trades"), but all the emphasis is on the end state, and there is in fact no process in neoclassical narratives.[5] But if starting prices can in principle be anything, Mirowski nonetheless insists that they cannot go on being "incoherent." That is, there are system properties that must obtain eventually. Thus prices may be thought of as random distributions, but if psychological values are such that individuals consistently lose (Dutch Book can be

---

4. It is not accidental that Hicks's early exposition of national income accounting was called *The Social Framework*. For a 1930s geometrical device for tracing world trade and payments flows that looks remarkably like an instance of Mirowski's directed graph formalism see De Marchi 1991, 163.

5. A recent example is Larry Neal's *Rise of Financial Capitalism* (1990), which finds evidence that eighteenth-century financial markets were efficient in the modern sense and uses this to (largely) eschew all discussion of the *emergence* of the markets and their associated institutions. The title is thus quite misleading. As noted earlier, this is, of course, a limitation of Mirowski's formalisms as well. My comments do not imply that neoclassical stories are entirely detached from history and historical institutions. Thus Walras's auctioneer is a theoretical fiction, but probably drawn after the discrete call procedures that were followed on the Paris Bourse at the time, prior to the announcement of a trading price. See Kregel 1992.

made against them, in Mirowski's usage), presumably there will be a process of elimination. He is not very explicit on the evolutionary dynamics here, and my interpretation may not be reliable. His clear hope, in any event, is that something like "fair game" conditions will make themselves felt; that actual market price can be modeled as a stochastic process and the arbitrage-free state of price as another such process, and that the necessary distributional conditions will obtain for the arbitrage variable itself to be a martingale. In short, at the individual level value is intrinsically random, but (somehow) systemwide symmetry will prevail; though how that last should be modeled is, Mirowski admits, an empirical question. This probabilistic element in the social theory of value is less satisfactorily developed than the arbitrage properties discussed earlier, but it is given prominence by Mirowski as his preferred way of introducing real time, novelty, freedom, and path dependence as elements of the new theoretical framework.

What Does the Social Theory of Value Hold for Historical Inquiry?

My concern with the social theory of value is twofold. First, it is Mirowski's third alternative to the two value traditions he explores, criticizes, and rejects in *More Heat than Light*: the substance theory and the subjective value theory. One cannot appreciate the book without knowing something about that third alternative—hence my attempt to restate his views. Second, since the social value alternative is, in Mirowski's eyes, a new research program in its own right, I want to know whether it holds the promise of fresh insights into the history of economics. Here too Mirowski has given the matter a lot of thought, and we can to some extent follow and evaluate the suggestions he makes in "Symmetries." I shall in fact mix his and my own ideas without trying to distinguish origins; at this point therefore I leave off trying faithfully to convey his views.

(1) The first lesson of the social value approach is that the choice of formalism is indeed that, a choice. Historians of economics therefore may find it fruitful to examine the choices that have been made in economics. In a sense this is Mirowski's own chosen theme in *More Heat*: the thesis that "conservation principles reify certain analytical prejudices" (160). But there are numerous subthemes, which may hold for particular periods, and which need not have to do with valuation or conservation in any obvious way. One that cries out for treatment is why the

choice was made against the probabilistic calculus and for deterministic mathematical formalism as *the* method for "moral" (social scientific) questions over the course of the eighteenth century and in the early nineteenth.[6] A related, equally important and no less neglected topic is the formalization of economics in the last four decades. This can be treated as a study in itself, or as part of a larger project on the Americanization of economics since the Second World War.[7]

(2) Second, Mirowski offers a new perspective on the role of empirical work in economics. If market participants can and do start with arbitrary prices and engage in "false" trades, we must recognize that at every step they also change the systemwide arbitrage-free state: with every change in quantities chosen, all prices of all commodities alter, just as if all forces really did change when one changed. This need not preclude ultimate convergence, but in any case we have to do, not with the approach to a fixed end-state, but with convergence involving a shifting target. Empirical work, on this view, is quite different from the way we have thought about it within the hypothetico-deductive tradition. There one theorized about "reality," or "nature," postulated an ideal exact or "true" function, and tested for goodness of fit. On the alternative view— Mirowski's, though he takes this particular point from Mandelbrot— actual price, the arbitrage-free price, and the convergence variable are all stochastic, possibly martingale processes.[8]

For the historian of economics the implications are dramatic. Impelled by the economist colleagues looking over our shoulders to write histories that show how present verities came to be selected, we have been

---

6. A beginning was made on this broad issue in Ingrao and Israel's *The Invisible Hand* (1990), but a more detailed treatment is to be found in Israel's "The Two Paths of the Mathematicization of the Social and Economic Sciences" (1991). The whole tradition of political arithmetic has been somewhat neglected by historians of economics, though the question has begun to be asked: Why was there no probabilistic revolution in economic thought? That question is the title of a contribution by Claude Ménard (1987) and informs ongoing work by Mirowski devoted to Edgeworth and Koopmans.

7. I know only of selected work in progress in these areas. Bob Coats is beginning to explore the Americanization issue; Mirowski's work (jointly with Albert Jolink) on Koopmans promises to touch on aspects of the formalization question, as his published work on Samuelson has done already (see, e.g., his commentary in this volume). Part of the background necessary for grasping Samuelson's contribution is provided in Weintraub's *Stabilizing Economic Dynamics* (1991), and he is just getting started on a project dealing with Debreu and the Bourbaki tradition.

8. Mirowski is not alone in his conviction that martingales are a promising way of unifying economic theory and empirical work. John McCall of the University of California, Los Angeles, has been exploring this and related themes for years.

grateful for the positivistic assurance that there is a world of theory and a world of facts, since in that case the two can be confronted and we have a criterion for weeding out theoretical error.[9] But if theory itself is stochastic, and if the way we represent both actual and "equilibrium" variables is very much a matter of empirical exploration, the lines between theoretical and empirical economics become blurred. At the very least the long tradition that the history of economics is best written as the history of theory, more or less in isolation, has to be rethought. Apparently straightforward questions have to be regarded differently. Was Smith right about the price-smoothing role of the inland corn dealer? Did Ricardo correctly read recent price history in his investigations of 1809–10? "Rightness" and "correctness" here will be found to turn not on a confrontation of hypotheses with hard facts, but on the ways, possibly multiple, in which we devise empirical models that capture parts or all of our theory, and on the links we can establish between these empirical models and the statistical models we adopt to represent features of the numbers we possess.[10] In addition to this major methodological reorientation, numerous particular historical questions arise directly out of the new perspective. To take illustrative examples from recent work that I happen to know about: Why was Tinbergen's econometric work *not* stochastic? What were the circumstances surrounding the work of an unknown like K. G. Hagstroem, who in 1938 *did* construct a stochastic exchange model?[11]

(3) A different aspect of acknowledging that "the empirical" is not a given, not part of a fixed nature, is that questions are raised about the boundaries between the physical (or, more broadly, the natural) and the social (or, more narrowly, the economic).[12] There has been a tendency

---

9. Salutary reading for historians of economics is Peter Novick's *That Noble Dream* (1988), esp. chs. 15 and 16.

10. The future historian of economics thus must be analytically able and empirically competent as well. Contributions along the lines that I see as inevitable are surfacing in small but increasing numbers: for example, Kim (1990) and his as yet unpublished work on Jevons (1992); Arnon's work on Ricardo and on Tooke (1989, 1991); Mirowski's own investigation of Smith (1984). Now that Marshall's "Red Books" (his own records of historical series) have been rediscovered, a whole new era in empirically based Marshall research could open up.

11. Hagstroem was unknown to me until I learned of him through the work of my student Mike Lail, who is investigating how theoretical statistics entered econometrics. Tinbergen's intellectual history is available for the first time in the dissertation of Marcel Boumans, of the University of Amsterdam (Boumans 1992).

12. Mirowski has a conference volume on these issues in press.

among historians of economics to assume that the natural (!) course of things is an economics that borrows its methods and its images from mathematics, physics, and perhaps biology. What are the resistances to movement in the reverse direction? What characterizes those historical examples—Mandeville's physiology and his economics constitute one such—that illustrate a reverse or even a two-way flow? (See de Marchi 1992b.)

(4) If exchange is a group activity and if exchange rates are targeted and to some extent set by group intervention, the study of market practices becomes a priority. We should, for example, be able to isolate the economic problem of specific groups, identify (in many cases) their rationalization of it—this will often take the form of a statement on valuation—and predict how they will act so as to achieve the price that "fits" their need. To use yet again the example of the art market, art dealers, we have seen, "must" act so as to secure for themselves a price appreciation at least equal to the rate of interest on bonds; painters of no special talent "must" be concerned about covering costs; specially talented painters, however, may be expected to extract a quasi-rent by manipulating and exploiting the demand curve; and so on. We will understand how this particular market operates only when we grasp the problem peculiar to each sort of participant and study the practices they invent to address their particular needs. Mirowski's interest, as theoretician, is in the properties of arbitrage-free exchange; I am much more interested in the groping, stumbling efforts that go into constructing a market, hence in the *emergence* of practices and institutions. But his social theory of value formalism helps me specify historical questions along the lines I have indicated.

(5) If actors choose and shape their own conventions for meeting the need for invariance, the study of accounting operations becomes critical. The somewhat neglected, if not maligned, tradition of political arithmetic then takes on fresh significance, as do more familiar methods of bookkeeping. Marx, Mitchell, Hicks, and Boulding have all made accounting frameworks in some ways the centerpieces of their economics, yet their example (in this respect) has not been studied especially, much less followed.[13]

---

13. Ted Porter at the University of California, Los Angeles, is pursuing the history of accounting as part of a more general study in the history of quantification.

Summary and Conclusions

I conclude with a summary and brief comments, in the form of three questions and my own answers to them.

(1) First, *More Heat than Light* is an attempt to rewrite the history of economic thought by focusing on the struggles associated with theorizing about value. Do we understand the undertaking better for knowing something of Mirowski's third alternative, the "social" theory of value? Clearly the answer for me is yes. The history in *More Heat* is difficult to follow because it is so unconventional. Value as "substance" is not the way we are used to having preclassical and classical thought represented, and to get used to it requires that we learn to think in terms of value theory as one expression of a then-dominant metaphor: matter as substance in motion. The successor approach of the nineteenth century, value as "energy," seems equally obscure, until we become accustomed to the idea that there arose a new dominant metaphor, the energy "field," with its associated formalism, which economists borrowed to explicate the maximizing of "utility." But not only is the history of *More Heat* difficult, it stops at this second dominant metaphor, leaving the impression that economics is beholden to an outdated physics. The criticism of incoherence that Mirowski levels at neoclassical economics in the later chapters of *More Heat* stems, after all, from the weaknesses inherent in sticking with that connection. Having the social value theory alternative before us is a useful reminder that the cultural evolution of economics did not have to stop with the energetics connection and field formalism. Moreover, emphasizing the *social* in thinking about value has a double effect: it reminds us that the history of economics in *More Heat* is indeed a story of *cultural* evolution—metaphors are expressions of a culture—and it keeps us aware that *More Heat* is a postmodern work: it offers us a reading, stressing coherence, rather than being a tale of professionalization or a narrative of analytical advance.

(2) Without a social theory of value could we have discovered reasons for undertaking possible fresh historical inquiries like those indicated earlier? Certainly; but it helps focus some of the issues and provides a rationale, if justification is needed, for taking a different view on certain topics. In fact, justifications can always be manufactured; what is difficult is to imagine things differently in the first place. Thus it is often asserted that studying the history of economics helps keep alive neglected alternatives to the dominant mainstream approach. That may be, but how

do we avoid seeing alternative figures as mere "also rans," or intellectual Luddites, if we start off with the idea that the history is necessarily disciplinary history, and that "progress" must be measured by the criterion of current verities? The social theory of value, and Mirowski's constructivist approach in general, help break down presumptions about the natural and the social, about the fixity of disciplinary boundaries, and about the inevitability of economics as we know it.

(3) But is the social theory of value a useful new research program in and of itself? The formal properties of arbitrage-free exchange circuits seem rather familiar. Mirowski would disagree: he suggests that the question of the linearity of prices has never been asked "in the whole history of economic thought" ("Symmetries," 1991b). Be that as it may, the formalism is newly adapted (and untainted);[14] the constructivist reading, I have just argued, is a great help in breaking out of old forms; and the space opened up for "false" trades may be a genuine step forward in the study of how markets work. The constructivist view of knowledge (and of trading circuits) is separable from the formalism of groups and directed graph theory, however; and the discussion of the randomness of value (which allows "false" trades) is at this stage relatively underdeveloped. Even with more work, the question whether convergence occurs, and how, seems unlikely to be solved except by imposing some "evolutionary" mechanism in the form of distribution constraints. We are thus left with the formalism of exchange itself, which is not enough: measurement and conservation issues do not embrace all the interesting questions. For one, growth finds no place here except via the not very promising concession that there can be no increase of value without a breaching of the (nominally given) invariance conditions, requiring an expansion of money. Even if formally correct, that gives us no way

---

14. As a purely practical matter, I am not sure how much difference to anybody's behavior is made by Mirowski's More Coherent Than Thou crusade against neoclassical economics. The last victor in a strictly-more-coherent battle was Piero Sraffa. It is all too easy for practitioners in the neoclassical tradition to step out of the line of fire by claiming: Well, we don't really think of utility as potential energy, so we're not strictly bound by our borrowed metaphor and its associated mathematics. An example of how to make that move is to be found in Hal Varian's (1991) review of Mirowski's *More Heat*. For a very clear exposition of how a well-trained physicist—Tinbergen—saw the need for *added* binding conditions to make sense of exchange when the problem is set up initially as one in which the mathematics of energy is transferred to the utility "field," see Boumans (1992, ch. 2.2). Tinbergen did not hesitate to make the needed changes; and since he was not beholden to the field metaphor or its formalism *or* the utility theory of exchange value, it is hard to fault him.

into such old questions as how wealth arises. A focus on the arbitrage-free state in developed markets tells us nothing in particular about the emergence of profit-producing strategems.

References

Arnon, Arie. 1991. *Thomas Tooke: Pioneer of Monetary Theory*. Ann Arbor: University of Michigan Press.
Arnon, Arie, and Y. Tsur. 1989. The Bullion Debate Once Again. Mimeo.
Baker, Wayne E. 1984. The Social Structure of a National Securities Market. *American Journal of Sociology* 89.4:775–811.
Boulding, Kenneth. 1950. *A Reconstruction of Economics*. New York: Wiley.
Boumans, Marcel. 1992. A Case of Limited Physics Transfer: Jan Tinbergen's Resources for Re-shaping Economics. Ph.D. dissertation, University of Amsterdam.
Christensen, Paul. 1991. Quesnay: Natural Philosophy, Physiology, and Economics. Mimeo. Hofstra University.
de Marchi, Neil. 1991. League of Nations Economists and the Ideal of Peaceful Change in the Decade of the Thirties. Annual supplement, *HOPE* volume 23, 143–78.
———. 1992a. Review of *More Heat than Light*, by Philip Mirowski. *Economics and Philosophy* 8:163–69.
———. 1992b. The Creative Work of Digestion and Artifice: Mandeville's Animal Oeconomy. Mimeo. Duke University.
de Marchi, Neil, and Christopher Gilbert, eds. 1989. *History and Methodology of Econometrics*. Oxford: Clarendon Press.
Hicks, J. R. 1942. *The Social Framework: An Introduction to Economics*. Oxford: Oxford University Press.
Ingrao, Bruna, and Giorgio Israel. 1990. *The Invisible Hand: Economic Equilibrium in the History of Science*. Cambridge: MIT Press.
Israel, Giorgio. 1991. The Two Paths of the Mathematicization of the Social and Economic Sciences. Mimeo. University of Rome.
Kim, Jinbang. 1990. Discovery and Testing in Economics: The Case of Job Search Theory. Ph.D. dissertation, Duke University.
———. 1992. A Note on Jevons's Curve Fitting. Mimeo. University of California, Riverside.
Kregel, Jan. 1992. Walras' Auctioneer and Marshall's Well-Informed Dealers: Time, Market Prices and Normal Supply Prices. *Quaderni di Storia dell'Economia Politica* 10:531–51.
Ménard, Claude. 1987. Why Was There No Probabilistic Revolution in Economics? In *The Probabilistic Revolution*, vol. 2, *Ideas in the Sciences*, edited by Lorenz Kruger, Gerd Gigerenzer, and Mary S. Morgan. Cambridge: MIT Press.
Mirowski, Philip. 1984. Adam Smith, Empiricism, and the Rate of Profit in Eighteenth-Century England. *HOPE* 14:178–98. Reprinted in *Against Mecha-*

nism: Protecting Economics from Science, edited by Philip Mirowski. Totowa, N.J.: Rowman & Littlefield, 1988.

———. 1986. Mathematical Formalism and Economic Explanation. In *The Reconstruction of Economic Theory*, edited by Philip Mirowski, 179–240. Dordrecht: Kluwer.

———. 1989a. Lecture Notes on an Institutionalist Theory of Value. Mimeo. Tufts University. October.

———. 1989b. *More Heat than Light: Economics as Social Physics, Physics as Nature's Economics*. Cambridge: Cambridge University Press. [Citations are abbreviated *MHL*.]

———. 1990. Learning the Meaning of a Dollar: Conservation Principles and the Social Theory of Value in Economic Theory. *Social Research* 57.3:689–717.

———. 1991a. Postmodernism and the Social Theory of Value. *Journal of Post-Keynesian Economics* 13.4:565–82.

———. 1991b. Symmetries, Arbitrage and the Social Theory of Value. Mimeo. November. Forthcoming in *New Directions in Analytical Political Economy*, edited by Amitava Dutt. Dordrecht: Kluwer.

Neal, Larry. 1990. *The Rise of Financial Capitalism: International Capital Markets in the Age of Reason*. Cambridge: Cambridge University Press.

Novick, Peter. 1988. That Noble Dream. In *The "Objectivity Problem" and the American Historical Profession*. Cambridge: Cambridge University Press.

Varian, Hal R. 1991. Review of *More Heat than Light*, by Philip Mirowski. *Journal of Economic Literature* 29:595–96.

Weintraub, E. Roy. 1991. *Stabilizing Economic Dynamics: Constructing Economic Knowledge*. Cambridge: Cambridge University Press.

Williams, Jeffrey. 1986. *The Economic Function of Futures Markets*. Cambridge: Cambridge University Press.

Wulwick, Nancy J. 1989. Phillips' Approximate Regression. In de Marchi and Gilbert 1989, 170–88.

After Mirowski, What?

E. Roy Weintraub

There is a danger in any important book. That danger is manifest in an image of a huge dark rock, dozens of feet high, which appears suddenly in the middle of a forest clearing. The forest inhabitants approach the rock fearfully, for the rock is powerful, awful, and menacing. They try to explain the rock, to make it sensible, to make it appear usual, but its strength unsettles them. They move around it skittishly, approaching and running away, approaching and running away.

More Heat than Light is an important book. The conference* tippy-toed around the menace, attempting to dismiss it, domesticate it, and place it in familiar categories. In this brief note I indicate the dimensions of its threat to the settled order and why I believe that historians of economics cannot return to the intellectual forest they had lived in so peacefully.

Let me be clear. *I contend that the most subversive feature of* More Heat than Light *is its historiographic stance, one which denies the separate disciplinary status of the history of economic thought. The book forces historians of economics to become historians first, economists second.*

The argument of the work is easily placed: it is a narrative reconstruction of the history of economics as a set of texts connected to sets of texts in what we commonly, now, refer to as physics, chemistry, biology, mathematics, psychology, philosophy, sociology, etc. In

---

*The Duke Economic Thought Workshop Symposium "Rethinking the History of Economics in the Light of *More Heat*," Durham, 1–3 March 1991, where the papers that appear in this volume were first presented.—*Ed.*

Mirowski's book economic writings are read against, contextualized by, writings in mathematics, physics, archival records, private correspondence, popular accounts, and so on. This reconstruction of the narrative called the history of economic thought forces one to deny that neoclassical economic theory can be presented, coherently and accurately, as having developed exclusively from a problematic defined, and driven, by economic texts. The history of economics is but one part of a larger and more comprehensive history of ideas, and of a more extensive social history than one which focuses on various neoclassical revolutionaries like Jevons, Menger, and Walras. In literary-theoretic jargon, Mirowski has provided a strong reading of the neoclassical canon, a reading that permanently alters subsequent readings of that set of documents. It is no longer possible to view a reading of Walras as satisfactory, say, if it ignores the mathematico-physical content of the formal apparatus employed by Walras and ignores the moves, in all areas of intellectual discourse, to legitimize representations of the economy by reconstructing the economy in terms of the successfully constructed natural world.

Too innocent of ideas outside the economics lecture hall, historians of economics have produced a history of equilibrium constituted from the canonical economics texts—where precisely can we locate the influence of Cournot on Marshall?—or a history of utility developed from nuggets in Smith and classical (!) economists. More comprehensive reconstructions of value, its social history say, or the representations of social equilibrium in the social order, were best left to intellectual or social historians, which meant that they were not language games historians of economists played. And given the lack of interest expressed by intellectual and social historians in the themes which concerned economists, what was left to others was left to no one in particular.

Mirowski's book is a remarkable frontal attack on this entrenched historiography. His interweaving of mathematics with physics, his understanding that the mathematics of the neoclassical revolution was the formally instantiated energetics of the earlier time, and his construction of a narrative to encompass the interrelated fields of scholarship which shared language, formalism, and imagery (albeit with incommensurability problems, and translation failures) make a history of economic thought which cannot be ignored. Once a connection is demonstrated, and argued, and seen, it cannot be unseen. Some genies will not go back in their bottles; of course, for some readers the metaphor is instead that of Pandora's box. *What Mirowski has accomplished is nothing less than a redefinition of what might constitute a convincing account of some feature, or other, of economic analysis.*

The usual historical account of the consumption function, or the natural rate hypothesis, or the optimal tariff, or the efficiency of the competitive equilibrium, has consisted of an internalist discussion of the sequence of texts which led to the idea in question, or an examination of the internal logic of the ideas which eventuated in the analytic edifice. Narratives have been structured by the development of the ideas, or the authorial constructions, of the economists. They have also been structured by a specific methodological discussion of how economics must have developed. One can tell Kuhnian stories of revolutionary episodes or normal problem solving. One can provide Lakatosian accounts of progress achieved or unattained. One can provide accounts to illustrate one or another meta-accounting rule like "any successful theory must have overcome hurdles A, B, C, etc." But what one is not accustomed to do in the history of economics is to account for a bit of economic analysis, or an economic idea, by locating it in contexts outside economics. This said, I note that externalist accounts of the development of economic ideas have focused primarily on the notion that economic theories are "caused" or conditioned by the real or actual economy however that is construed. The context of an idea is generally of limited interest.

The conference played a leitmotif of "So what if neoclassical analysis *is* 'connected' to nineteenth-century physics? The analysis is still best understood by its successes, and presented through its development as *economic* analysis." What Mirowski has problematized is the phrase "best understood." He has called into question the intellectual isolation of historians of economics and, by so doing, forces a reader to attend to the implicit historiographic assumptions which have defined history of economic thought as a subfield of economics. If Mirowski is convincing, that subfield must establish connections to the history of science, and thence to intellectual and social history proper. Accustomed as historians of economics are to seek approval only from one another, this is a frightening prospect indeed.

Part 5 The Enterpriser Responds

The Goalkeeper's Anxiety at the Penalty Kick

Philip Mirowski

> Historians undertake to arrange sequences—called stories or histories—assuming in silence a relation of cause and effect. These assumptions, hidden in the depths of dusty libraries, have been astounding, but commonly unconscious and childlike; so much so, that if any captious critic were to drag them to light, historians would probably reply, with one voice, that they had never supposed themselves to know what they were talking about. Adams, for one, had tried in vain to find out what he meant.—*The Education of Henry Adams*

1. The Education of Philip Mirowski

The purpose of this conference,* for the existence of which I owe a great debt of gratitude to Neil de Marchi, Craufurd Goodwin, and Roy Weintraub at Duke, has been to discuss my book *More Heat than Light*. While every author must be pleased and gratified when an illustrious group of talented souls take the time and effort to understand and discuss his or her work, I must confess I there contracted an anxiety attack which I have yet to shake. It began almost inadvertently, when I thought I heard people discussing me in the third-person past tense, as if I were long dead, or at the least as though I were observing the proceedings from a very great distance. And then, after the conference, there came the unabashedly *ad hominem* reviews, the ones that telegraphed the impression that things might be better off if I were indeed dead. And so, after resorting to

---

*The Duke Economic Thought Workshop Symposium "Rethinking the History of Economics in the Light of *More Heat*," Durham, 1–3 March 1991, at which the papers that appear in this volume were first presented.—*Ed.*

every subterfuge and procrastination available to my unconscious, here I find myself setting out to play the tedious and unsympathetic role of the spurned and misunderstood author, buttonholing all and sundry passersby with my pathetic plea that I have not been read either correctly or sympathetically; when all along, the truth is that I silently wonder what it was that I myself meant by all this.

I am not trying to be disingenuous or Derrida-esque here: of course I had a plan and specific ideas and made conscious choices along the way; and moreover, I more or less fully anticipated the wrath of the orthodox neoclassical economics profession. Had I been trying to ingratiate myself with that crew, I should have done things differently from the very beginning, well before *More Heat* was conceived in 1981. The rules of the academic game are such that if you are off-side, even if you manage to score, you must face up to the penalty kick without whinging or whining. No, the anxiety I refer to here is something closer to what Henry Adams obliquely referred to in his curious text *The Education*, which is largely a historical narrative about energetics and the onrushing juggernaut of science at the beginning of the century which now draws to a close, although it masquerades as an autobiography. My book is also something masquerading as something else, an assertion I shall flesh out shortly. The anxiety which Henry and I seem to share has instead to do with our uncertainty over how much of the historical trends which we thought we had identified could or should be written off as personal idiosyncrasy, how much are the contingent products of a particular path of inquiry, and how much are the end product of interactions with other scholars, living and dead. I personally believe, along with Wilhelm Dilthey, that hermeneutics has to do with readers understanding an author better than he is capable of understanding himself; nothing I can do or say will definitively settle the issue to anyone else's satisfaction. The text has a life of its own, and spawns more than a few Philip Mirowskis that I have certainly never encountered before; perhaps some of them do invite a stake through the heart. This explains some of my feeling like an unwelcome specter at the wake; but only partly.

I also fear any attempt to stabilize a project that is still evolving in its conception, its content, and in its fancied audience. When I started out, I intended primarily to address historians of economic thought, which accounts for many of the names on the roster at this conference. Yet very quickly I sought to broaden the audience to include those economists disaffected from modern orthodox economics; but as that is a very heterogeneous category, the demands made upon the project started pulling it in different directions. Then a third potential audience loomed on the horizon, namely, the history of science community. Their many and varied contributions have been one of the splendid bright spots in a sometimes rather dull academic landscape in the late twentieth century; and the prospect of having them become interested in these questions was too enticing to pass up. Nevertheless any moves made in their direction would entail an entirely different treatment of the history of physics from the one which adopted the less ambitious format of a plodding tutorial for the unwashed, those hanging out on the wrong side of the fence separating the "two cultures." And now it seems there is yet a fourth potential audience, the philosophers of social life who have avidly read such authors as C. S. Peirce, Michel Foucault, Ludwig Wittgenstein, Max Black, Richard Rorty, Bruno Latour, Michel Serres, Mary Douglas, Jürgen Habermas, Hans-Georg Gadamer, Ian Hacking, Peter Galison, and a host of others. This audience is larger than one might initially anticipate and an author neglects the implied scale economies at his peril.

Consequently the original prospectus sent to Cambridge University Press envisioned three volumes, in a rather different configuration from what eventually ensued. The first volume would look something vaguely like *More Heat*, but without the first three chapters and augmented with a much more detailed narrative of the struggles to render economics a "science," both before and after 1870. A history of economic theories of value would provide a second parallel narrative track, without actually resolving the tensions inherent in two such disparate story lines. The second volume was then intended to explicate this tension by sketching a similar tension in the rather more respected project of physics: even there, I would suggest, the quest for scientific status was just as bound up with competing ideas of invariance and value, which were themselves often buttressed with economic metaphors and concepts. In effect this would have been the present chapters 2 and 3, augmented by extensive consideration of such writers as Emile Meyerson, Emile Durkheim, Mary Douglas, David Bloor, and others not present in the published book.

The purpose of the second volume would have been to impart the idea that the imitation of physics by economists was *not* simply some pathetic tic found in assorted snivelling, depraved individuals desperate for the status, prizes, and recognition of their intellectual superiors, but rather an integral part of an interlocking system of anthropomorphic reasoning which served to reify and stabilize invariance in an unstable world. The juxtaposition of the two fields was then intended to provoke the question of what exactly it was that had led to a "success" in one case and not in the other, since at least in this fundamental sense they both had recourse to the "same method." The multiform deliberations over this issue found in the now neglected literatures of the German Historicist and American Institutionalist schools would have revealed that these are old questions in economics, and that neoclassicism is unique in that it finds itself unable to sustain a language within which to pose them.

The third volume, whose contents never made it into *More Heat*, would have been an attempt to resolve the tension and tender an answer to the previous question by locating the problem of invariance in the larger context of symmetry principles. Just as the process of mathematical formalization in physics was predicated upon postulation of ever more elaborate symmetries—from spatial symmetry to temporal symmetry to more inaccessible gauge symmetries—so too must economics settle upon what it is that particularly characterizes the symmetries inherent in their own specific subject matter. One does not get this from imitation of physical models or any putative "scientific method," but rather from specific philosophical considerations generated from within the discipline of economics.

This hidden agenda of providing economics with its own intrinsic rationale would probably help explain the fascination with value theory found in *More Heat* which some commentators found arbitrary or even a bit oldfashioned; it also explains the critical thrust in what struck many as an incongruously relativist text. I have suggested in some subsequent papers published elsewhere that the symmetry intrinsic to the description of markets is the principle of arbitrage, which is not at all central to the neoclassical tradition and which, moreover, requires a radically different style of mathematics for its formalization.[1] Here I grant that I may not have done the readers of *More Heat* much of a favor by leaving out the entire upbeat side of my message; but then again, Cambridge University Press did ultimately demand a discrete single volume as a condition of publication, and the book was slated to be included in a series entitled "Historical Perspectives on Modern Economics." And yet, given my desire *not* to have the message of the book become regarded as the trivi-

---

1. Mirowski 1991a and in press, b.

ally uninteresting and fallacious thesis that "economics copied physics and that's patently wrong," I included a fair amount of material suggesting that conservation principles were not all that stable or rock-solid in the history of physics, and that earlier physicists had no compunctions about resorting to economic metaphors in order to try and stabilize their own discourse. The extremely compressed version of this component of the argument accounts for the crystalline trialectic found on page 107, a synecdoche which apparently nobody liked. In retrospect I realize how much Hegel seeped in here via Meyerson, and how poorly such themes can be reconciled with the present intellectual climate.

In my less confident moments I now wonder whether this entire expository strategy (but not the ideas themselves) was ill conceived. When Thorstein Veblen was asked whether he was the infamous author of *The Theory of the Leisure Class*, he replied that he had to plead guilty, but that if it were any consolation, he would promise never to do it again. If it is any consolation, I will also take the pledge.

2. An Anatomy of Physics Envy

It has been an uphill struggle even to convince economists and historians of thought of the importance of the history of physics in beginning to understand the evolution of economics. I find the accusations that I have an "obsession with physics and neoclassical economics" or that I have somehow misrepresented the work of Paul Samuelson to be astounding, given that I regard this particular aspect of *More Heat* to be thoroughly unoriginal on my part. Many people with serious backgrounds in physics, having gone on to undertake equally serious study of the social sciences, have made the same points frequently. I made reference to Nicholas Georgescu-Roegen in this regard in the book, but with only minor efforts I can come up with other examples. Take, for instance, Harrison White. He holds a Ph.D. in theoretical physics from MIT, but then went on to take a Ph.D. in sociology, and has subsequently had a distinguished career as a sociologist at the University of Chicago and at Harvard. I reproduce the following quote from a recent interview:

> I took a year of graduate mathematical economics from Paul Samuelson. . . . Samuelson's *Foundations of Economic Analysis* was clearly taking over economics in the 1950s and moving it, as far as I was concerned, in the wrong direction. . . . Samuelson had the bad luck to

form his ideas in the environment of the early 1940s, when the natural model to follow in science was field theory in physics. And to me that is a singularly inappropriate analogue to economic phenomena. . . . Since the economists had killed off the institutionalist tradition, there was in effect no intellectual basis for young economists to grow some theory out of a historical background without being trapped by it. It was hard for them to approach the problem of the theory of the market historically and see its evolutionary pattern.[2]

Since such impressions are hardly novel or earthshaking and, indeed, can be discovered as far back as the writings of Veblen, what accounts for the various manifestations of pollution taboo behavior that have greeted *More Heat*? Everyone is free to propose hermeneutic clarifications, but in the interests of getting the conversation going beyond what we experienced at the conference, I suggest three theses, and a digression on style:

1. Orthodox neoclassical economics is experiencing severe pangs of self-doubt at the moment, provoking neurotic overkill in response to any critique which is regarded as having deleterious implications for funding or other legitimation procedures.
2. Various cultural outlets such as *Science*, *Scientific American*, and *Physics Today*, claiming to represent the interests of the sciences as a whole, reveal a willingness to intervene much more directly in the affairs of economics than has previously been the case.
3. The economics profession has been progressively sloughing off the history of economic thought (as physics has successfully dispensed with its own history) as a subject suitable for graduate curricula, and therefore it is deemed doubly impossible that any significant ideas or theoretical contribution might originate there.

Let us briefly consider each influence in turn, and begin with the standard response: "Crisis? What crisis!??" I shall merely refer to the ubiquity of the wringing of hands and the gnashing of teeth in a footnote, and move on to more substantive symptoms.[3]

---

2. Interview with Richard Swedberg (in Swedberg 1990, 79, 84). I have further discussed the importance of Nicholas Georgescu-Roegen in Mirowski 1992a.

3. Leontief 1982; Morishima (in Wiles and Routh 1984); Hahn 1991; *The Crisis in Economic Theory* 1977 (special issue of *The Public Interest*); Coats 1977; Kirman 1992; Summers 1991. Of course, it takes an outsider not to mince words: "Within fifteen years, by the year

The crisis at the heart of the orthodoxy is poignantly revealed by the sequence of its preferred English-language graduate micro texts, from Marshall (1890) to Henderson and Quandt (1958) to Varian (1978) to Kreps (1990). The first, as many are well aware, relegated the physics appropriations to the appendices, in favor of numerous digressions concerning organic metaphors, industrial organization, the distribution of income, folk psychology, and the like. Of course, much of this was intended to foster the impression of a smooth continuity between classical and neoclassical value theory that just was not there, but it did have the charm of a certain crusading spirit and seeming relevance to the concerns of those initially attracted to economics. Henderson and Quandt, while sporting a much closer resemblance to an undergraduate classical mechanics text, still followed in the hallowed Marshallian tradition of supply and demand, although the discussions of psychology were now notably absent, and in their place one dived right into something called "consumer theory." Dynamics were unabashedly Marshallian, with no Hamiltonians anywhere in sight, and concessions to relevance came through chapters on imperfect competition and welfare economics. By the time we get to Varian, the Marshallian component is only an embarrassing remnant; but more significantly, "consumer theory" is itself relegated to a delayed appearance in chapter 3. The student gets the message that it is nothing but optimization all the way down, being informed on page 1 that a simple application of the Kuhn-Tucker theorem will always do the trick; but the poor student has to turn to appendix 7 to find how to actually do the trick. Dynamics now gets hidden away on a few pages (188–93), where the hard-edged rhetoric of theorem-lemma-proof gives way to "sketches," impressions, and "plausible" stories. Concessions to "reality" come now in the format of a chapter on "econometrics and economic theory," but instead of giving us examples of some technological regularities or laws of consumer behavior that economists have successfully uncovered in their empirical endeavors, it is all a run-

---

2000 or so, economics as we know it will have gone through a major crisis. And it won't have been brought on by outsiders like me. There will come a time when the machine just kind of collapses out of frustration with itself. Just look at those Nobel Prizes they are handing out every year. These supposed achievements really make you wonder" (Harrison White, in Swedberg 1990, 86). My all-time favorite is Frank Hahn's "reflections" upon his retirement from the University of Cambridge: "Economics is not in crisis. . . . There is no point discussing the use of mathematics in economics. . . . Here is an old man's advice—don't worry" (*Royal Economic Society Newsletter*, April 1992, 5). It must feel swell to retire just now.

up to the admission that "any continuous function that satisfies Walras' Law can be generated by some set of preference-maximizing consumers with some distribution of income" (134). The wording is ambagious, if not intentionally misleading, but what it all comes down to is that the non-Marshallian price theory provides hardly any significant empirical restrictions at all. (See section 4 below.) No accommodation or quarter is given in actually justifying why anyone should persevere beyond that chapter, or indeed in their graduate education. When we finally arrive at Kreps, we are in a brave new world. Marshall is unceremoniously dumped (37, 279). All sorts of revealing admissions are made: von Neumann–Morgenstern expected utility fails most empirical tests; the Walrasian model does not describe how a market actually works (195); Walrasian economies generally have infinite numbers of equilibria (215); Arrow's (im)possibility theorem suggests that optimality is incompatible with democracy—and a whole raft of others. But not to worry: the entire discourse will now be stabilized around the alternative organizing principle of game theory, though the absence of any fundamental consensus in game theory over solution concepts might be thought to put a crimp in the enthusiasm of the tyro student, if not the author himself.

I think it is clear we are indeed in a different world, and those neoclassicals who pine for the nostalgic verities of Marshall (or Marshallians such as Friedman, or—and I shudder to think of the enemies I am making here—Keynes) are either deluding themselves or living in the past. By this I do not mean that Marshall's system was analytically superior: far from it.[4] Rather, one can make the historical case that Marshall's curves of demand and supply were ancillary to the program of imitation of energetics, the Trojan Horse that got it into the academy, and therefore had to be progressively abandoned in theory textbooks at the graduate level; but once that was accomplished, the Walrasian variant, the social physics, *the right stuff*, really had nothing equally compelling or inspirational to put in its place. This is nicely illustrated by the book by Arjo Klamer and David Colander on the vacuity at the heart of American graduate economics education. Once the Sonnenschein-Mantel-Debreu results had sunk in, it has become apparent, in the words of Alan Kirman, that "the emperor has no clothes."[5] In fact one could make the

---

4. This argument is presented in more detail in Mirowski 1990c. The ambivalent use of biological metaphor is discussed further in Schabas, in press.

5. Klamer and Colander 1990; Kirman 1989. The original paper in this literature was Sonnenschein's "Market Excess Demand Functions" (1972). A good survey of the various

case that the compulsive shift to game theory is a direct consequence of the utter disintegration of the program of methodological individualist determinism in the Walrasian general equilibrium program. So perhaps at least some of us can agree that there really is a crisis in neoclassicism, and that pointing out the physics origins of marginalism as a prelude to diagnosis may therefore elicit something more than antiquarian ennui.

And then there are those who would insist that whatever the present status of neoclassicism, its origins in energy physics or pushpin or poetry are entirely irrelevant, since economists have managed to outgrow or transcend or sublimate their physics envy in the interim. Again, I am astounded at this attitude, since the slightest empirical inquiry would demonstrate otherwise. I produce the following passage from *Science* magazine of August 1989—and please note well the use of sexual innuendo:

> Over the past 2 years, [Philip] Anderson and [Kenneth] Arrow have worked together in a venture that is one of the oddest couplings in the history of science—a marriage, or at least a serious affair, between economics and the physical sciences. If this unlikely liason bears fruit, the result could be a hybrid theory that imparts to economics some of the tools and techniques developed for such fields as physics and biology. . . . In 1986, John Reed, chairman of Citicorp, found himself dissatisfied with state-of-the-art economic forecasting. . . . Having a degree in metallurgical engineering himself, Reed looked to the physical sciences for help, and he asked the Santa Fe Institute to find ways to improve economic forecasting.[6]

---

problems organized under the rubric of the problem of "microfoundations" is Rizvi 1992a; an excellent history of the problem is in Ingrao and Israel 1990.

6. Pool 1989. Just in case one is interested in gender identification, one discovers the further statement down the page: "Anderson and the other scientists in the project think they have something to offer because, like economists, they deal with complex systems whose many parts interact nonlinearly. The economists are not quite so sanguine, but they are definitely interested in seeing what their counterparts can offer." An unnamed but reliable inside source informs me that John Reed should not be regarded as just another pushover for any physicist who comes sauntering around the block: "Actually, Reed is far more of a mystic/visionary type than a hardboiled quant. On a CEO list of books recently read, where most focused upon Michael Porter, military history, power-of-persuasion, Bible and so on, Reed was reading in Russian art history of the Middle Ages because he thought it had gotten short shrift in standard histories, was boning up on his microbiology to help him on the board of Monsanto, was installing a major Zen garden in the middle of the remarkable 2nd floor executive suite at 399 Park Ave." But really, who better to act as chaperone on a blind date, especially if conversation starts to flag?

Be it legitimate marriage or one-night stand, neoclassicals have never spurned the advances of physics, especially not when accompanied by the requisite flowers and chocolates. One insistent theme of *More Heat* is that history matters, whether it be in physics, or economic theory, in the writing of histories, or in the self-understanding of the economics discipline itself.

Now that I have distressed a goodly portion of my audience, let me try to alienate the rest. None of the above has anything to do with standard methodological concerns about "realism," be it of assumptions or predictions or concepts or what-have-you. Neoclassicism has encountered serious difficulties in stabilizing its own empirical practices; and this is a historical phenomenon I have been most recently concerned to document, using much the same approach of bringing the history and sociology of science to bear upon that sadly neglected topic, in the same general spirit as *More Heat*.[7] The lack of this empirical aspect in *More Heat* did make the book look excessively internalist or idealist, as a number of conference participants have complained. Nevertheless I feel impelled to counter that this absence was part of the point: changes in "the economy" or specific empirical inquiries have had very little to do with the larger transformations in value theory and, therefore, with the structural framework of economic theory. The contemporary crisis in orthodox economics ultimately derives from the analytical observation, rooted in the Sonnenschein-Mantel-Debreu literature, that its value theory is empirically empty, which (I claim) in turn derives from its provenance as an imperfect imitation of physics. I elaborate upon this claim further in section 4 below, on integrability and symmetry.

This brings us to the second observation, namely, we are not talking about a bunch of cloistered monks poring over the arcane cabala of fixed-point theorems and separating hyperplanes, but about a discipline embedded in a larger scientific culture. If science indeed depends upon a social context, then the legitimacy of that science requires the persistent intervention of other scientists to shore up its boundaries and pretensions, everywhere from the government funding sources to the organs of the popularization of science. While I knew this intellectually, it was brought home in a visceral manner by some subsequent reactions to *More Heat*. Shortly after publication and a favorable notice in the

---

7. Mirowski 1989a, 1989c, 1989d, 1990b; in press, c. The demonstration that empirical events have very little impact upon major developments in economic theory dates back to my early article on Adam Smith (see Mirowski 1988, chapter 11).

Boston Globe, I was approached by both *Science* and *Scientific American* to prepare some short precis of the book for a general audience. Clearly neither of the staff persons who had contacted me had bothered to read it, undoubtedly mistaking it for yet another candidate in that commonplace genre of physico-economic treatises. When they finally did discover that it was simultaneously a critical history of energy and of orthodox economics, couched within the overall problematic of scientism, they both rather rudely dropped the project. And yet those publications imperiously assert the capacity to pronounce on what constitutes "good science" in standard economics, even though it may on occasion be patently false[8] or blatantly naive.

An example of the latter stance is an article in a recent *Scientific American* chosen (honestly!) at random, entitled "Coping with Math Anxiety."[9] The article notes that "some economists have worried that the explosion of work in high-powered mathematics has outpaced research on fundamental theory." The subsequent mollification of such worries, effectively nothing more than an inept series of non sequiturs interspersed with Nobelist quotes, deserves a separate detailed rhetorical analysis which we cannot give it here. The present point at issue is, rather, who or what endowed *Scientific American* with the right, the competence, or even anything other than a passing fancy, to intervene in this methodological debate? Can armchair physicists really soothe our fevered brows? The answer is neither deep nor subtle: for more than a century the primary motor of economic discourse has been the achievement and maintainance of a scientific demeanor. This must needs be accomplished by innuendo, indirection, and mathematics; it cannot be openly discussed in polite company. The major function of *Scientific American* appears to be that of spin doctor of the scientific disciplines and their "wannabe" cousins. Apropos of our present concerns, why would this economists' internal spat have been anything more than a superfluous bit of cultural folderol, unless there were actually something at stake here, some sneaking suspicion that something can look very much like a science (and that is an eminently historical question) and yet not really make the grade?

The third thesis has to do with the recent sociology of the economics

---

8. "The success of risk management policies should be judged in terms of their effect on [von Neumann–Morgenstern] expected utility, the only well-developed prescriptive framework for choice under uncertainty" (Zeckhauser and Viscusi 1990, 559).

9. Corcoran and Wallich 1992.

profession. Everyone is aware that in the last generation graduate studies in economics have grown more fixated upon mathematical competence, more homogeneous in terms of topics covered, and less tolerant of diverse perspectives drawn from other literatures. This is not only true in the United States, but also in Europe, where the MIT model can now be found in almost any large research institution. From one vantage point, this is evidence of the final triumph of scientific economics, the Hegelian "end of history." A corollary is often drawn that it is also the end of the history of economic thought as a credible subdiscipline of economics. It has recently even been suggested that historians of thought should gird up their loins and gather up their tattered remnants in preparation for a mass exodus to departments of the history of science.[10] While I doubt historians inhabit anything even remotely resembling the Promised Land on college campuses, it does give some indication of the tenuous status of knowledge of previous traditions under the MIT model.

One implication of this trend is that, by definition, work in the history of economic thought could never make any relevant contribution to economics at this late date. Its only residual function, other than to provide a pasture in which over-the-hill neoclassical theorists could ruminate, is to provide those paragraph-long vignettes in undergraduate textbooks, the better to spur the neophyte onwards in emulation of past genius, or else to posit the "rational reconstruction" and the "canonical model" of this or that classical author, revealing him as progenitor, witting or otherwise, in the One True Line of economic thought. The very idea that a history could gather together long-suppressed concerns and failures and knit them together into a coherent narrative is just beyond the realm of possibility, given the present situation in economics departments. This conviction, perhaps more than anything else, lay behind the shrill tones of outrage and incredulity which one finds in economists' reactions to *More Heat*.

I am unhappy to report that the historians are not such innocent victims caught up in the sweep of events as they might like to think. Instead they have oftentimes been the complicit accomplices in promulgating the attitude that history is bunk, in all of the various senses of that Fordist catch-phrase. How else can one interpret such pronunciamentos as "The historian of economic thought cannot add to the unalterable body of past writings with which he deals," or "Knowing H. L. Moore's exposition of general equilibrium equations is of no importance for cur-

---

10. Schabas 1992.

rent general equilibrium theory," or "Economic facts and events are not philosophical issues"?[11] Or how is it that any university press would be interested in a "history" that unabashedly asserts that "whatever in the past literature . . . [that] has not become part of the modern mainstream will at most be mentioned in passing" or that "economic thought is as old as mankind. Since the expulsion from paradise man has been confronted with the same basic problems of scarcity, resource allocation and exchange."[12] Richard Rorty has an apt term for this sort of text: *doxography*, defined as "the desperate attempt to make [Smith and Arrow, Marx and Walras, Commons and Coase, etc.] talk about some common topics, whether the historian and his readers have any interest in the topics or not. . . . The real trouble with doxography is that it is a half-hearted attempt to tell a new story of intellectual progress by describing all texts in terms of recent discoveries."[13]

The reason doxography is so pernicious is that it encourages a tendency (already endemic in callow youth) to believe that there is nothing interesting or significant in the particular past endeavors of human beings who have struggled to constitute a rational discourse revolving around the "economy." This belief in a context-free character of received orthodox doctrines is itself a heritage of Western physics, reducing all that hard work to some generic "scientific method" in which each and every faceless historical personage waltzed through the same stereotyped motions. I find it most ironic that many feel so strongly that I have maligned and misrepresented their heroes in the history of neoclassical thought, for there were no living, breathing personalities in previous orthodox histories of economic thought, so far as I was aware.[14] The task of breathing life into them was not one of the immediate aims of *More Heat*, although it may ultimately help serve that purpose (see section 5 below).

3. Hopeful Monsters

Moving beyond the various defensive neoclassical reactions to *More Heat*, there are some legitimate questions raised by sympathetic par-

---

11. All quotes are from Walker 1988, 100, 105, 109. A bit of history which contradicts all three assertions may be found in Mirowski 1990b.
12. Niehans 1990, 2, 15.
13. Richard Rorty, in Rorty, Schneewind, and Skinner 1984, 62–63.
14. Or perhaps more sadly, this conception of history has prevented the few instances where the human being threatened to break through the mummified husk of the "scientist," as in the case of William Jaffé's abortive biography of Walras (see Tarascio 1988).

ticipants in this symposium about writing a disciplinary history while denying that such a thing as a discrete discipline with a well-defined "inside" and "outside" exists. In particular, Neil de Marchi and Rob Leonard are disturbed by the coexistence of the language of imperative and of choice, of the unconscious and the conscious, the repression and the subterfuge, Hegelian telos and postmodernist fragmentation. Elsewhere I have been accused by Norton Wise and Margaret Schabas of excessive praise of the physicists, whereas others instead saw a lack of respect that betokened nihilism. I have gotten fan mail from those who believe me an advocate of up-to-date appropriation of physical models, and those who detect a kindred spirit wishing a pox on all science. Since I have never actually tried to develop the political skill of telling everyone what they think they want to hear, I chalk some of this up to the truncation of the manuscript mentioned in section 1; but the problem runs deeper than that.

For the previous generation of social scientists in the American context, the only "methodological" question that seemed worthwhile to entertain was whether or not they had attained the status of a science. The richer continental discussions regarding the *Geisteswissenschaften* and the *Naturwissenschaften* were lost in the backlash to World War II; and the atomic bomb lent an inflated estimate of prestige and power to the knowledge claims of the physicists. The flowering of the history and philosophy of science in the last two decades has counteracted that trend to a certain extent; yet there still persists amongst social theorists a rather circumscribed set of preconceptions governing discourse when the topic of "science" is broached. Basically, the range of sanctioned opinion runs from a bald assertion of the unity of all science to allowing some epistemological excuses why the human sciences should be granted a handicap or two to compensate for their rather poor showing, relative, of course, to physics.[15] Precisely because these positions mark the horizons of modern interpretation of any text which sets out to recover and reconfigure the earlier heritage of continental thought (and its American derivatives), a certain intolerance is quick to surface for what is variously perceived as ambivalence or, even worse, contradictory statements concerning science.

Although this is not the place for an extended dissertation, I suggest that the problem of constructing such a historical narrative about any

---

15. For an example of the former see Glymour 1983; for the latter see Searle 1991.

one intellectual discipline is intimately bound up with the preconception of the boundaries of the Natural and the Social, and that the possible positions that can be staked out are effectively quite numerous. To save time, I sketch out an outline taxonomy, with names attached to provide pointers for the curious:

1. The Natural and the Social are identical in
   a. every respect (materialist reductionists)
   b. laws (Churchland, Rosenberg)
   c. epistemic methods (Glymour, most neoclassicals)
   d. metaphorical structures (early Pareto, Edgeworth).
2. The Natural and the Social are disjunct but severally lawlike due to
   a. epistemic status (Windelband, Rickert, Weber)
   b. ontological status rooted in psychology (Dilthey, Taylor, Searle)
   c. purposes (Habermas, Dreyfus).
3. The Natural is objectively stable, whereas the Social is patterned upon it but is not; implying
   a. sociology of collective knowledge (Durkheim, Mannheim)
   b. sociology as epistemology (Douglas, Bloor, Shapin).
4. The Natural and the Social are both unstable and jointly constructed
   a. out of interests (Latour, Haraway, Knorr-Cetina)
   b. out of practices (pragmatists, Rouse)
   c. out of will (Nietzsche, Foucault).

Those whose horizons can only encompass categories 1 + 2a will definitely have trouble making sense of *More Heat*. For instance, they will think the poor addled author of that text simply could not make up his mind whether he wanted to assert that the economists' use of the physics was defective, or that the physicists were themselves mistaken about conservation principles, or that there is some empirical claim being made about the nature of the conservation of economic phenomena.[16]

---

16. Walker 1991. While I'm at it, I should also like to register my amazement at those who think that even the title of the book can be used against me, as if I were entirely oblivious to the fact that some might feel that rhetoric egregiously dominated "content" here. The title is an explicit challenge to those who want to use that metaphor: if "hard" content is thought to be distinct from and quantitatively commensurate with angry discourse, such that one could confidently attribute deficit and surplus, then where is the relevant conservation principle or Meyersonian invariant? The very idea that scientists should repress their disputes so that they could be settled by Nature was itself the outcome of a particular set of historical practices: cf. Shapin and Schaffer 1985.

Or perhaps they will quail at the mixture of the language of choice and imperative, often used with regard to the same historical figure. What is significant here is that the full range of options are not considered part of the economist's "tool kit," and therefore I was hesitant to indicate directly in the text that *More Heat* would most comfortably fit under heading 4b, while making use of some of the theses of authors located under 3b.

To begin, let me briefly suggest the parts of the work of Mary Douglas, building upon Durkheim and Mauss's classic book *Primitive Classification*, from which I have drawn inspiration.[17] Durkheim was intent upon demonstrating the existence of "social facts," which he defined in his *Rules of Sociological Method* as "any way of acting, whether fixed or not, capable of exerting over the individual an external constraint; which is general over the whole of a given society whilst having an existence of its own, independent of its individual manifestations." In the book with Mauss, he believed he had found just such a social fact in "primitive" societies in the principle that the "classification of things reproduces the classification of men." As they wrote there about the isomorphisms they thought they had uncovered in various totemic systems:

> whereas for us they are hardly more than metaphors, originally they meant what they said. Things of the same class were really considered as relatives of individuals of the same group. . . . Things are above all sacred or profane, pure or impure, friends or enemies, favorable or unfavorable; their most fundamental characteristics are only expressions of the way in which they affect social sensibility. (84–86)

Methodological individualists such as Gabriel Tarde reacted with horror to this suggestion that there was some ghostly something hovering outside the personal consciousness; others complained that restricting the discussion to "primitive societies" tended to leave modern science with its impersonal objective character a deus ex machina.

Mary Douglas and David Bloor aimed to avoid those drawbacks and thus to provide a less static picture of the process of classification by rendering it into a functionalist story of interests and their mediations.

---

17. Durkeim and Mauss 1963; Bloor 1982; Douglas 1984, 1973, and 1986. Notice I do not make use of the grid-group analysis found in Douglas's *Natural Symbols* (1973, chapter 4), because I find it excessively Cartesian and deterministic. I also ignore the positive evaluation of neoclassical economics which she gives in *In the Active Voice* (Douglas 1982).

Bloor attempts to marry Durkheim and philosophers of science such as Quine and Hesse by asserting that

> the social message comprises the coherence conditions, while the negotiability of the network provides the resources for reconciling those demands with the input of experience. The idea that knowledge is a channel which can convey two signals at once requires us to drop the assumption that nature and society are polar opposites . . . the similarity of structure between knowledge and society is the effect of the social use of nature. (1982, 293, 297)

The later Douglas produces a more nuanced view of the role of natural metaphors in a social context, first by stressing how a modicum of distance is achieved from mundane direct interests through metaphorical intermediation and, second, by locating the primal act of categorization in the assignment of invariance and identity:

> Before it can perform its entropy-reducing work, the incipient institution needs some stabilizing principle to stop its premature demise. That stabilizing principle is the naturalization of social classifications. There needs to be an analogy by which the formal structure of a crucial set of social relations is found in the physical world, or in the supernatural world, or anywhere, so long as it is not seen as a socially contrived arrangement. . . . The effort to build strength for fragile social institutions by grounding them in nature is defeated as soon as it is recognized as such. That is why founding analogies have to be hidden. (1986, 48, 53)

> It is naive to treat the quality of sameness, which characterizes members of a class, as if it were a quality inherent in things or as a power of recognition inherent in the mind. . . . Institutions bestow sameness. Socially based analogies assign disparate items to classes and load them with moral and political content. (1986, 58, 63)

I see the useful pointers inherent in this work as the insistence upon natural metaphor as a resource in stabilizing practices which are embodied in institutions—and the attendant taboo and pollution violation reactions when these simple metaphors are exhumed—as well as the equation of stable institutions with the postulation of invariants in social classifications. The latter aspect links up rather nicely with Emile Meyerson's work on the Western taming of change by reducing it to motion and

322   Philip Mirowski

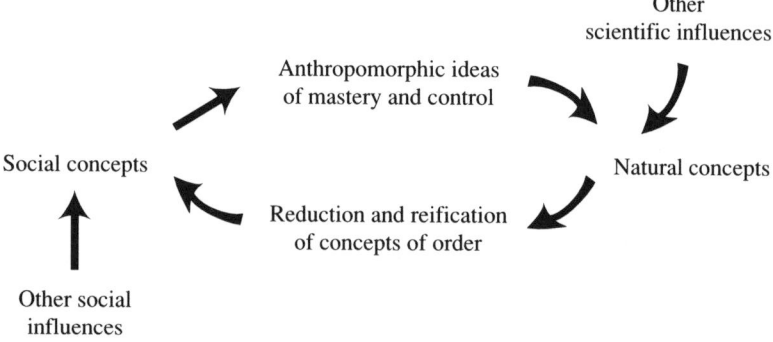

Figure 1

invariance, and of course, my own chosen topic, the history of conservation principles in physics and economics. However, I also believe that Douglas's work has a much wider sphere of application than the narrow (but fascinating) range of nineteenth-century energy physics and neoclassical economics. To sketch this out, and to make the dynamic aspect of these suggestions stand out more starkly, I have in the past made use of what I have called the "Durkheim/Mauss/Douglas" thesis (figure 1).

In order to wrest the work of Durkheim, Mauss, and Douglas out of the camp of the sociology of knowledge and bring it into the constructivist camp, a number of amendments are necessary. First, as has often been noted,[18] these theorists allow an asymmetry in their treatment of "Society" versus "Nature," either because they take successful modern science as an unproblematic given, or else because they posit certain macrosocial entities like "interests" or "ideology" as self-sufficient entities. Rather than posit two alien transcendental principles which then never can be reunited in any rational fashion, the constructivist school proposes to inquire how the boundaries were ever conceived in the first place and to ask if the distinction remains stable for very long. Second, the whole rigamarole of "social facts" is jettisoned in favor of "local knowledge," which then becomes promulgated through networks of interaction, primarily through concrete instruments, specific practices, and codified institutions. Third, the resulting impression of a "view from nowhere" is produced by means of the technologies of the discourse, such as the standard format of the scientific paper, the assertion of the

18. Latour 1990; Rouse 1987; Pickering 1992; McMullin 1992.

possibility of replications, the use of self-effacing idiom, the twenty-four-carat diploma, the austere mathematics of theorem-lemma-proof, and so forth; and it is this which serves to erase the founding metaphors from immediate consciousness, and not any conspiracy by Big Brother.[19]

The beauty of the revised Durkheim-Mauss-Douglas (DMD) thesis is that it can begin to account for change and invariance across the history of diverse intellectual disciplines. Following Meyerson, Westerners can only tell if something is "different" if something else remains the "same." The invariance in traditions enters here precisely through the naturalization of social thought, which implicitly provides reassuring definitions of order and man's priviledged place in the universe, while the use of society to suggest natural concepts helps render the ineffable "other" of the external world comprehensible to human purposes and desires. Hence severe ruptures in physical or social theory can still be recognized as part of the "same" project, even if their specific analytical content makes them hard to reconcile with previous thought. For example, in this way of thinking, both classical and neoclassical economics were part of the same explanatory project, even though their value theories and the very languages in which they were expressed (moral philosophy versus mathematics) seemed to dictate an unbridgable gulf. But most importantly, the DMD thesis also explains the persistence of relentless unresolved disputes over the meaning of the Natural and the Social in Western intellectual history. In this view, there are no special ontological or epistemological distinctions which characterize the duality; rather, the difference stems from a historical division of labor in forms of inquiry (i.e., the Cartesian mind–body dichotomy), while the pressure for identity comes from the metaphorical dynamic and its functions of promoting order and convictions of simplicity and efficacy.

Some brief illustrations of this theory of metaphorical reasoning may indicate how it could be fruitful in the history of science. One trajectory of the spiral encompasses the interplay of political economy and Darwinian evolution. Malthus began his essay by comparing people to animals in order to justify his conception of population pressure upon resources. Darwin, as is well known, read Malthus and the political economists, and this prompted him to see competition and the division of labor in animal Nature.[20] As Darwinism became the new battle cry

---

19. Nagel 1986; Shapin and Schaffer 1985; Mirowski and Sklivas 1991.
20. Young 1985; Desmond and Moore 1991; Schweber 1980.

of the professionalizing classes, "Social Darwinism" was elevated into a scientific doctrine explaining Society. Mix together Social Darwinism and some simple Marshallian microeconomics, and you arrive at E. O. Wilson's sociobiology; whereas if you opt instead for game theory, you get the new population ecology.[21] And, as if that were not enough, mix the new evolutionary synthesis and varying proportions of population biology and ecology with previous strains of economics, and you end up with either a slightly less mechanistic Marshallianism, or else a version of a rejuvenated Institutionalism.[22] And so it goes.

Another example, possibly equally freighted with immediate significance for economics, might go like this. Early notions of probability appeared in legal contexts of the plausibility of evidence and the division of partnership stakes in risky undertakings; quantitative probability arose based upon the model of fair division of expectations. When shifted to an astronomical context, mathematical expectation was reconceptualized as a "law of error," describing a natural distribution of observations around a true value. The Gaussian or "Normal" was then reflected back into the social sphere by Quetelet and his *homme moyen*. Upon reading Herschel on Quetelet, James Clerk Maxwell transposed the image of order in the midst of a population exhibiting seeming randomness back into nature with his gas laws.[23] From there stochastic formalisms spread to thermodynamics, quantum mechanics, and beyond—to the extent that it became *de rigueur* to believe that all the basic laws of Nature were at bottom probabilistic. At that point a number of scientists moved over into economics from physics and created something now known as "econometrics."[24] And so it goes.

A third example focuses upon an instrument rather than a theory. Early nineteenth-century astronomical observations required massive amounts of calculations to reduce the data to fixed stellar positions. Upon reading Adam Smith, both Prony in France and Airy in England set out to organize the process along a strict division of labor to get rid of "personal error," with skilled workers assigned to the more delicate calculations. Charles Babbage in the 1820s sought to mechanize the calculation of astronomical tables, and this, in conjunction with some inspiration from

21. Bannister 1979; Kingsland 1985; E. O. Wilson 1975.
22. Nelson and Winter 1982; Mirowski 1988, chapter 9; Hodgson, in press; Limoges and Menard, in press.
23. Daston 1988; Porter 1986; Herschel 1857, 365–465.
24. Porter 1981; Mirowski 1989c.

the Jacquard loom, resulted in one of the earliest models of a mechanical calculation device. Development of these devices proceeded apace, adopting new forms of electronic circuits and telephone switching banks, which in turn became metaphors for the working of the brain by the 1930s. These images not only led to the further development of the computer by John von Neumann in the 1940s but also informed the structure of the development of game theory.[25] Now that there is a computer on every desk, many people called "cognitive scientists" seem to think that the computer provides an excellent model for human cognition. And so it goes.

I hope this gives some indication of what all the cryptic references to Bloor and Douglas in *More Heat* were all about, and also why I think they provide an alternative model to the conventional Whig standard of writing the history of economics. I do not believe, however, that this encourages the generation of some late-Hegelian monsters of idealist historiography, contrary to the suggestion of some conference participants. In this conception, any particular historical persona can be busily at work "constructing" the meaning of the economy, or prices, or capital, or whatever, and yet be driven by certain imperatives concerning which he (or she) may not be fully aware. Metaphors, as philosophers never tire of pointing out, do not have fixed referents or fixed rules. If one insists upon regarding them as an analogical syllogism A:B::C:D where B and C are omitted as being "understood," there is plenty of room to substitute myriad intervening links besides those originally "intended." Nevertheless, upon adopting the *mathematics* of the other language community, we have now imported much more structure—hence the claim that mathematics is the premier mode of metaphorical transfer—such that we can more clearly perceive C:D and can more readily work backwards to B. The imperative comes in the naturalization of the social phenomenon; the mathematics, far from enforcing clarity or "rigor," is instead something that must be gotten around, usually by altering the original implied conservation principles. It is the contingent interplay of the DMD thesis and mathematical appropriation that produces the narrative of imperative/inertia in *More Heat*, and not any conviction that I am writing about puppets or zombies. Perhaps they are instead hopeful monsters.

This is a story of intercalated layers of determination, where people's

---

25. Schaffer 1988; Aspray 1990, esp. 179–80; Mirowski 1992b.

free choices ultimately lock them into a small number of analytical options in a specific historical period, here roughly pre-1940. At the most rarefied level, we are discussing people who buy into something like the DMD dynamic. Those who oppose the naturalization of society, like the first generation of American Institutionalists or certain members of the German Historicist school, need not apply. Second, we have the subset of the above who are dead keen to be considered the "scientists" of society, which usually means they have some exposure to the socialization and training of natural scientists in their era, which until recently, meant rational mechanics. Third, we have the subset of the above who are dead certain that the mere use of mathematics renders a discipline scientific, but whose sole exemplar in this regard is rational mechanics. Hence, contrary to some comments at the conference, these economists' (who, by no accident, all happen to be neoclassicals) explicit references to rational mechanics are not unspecific testimonials to "mathematics" as a generic species of rational discourse, since (1) there is no such thing (mathematics is plural rather than singular); (2) they almost never reveal any awareness that there exists any mathematics other than that associated with rational mechanics;[26] and (3) they never feel the need to justify their chosen mathematics with regard to the posited ontological character of the economic phenomena of interest. All these layers of determination weigh heavily upon the shoulders of the protagonists in our narrative, and within the narrow range of freedom opened up by their own powers of metaphorical invention, I think it is safe to say that their responses travel in certain well-worn grooves.

4. Integrability and Symmetry

While we are on the topic of mathematics, it may be germane to address the format of the mathematical exposition in *More Heat*. One of the implications of expanding the potential audience was to curtail the detail in which the mathematical problems of neoclassical economics would be discussed. Explicit Hamiltonians were thus relegated to an appendix, and many of the fine points of field theory were eliminated. In particular, many statements about the integrability problem were tele-

---

26. The "almost" refers here to the single exception of probability theory; but their response to this area reveals their unwillingness to condone the use of a mathematical structure before it has been sanctioned by use in physics. On this issue see Mirowski, in press, d.

graphed as citations of economic authors who had admitted the parallels with physics; and the limited use of mathematics on pages 226–33 was intended as more suggestive than exhaustive of the issues at stake. Nevertheless I should have realized that interested readers would have wanted the Slutsky conditions written out and painstakingly compared point by point with the standard field formalism in the discussion on integrability, which would have then embroiled the narrative in all sorts of tangential questions, such as: Where are the mass terms? the multiple integrals? What happens when you append the law of one price, which is not a part of the physics? The unfamiliar terminology of divergence, curl, and gradient is conventionally used with Maxwell's equations, so why doesn't neoclassical theory look like electrodynamics? I thought I could get away with directing the reader to various texts where the comparisons to physics were made directly (366–67), but I should have anticipated that hostile readers would not deign to look them up, eager to convict me of the one sin which can flunk you out of economics graduate school: making mathematical mistakes. Fortunately, Wade Hands has developed a way to talk about the crucial mathematical issues without getting bogged down in minutiae, in such a way that the actual historical character of the argument can shine through.

There seem to be at least two issues in the history of science which are sticking points, which then translate into controversy over what precisely it was that the neoclassicals appropriated, and when it was that they took it. One is the timing of the transition from force functions to potentials to fields, and the relationship of French eighteenth-century mechanics and extremum principles to these transitions; and the other is the related issue of the conceptualization of statics and dynamics, and the attendent importance of the conservation of energy.[27] The earlier back we push the mathematical inspiration, the claim goes that potentials but not fields were central to neoclassicism, and since there were no mass terms or integrals over the entire space, there was no kinetic energy, no dynamics, and no *More Heat*. The neoclassicals are effectively off the hook, since all they putatively cared about were some static potentials summed over virtual motion in commodity space: no big deal.

While I will confess that I now dislike the passages in *More Heat* where I read energy back into the original Lagrangian formulation, strangely enough, I think the above version of events is even more ahistorical

27. Wise 1992.

and arbitrary. The problem, put crudely, is this: in the heat of events, there were many strains of mechanics mixing and matching all these possible components in a motley of mixed mathematics. Some favored extremum principles (Euler, Maupertuis, Hamilton), and some did not (Lagrange, Laplace, Poisson); some distinguished potentials and fields, and some did not; some held out the hope of reducing dynamics to statics (Lagrange), whereas others sought to reduce statics to dynamics (Kelvin); and so forth. Outsiders such as Jevons, Walras, Pareto, Fisher, et al. were certainly not privy to such fine distinctions; and, moreover, they were not the reason why the appropriation was successful. The language of metaphor is used insistently in the book in order to telegraph it was the *image* of desire suffusing commodity space subject to constraint which fired their imaginations; and that, in turn was a cultural phenomenon conditional upon the widespread energetics movement in the later nineteenth century. Sorting out the relevant distinctions between forces and potentials and fields and, by implication, the relation of statics to dynamics, was a task bequeathed to future generations; and it is the story of their uneasy relationship to energy physics which then gets told in *More Heat*.

To give the reader just the barest taste of the complexity involved, I reproduce as figure 2 a schematic claiming to represent the pedigree of the concept of vector potential in the history of physics.[28] A few relevant things are immediately apparent. Much of the work distinguishing the formalisms happens in the 1830s to 1860s; one of the key issues is the question of a scalar versus a vector potential; and much effort goes into trying to decide whether potentials actually represent physical entities or whether they are simply convenient modes of representation of something much more complicated; issues of the invariance of potentials under various transformations grow in importance; and much of the integrability requirements and so on are worked out in the context of electromagnetism. All of these controversies (with the exception of the adoption of Maxwell's equations) get played out in the neoclassical context in the twentieth century. These turn up under the rubrics of integrability, cardinal versus ordinal utility, the rejection of utilitarian psychology, and the recoverability of preference orderings.

As Hands shows, the symmetry of prices in a conservative vector

28. The figure is from Roche 1990, 146. Other sources which are helpful in beginning to sort out this morass are Grattan-Guinness 1990; Kennedy 1990; Smith and Wise 1989.

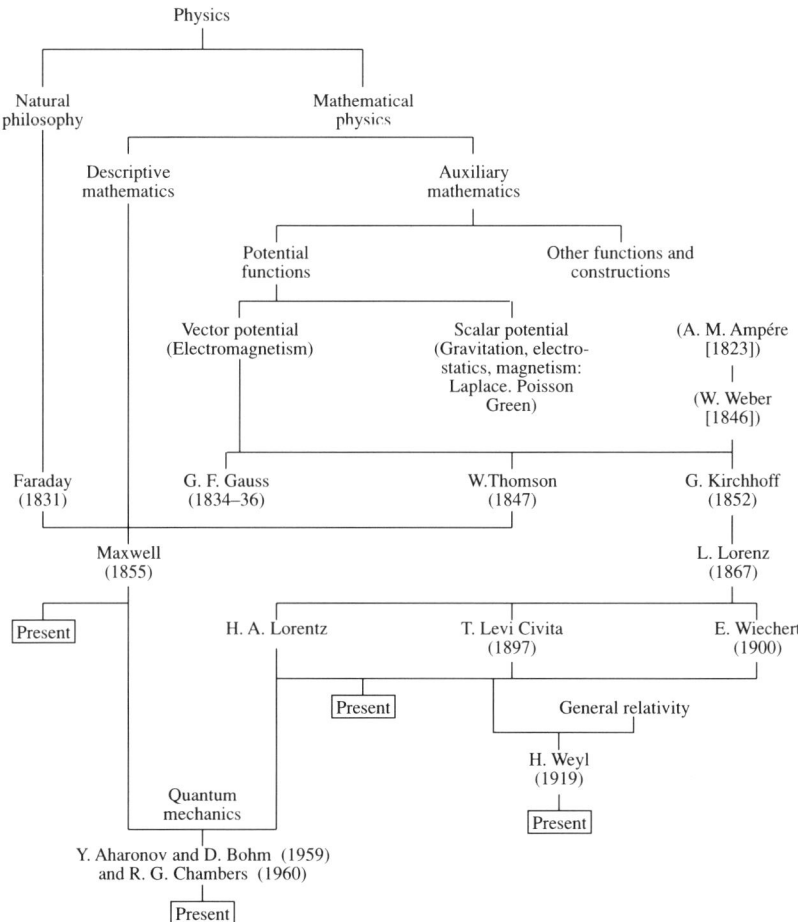

Figure 2

field does not by itself imply the standard Slutsky restrictions, although, as he also notes, it was the starting point for many early neoclassicals' trying to clarify the empirical implications of the physics metaphor. A pure symmetry condition like $\partial p_j/\partial x_i = \partial p_i/\partial x_j$ [*] imposed upon the phenomenological demands would tend to make the entire model more like a gradient problem; but in that case it runs afoul of the law of one price, an extra condition—nowhere present in the physics—that small changes in position in commodity space force a revision of the price paid for *each* unit of the relevant commodity, and therefore the income available to purchase all other commodities, and in consequence, all other prices. It would be as if in the physics, any marginal change in one force, through some external hidden variable, changed all the other forces in the problem. This is entirely an artifact of the imposition of the external arbitrage requirement of the "law of one price," which, to repeat, has no analogue in the physics. An initial reaction might be: okay, so what's the problem if the neoclassicals showed a little initiative and had the gumption to change some of the math to fit the economic circumstances?

The answer is that this little amendment was the beginning of the end of the intelligibility of the neoclassical model, and it can be traced back to the mistaken treatment of conservation principles. As explained in *More Heat*, unwillingness to directly confront the conservation of energy led instead to imposing two separate conservation principles: that of invariance of tastes and invariance of the budget.[29] To make the budget invariant and impose the law of one price, one is forced to posit that essentially all existing prices change with each marginal bilateral adjustment. This in turn dictates that the simple symmetry above must be amended to read: $\partial x_i^*/\partial p_j + x_j^* \partial x_i^*/\partial M = \partial x_j^*/\partial p_i + x_i^* \partial x_j^*/\partial M$ for all i, j [**]. These are *Slutsky's* symmetry conditions. It is easy to see this as an augmented symmetry, with linear terms added to both sides. A physicist would immediately recognize this as a common trick of changing the "space" in which the symmetry is evidenced by means of a linear transformation of the axes of the original problem; this is the way linear constraints traditionally have been built into physics problems. But unlike the common situation in the physics, this version demolishes any hope for a serious dynamics, and therefore any serious prospect of a credible economic theory.

29. I must register here a certain amount of displeasure with those who maintain that I fabricated the concern over integrability and conservation out of whole cloth with respect to Irving Fisher. While I was careful to say there is no "smoking gun" in the form of a memo from Gibbs to Fisher on the issue, there is some evidence, as clearly cited on the first line of *MHL*, 243. Edwin Bidwell Wilson, Gibbs's last student and coauthor of one of his final works, wrote in a review of Pareto (Wilson 1912, 467) that Volterra's complaint over integrability had some merit and that "the same suggestion [as Pareto's] was made already in 1892 by Fisher . . . on mathematical grounds; but I believe that considerations indicated by Gibbs have since led him to abandon the suggestion."

One cannot achieve an understanding of this from reading modern neoclassical textbooks—a travesty I shall comment upon shortly. One cannot even find a serious discussion of the economic meaning of integrability anywhere, a situation bemoaned on page 370 of *More Heat*. The one sterling exception is Sidney Afriat's underappreciated book on the Slutsky matrix.[30] There he recounts that, under the sway of the textbooks, he had unthinkingly associated the Slutsky conditions with the classical integrability conditions for a linear differential form found in Frobenius (i.e., [*]); but upon reflection, he realized that they did not permit an integration giving a utility function in commodity space, but rather one in "budget space." Following up a hint by Frisch in a 1959 *Econometrica* article suggesting that integrability be identified with a transitivity condition, he worked through the mathematics and discovered (61 ff.) that the symmetry and negative definiteness of the Slutsky matrix [**] implied two different invariance conditions: the first is the standard field invariance mentioned above; the second permitted invariance of the utility function when transposed from budget space to commodity space. While Afriat leaves matters there, it is tempting to read into one of his comments an awareness of the damning character of his result: "Though utility is talked about a great deal, there seldom comes a point where we have a real utility function, a specific one stated in computable terms and known to belong to some identifiable agent. . . . Schemes offered for empirical utility construction serve a wish for constructability but not a serious practicality" (7).

Why not? I shall try to phrase this as clearly as I am able, so even a hardened neoclassical theorist can understand it. If you have a situation where any possible motion in a space not only alters all future motions, but also the space in which it is embedded, and you have relinquished any invariants in the ways in which the space is changed by the motion, then you have effectively renounced all pretense to determinacy in your mathematics. Sometimes repetition helps, so let me try again. Why is it that after all these years and all those high-powered rigorous folks getting involved, neoclassicals have been able to prove "existence" of equilibrium, but not provide satisfactory uniqueness or stability results? The answer is simple. In copying field physics but opting not to follow the physics lead in positing the joint conservation of income and utility (kinetic and potential energy), the only invariance left in the prob-

---

30. Afriat 1980.

lem is quite literally "in people's heads." They "think" their income's constancy will not be affected by their choices; and they "think" that contemplating bundles in different orders will not change their final determination of the bundle that they prefer most. If we as analysts treat everyone as similarly constituted Leibnizian monads, we can guarantee the existence of some "equilibrium" with everyone "thinking" similar things at once; but if we actually allow them to trade, they will soon discover the error of their rational economic solipsisms: their anticipations have no fixed referent. There is absolutely no reason for them or for us to believe that equilibrium is unique or path-independent as long as the budget space undergoes cosmic warp contortions, even if we generously allow the unlikely hypothesis that the actors conveniently come "hardwired" with nicely shaped, stable preference fields. It is this obstruction which blocks the achievement of any credible neoclassical market narrative.

Let me try to explain it one more way, the way it actually happened: the history.[31] When Laurent queried Walras, and Volterra chided Pareto, they were asking explicitly about the classical integrability conditions [*] for a linear differential form; one reason each encounter ended in mutual frustration was a lack of recognition of the implied change from commodity space to budget space [**]. In other words, they started from the physics metaphor, but did not themselves realize how their postulate of the law of one price and the conserved budget constraint forced them to diverge from it. Then in the 1920s and 1930s a number of people became interested in locating the precise restrictions which neoclassical utility theory imposed upon observed price-quantity interactions. Harold Hotelling and Henry Schultz, for instance, explicitly debated the integrability conditions in private correspondence, starting with the simple symmetry [*] conditions $\partial p_i/\partial x_j = \partial p_j/\partial x_i$. But Schultz rejected that condition as empirically silly, and later lit upon the Slutsky conditions. This was not the happy ending of that story, however; the Slutsky restrictions did not pass his empirical tests. Modern neoclassicals' contempt for all history prevents them from noticing that Schultz *explicitly saw this failure as the impasse in the project of the imitation of energy physics.*[32]

---

31. This next paragraph is based upon some ongoing collaborative work being done with Wade Hands. The Hotelling-Schultz correspondence can be found in the Harold Hotelling papers in the Columbia University Manuscripts archive.

32. "But what equations of motion and what laws of conservation of comparable scope do

Lots of other people—Boninsegni, Antonelli, Fisher, Griffith Evans, E. B. Wilson—struggled down the same path, from energy fields to something rather less economically intuitive and thus less satisfactory. Paul Samuelson, as usual, played a major role in stabilizing the orthodox discourse about the integrability problem, ridiculing the simpler physics symmetry [*][33] but ultimately entirely obscuring the importance of the Slutsky construction [**] for the economic interpretation of the problem. The net result is an MIT textbook orthodoxy where the integrability conditions are treated as a two-page throwaway in graduate price theory, an abstruse bit of mathematics guaranteeing the never-to-be-witnessed recovery of a utility function from a demand curve.[34]

The beauty of Hands's recent work is that he opens up consideration of many of the ways that the "stabilization" of integrability was a harbinger of so many impasses in modern orthodox economic thought. For instance, some neoclassicals could simply damn the torpedoes and blast ahead with compensated prices as a conservative vector field and—*eh voilà!*—we have the Chicago pragmatic tradition of ignoring income effects, not to mention an explicit reason why Samuelson is persona non grata around his old stomping grounds. Or, we can see that Samuelson's "correspondence principle" was an attempt to preserve all the nice aspects of a simple gradient model without really hewing to the field formalism. Or, most significantly, we can see how the failure of the search for a dynamic microfoundations for the Walrasian system is itself a playing out of the implications of the hobbled physics metaphor.[35]

The Sonnenschein-Mantel-Debreu (SMD) results are the most important negative findings in the orthodox economics literature of the last generation, although their significance has yet to filter down to *hoi polloi*

---

we have in economics? To ask the question is to answer it. There are none that have the definiteness and universal demonstrability of the corresponding physical laws" (Schultz 1938, 57). Estimation of demand systems that check for the Slutsky restrictions still find them violated, even today. See, e.g., Gilbert 1991. You don't read about that in any neoclassical price theory textbook, do you?

33. Samuelson 1965, 270–71 n. 14.

34. Varian 1978, 100–101. I do hope this explains why a certain textbook writer would be more interested in giving me a failing grade in maths than in understanding a historical argument. See Varian 1991, 595–96. In the same sense that Roy Weintraub claims (1991) that Samuelson "stabilized" the referent of the multivalent term "dynamics" in the postwar period, I am claiming that he also "stabilized" the meaning of the "integrability problem," which had competing interpretations prior to that period.

35. These were all first mentioned in Hands 1992.

in the neoclassical trenches.[36] Almost everyone is aware there have been a number of proofs of the existence of a Walrasian competitive equilibrium set of prices p^* and allocations x^* for each consumer such that each excess demand is zero or negative (allowing free goods with negative prices): $z(p) \leq 0$. It took an inordinately long time in the neoclassical tradition to realize that it is *aggregate* excess demands that matter in their theory; so it was not until the 1970s that theorists looked into the shape of $z(p)$. The derivable properties of Walrasian aggregate excess demands are:

1. Continuity: $z(p)$ is continuous for all strictly positive prices p.
2. Walras's Law: $p\,z(p) = 0$.
3. Homogeneity: $z(\lambda p) = z(p), \lambda > 0$.

The major implication of the SMD results are that there are basically no other restrictions upon $z(p)$ imposed by Walrasian theory, disregarding a few anomalous cases. This result is quite robust, even in the face of attempts to tinker with preference and endowment attributes; it even seems that this is the case in putative "non-Walrasian" models, such as those with fix-price rationing schemes and forms of price-setting. The significance of this literature for our present concerns is that it renders more conspicuous the reasons why uniqueness and stability have seemed to elude the neoclassicals' grasp. Lacking well-behaved aggregate excess demand functions, it is unlikely that markets can home in on some jointly understood "equilibrium" that makes everyone fat and contented. But more significantly, the legacy of the physics metaphor makes its appearance through the modality of these results. As Hands indicates, if the neoclassicals had been willing to retain the simpler symmetry restriction [*] taken from the physics, they would not encounter all the problems entailed by the SMD results. What he does not notice is that the primary SMD implication for aggregate excess demand functions is *Walras's Law*, that is, the one conservation principle crowbarred into the problem in order to avoid the legitimate physical conservation principle. Hence, by ignoring the conservation of energy, neoclassicals end up bereft of the determinate structure they so admired and envied in the physics. Moreover, this is a deep structure of the project, not so

---

36. The seminal papers were Sonnenschein 1972 and 1973; Mantel 1974; Debreu 1974. Parenthetically, I should like to register some dismay that Roy Weintraub did not include consideration of this literature in his otherwise seminal history, *Stabilizing Dynamics* (1991).

expendable or easily repudiated as the various doctrines concerning production and capital which are also artifacts of the original appropriation.

I hope this provides some pause to all those who bear such contempt for their own history that they feel any discussion of intellectual origins is prima facie evidence for commission of the genetic fallacy. The physics metaphor lives on today in the very entrails of neoclassical economics, whether the protagonists are aware of it or not. And indeed, given that orthodox textbook writers are so willfully oblivious to these trends, I cannot think what miracle will transform a generation of *idiots savants* nurtured upon those chitterlings into social theorists.

5. Skin and Bones, Flesh and Blood

> History is written by men, and accordingly I think the criteria governing history of science are disputable. Every change in criteria, of course, modifies judgment.—Maffeo Pantaleoni (1923)

Sometimes I get the feeling people think I am not interested in writing real history, but rather hanker after some sort of flippant narrative that need not be held accountable to the agreed-upon sources and other forms of data. Neil de Marchi, in an earlier version of his contribution, worried about being "Philfooled." Perhaps this has to do with matters of writing style or the depth to which cherished preconceptions are challenged; in any event, it is not an attitude I hold or would ever wish to foster. I think of myself first and foremost as a historian, and then only secondarily as an economist, if those categories really do exist as discrete entities. The one thing which would make me break out in a cold sweat would be strongly disconfirming bits of evidence from the lives of the protagonists of the drama with which we are all concerned. To give one example which has surfaced since publication, I now feel impelled to retract my statement on page 235 that neoclassicism "has nothing to do with subjective psychology or the mind" as too insensitive to historical nuance. Michael White's outstanding paper on Richard Jennings and William Stanley Jevons[37] has convinced me that physiological psychology was a major motivating concern in Jevons's work; and if this is true for Jevons, it may also be true for other key neoclassicals. Norton Wise has made me worry that I may have misrepresented Kelvin and Maxwell on variational

---

37. M. White, in press. See also Rizvi 1992b.

principles in their relation to the historical program of field theory.[38] All this is to the good, as far as I am concerned, since it leads us back to historical work and the need to construct more finely textured narratives.

However, I must confess that I did not see very much of that finely textured historical work at this conference. Albert Jolink makes various statements about Walras's supposed intentions without once confronting the critical story, identified as such by Jaffé, of his tutelage by the engineer Antoine-Paul Piccard in the mathematics of fields; nor does he address the structure of the mathematical arguments made by Walras; nor the profoundly important attempt at the end of his life to convince all and sundry that his theory of equilibrium was practically isomorphic to that found in mechanics.[39] Cliff Gaddy has provided some fascinating biographical background on Knut Wicksell, but when it comes to the central questions about his attitudes toward and familiarity with physics, we are left without much in the way of evidence one way or another. Since the conference, I have learned that there is a vast archive of Wicksell's correspondence and papers at Uppsala, much of it not explicitly about economics; an archive not even touched by the biographers of Wicksell. Marcel Boumans identifies another key incident in the influence of Paul Ehrenfest upon his protégé Jan Tinbergen; but the story needs further elaboration, given Tinbergen's relative agnosticism when it came to neoclassical price theory.

As previously indicated, there is a problem of trying to decide whether I have gotten any particular protagonist right, if they rarely had any flesh and bones to start with in the history of economic thought. It certainly is the case that there are no flesh-and-blood human beings in *More Heat*; but that is mainly because it is a different sort of genre, what Rorty calls *Geistesgeschichte*. Since then, I have become more drawn to the genre of biography, because the narrative of a person's life is always more edifying, though perhaps less pedagogical, than such abstract stories of the movement of Thought. The lives and the narratives built up around them are always informed by Guiding Principles and Coherent Threads, but the beauty of biography is that the unruly stuff of life generally pokes through the netting. Once the loose ends and the batting are on display, something happens to the organizing narrative, and the result can set in

---

38. Wise 1992.

39. The text of Walras's "Économique et mécanique" is translated in Mirowski and Cook 1990.

motion real historical research. I have already had this experience in researching the life of Henry Ludwell Moore, finding that the conventional scarecrow bumbler with regard to the "identification principle" slowly became a lumpier, crankier but unambiguously smarter mannikin. My fondest hope is that *More Heat* might induce some similar experiences with other figures in the history of economic thought. While it is one thing to make a list of prime candidates for the kiss of life—some personal favorites are Francis Ysidro Edgeworth,[40] the really brilliant British neoclassical thinker; William Thornton, who was singlehandedly responsible for motivating Jevons, Marshall, and Fleeming Jenkin to put pen to paper; and Tjalling Koopmans, who, I believe, even more than Samuelson, set the pattern for neoclassical practice in the United States for the subsequent generation[41]—it is probably more worthwhile to give a few explicit examples of the sorts of things that need to be done. For the sake of not overtaxing my already overly generous allocation of space, I concentrate here upon one unknown and one stellar performer: Edwin Bidwell Wilson, and Paul Samuelson.

E. B. Wilson (1879–1964) was the man who singlehandedly brought rigorous neoclassical theory to Harvard. You can search high and low in all the usual places, like Blaug or Schumpeter, or *HOPE*, and you would never get a hint of it; in Schumpeter's case, because he managed to foster the impression that he was the sole bearer of scientific tidings at Harvard; in other cases, because Wilson seems such an unlikely figure. With degrees in mathematics from Harvard and Yale, he started out as

---

40. An attempt to situate Edgeworth in his biographical context appears in Mirowski 1993. I assert there that he is the smartest neoclassical of his generation precisely because he explicitly discusses the drawbacks of analogies to rational mechanics, and saw the future of neoclassicism in probability theory.

41. For instance, very early on Koopmans innovated the now common position that modern mathematical neoclassicism had somehow freed itself from the early fetters of physics envy. The following quote is from his *Three Essays on the State of Economic Science* (1957, 175–76): "This particular development is one instance of a more general phenomenon which has by no means run its full course: the emancipation of the social sciences, in the choice of mathematical tools, from the precedents of the more classical parts of the physical sciences. Many other instances come to mind. A utility function of a consumer looks quite similar to a potential function in the theory of gravitational or electrical fields. But there is no counterpart in the physics to the more general concept of a preference ordering, not necessarily representable by a utility function." He also mentions game theory as another example, on the next page. However, as we have seen from our discussion of the SMD results above, orderings only get you existence, and that is hardly good enough to dispose of the original conception of a potential field. As for game theory, the commonplace idea that it escapes physics envy is critically discussed in Mirowski 1991b and 1992b.

a mathematics instructor but then underwent more perigrinations in one lifetime than a Bedouin nomad.[42] After helping Willard Gibbs to turn his lectures on vector analysis into a textbook, he moved to MIT, where he eventually began teaching physics as well as mathematics. During World War I he began teaching aeronautical engineering; after 1922 he moved to the Harvard School of Public Health to take a chair in Vital Statistics. The Harvard chair was not the sort that constrained the occupant to remain within any particular sphere of endeavor; thenceforward he was engaged in the most remarkably diverse set of intellectual projects, from the "Pareto Circle"[43] to epidemiology, from sociology to the philosophy of C. S. Peirce, and, not least, from economic statistics to mathematical economics. His position at the center of the National Academy of Sciences put him in the midst of a vast web of patronage and academic clout in the 1930s; and he was one of the powers behind the scenes in the formation of the Econometric Society. Roy Weintraub is the first historian of economics to note his significance for the evolution of neoclassicism, and he has only begun to scratch the surface.[44]

My interest in Wilson has obvious roots in his role as a carrier of physical metaphor into the economics profession; but as is usual with biography, a little bit of digging leads to much more than one originally anticipated. First, one gets a sense of what would attract such a person to neoclassical economics. In a very important review of Pareto's *Manuel* in a mathematics journal in 1912 (!) one finds the observation that counting equations and unknowns is not rigorously correct, but is very similar to the way physicists treat mathematics; that integrability is a sticking point in Pareto's exposition; and that "much as the author's scientific economics appeals to us, we must say that his sturdy vision into society and social evolution are [sic] even more to our liking."[45] In the early 1930s he was teaching graduate statistics for the Harvard Economics Department, and in 1935 they importuned him to also teach graduate mathematical economics. With the bold panache of the outsider who knows what he likes when he sees it, Wilson promptly set out to define that previously nebulous entity:

42. Hunsaker and MacLane 1973. There seems to be no other major source on Wilson's life. See also Wheeler 1951.
43. See Heyl 1968.
44. See Weintraub 1991, chapter 3.
45. See Wilson 1912, 474.

The department of economics is going to ask me next year to replace my course on mathematical statistics by a course on mathematical economics . . . [so that] they will not be frightened by the peculiar language and can read easily things that Edgeworth and Marshall have written and some others. I don't expect to get up where they can read Hotelling and Roos . . . I think that Marshall's appendeces [sic] are not numerous enough nor connected enough from a pedagogic point of view. . . . The same is true of Edgeworth's papers . . . I don't like Evans' book. What the student needs to learn is to hang an economic argument on a general mathematical formulation . . . and this it seems is what Evans doesn't teach him to do. He takes some dinky little artificial problem and solves it.[46]

The key, of course, is that the mathematical economics which Wilson found pedagogically salubrious just happened to be that which most closely corresponded to his own training with Gibbs. Hence he tended to reject work like that of the pure mathematician Evans, which was skeptical of the virtues of utility theory. He told Hutchins Burbank, chair of the Harvard economics department, that he would "give as I did last time a general theory of equilibrium such as this is understood by physical chemists including the phase systems of Willard Gibbs. Most of our equilibrium theory in economics really has for its background the notions of equilibrium which arise in mechanics. . . . It is pretty high-brow stuff. Mathematically or physically it isn't any more high-brow than things which I long taught at Yale University and at the Institute of Technology."[47]

Wilson was a plainspoken Yankee, and his own peripatetic career had taught him the lesson that the man of science is at home everywhere, while the philosopher and the historian are more like those freeloading cousins you wish would stay at home: "I have never understood what John Dewey meant, if he really meant anything, by saying that the social sciences must not imitate the natural sciences in their methodology but must develop their own methodology."[48] In the ambit of one

---

46. E. B. Wilson to W. C. Mitchell, 9 May 1934, HUG 4878.207. This and all his letters cited subsequently are in Wilson Correspondence, Wilson Papers, Harvard University Archives.

47. Wilson to H. H. Burbank, 20 December 1938, Wilson Correspondence, HUG 4878.203.

48. Wilson to L. J. Henderson, 4 November 1938, Wilson Correspondence, HUG 4878.203.

and the same letter, no-nonsense attitudes about philosophy cohabited with no-nonsense ideas about the Depression:

> We know very little about social science, and I take this to be chiefly the fault of historians who seem to divide themselves mainly into two lots, the dry-as-dust-ers and the raconteurs, the people who grub for possible meaningless facts and the story tellers. For both these types the main conclusion can be no other than that history does not repeat itself and yet there can be no social science as far as I can see unless history does repeat itself . . . the economist is likely to keep on with logic-chopping disputations and the sociologist is likely to keep writing very bad romances. . . . My wife says it is harder this past year to get a satisfactory maid than it has been at any time in the last 25 years. Part of this situation is due to the large amount of relief money in the hands of our federal government and the stupid way in which it is spent.[49]

One can easily observe the DMD thesis of order in social life being informed and defined by very specific images of natural order in particular local circumstances.

> I take it that societies could not exist unless they were in a state of quasi equilibrium by which one means that any force applied to the system distributes its effects fairly widely over the system so that the first order responses are much less than might be figured . . . if we apply enough force to get any major change of the first order we may produce in the second or higher orders such large changes as will induce a catastrophic condition and break down the whole system. This will of course be obvious to everybody and is decidedly a matter of regret to most people having the temperament leading them to desire rapid changes in the socio-economic system.[50]

But then, as usual, dogged persistence in research reveals not a rigidly consistent protagonist, but rather someone who defies our expectations from time to time—a cantankerous cosmopolitan chrestomath; someone we might like to know a bit better:

---

49. Wilson to Arthur Schlesinger, 9 June 1936, Wilson Correspondence, HUG 4878.203.
50. Wilson to Edward S. Mason, 20 December 1935, Wilson Correspondence, HUG 4878.203.

> *Econometrica* is doing just what I should expect a journal run by Frisch would do. It is being run away with by mathematicians. Now mathematics is merely a more complicated and less intelligible type of logomathy, except it is founded more substantially upon facts than is the literary type of logomathy.[51]

Or:

> I remember very clearly with what interest and instruction I read those early papers of Pearson while studying statistical method with a brilliant young Yale economist in the years 1899–1902. They seemed to open up large possibilities for a scientific basis for political economy quite different from that other scientific method followed by Walras, by Pareto and Irving Fisher in one of his notable early papers. On the whole, however, it is my judgment that up to the present time it has been not the economist but the student of biology who has availed himself of these newer statistical methods.[52]

Perhaps I have made my point, that historians of economic thought should try to kick their Smith/Ricardo/Walras habit and start looking into the flesh-and-blood people who actively constructed the neoclassical orthodoxy with which we are saddled today.

One person drew extended attention in *More Heat*, and that was Paul Samuelson. More than one reader thought I was inexcusably rude in my treatment of one of the most famous economists of the twentieth century and that I misrepresented him. My response would be that I have not done justice to the *man* at all; again, that was not my intention. Basically, I was just treating Samuelson as he treats most other figures in the history of economic thought: hectoring them for their failures, handing out little prizes and demerits for his construction of what they must have meant; deploying his very subtle command of English to telegraph his notions of science and progress without being held to any explicit standards of generosity or empathy; and hewing as close as possible to the published record. Paul and his MIT confreres persist in scorning historians of economic thought as mushbrains, but they should wise up: someday he will be absent, and what will prevent the historians from gaining their revenge then?

51. Wilson to Carl Snyder, 19 February 1934, Wilson Correspondence, HUG 4878.203.
52. Wilson 1923, 94.

Of course, we as historians would like to have access to much more than the published record, because it really would be interesting to find out what makes Samuelson tick. Thanks to the Sloan Foundation's program of commissioning autobiographies from Nobelists, we should soon have his own version of events, as well as the narrative structure by which he would like to be remembered. Perhaps after that event, we will be allowed to scan the papers and correspondence from his early career, because now, even though there is a Samuelson archive at MIT, none of those materials from the active years are in it. The sanitized and objectified version of events will clearly not suffice, since Samuelson's role in the stabilization of the neoclassical orthodoxy is so monumental and far-reaching that it would be fair to say that we do not understand American neoclassicism until we can understand Samuelson. Roy Weintraub, as usual, has been the first to discern this fact; the rest of us will follow.

I would like to close with a suggestion as to what this may look like, and its relationship to the thesis in *More Heat*. This will be a bit crude given all I have said above about the bracing influence of biographical research, but one has to start somewhere, with the materials available at this juncture. My hunch from reading Maila Walter's marvelous biography of the physicist Percy Williams Bridgman (1882–1961) and working through the Wilson archive is that Samuelson's scientific persona is a convex combination of Bridgman and Wilson.[53] Bridgman, like Wilson, was a Yankee and an upright man; both were searching for

> something stable, an island of permanence, in the midst of the change that was so rapidly transforming physics. . . . We should now make it our business to understand so thoroughly the character of our permanent mental relations to nature that another change in our attitude, such as that due to Einstein, shall be forever impossible. It was perhaps excusable that a revolution in mental attitude should occur once, because after all physics is a young science, and physicists have been very busy, but it would certainly be a reproach if such a revolution should ever prove necessary again. (Walter 1990, 107–8)

Samuelson's explicit endorsement of Bridgman's "operationalism" is of course well known, but what I think is less well appreciated is that Bridgman's specification of the operationalist program reads point-for-point like the theory of revealed preference. But what is especially

---

53. Walter 1990.

poignant is that the coherence of "operationalism" fell apart in Bridgman's hands by the 1940s, and its disintegration exactly mirrors the disintegration of the program of revealed preference in the same era.

> Instead of providing a clear line of demarcation between the "real" and the "metaphysical," operations blurred the distinction among metaphysics, epistemology, psychology, language and behavior. . . . Energy, as Bridgman discovered to his obvious dismay, is as much an affair of metaphysics as of laboratory operations . . . the basic failure of operationism was the failure to recognize the role of communication, the transmission of a signal, in creating knowledge. Operationism did not succeed in making the distinction between the classical logic of the "now present" categories and the logic of time-dependent processes. It was still based on the epistemology of intuition, on the expectation of knowledge unmediated by the process of communication. (Walter 1990, 112, 231, 244)

These are precisely the failures discussed in *More Heat*. Bridgman and Wilson wanted a return to simple nineteenth-century energy physics, perhaps augmented by the modern formalisms of Gibbs's vector analysis. They disliked almost everything about twentieth-century science and its world-destabilizing discourse and were suspicious of probability and creeping indeterminism; Bridgman openly spurned "physicists such as Einstein and von Neumann, whose cocksureness I have always found profoundly irritating."[54] But they could not banish Einstein, von Neumann, et al. from science, so they instead attempted a rearguard action to absorb the newer doctrines within the older structures. This, I would argue, is the style of reasoning they bequeathed to the young Paul Samuelson.

But I might go even a bit further. Samuelson very much encouraged the now prevalent attitude that economics is what economists do, as long as it looks scientific. This too has its origins in a principled stance of Bridgman's:

---

54. Bridgman to Arthur Bentley, 12 August 1936, quoted in Walter 1990, 160. Samuelson's persistent disparagement of von Neumann is documented in Mirowski 1992b. Von Neumann returned the favor, refusing to review Samuelson's *Foundations* because "one would think the book contemporary with the time of Newton" and that he "has murky ideas about stability. He is no mathematician and one should not ascribe the analysis to him. And even in 30 years he won't absorb game theory" (Oskar Morgenstern Diaries, 8 October 1947, Oskar Morgenstern Papers, Duke University Archives). And as for Einstein, when asked what the economists were doing at Princeton, he responded: "Dreck" (Morgenstern Diaries).

> In some ways Bridgman spoke in concert with a number of his colleagues who also argued that science is done for its own sake, but . . . they did not recognize the Puritan cunning behind his reasoning . . . the universe of the Puritan is ruled by an inscrutable, unpredictable God whose ways are forbidden to human knowledge. . . . The Puritan intellect is constrained to activity in a concrete, practical, this-worldly theatre. It is entitled, indeed obligated, to seek into the meaning of the manifest Word of God, but it does not inquire into His actual working . . . the fear of social chaos concentrated attention on the means rather than the end. (Walter 1990, 262–64)

Of course, Samuelson did not literally share their Protestant faith; but replace God with the Invisible Hand and one can begin to understand the disdain for the historical and the philosophical, the stress on mathematical method as an antidote for disputed meanings, and the willingness to live with all sorts of comparative static stories as palliatives for answers to questions about how the market really works. As Walter says about Bridgman, "The responsibility is not in the first place to society. It is to science."

Bridgman provided the attitudes, and Wilson provided bits of formalism and smoothed the way. Weintraub's thesis that Gibbs's formalisms by way of Wilson informed much of the early work is seconded by letters from Samuelson where he works through "the Gibbs approach."[55] Wilson was chair of Samuelson's thesis examination, essentially because no one else was deemed competent to evaluate his mathematical economics.[56] And when the time came to find Samuelson a place in the universe of economic discourse, it was Wilson who saw his protégé clearly:

> . . . not many people want a mathematical economist. Moreover, it seems to me that Samuelson thinks rather as a mathematician than as an economist. He tends to go into equations rather than into a literary form of expression without equations. While he has a very fine training in mathematics and is entirely able to pick up what mathematics he needs he isn't as much a mathematician in the sense in which most departments of mathematics define the term just as he isn't as such an

---

55. Paul Samuelson to Wilson, 25 January 1938, Wilson Correspondence, HUG 4878.203.
56. Wilson to E. Chamberlin, 22 November 1940, Wilson Correspondence, HUG 4878.203.

economist in the sense in which most departments define the term. . . . If I were in charge of the economics department at a place like the Mass. Inst. of Technology where every student has to take economics in his Junior year after he has two years of physics and two years of mathematics and a year of chemistry . . . one of the first persons I should think of to have on my staff would bee [sic] Samuelson.[57]

It has taken a long time to make the world safe for Samuelsons, but Wilson was prescient when he imagined his ideal MIT curriculum. Now it is scattered throughout universities all over the world. For who can deny that it is precisely the ideal preparation for someone to really understand modern orthodox economics?

I thank Wade Hands for many helpful conversations on these issues, and the following people for detailed comments: Neil de Marchi, Bob Coats, David Moore, and Alexander van Altena.

References

Afriat, S. N. 1980. *Demand Functions and the Slutsky Matrix*. Princeton: Princeton University Press.
Aspray, William. 1990. *John von Neumann and the Origins of Modern Computing*. Cambridge: MIT Press.
Bannister, Robert. 1979. *Social Darwinism*. Philadelphia: Temple University Press.
Bloor, David. 1982. Durkheim and Mauss Revisited. *Studies in the History and Philosophy of Science* 13:267–97.
Coats, A. W. 1977. The Current "Crisis" in Economics in Historical Perspective. *Nebraska Journal of Economics* 16.3:3–16.
Corcoran, Elizabeth, and Paul Wallich. 1992. Coping with Math Anxiety. *Scientific American* 266 (January).
The Crisis in Economic Theory. 1980. Special issue of *The Public Interest*.
Daston, Lorraine. 1988. *Classical Probability in the Age of the Enlightenment*. Princeton: Princeton University Press.
Debreu, Gerard. 1974. Aggregate Excess Demand Functions. *Journal of Mathematical Economics* 1:15–21.
Desmond, Adrian, and James Moore. 1991. *Darwin*. London: Michael Joseph.
Douglas, Mary. 1973. *Natural Symbols*. London: Barrie & Jenkins.
———. 1982. *In the Active Voice*. London: Routledge & Kegan Paul.
———. 1984. *Purity and Danger*. London: Ark.
———. 1986. *How Institutions Think*. Syracuse: Syracuse University Press.

57. Wilson to Griffith Evans, 31 March 1939, Wilson Correspondence, HUG 4878.203.

Durkheim, Emile, and Marcel Mauss. 1963. *Primitive Classification*. Translated by Rodney Needham. Chicago: University of Chicago Press.

Gilbert, Christopher. 1991. Do Economists Test Theories? In *Appraising Economic Theories*, edited by Neil de Marchi and Mark Blaug. Aldershot: Edward Elgar.

Glymour, Clark. 1983. Social Science and Social Physics. *Behavioral Science* 28:126–34.

Grattan-Guinness, Ivor. 1990. The Varieties of Mechanics by 1800. *Historia Mathematica* 17:313–38.

Hahn, Frank. 1991. The Next Hundred Years. *Economic Journal* 101:47–50.

Hands, D. Wade. 1992. More Light and Less Heat. *Philosophy of the Social Sciences* 22:102–3.

Herschel, John. 1857. *Essays from Edinburgh and Quarterly Reviews*. London: Longman, Brown.

Heyl, Barbara. 1968. The Harvard Pareto Circle. *Journal for the History of the Behavioral Sciences* 4:316–34.

Hodgson, Geoff. In press. *Economics and Evolution*. Oxford: Basil Blackwell.

Hunsaker, Jerome, and Saunders MacLane. 1973. Edwin Bidwell Wilson. *Biographical Memoirs of the National Academy of Sciences* 43:285–320.

Ingrao, Bruna, and Giorgio Israel. 1990. *The Invisible Hand*. Cambridge: MIT Press.

Kennedy, J. B. 1990. The Field Concept in Recent Physics. Reilly Center Discussion Paper, University of Notre Dame.

Kingsland, Sharon. 1985. *Modelling Nature*. Chicago: University of Chicago Press.

Kirman, Alan. 1989. The Intrinsic Limits of Modern Economic Theory. *Economic Journal* 99:126–39.

———. 1992. Whom or What Does the Representative Individual Represent? *Journal of Economic Perspectives* 6:117–36.

Klamer, Arjo, and David Colander. 1990. *The Making of an Economist*. Boulder, Colo.: Westview Press.

Koopmans, Tjalling. 1957. *Three Essays on the State of Economic Science*. New York: McGraw-Hill.

Latour, Bruno. 1990. Postmodern? No, Simply Amodern. *Studies in the History and Philosophy of Science* 21:145–71.

Leontief, Wassily. 1982. Academic Economics. *Science* 217:104–7.

Limoges, C., and C. Menard. In press. Organization and the Division of Labor. In Mirowski, in press, a.

McMullin, Ernan, ed. 1992. *The Social Dimensions of Science*. Notre Dame, Ind.: University of Notre Dame Press.

Mantel, Rolf. 1974. On the Characterization of Aggregate Excess Demand. *Journal of Economic Theory* 7:348–53.

Mirowski, Philip. 1988. *Against Mechanism*. Totowa, N.J.: Rowman & Littlefield.

———. 1989a. The Measurement without Theory Controversy. *Economies et sociétés*, no. 11:65–87.

———. 1989b. *More Heat than Light: Economics as Social Physics, Physics as Nature's Economics*. Cambridge and New York: Cambridge University Press.

———. 1989c. The Probabilistic Counter-revolution. *Oxford Economics Papers* 41:217–35.

———. 1989d. 'Tis a Pity Econometrics Isn't an Empirical Endeavor. *Ricerce Economiche* 43 (June–July): 76–99.

———. 1990a. Learning the Meaning of a Dollar: Conservation Principles and the Social Theory of Value in Economic Theory. *Social Research* 57:689–717.

———. 1990b. Problems in the Paternity of Econometrics: Henry Ludwell Moore. *HOPE* 22:587–610.

———. 1990c. Smooth Operator: How Marshall's Demand and Supply Curves Made Neoclassicism Safe for Public Consumption but Unfit for Science. In *Alfred Marshall in Retrospect*, edited by Rita McWilliams Tullberg. Aldershot: Edward Elgar.

———. 1991a. Postmodernism and the Social Theory of Value. *Journal of Post-Keynesian Economics* 13:565–82.

———. 1991b. When Games Grow Deadly Serious. In *Economics and National Security*, edited by Craufurd D. Goodwin, 227–55. Annual supplement, *HOPE* volume 23.

———. 1992a. Nicholas Georgescu-Roegen. In *New Horizons in Economic Thought*, edited by Warren Samuels. Aldershot: Edward Elgar.

———. 1992b. What Were von Neumann and Morgenstern Trying to Accomplish? In *The History of Game Theory*, edited by E. R. Weintraub, 113–47. Annual supplement, *HOPE* volume 24.

———. 1993. Marshalling the Unruly Atoms. In *Ysidro Ycheued: Edgeworth on Chance, Economic Hazard and Statistics*, edited by Philip Mirowski. Totowa, N.J.: Rowman & Littlefield.

———. In press, a. *Natural Images in Economics: Markets Read in Tooth and Claw*. Cambridge: Cambridge University Press.

———. In press, b. Symmetries, Arbitrage and the Social Theory of Value. Forthcoming in *New Directions in Analytical Political Economy*, edited by Amitava Dutt. Dordrecht: Kluwer.

———. In press, c. Three Ways of Thinking about Testing in Econometrics. *Journal of Econometrics*.

———. In press, d. *Who's Afraid of Random Trade?* Princeton: Princeton University Press.

Mirowski, Philip, and Pamela Cook. 1990. Walras' "Economics and Mechanics": Translation, Commentary, Context. In Samuels 1990.

Mirowski, Philip, and Steven Sklivas. 1991. Why Econometricians Don't Replicate (Although They Do Reproduce). *Review of Political Economy* 3:146–63.

Nagel, Thomas. 1986. *The View from Nowhere*. Oxford: Oxford University Press.

Nelson, Richard, and Sidney Winter. 1982. *An Evolutionary Theory of Economic Change*. Cambridge: Harvard University Press.

Niehans, Jurg. 1990. *A History of Economic Thought*. Baltimore: The Johns Hopkins University Press.

Pantaleoni, Maffeo. 1923. Obituary: Vilfredo Pareto. *Economic Journal* 33:582–90.

Pickering, Andrew, ed. 1992. *Science as Practice and Culture*. Chicago: University of Chicago Press.
Pool, Robert. 1989. Strange Bedfellows. *Science* 245 (18 August):700–703.
Porter, Theodore. 1981. A Statistical Survey of Gasses. *Historical Studies in the Physical Sciences* 12:77–114.
———. 1986. *The Rise of Statistical Thinking*. Princeton: Princeton University Press.
Rizvi, Abu. 1992a. Microfoundations and the Arbitrary Nature of Aggregate Excess Demand Functions. Paper presented at the ASSA meetings, New Orleans, 5 January.
———. 1992b. Utility and Value in the Classical Economists. Paper presented at the meetings of the History of Economics Society, George Mason University.
Roche, John. 1990. A Critical History of the Vector Potential. In *Physicists Look Back*, edited by John Roche. Bristol: Adam Hilger.
Rorty, Richard, J. B. Schneewind, and Quentin Skinner. 1984. *Philosophy in History*. Cambridge: Cambridge University Press.
Rouse, Joseph. 1987. *Knowledge and Power*. Ithaca: Cornell University Press.
Samuels, Warren J., ed. 1990. *Economics as Discourse*. Boston: Kluwer.
Samuelson, Paul. 1965. *Foundations of Economics*. New York: Atheneum.
Schabas, Margaret. 1992. Breaking Away. *HOPE* 24:187–203.
———. In press. The Greyhound and the Mastiff. In Mirowski, in press, a.
Schaffer, Simon. 1988. Astronomers Mark Time. *Science in Context* 2:115–46.
Schultz, Henry. 1938. *The Theory and Measurement of Demand*. Chicago: University of Chicago Press.
Schweber, Silvan. 1980. Darwin and the Political Economists. *Journal of the History of Biology* 13:195–289.
Searle, John. 1991. Intentionalistic Explanations in Social Science. *Philosophy of the Social Sciences* 21 (September): 332–44.
Shapin, Steven, and Simon Schaffer. 1985. *Leviathan and the Air-Pump*. Princeton: Princeton University Press.
Smith, C., and M. N. Wise. 1989. *Energy and Empire*. New York: Cambridge University Press.
Sonnenschein, Hugo. 1972. Market Excess Demand Functions. *Econometrica* 40:549–63.
———. 1973. Do Walras' Identity and Continuity Characterize the Class of Community Excess Demand Functions? *Journal of Economic Theory* 6:345–54.
Summers, Larry. 1991. The Scientific Illusion in Empirical Macroeconomics. *Scandinavian Journal of Economics* 93:129–48.
Swedberg, Richard. 1990. *Economics and Sociology*. Princeton: Princeton University Press.
Tarascio, Vincent. 1988. Jaffé's Walras. *History of Economics Society Bulletin* 10 (Fall): 171–74.
Varian, Hal. 1978. *Microeconomic Analysis*. New York: Norton.

———. 1991. Review of *More Heat than Light*, by Philip Mirowski. *Journal of Economic Literature* 29:595–96.
Walker, Donald. 1988. Ten Major Problems in the Study of the History of Economic Thought [1988 Presidential Address]. *History of Economics Society Bulletin* 9 (Fall).
———. 1991. Economics as Social Physics. *Economic Journal* 101:615–31.
Walter, Maila. 1990. *Science and Cultural Crisis*. Stanford: Stanford University Press.
Weintraub, E. Roy. 1991. *Stabilizing Economic Dynamics: Constructing Economic Knowledge*. Cambridge: Cambridge University Press.
Wheeler, Lynde. 1951. *Josiah Willard Gibbs*. New Haven: Yale University Press.
White, Michael. In press. The Moment of Richard Jennings. In Mirowski, in press, a.
Wiles, P., and G. Routh, eds. 1984. *Economics in Disarray*. Oxford: Basil Blackwell.
Wilson, E. B. 1912. Review of Pareto. *Bulletin of the American Mathematical Society* 18.
———. 1923. The Statistical Significance of Experimental Data. *Science* 58 (10 August): 93–100.
Wilson, E. O. 1975. *Sociobiology*. Cambridge: Harvard University Press.
Wise, M. Norton. 1992. Does the History of Physics Help Him? *Philosophy of the Social Sciences* 22:122–30.
Young, Robert. 1985. *Darwin's Metaphor*. Cambridge: Cambridge University Press.
Zeckhauser, Richard, and W. K. Viscusi. 1990. Risk within Reason. *Science* 248 (4 May): 559–64.

Index

ABC curves, 139
Abel, Niels Henrik, 190
Aboriginal tribes, 29
Abortion, 255
Absolute presuppositions, 114
Abstract expressionism, 236, 241
Abstract representation, 244
Academic art, 243
Academy of Science (Paris), 59
Academy of Science (Sweden), 199
Accounting, 65–66, 290, 291, 295
Accounting, Organizations, and Society (periodical), 65n
Acta Mathematica (periodical), 188, 189–90, 196, 197
Adams, Henry, 234, 236, 305, 306
Adaptation, parallel, 12n
Adiabatic method, 132–33
Adiabatic theorem, 154
Afriat, Sidney, 331
African masks, 240
Agricultural products, 149–50
Air pumps, 59, 62
Airy, G. B., 324
Alchian, Armen A., 38–40
Alembert, Jean Le Rond d', 33. *See also* D'Alembert's principle
Alfred Marshall in Retrospect (Tullberg), 3

Algebra, 17–18, 184
Amariglio, Jack, 227n
Amateurs, 63
American abstract expressionism, 236, 241
American Constitution, 8
American Economic Association, 173
The American Heritage Dictionary, 25n
American Institutionalists, 46, 72, 272, 308, 324, 326
Analogia, 36
Analogical grammar, 94
Analogical syllogisms, 325
Analogies, 12–15; biological, 38–40; Coats on, 274n; homologies and, 11–12, 16–24, 37; inappropriate, 32–34; McCloskey on, 224–25; Marx and, 46; metaphors and, 11, 35–36, 38. *See also* Physical analogies
Analogues, 36
Ancient trade, 260
Anderson, Benjamin, 286
Anderson, Philip, 313
Animals, 29
Anomalies, 258
Anthropology, 249, 250, 255
Anthropomorphics, 86–87, 88, 308
Antipodean Idealization Model (AIM) 103–5, 110

Antonelli conditions, 118, 120, 121, 216
Ants, 12
Appell, Pierre, 189, 190
"The Application of Mathematics to Political Economy" (Walras), 26–27, 169n
Approximation, 101
A priori knowledge, 96
Arbitrage, 308
Arbitrage-free prices, 284, 292, 293, 295, 297, 298
Architecture, 233
Aristotelian cosmology, 34
Aristotle, 34, 36, 85, 260
Arnon, Arie, 294
Arrow, Kenneth, 284, 312, 313
Artificial intelligence, 73
Art/Arts: markets for, 285–86, 288–90, 295; Modernist, 231–35, 236, 237–41, 243, 244, 246; Szostak on, 227n
Astronomy, 324. *See also* Celestial mechanics
Atomic bomb, 318
Atomic structure, 17
Atomism, 89
Åttiotalisterna, 182, 187
Attractions, 15
Austrian economics, 112
Automobiles, 236
Avery, John Lubbock, 12

Babbage, Charles, 324–25
Bailey, Samuel, 263, 272n
Balance of trade, 278, 279n
Barbon, Nicholas, 272n
Barnes, Barry, 250, 255–56
Baudelaire, Charles, 237, 238
Bauhaus movement, 233, 235
Beardsley, Monroe, 25n
Belgian Congo, 252
Beliefs, 252, 253, 254, 255, 256, 267
Bentham, Jeremy, 13
Bentley, Arthur, 343n
Bergson, Henri, 236

Berkeley, George, 9
Berlin Institut für Konjunkturforschung, 139, 140
Berman, Marshall, 236
Bernoulli, Daniel, 230
"Bestimmung und Deutung von Angebotskurven" (Tinbergen), 147–48
Beyond the Pleasure Principle (Freud), 13n
Biagioli, Mario, 58–59
Bibliothèque de la Philosophie Scientifique (Le Bon), 172
Biography, 336–37, 342
Biology: economics and, 23–24, 38–40; sociology and, 9–10, 27–28, 32; terminology of, 11; E. B. Wilson on, 341
Bird prototypes, 77, 78
Birth control, 180
The Birth of the Business Cycle (Mirowski), 276, 278n
Black, Max, 35
Blaug, Mark, 245, 337
Bliss, Christopher J., 212–13
Blood circulation, 30, 260
Bloodletting, 170
Bloor, David, 249–70, 320–21, 325
The Blue and Brown Books (Wittgenstein), 257
"Blue moons," 35n
Bluntschli, Johann Caspar, 27
Bluntschli, Otto, 10
Body-motion-value simplex: Birner on, 86–87, 88, 89; Coats on, 272, 274n; A. J. Cohen on, 205, 206, 216–17; Leonard on, 259–60, 266; Mirowski on, 309; Porter on, 55, 57–58
Böhm-Bawerk, Eugen, 192, 199, 208n
Bohr, Niels, 265
Boltzmann, Ludwig, 136–37
Bond interest rates, 286, 295
Bookkeeping, 2–3
Booth, Wayne, 35
Borges, Jorge Luis, 52
Boumans, Marcel, 294n, 336
Bourbaki, Nicolas, 293n

Boutroux, Emile, 172
Bowley, A. L., 138
Boyd, Richard, 70, 73
Boyle, Robert, 59, 62
"Une branche nouvelle de la mathématique" (Walras), 165
Braque, Georges, 240
Brazilian coffee valorizations, 150
Breuer, Josef, 13n, 28n
Brewster, David, 12
Bridgman, Percy Williams, 342–44
British economy, 277
British mercantilism, 279
Buchdahl, G., 94
Bullock, Charles J., 139
Burbank, Hutchins, 339
Bushmen, 29
Business cycles, 139–40, 144–47

Calculation devices, 325
Calculus: analogous applications of, 13; Evans on, 143; Jevons on, 37; marginalist revolution and, 2, 192; standard model for, 99; Walras and, 169. *See also* Constrained maxima; Differential equations
Calder, Alexander, 232
Calvin, John, 233
Cambridge capital theory debate, 107, 202–19, 273
Canadian settlers, 75
Cannon, Walter Bradford, 27, 29–30, 32
Canoes, 76
Cantor, Georg, 176n, 177, 178, 190–91
Capital: A. J. Cohen on, 208, 209, 210, 211; interest rates and, 213n, 214, 215; Leonard on, 264
Capital (Marx), 262
Capitalism, 51–52, 80
Carey, Henry C., 11, 24–25, 31
Carlyle, Thomas, 27–28
Carroll, Lewis, 159
Cartesianism: Bloor on, 257; I. B. Cohen on, 34; Klamer on, 227–28, 231, 234, 235–36, 237, 239; Leonard on, 260, 262, 266; Mirowski on, 323
Cartwright, Nancy, 63
Cassirer, Ernest, 229
Catallactics, 284
Causality, 74, 75, 87, 287
Celestial mechanics, 9, 18, 31, 263
Cell theory, 16
"Cellular pathology" doctrine, 10
Centrifugal force, 31
Centripetal force, 31
Cézanne, Paul, 239, 240
Chamberlin, E. H., 148, 152
Chebyshev, P. L., 189
Chicago school, 125, 216, 333
Circulation (physiology), 30, 260
City populations, 28
Civil disturbances, 28
Clark, John Bates, 213, 280, 286
Classical architecture, 233
Classical art, 238
Classical dynamics, 132, 133, 140, 154, 327, 328. *See also* Dynamics (economics)
Classical economics: Leonard on, 260, 266; physics and, 112, 263; substance theory of value in, 205, 206, 217, 292; Weintraub on, 301; Wicksell and, 183
Classical mechanics: Carey and, 11, 25, 31; I. B. Cohen on, 32–34; Hertz on, 135; Jolink on, 165; Klamer on, 234; Ricardo and, 112; A. Smith and, 266. *See also* Celestial mechanics; Gravitation, law of
Classification, 77, 320, 321
Clay tablets, 78
Coats, A. W. (Bob), 64n, 293n
Coffee valorizations, 150
Cognition, 73, 325
Cognitive dissonance, 78
Cognitive psychology, 77
Coherence, 268
Colander, David, 312
Collingwood, R. G., 113–14
Collins, Harry, 250

Columbia University, 173
Common descent, 15n
Commons, John Rogers, 286
Communal authority, 255
Communication: Douglas on, 255; Fuller on, 74, 75, 76–77, 78–79; Porter on, 60–61; Walter on, 343
Communication technology, 236–37
Communities: primitive, 252–53, 320; scientific, 59–60, 62–63
Compensated demand functions, 123, 124
Compensated prices, 124, 129
Competition, 148, 153, 217
Computers, 73, 325
Comte, Auguste, 80, 87n
The Concise Oxford Dictionary, 25n
Concretization, 101
Conditional method, 112
Conservation of energy: Birner on, 91; Coats on, 273; I. B. Cohen on, 16–17; de Marchi on, 287; Fisher and, 21; Jolink on, 165; Mirowski on, 334; Porter on, 56–57; Walras on, 166, 172
Conservation of matter, 163
Conservation of motion, 260
Conservation principles: Birner on, 86, 87, 88, 90, 91, 93; Boumans on, 131; Coats on, 277, 279; A. J. Cohen on, 202, 204–5, 206, 210, 211–12, 216, 217; de Marchi on, 287, 292; Fuller on, 70; Jolink on, 162, 169; Leonard on, 260, 262, 264, 265, 267; Marx and, 45, 46; Mirowski on, 309, 319, 325, 330; Porter on, 55, 56, 57, 58; Schabas on, 49; Schultz on, 332–33n
Consolidator economists, 177
Constrained maxima, 56, 91, 138, 167, 168–69, 175–76
Constructivism, 322
Consumer choice problem, 122, 127, 128
Consumer theory, 311
Consumption, 107, 121, 205, 210, 255
Contracts, 285

"Coping with Math Anxiety," 315
Le Corbusier (C.-E. Jeanneret), 233, 241
Correspondence Principle, 265, 333
Correspondence strategy, 102–3, 110
Cosimo II of Florence, 59
Cosmologies, 253, 254–55
Cotton shortages, 262
Cournot, Augustin, 148, 152, 183, 225, 230, 301
Craig, John, 33
Crelle, August Leopold, 190
Criticism, 103, 104–5
Crum, William L., 139
Cubism, 239, 240, 241, 244
Curl conditions, 120
Cyclic problems, 139–40, 144–47

Dada movement, 236, 241
D'Alembert's principle, 22
Danziger, Kurt, 63n
Darwin, Charles, 14–15, 24, 234–35
Darwinian evolution, 12n, 15n, 23, 235, 323–24
Davidson, David, 184–85, 188
Death, 255
Debreu, Gerard, 284, 293n. *See also* Sonnenschein-Mantel-Debreu literature
Dedekind, Richard, 176, 177, 191
Deductive reasoning, 138
De jure belli et pacis (Grotius), 8
De Kooning, Willem, 232, 241
Demand/supply diagrams, 223
Demand theory, 121, 122–26
De Marchi, Neil, 318, 335
Demoiselles d'Avignon (Picasso), 239–40
Denis, Maurice, 239
Derrida, Jacques, 76, 306
Desaguliers, J. T., 32–33
Descartes, René: Jevons on, 18; Klamer on, 227–28, 230, 231, 234, 240, 241; Le Corbusier and, 233; *Regulae ad Directionem Ingenii*, 169; theology of, 94n. *See also* Cartesianism

Des méthodes dans les sciences de raisonnement (Duhamel), 168
Determinists, 255n
Dewey, John, 228, 236, 339
Differential equations, 18, 37, 191n. *See also* Lagrange equations
Dilthey, Wilhelm, 306
Dimensional analysis, 20
Directed graph formalism, 291, 297
Discourse, 226–27, 239, 266. *See also* Language; Rhetoric
Doesburg, Theo van, 242
Domain strategy, 103–4, 105, 110
Douglas, Mary, 2, 249–70, 320–21, 322–23, 325. *See also* Durkheim/Mauss/Douglas thesis
Doxography, 317
Dual expenditure minimization problem, 123
Dualism, 228–29
Duchamp, Marcel, 241
Duhamel, Jean-Marie-Constant, 168
Duhem, Pierre, 135
Dumez, Hervé, 65
Dupouy, Edmond, 28n
Durkheim, Emile, 2, 250, 251; Bloor and, 321; Douglas and, 256; *Elementary Forms of Religious Life*, 253; *Primitive Classifications*, 320; *Rules of Sociological Method*, 252, 320; Wittgenstein and, 257
Durkheim/Mauss/Douglas thesis, 322–23, 325, 340
Dutch Central Bureau of Statistics (CBS), 139
Dynamics (economics), 140–51, 311
Dynamics (physics), 132, 133, 140, 154, 327, 328
Dynamos, 236

Eco, Umberto, 159
Ecole des Mines (France), 164
Ecole Normale (France), 29
Ecole Polytechnique (France), 29, 164
Econometrica (periodical), 341
Econometrics, 265, 324

Econometric Society, 338
Economics, Philosophy, and the Physics (Hsieh and Ye), 226
"Economique et mécanique" (Walras), 18, 55, 166, 167, 168
Edgeworth, Francis Ysidro: on analogies, 18n; I. B. Cohen on, 36; de Marchi on, 293n; Gaddy on, 193; Leonard on, 263; Mirowski on, 337; E. B. Wilson on, 339
Edgren-Leffler, Anne Charlotte, 185, 186–87, 188, 197
The Education of Henry Adams (Adams), 234, 305, 306
Ehrenfest, Paul, 131–56, 265, 336
'80s Generation, 182, 187
Einstein, Albert, 52, 237, 342, 343
Elections, 28
Electrodynamics, 327
Electromagnetism, 133–34, 328
Electron theory, 17
Elementary Forms of Religious Life (Durkheim), 253
Eléments de statique (Poinsot), 56, 168
Eléments du calcul infinitésimal (Haton de la Goupillière), 168
Elements of Pure Economics (Walras), 20, 37, 165, 183
Elfving, Gustav, 178n
Elster, Jon, 79
Empirical economics, 293, 294
Empirical knowledge, 95, 96
Encyclopaedia of the Social Sciences, 8
Encyclopedia of Philosophy, 26n, 115
Endogenous motion, 145, 146–47
Endowments, 206, 208, 209, 212n
Energy, conservation of. *See* Conservation of energy
Energy metaphor: Boumans on, 131; A. J. Cohen on, 204, 206; Gaddy on, 194; Hands on, 124–25; Jolink on, 162, 163, 170; Schabas on, 48, 50. *See also* Proto-energetics metaphor
Energy physics, 16, 33, 36–37, 263, 332, 343
Energy-utility relationship, 1, 2; Birner

Energy-utility relationship *(continued)* on, 86; Coats on, 275; A. J. Cohen on, 206, 208n; de Marchi on, 287, 296, 297n; Fuller on, 70; Gaddy on, 193; Hands on, 118, 128, 129; Leonard on, 249–50, 263, 264; Schabas on, 47, 51
Energy-value relationship, 20, 72, 230
Engels, Friedrich, 236
England, 27, 62
English classical economics. *See* Classical economics
English natural philosophy, 59
Enlightenment, the, 229, 231, 242, 243
Entrepreneurial demand functions, 126–29
Entrepreneurship, 80, 154
Envy, 52
Epistemology: Coats on, 276; Klamer on, 237, 238, 240, 241, 242, 244; positivist, 229; Walter on, 343. *See also* Knowledge
Equations, 36; differential, 18, 37, 191n; Euler, 141, 142, 150, 151, 152; Hamiltonian, 140, 142, 153; Lagrange, 134, 135, 140, 141, 142, 153; Laplace's, 173; Maxwell's, 327, 328; simultaneous, 214–15
Equilibrium: A. J. Cohen on, 204n, 212, 213, 216; de Marchi on, 284; Ehrenfest and, 131–32; Mirowski on, 316–17, 331, 332; Pareto on, 19; Roos on, 143; Tinbergen and, 138, 142, 143; Walras on, 336; E. B. Wilson on, 339, 340. *See also* Homeostasis
Erlanger Program, 176–77, 189
Error, law of, 324
Essays in the Sociology of Perception (Douglas), 258
Etner, François, 65
Euclid, 263
Euler, Leonhard, 33
Euler equations, 141, 142, 150, 151, 152
Euler Theorem, 258

Eulerian hydrodynamics, 137
European mensuration, 61
European trade, 277
Euthanasia, 255
Evans, G. C., 142–43, 339
Evans-Pritchard, Edward, 257
Evolution, 12n, 15n, 23, 235, 323–24
Exchange rates, 289
Exchange value, 164–65, 169, 208n
Expenditure function, 123
Experimentation, 50, 60, 62, 79
Exposition Universelle de St. Louis (1904), 167, 174
Eye evolution, 12n

Fable of the Bees (Mandeville), 52
Factualization, 101
Fallacies, 25–26n
Falsification, 50, 274n
Faraday, Michael, 15, 263
Fawcett, Henry, 280
Female figure, 240
Field theory: Birner on, 92; conservation principles and, 93; Jolink on, 162; Mirowski on, 326; Porter on, 57; of value, 205–6, 207–12, 215–16
Financial crises, 28
Financial markets, 291n
Finitism, 257
Finland, 188
Finnish mathematics, 178n
Fisher, Irving: Birner on, 99, 112; I. B. Cohen on, 36, 37; Klamer on, 231; *Mathematical Investigations into the Theory of Value and Prices*, 21, 264; Mirowski on, 330n; E. B. Wilson on, 341
Fluids, 137
Force (physics), 15, 21, 135
Ford, Henry, 234
Forecasting, 271, 313
Formal analogies, 17
Formalism: Birner on, 91, 92; Boumans on, 131; de Marchi on, 286–93, 297; Klamer on, 243; Tinbergen and, 132. *See also* Mathematical formalism

Forward contracts, 285
Foucault, Michel, 54, 226
Foundations of Economic Analysis (Samuelson), 309, 343n
Fourier, Charles, 12
Fowler, H. W., 25–26n
Free trade, 278, 279n
French economics, 65
French mathematics, 189
French Physiocrats, 230
Freud, Sigmund, 13–14, 28n, 240
Freudianism, 45, 72
Friction problems, 143, 145
Fried, Michael, 240–41
Friedman, Milton, 125, 312
Frisch, Ragnar, 331, 341
Frobenius, Ferdinand Georg, 331
Frölander, Theodor, 184
Fuchs, Lazarus, 189
Funerals, 255
Fur trade, 75–76
Futures markets, 285

Gaddy, Cliff, 336
Galileo Galilei, 8, 58–59
Game theory: A. J. Cohen on, 216; Mirowski on, 312, 313, 324, 325, 337n; Porter on, 55; Samuelson and, 343n; Schabas on, 47
Gärdlund, Torsten, 178n, 183, 185, 186n, 195
Gases, kinetic theory of, 17
Gaussian distribution, 324
The General Theory of Employment, Interest and Money (Keynes), 244
Geometry, 8, 17–18, 95–96, 176
Georgescu-Roegen, Nicholas, 309, 310n
German Historical School, 235, 272, 308, 326
German mathematics, 189
Gestalt psychology, 273
Giacometti, Alberto, 232
Gibbs, J. Willard, 21, 330n, 338, 339, 343, 344
Giffen, Robert, 129

Global analysis, 99
God, 94n, 344
Gold market, 289
Gossen, Herman Heinrich, 183, 230
Grain storage, 285
Grammatology, 76
Gravitation, law of: Carey and, 11, 12, 24–26, 31; Fourier and, 12; Jevons on, 20; misapplication of, 31–32, 193; social sciences and, 34; Walras and, 26–27
Gravitational mass, 26n
Great Exposition (1900), 236
Greek geometry, 8
Greek tragedies, 13
Greenberg, Clement, 241–42
Grid-group analysis, 253–54, 258, 320n
Gropius, Walter, 233
Grotius, Hugo de, 8, 230
Group solidarity, 253–54
Grundlagen einer allgemeinen Mannigfaltigkeitslehre (Cantor), 191n
Guerlac, Henry, 33n29
Guilds, 289

Hagstroem, K. G., 294
Hahn, Frank H., 214, 311n
Hamilton, William Rowan, 20, 33
Hamiltonian analysis, 47
Hamiltonian concept, 131, 135, 265, 326
Hamiltonian determinism, 2
Hamiltonian dynamics, 91
Hamiltonian equations, 140, 142, 153
Hamiltonian formalism, 132, 140
Hamiltonian functions, 16
Hamilton's principle, 141, 148
Hanau, A., 140
Hands, D. Wade, 212n, 216n, 327, 328, 333, 334
Harmonic oscillations, 154
Harrington, James, 8
Harvard Economic Service, 139
Harvey, David, 236
Harvey, William, 8

358 Index

Haton de la Goupillière, Julien Napoléon, 168
Heat, 15, 18
Hegel, G. W. F., 309
Heisenberg, Werner Karl, 154
Helmholtz, Hermann von, 49, 52, 135, 172
Helsinki University, 187–88
Hempel, Carl, 45
Henderson, James, 311
Henderson, L. J., 339n
Henry, C., 191n
Hermeneutics, 86, 88–89, 98, 113, 306
Hermite, Charles, 189, 190
Herschel, Sir John Frederick William, 324
Hertz, Heinrich, 64, 135–37
Hessen thesis, 272
Heterogeneous commodity production function, 211–12
Heuristics, 104, 105–6, 109, 110
Hicks, J. R., 284, 291n
Historiography: Adams on, 305; de Marchi on, 292–95; Fuller on, 69; Jolink on, 171; Klamer on, 234–35, 246; Leonard on, 249; Mirowski on, 310; Pantaleoni on, 335; Weintraub on, 301, 302. *See also* Science: history of
A History of Economic Thought (Niehans), 4
Hobbes, Thomas, 62
Hobbs, Michael, 71, 72
Holland, 148. *See also* Netherlandish art markets
Homeostasis, 30, 39. *See also* Equilibrium
Homologies, 11–12, 16–24, 24–30, 31, 37, 39- 40
Homothetic preferences, 121
Hotelling, Harold, 126–29, 332, 339
Houthakker, Hendrik, 265
Hsieh, C. Y., 226
Hugo de Grotius, 8, 230
Humanities, 235, 243
The Human Motor (Rabinbach), 233–34

Hume, David, 229, 230
Hurwicz, L., 125
Hurwitz, Alfred, 189
Hutchison, Terence, 2
Huxley, Thomas Henry, 10n
Hydras (zoology), 29
Hydrodynamics, 137
Hydrostatics, 21
Hysteresis, 79
Hysteria, 28

Ibsen, Henrik, 186
Idealization, 100–102, 103
Identity, 9–10, 58, 87, 88, 95
Identity and Reality (Meyerson), 54, 56
I krig med samhället (Edgren-Leffler), 187
Immunizing strategems, 105
Implicit Meanings (Douglas), 255–56
Impressionist painting, 238–39, 240, 244
Income, 57, 124, 125, 212n
Induction (logic), 138
Induction (physics), 80
Inertial mass, 26n
Information processing, 73
Ingrao, Bruna, 293n
Ingres, Jean-Auguste-Dominique, 238, 240
Innis, Harold, 75, 76, 78, 79
Institut für Konjunkturforschung, 139, 140
Institutionalists, 46, 72, 272, 308, 324, 326
Institutions, 256, 257, 266, 321
Institut Mittag-Leffler, 186n
Integrability, 118–30, 206n, 265, 326–35, 338
Intentional fallacy, 25n
Interest rates: on bonds, 286, 295; Cambridge capital theory debate on, 107; capital and, 213n, 214, 215; A. J. Cohen on, 208, 209, 210, 211
International Encyclopedia of the Social Sciences, 8
International Style (architecture), 233

Index   359

Internuncial agencies, 29
Interpretation of Dreams (Freud), 13
In the Active Voice (Douglas), 320n
Invariance: de Marchi on, 287–88, 289, 291, 295, 297; Mirowski on, 308, 323, 330, 331–32
Inventory problems, 143, 145–46, 150–51, 153
Investigations on Method (Menger), 112
Irrational numbers, 96
Irreversibility, 204n
Isherwood, B., 255
Israel, Giorgio, 293n
Italian bookkeeping, 2–3

Jacobian matrix, 120, 121, 122
Jacquard loom, 325
Jaffé, William, 169n, 317n, 336
Jenkin, Fleeming, 337
Jennings, Richard, 335
Jevons, William Stanley: Coats on, 280; I. B. Cohen on, 20, 36, 37; de Marchi on, 284; Fisher and, 21; Fuller on, 80; Gaddy on, 175, 177, 183, 193, 194; Jolink on, 161, 163, 171; Klamer on, 225, 230, 234; Leonard on, 263; on mathematics, 17–18; physiological psychology and, 335; Porter on, 56; prime-minister analogy of, 36; *Theory of Political Economy*, 18, 37, 183, 263; Thornton and, 337; Weintraub on, 301
Johns, Jasper, 232
Johnson, Mark, 35
Johnson, Philip, 233
Jolink, Albert, 207–8n, 293n, 336
Joule, James Prescott, 263
Joyce, James, 231, 236
Jupiter (planet), 14
Justificationism, 98–99, 110–11

Kandidat degree, 178n
Kandinsky, Wassily, 241, 242
Kant, Immanuel, 96, 113, 229–30
Kathedersozialisten, 182, 186

Kautsky, Karl, 184
Kelvin, William Thomson, Lord, 134–35, 335-36
Kern, Stephen, 236
Keynes, John Maynard, 236, 244, 245, 264, 286, 312
Kiefer, Anselm, 232
Kim, Jinbang, 294n
Kinetic theory of gases, 17
Kirman, Alan, 312
Klamer, Arjo, 312
Klein, Felix, 176, 189
Klein, Martin J., 137
Knight, Frank, 236
Knowledge: belief and, 255, 256; Bloor on, 267, 321; Douglas on, 253, 256; Enlightenment philosophes and, 229; Leonard on, 268; sociology of, 251, 252, 322; Walter on, 343. *See also* Epistemology
Knowledge and Social Imagery (Bloor), 256
Koopmans, Tjalling Charles, 293n, 337
Kovalevskaya, Sonya, 181, 185, 187–88, 189, 191n
Krajewski, W., 100, 105
Kreps, David, 311, 312
Kuhn, Thomas, 69, 85, 86, 226, 273, 302
Kuhn-Tucker theorem, 311
Kula, Witold, 61, 88, 259, 277

Labor, 209, 233–34
Labor theory of value, 204, 213, 249, 262
Lagrange equations, 134, 135, 140, 141, 142, 153
Lagrange, Joseph-Louis, 20, 33, 197
Lagrangian analysis, 47
Lagrangian formalism, 132
Lagrangian functions, 141, 148
Lagrangian hydrodynamics, 137
Lagrangian virtual displacements, 16
Lail, Mike, 294n
Lakatos, Imre: Birner on, 85, 86, 99, 105–6; Bloor and, 258; Fuller on,

Lakatos, Imre *(continued)*
69, 73, 80; *Methodology of Scientific Research Programmes*, 105–6, 109; PR+ and, 111; *Proofs and Refutations*, 99n, 105, 108, 109; Weintraub on, 302
Laksov, Dan, 186n
Language, 257, 258. *See also* Discourse; Rhetoric
Laplace, Pierre-Simon de, 2, 33, 208n; I. B. Cohen on, 20, 33; Schabas on, 48, 49, 50; *Système du monde*, 14
Laplace's equations, 173
Latour, Bruno, 78–79, 250
Laudan, Larry, 69
Laurent, Hermann, 193, 194, 264, 332
"Learning the Meaning of a Dollar" (Mirowski), 284
Least curvature, principle of, 135
Le Bon, Gustave, 172
Le Chatelier Principle, 265
"Lecture Notes on an Institutionalist Theory of Value" (Mirowski), 284
Leffler, Anne Charlotte, 185, 186–87, 188, 197
Leffler, Gösta, 185, 188
Leffler, Johan, 185, 186, 198
Leger, Fernand, 242
Leibniz, Gottfried Wilhelm, 8–9, 332
Lele tribe, 252
Leonard, Rob, 318
Lever, 18, 263
Licentiat degree, 178n, 179, 181, 182
Lichtenstein, Roy, 232
Lie, Sophus, 176, 189
Life cycle analogy, 39
Light, 134
Lilienfeld, Paul von, 9, 27, 28
Lineamentric measurement, 88, 262
Literary writing, 77, 273
Locke, John, 233
Logic, 99, 257
Logical positivism, 235
Logomathy, 341
London, 62, 289

Lorén, Viktor, 184, 185, 188
Lorén Foundation, 184–88, 191n, 199
Lorenz, Konrad, 12n, 172
Louis, Morris, 232
Lowell, A. Lawrence, 27
Lucas, Robert E., Jr., 245
Lumber trade, 75–76
Luytelaer, Th. van, 150
Lyapunov, A. M., 189, 191n
Lyotard, J. F., 242

McCall, John, 293n
McCloskey, Donald, 36, 63–64, 71, 72, 224–25, 250n
McCulloch, John Ramsey, 280
Machine metaphors, 10, 233–34, 243
McLuhan, Marshall, 75, 76
Malevitch, Kazimir, 241, 242
Mall, T., 197
Malmsten, Carl Johan, 190
Malthus, Thomas, 14–15, 183, 323
Malthusianism, 179–80, 182, 184
Malvinaud, Edmond, 207, 211, 215
Manasse, Georg, 185n
Mandelbrot, Benoit, 293
Mandeville, Bernard, 52, 295
Manet, Edouard, 238–39, 240, 241
"Manifest and Latent Functions" (Merton), 30
Marcet, Jane, 280
Marginalist revolution, 1–2; Coats on, 64n; A. J. Cohen on, 208n; I. B. Cohen on, 20; Fuller on, 72, 73; Gaddy on, 175, 177, 178, 182–84, 192–94; Jolink on, 161; Leonard on, 263; Stigler on, 63
Marine animals, 29
Market graph formalism, 290
Markets, 285, 295, 308
Markov, A. A., 189
Marriage, 14
Marshall, Alfred: on analogies, 23–24; Coats on, 280; de Marchi on, 284, 294n; Gaddy on, 194; Jolink on, 161; Mirowski on, 312; *Principles of Economics*, 24, 311; Thornton and,

337; Weintraub on, 301; E. B. Wilson on, 339
Marshallian economics, 125, 208–9, 264, 311, 324
Martineau, Harriet, 280
Martingale processes, 293
Marx, Karl: Berman on, 236; *Capital*, 262; conservation principles of, 45, 46; de Marchi on, 284; epistemology and, 240; Klamer on, 234, 235; Leonard on, 260, 262; Rabinbach on, 233; value theory of, 204
Marxism, 51, 72, 255n
Mass (physics), 26, 31
Massachusetts Institute of Technology, 316, 345
Mathematical anomalies, 258
Mathematical economics, 338–39. *See also* Econometrics
Mathematical formalism: Birner on, 94, 99, 110; Jolink on, 164, 168–69; "lines of force" theory and, 15; metaphors and, 93, 94; Wicksell and, 194
"Mathematical Formalism and Economic Explanation" (Mirowski), 192–93, 267, 284
The Mathematical Groundwork of Economics (Bowley), 138
Mathematical Investigations into the Theory of Value and Prices (Fisher), 21, 264
Mathematical models, 245
Mathematical physics, 16, 17, 18, 38, 54–68
Mathematics: heuristics and, 105–6; justificationism and, 98–99, 110–11; metaphor and, 90–95, 325; Meyerson on, 95–98, 110; nonneutrality of, 2, 90–95, 258; physics and, 97–98, 177; Porter on, 62–63, 64; Swedish, 178; E. B. Wilson on, 341. *See also* Algebra; Calculus; Equations; Geometry
Mathematics-economics relationship: Fuller on, 72; Gaddy on, 177–78, 183, 194n; Jolink on, 167, 168, 170; Mirowski on, 316, 326; Pareto on, 19; Porter on, 63, 64, 65, 66
Matisse, Henri, 239, 240
Matter, conservation of, 163
Mauss, Marcel, 2, 250, 251, 252–53, 320. *See also* Durkheim/Mauss/Douglas thesis
Maxwell, James Clerk: analogies and, 14, 15, 133–35, 136; Boltzmann and, 136; gas laws of, 324; Hertz and, 64, 135; homology and, 18; Jevons and, 20, 263; Mirowski on, 335–36; Walras on, 172
Maxwell's equations, 327, 328
Mazzola, Ugo, 198
Measurement, 61, 88
Measures and Men (Kula), 61
Mechanical calculation devices, 325
Mechanical metaphors, 10, 233–34, 243
Mechanics. *See* Classical mechanics; Rational mechanics
Mechanism, 89
Meek, Ronald L., 203
Mémoire sur les courbes définies par une équation différentielle (Poincaré), 191n
Mémoire sur les fonctions fuchsiennes (Poincaré), 190
Memory, 13
Ménard, Claude, 293n
Menger, Carl: Birner on, 112; Coats on, 280; Gaddy on, 177, 194; Jolink on, 161, 163, 171; Weintraub on, 301
Mercantilism, 260, 266, 277, 278–79
Merleau-Ponty, Maurice, 77
Merton, Robert, 30
Metanarratives, 242, 243, 244, 245
Metapherein, 36
Metaphorical simplex. *See* Body-motion-value simplex
Metaphors, 34–38; absolute presuppositions and, 114; analogies and, 11, 35–36, 38, 39; Birner on, 90–95, 98–99; Boyd on, 70; Coats on, 273,

Metaphors *(continued)*
274; Fuller on, 71–79; Jolink on, 171; McCloskey on, 224–25; mathematics as, 90–95, 325; Mirowski on, 309, 325; Schabas on, 46, 48. *See also* Energy metaphor; Proto-energetics metaphor
Metaphysics, 94, 113–14, 172, 343
Metaphysics (Aristotle), 85
Methodology of Scientific Research Programmes (Lakatos), 105–6, 109
Metric system, 61
Meyerson, Emile: Birner on, 87–88, 89, 114; causality and, 52, 87; A. J. Cohen on, 204; de Marchi on, 2; empirical reality and, 115; Hegel and, 309; hermeneutics and, 94, 113; *Identity and Reality*, 54, 56; justificationism of, 110; Lakatos and, 111; on mathematics, 95–98; Mirowski on, 319n, 321–22, 323; Samuelson and, 210, 212; on time, 147
Microeconomics, 119, 125
Mies van der Rohe, Ludwig, 233, 235
Mill, John Stuart, 80, 182, 183, 276
Minimumproblemen in de natuurkunde en economie (Tinbergen), 132
Minimum problems, 140–44
Miracles, 33
Misplaced concreteness fallacy, 25
Mitchell, Wesley Clair, 278n, 339n
Mittag-Leffler circle, 175–201
Models, 36, 100–105, 109–10, 135–36, 245
Modern English Usage (Fowler), 25–26n
Modernism, 223–48
Mohring, Herbert, 57n
Monarchy, 31
Mondrian, Piet: on abstraction, 223; aims of, 242; art of, 235, 239, 241; Samuelson and, 226, 244–45
Monopolies, 138, 144, 146, 148, 153
"Monster-barring," 258
Montesquieu, Charles, 31
Moon, 35n

Moore, Henry Ludwell, 167, 172–74, 316–17, 337
Morality, 229–30, 234
Morgan, Mary, 63n
Morris, Charles R., 271
Morris, William, 235
Moses and Monotheism (Freud), 14
Motion (economics), 144–45
Motion (physics), 260, 277, 278. *See also* Perpetual motion
Murray, John Middleton, 35
Musgrave, A., 100, 103–4, 105
Mutation analogies, 39, 40
"My Economic Endeavors" (Mirowski), 21
Myrdal, Gunnar, 276, 286
"Mystic Writing-Pad," 13

Nagel, Ernest, 15–16n, 17
National Academy of Sciences (U.S.), 338
National Gallery (Washington, D.C.), 231–33
Natural law, 216
Natural sciences, 2, 7–44, 86, 339
Natural selection analogy, 14n, 39
Natural Symbols (Douglas), 320n
Nature, 238–39. *See also* Social-Natural relationship
Neal, Larry, 291n
Negligibility strategy, 103, 104, 105
Neoclassical economics: Cambridge capital controversies and, 215–16; demand theory of, 121; Douglas on, 249; global theories of, 99; Hands on, 124–25; integrability and, 120, 126; Jolink on, 161–64; Leonard on, 267–68; production theory of, 205, 206; Schabas on, 46; value theory of, 205–6, 207–12, 215–16; Weintraub on, 301; Wicksell and, 182–83, 191. *See also* Marginalist revolution
Neoclassical economics–physics relationship, 1; Birner on, 86, 90–92; Coats on, 274–75, 280; A. J. Cohen on, 216n; I. B. Cohen on, 7, 16–17,

20, 36–38; de Marchi on, 287; Fuller on, 70–71; Gaddy on, 175–77, 192–94; Jolink on, 160, 170, 171; Klamer on, 225–26, 231; Leonard on, 249–50, 258n, 265, 266, 267; Mirowski on, 314, 327–28, 334; Porter on, 55–56, 62; Schabas on, 47, 51
Neo-Malthusianism, 179–80, 182
Netherlandish art markets, 285–86, 288–90
Neurosis, 14, 49, 72
Newman, Barnet, 232
Newton, Isaac: Descartes and, 228, 260; Enlightenment philosophes and, 229; Klamer on, 231; *Philosophiae Naturalis Principia Mathematica*, 33, 34, 37
Newtonian mechanics. *See* Classical mechanics
The Newtonian System of the World (Desaguliers), 33
New York Stock Exchange, 289
Nicholson, Margaret, 26n
Niehans, Jurg, 4
Nietzsche, Friedrich, 235
Nihilism, 188n
Nobel Prizes, 311n
Non-Euclidian geometries, 96, 176
"The Notions of Horizon and Expectancy in Dynamic Economics" (Tinbergen), 148–49
Nowak, L., 100, 105
Number system, 95

O'Brien, Denis, 3
Obsessional neurosis, 14
Obshchaya zadacha ob ustoychivosti dvizheniya (Lyapunov), 191n
Oceana (Harrington), 8
Oedipus complex, 14
"On Checking Root Equations" (Wicksell), 179
One-commodity surrogate production function, 209–11, 213, 214
One price, law of, 91, 287, 291, 330, 332

On Liberty (Mill), 182
Ontological grammar, 94
Operationalism, 342–43
Ophelimity: Pareto on, 22, 23; Tinbergen on, 142, 143, 147, 148–49, 150
Organismic sociology, 9–10, 27–28, 32
Origin of Species (Darwin), 14–15, 24, 234–35
Oscar II, King of Sweden, 189
Overpopulation, 180, 323
Oxford English Dictionary, 25n

The Painter in Modern Life (Baudelaire), 238
Painting, 237–41, 244, 285–86, 288–90
Palme, J. H., 186n
Palme, Olof, 186n
Pangolins, 252
Pantaleoni, Maffeo, 335
Paper documents, 78
Parallel adaptation, 12n
Parapraxes, 72
Pareto Circle, 338
Pareto, Vilfredo: on analogies, 19–21; I. B. Cohen on, 36, 37; error of, 93; Gaddy on, 193; Leonard on, 263–64; philosophy of science and, 80; Roos on, 143; Tinbergen and, 138, 139; Volterra and, 332; E. B. Wilson on, 330n, 338, 341
Paris, 233
Paris Bourse, 291n
Paris Commune, 188n
Pathetic fallacy, 25n
Patronage, 58–59
Pearson, Karl, 341
Peel, J. D. Y., 29n
Pei, I. M., 232
Peirce, Charles Sanders, 80, 338
Penrose, Edith, 38–40
Perpetual motion, 80, 217
Perrier, Ed., 172
"The Personality of A. A. Cournot," 173
Persons, Warren M., 139

Petty, William, 57, 62, 230, 279n
Philosophes, 229, 231
Philosophiae Naturalis Principia Mathematica (Newton), 33, 34, 37
Philosophy of science, 79–80, 86, 114, 318
Philosophy of the Inductive Sciences (Whewell), 114n
Photography, 237
Physical analogies, 15–16n, 133–37, 192–93, 266, 275, 276. *See also* Energy metaphor; Proto-energetics metaphor
Physics, 52, 97–98, 177, 309, 317; energy, 16, 33, 36–37, 263, 332, 343; innovations in, 264–65, 342; mathematical, 16, 17, 18, 38, 54–68; quantum, 16, 154. *See also* Classical mechanics
Physics and Mathematics Society (Sweden), 179
"Physics and the Marginalist Revolution" (Mirowski), 192n
Physics-economics relationship: Birner on, 110–11; Coats on, 277, 281; A. J. Cohen on, 202; Fuller on, 74, 79; Jevons on, 18; Jolink on, 159; Klamer on, 244–45, 245; Leonard on, 249–50, 266; Marshall on, 23; Mirowski on, 307–8, 313, 319; Pareto on, 19; Schabas on, 48–52, 53; Walras on, 18; Harrison White on, 310. *See also* Classical economics: physics and; Neoclassical economics-physics relationship
Physics envy, 45–53, 72, 111–13, 118, 170, 309–17
Physics Today (periodical), 310
Physiocrats, 230, 260, 261, 279
Physiological psychology, 335
Picard, Charles-Émile: Hermite and, 189, 190; Walras and, 165, 167, 172, 173–74
Picasso, Pablo, 239–40
Piccard, Antoine-Paul, 169, 336
Pirandellian social constructivism, 79

Pissarro, Camille, 240
Planck, Max, 154
Planetary orbital motion, 9, 18, 31, 263
Poincaré, Jules-Henri: *Mémoire sur les courbes définies par une équation différentielle*, 191n; *Mémoire sur les fonctions fuchsiennes*, 190; Mittag-Leffler circle and, 189, 190, 191; Porter on, 55; Schabas on, 48, 49, 52; *La science et l' hypothèse*, 165, 166, 171–72; *Sur le problème des trois corps et les équations de la dynamique*, 191n; *Théorie des groupes fuchsiens*, 190; Walras and, 165, 166, 167, 170, 171–72
Poinsot, Louis, 56, 168
Pointillism, 240
Polanyi, Michael, 229n
Polish Idealization Model (PIM), 100–103, 104, 105, 110
Political science, 268
Pollock, Jackson, 241, 242
Polyps (zoology), 29
Popper, Karl Raimund, 80, 85, 86, 95, 104, 114
Popperian falsificationism, 50
Popular art, 243
Population ecology, 324
Population growth, 14, 180, 323
Pork market, 140
Porter, Michael, 313n
Porter, Ted, 295n
Positivist epistemology, 229
Posterior odds, 33n
Postmodernism, 244n
"Postmodernism and the Social Theory of Value" (Mirowski), 284
Potato flour, 147–48
Potential theory, 56, 328
Power (social science), 51, 52, 61, 235
$PR+$, 109–11
Pre-Raphaelites, 235
Pribram, Karl, 278n
Price expectancies, 149
Price potential, 128
Prices: arbitrage-free, 284, 292, 293,

295, 297, 298; as conservative vector field, 118, 119–21, 123–24, 216n; entrepreneurial demand and, 127; equilibrium of, 216, 334; income and, 212n; linearity of, 290; Newtonian law of gravity and, 26–27, 31–32; in one-product surrogate production model, 210; as random distributions, 291–92; supply regularization and, 147; symmetry of, 328–29; value theory and, 203–4, 206, 207–8. *See also* One price, law of
Price-substitution terms, 124
Primitive Classifications (Durkheim and Mauss), 320
Primitive societies, 252–53, 320
Principia Mathematica (B. Russell), 235
Principles of Economics (Marshall), 24, 311
Principles of Economics (Menger), 112
The Principles of Mechanics Presented in a New Form (Hertz), 135–37
The Principles of Scientific Management (F. W. Taylor), 234
Principles of Sociology (Spencer), 9–10
Probability, 33n, 166, 324, 326n, 337n
"Ein Problem der Dynamik" (Tinbergen), 148
Les Procédés de raisonnement dans les sciences naturelles et sociales (Perrier), 172
Production: A. J. Cohen on, 205, 206, 209, 210, 211; Hand on, 125n; Jolink on, 165; in labor theory of value, 204; neoclassical model of, 107, 109, 163, 264; Schabas on, 51; substance theory of, 207–12, 264; Tinbergen on, 152–53
Profit, 143, 144, 145, 148, 262
Profit-maximizing behavior, 39, 108
Programmatic guidance, 108
Progress, 69, 105
Prony, G.-C.-F.-M. Riche, Baron de, 324

Proof analysis, 106–7
Proofs and Refutations (Lakatos), 99n, 105, 108, 109
Prostitutes, 240
Protectionism, 279n
Proto-energetics metaphor: Birner on, 91–92; Coats on, 271n, 275; defined, 204n; Fuller on, 70, 79; Jolink on, 160, 163, 165, 166; Klamer on, 226; Leonard on, 263, 264, 266
Prototype recognition, 77, 78
Protozoa, 29
Proust, Marcel, 231, 236
"On Proving the Existence of a Root of a Polynomial Equation" (Wicksell), 182
Psychologism, 257
Psychology, 77, 244, 273, 311, 335
Ptolemaic system, 34
Pure exchange models, 207
Puritanism, 344
Pylyshyn, Zenon, 73

Quandt, Richard E., 311
Quantification, 61, 63. *See also* Mathematics
Quantity-substitution terms, 124
Quantum physics, 16, 154
Quesnay, François, 10, 57, 170, 260, 262
Quetelet, L. A. J., 324

Rabinbach, Anson, 233–34
Radnitzky, Gerard, 80
Raphael Sanzio, 237
Rational mechanics: economics and, 20–21, 33, 36–37, 38; Edgeworth and, 337n; Leonard on, 260; Mirowski on, 326; Pareto on, 19, 20–21, 22–23; social sciences and, 16; Walras and, 164
Rauschenberg, Robert, 232
The Realms of the Natural (Mirowski), 272
Reason: Birner on, 92; in Cartesianism, 228–29; Enlightenment philosophes

Reason *(continued)*
and, 229; Kant on, 229–30; Meyerson on, 87, 95; Tinbergen on, 138; Walras on, 172
Reed, John, 313
Regulae ad Directionem Ingenii (Descartes), 169
Reification, 56, 57
Relativism, 237
Relativity, 13, 16, 176
Religion, 14, 94n, 344
Remarks on the Foundations of Mathematics (Wittgenstein), 257
Rembrandt Harmenszoon van Rijn, 232, 289
Renoir, Auguste, 232
Replication, 60
Representation of reality, 242–43, 244
Repurchase agreements, 285, 286
Research communities, 59–60, 62–63
Retardation problems, 144, 145, 147
Revealed Preference Theory, 265
Rhetoric: Fuller on, 71–72; Klamer on, 240; McCloskey on, 63–64, 224–25, 250n; Porter on, 63–64, 66. *See also* Analogies; Metaphors
Rhetoric of Economics (McCloskey), 72
Ricardians, 65
Ricardo, David: de Marchi on, 284, 294; Klamer on, 230; Leonard on, 260, 262, 263, 266; Newtonian physics and, 112; Wicksell and, 183
Ricca-Salerno, Giuseppe, 198
Richards, I. A., 76, 77
Richards, Robert J., 29n
Ring Movement, 182, 186
Rise of Financial Capitalism (Neal), 291n
Robinson, Joan, 213n, 215
Rogin, Leo, 278n
Romantics, 235
Roos, Charles F., 142, 143, 339
Roosevelt, Theodore, 27
Rorty, Richard, 317, 336
Roscher, Wilhelm, 185, 186
Rosser, John Barkley, 99

Rothko, Mark, 232, 241
Rowland, Henry Augustus, 172
Royal Society (Britain), 62
Rubens, Peter Paul, 240, 289
Rubik's cube, 159
"Rules of Historical Evidence" (Craig), 33n
Rules of Sociological Method (Durkheim), 252, 320
Rule systems, 254
Ruskin, John, 25n
Russell, Bertrand, 235
Russian constructivists, 241
Russian Formalists, 77
Russian mathematics, 189
Russian nihilism, 188n
Russian Revolution, 242
Russian universities, 187

Sacredness, 252–53, 257
St. Lawrence River, 75–76
St. Louis World Fair (1904), 167, 174
The Salon of 1859 (Baudelaire), 237
Samuelson, Paul: Birner on, 99, 112; de Marchi on, 284, 293n; *Foundations of Economic Analysis*, 309, 343n; Hand on, 126; integrability problem and, 333; Jolink on, 160, 162; Leonard on, 265, 267, 269; Mirowski on, 341–42, 343–45; Modernist art and, 226; Mondrian and, 244–45; on political economy, 223; Porter on, 55; Schabas on, 50; surrogate production function thesis of, 202, 206–12; Walras and, 160; Harrison White on, 309–10
Santa Fe Institute, 313
Sartor Resartus (Carlyle), 27
Sax, Emil, 198
Say, J. B., 273
Scaly anteaters, 252
Scarcity: A. J. Cohen on, 204, 207, 208, 210, 211, 213, 217; Fuller on, 80
Schabas, Margaret, 71, 216n, 318
Schaffer, Simon, 59, 62, 79

Schäffle, Albert E., 27
Schröder, Erwin, 131
Schultz, Henry, 332–33
Schumpeter, Joseph, 45, 65, 80, 214n, 279, 337
Science: economics and, 295, 300, 310; entrepreneurship and, 80; epistemological problem in, 244; history of, 87; humanities and, 235, 243; incorrect, 31–32, 262; mathematics and, 95; metaphors and, 50, 88–89; metaphysics and, 113–14; methodology of, 74; Meyerson on, 56, 89; philosophy of, 79–80, 86, 114, 318; Porter on, 58; sociology of, 256–57, 258, 268, 314
Science (periodical), 310, 315
La science et l'hypothèse (Poincaré), 165, 166, 171–72
Science et Religion (Boutroux), 172
Science in Action (Latour), 79
La science moderne et son état actuel (Picard), 165, 172, 173–74
Scientific American (periodical), 310, 315
Scientific communication, 60–61
Scientific communities, 59–60, 62–63
Scientific historiography. *See* Historiography
Scientific progress, 69, 105
Scientific research, 273–74
Scientific Revolution, 8, 35
Scientific societies, 59
Scottish moral philosophers, 230
Seagram Building (New York), 233
Seasonal dependence, 146
Self-interest, 217
Self-regulation. *See* Equilibrium; Homeostasis
Seligman, Edwin R. A., 173
Seurat, Georges, 240
Sex, 10
Shannon, Claude, 74
Shapere, Dudley, 80
Shapin, Steven, 59, 62, 79, 250, 255–56

Shible, W. A., 35
Shipbuilding cycle, 133
Signs, 257
Simultaneous equations, 214–15
Single tax, 170
Sitte, Camillo, 233
Skandia (firm), 186n
Sloan Foundation, 342
Slutsky conditions: A. J. Cohen on, 216; compensated demand functions and, 123–24; conservation principles and, 264; consumer choice problem and, 122; integrability and, 118, 120, 121; Mirowski on, 327, 329, 330, 331, 332–33; Samuelson on, 126
Smith, Adam: Coats on, 273, 279–80; de Marchi on, 3, 284, 294; Leonard on, 260–61, 262; Mirowski on, 324; Porter on, 57, 65; *Wealth of Nations*, 31–32; Wicksell and, 183
Smith, Crosbie, 281n
"Smooth Operator" (Mirowski), 3
Snow, C. P., 235
Social classifications, 320, 321
Social constructivism, 52, 79
Social Darwinism, 324
The Social Framework (Hicks), 291n
Social gravitation, 25
Social hierarchies, 254
Social history, 301
Social institutions, 256, 257, 266, 321
Socialism, 132, 184
Social-Natural relationship: de Marchi on, 294; Klamer on, 225, 230, 235; Leonard on, 252; Mirowski on, 319, 322, 323
Social organization, 254–55, 257
Social power, 51, 52, 61, 235
Social relationships, 256
Social sciences, 7–44, 339, 340
"Social Theory of Value" (Mirowski), 267
Social value, 272n, 283–99
Social wealth, 165, 167
Societies, traditional, 252–53, 320
Sociology: of Carey, 11; of economics,

Sociology *(continued)*
315–16; of Fourier, 12; of knowledge, 251, 252, 322; Leonard on, 268, 269; organismic, 9–10, 27–28, 32; Porter on, 66; of science, 256–57, 258, 268
Solar system, 14, 17, 134
Sonnenschein-Mantel-Debreu literature, 312, 314, 333–34, 337n
Space perception, 236–37
Spencer, Herbert, 9–10, 27, 28–29
Spirit of the Laws (Montesquieu), 31
Sponges, 10n
Sraffa, Piero, 297n
Sraffian program, 109
Stability analysis, 63n
Stabilizing Economic Dynamics (Weintraub), 293n
Standardization, 60, 61, 237
State power, 61
Statics, 327, 328
Statistics, 61, 138
Steamboats, 75, 76
Steffen, G., 199
Stella, Frank, 232
Stetigkeit und irrationale Zahlen (Dedekind), 176
Stigler, George, 63
Stigler, Stephen, 33n
Stochastic processes, 166, 292, 293, 294, 324
Stockholm University, 181, 186, 188, 189, 195, 198
Stock options market, 285
Strindberg, August, 182, 186
"Strong program in the sociology of science" (SPSS), 256
Structuralism, 255n
Structure (biology), 11
Structure of Scientific Revolutions (Kuhn), 69
"Studies in Economics" (Columbia University), 173
Subjectivity, 229, 244
Substance theory of production, 207–12, 264

Substance theory of value, 205, 206, 217, 292
Substantive analogies, 17
Substitution effects, 120
Suicide, 255
Supply models, 150–54
Supply regularization, 147–50
Suprematist style, 241, 244
Sur le problème des trois corps et les équations de la dynamique (Poincaré), 191n
Surrealism, 236, 241
Surrogate production function, 202, 206–12
Swedberg, Richard, 310n
Swedish mathematics, 178
Swedish Parliament, 186
Syllogisms, 325
"Symmetries, Arbitrage and the Social Theory of Value" (Mirowski), 284, 287, 292, 297
Symmetry, 118–30, 308, 326–35
Syndetic measurement, 88
Synonymy, 36
Synthetic history, 69–70
Système du monde (Laplace), 14
Szostak, Rick, 227n

Tarde, Gabriel, 320
Taylor, F. W., 234
Technology: Coats on, 272; A. J. Cohen on, 206, 208, 212; Klamer on, 236–37; Leonard on, 264
Telegraph, 236
Telephone, 237
Tenacity, principle of, 274
Testimonies, 33
Theologiae Christianae Principia Mathematica (Craig), 33
Theology, 14, 94n, 344
Théorie des groupes fuchsiens (Poincaré), 190
Théorie mathématique des richesses sociales (Walras), 183
Theories. *See* Models

Index 369

Theory of Political Economy (Jevons), 18, 37, 183, 263
The Theory of the Leisure Class (Veblen), 309
Thermodynamics, 47–48, 131–32, 154, 172, 204n
Thomas Aquinas, 230, 260
Thornton, William, 337
Thoughts on the Social Science of the Future (von Lilienfeld), 9
Three Essays on the State of Economic Science (Koopmans), 337n
Thunen, Johann Heinrich von, 230
Tiden (newspaper), 182
Time perception, 236–37
Time variable, 142, 146, 147, 149, 204n
Tinbergen, Jan, 131–56, 294, 297n, 336
Titian (Tiziano Vecelli), 232, 237
Totem and Taboo (Freud), 14
Totemic systems, 320
Trade, 260, 278, 279n
Traditional societies, 252–53, 320
Transportation systems, 30, 74–75, 236
Treatise on Metaphysics (Voltaire), 229
Tullberg, Rita McWilliams, 3
Turgot, Anne-Robert-Jacques, 57, 272n
"The Two Paths of the Mathematicization of the Social and Economic Sciences" (Israel), 293
Tyndall, John, 12

Über die Ausdehnung eines Satzes aus der Theorie der triognometrischen Reihen (Cantor), 176n
Über Wert, Kapital und Rente (Wicksell), 185, 188, 198, 199
"Uncertainty, Evolution and Economic Theory" (Alchian), 38–40
University of Berlin, 187
University of Stockholm, 181, 186, 188, 189, 195, 198
Uppsala University, 180
Ur Lifvet (A. C. Leffler), 197

Utility: Afriat on, 331; Birner on, 91, 111; A. J. Cohen on, 204, 205, 206; Hands on, 118–30; Jolink on, 165, 169; Leonard on, 264–65; Pareto on, 23; Porter on, 57; Weintraub on, 301. *See also* Energy-utility relationship

Value: Birner on, 89; Coats on, 272, 273, 276, 277, 278; A. J. Cohen on, 202–17; energy as, 20, 72, 230; Fuller on, 80; Jolink on, 162, 164–65; labor theory of, 204, 213, 249, 262; Leonard on, 260, 262; Mirowski on, 308; Porter on, 57; social, 272n, 283–99; substance theory of, 205, 206, 217, 292; Walras on, 169n
Value, Capital and Rent (Wicksell), 185, 188, 198, 199
Vanishing income effects, 121, 125n
Varian, Hal, 297n, 311
Variational problems, 143, 144, 145
Veblen, Thorstein: Coats on, 278; de Marchi on, 286; Fuller on, 80; Mirowski on, 309, 310; Schabas on, 46–47, 52; *The Theory of the Leisure Class*, 309
Velocity, 147
Verein für Sozialpolitik (Kathedersozialisten), 182, 186
Victoria (firm), 186
Vienna Circle, 235
Viennese architecture, 233
Virchow, Rudolf, 10
Virtual displacements, 148
Virtual velocities, 18
Vision, 12n
Visual arts, 231–33
Vis viva, 47
Voltaire, 229
Volterra, Vito, 189, 193, 194, 330n, 332
Von Neumann, John, 325, 343
Von Neumann–Morgenstern expected utility, 312
Von Weizsäcker, Carl Christian, 214–15
Vortex and particle model, 134

Wage fund theory, 183m
Wagner, Otto, 233
Walras, Léon: "The Application of Mathematics to Political Economy," 26–27, 169n; Birner on, 91, 99; "Une branche nouvelle de la mathématique," 165; Coats on, 280; A. J. Cohen on, 207–8n, 216n; I. B. Cohen on, 36, 37; de Marchi on, 291n; "Economique et mécanique," 18, 55, 166, 167, 168; *Elements of Pure Economics*, 20, 37, 165, 183; Fisher and, 21; Gaddy on, 175, 177, 183, 192, 193, 194; Jolink on, 159–74, 336; Klamer on, 225, 230, 234; Laurent and, 332; Leonard on, 263–64; Mirowski on, 312, 313, 333; Newtonian mechanics and, 24–25, 26–27; on physico-mathematical sciences, 20; Porter on, 56; Roos on, 143; *Théorie mathématique des richesses sociales*, 183; Tinbergen and, 138, 139; on value, 207n; Weintraub on, 301; E. B. Wilson on, 341
Walrasian demand functions, 119, 120–21, 122, 123, 334
Walrasian prices, 124
Walras' Law, 312, 334
Walter, Maila, 342, 343, 344
Wang, Hao, 99
Want-curves, 169n
Warhol, Andy, 232, 244
Washington, George, 50
Watkins, J. W. N., 114
Wealth of Nations (A. Smith), 31–32
Weaver, Warren, 74
Weber, Max, 234, 272
Webster's New International Dictionary, 25n
Weierstrass, Karl, 187, 189, 190, 191n, 195, 199

Weintraub, E. Roy, 63n, 293n, 338, 342, 344
Wheat trade, 260
Whewell, William, 80, 114n
White, Harrison, 309, 311n
White, Hayden, 226
White, Michael, 335
Whitehead, Alfred North, 25, 235
Whitman, Anne, 33n30
Wicksell, Knut, 175–201, 336
Wieser, Friedrich von, 113
Wigner, E., 95
Williams, Jeffrey, 285
Will to power, 235
Wilson, Edwin Bidwell, 330n, 337–41, 342, 343, 344
Wilson, E. O., 324
Wimsatt, W. K., 25n
The Wisdom of the Body (Cannon), 30
Wise, M. Norton, 70, 79, 281n, 318, 335
Witchcraft, Oracles, and Magic among the Azande (Evans-Pritchard), 257
Witnesses, 33
Wittgenstein: A Social Theory of Knowledge (Bloor), 257
Wittgenstein, Ludwig, 236, 251, 256, 258
Women, 28
Woolf, Virginia, 231, 235, 236
Workers' Ring Movement, 182, 186
World Fair (1904), 167, 174
The World of Goods (Douglas), 249, 255
Worms, René, 27

X-rays, 236

Ye, M. H., 226

Zahar, Elie, 94, 97–98
Zola, Emile, 238

Contributors

Jack Birner is associate professor of economics at the University of Maastricht. He is the author of forthcoming books on the development of F. A. Hayek's research program in economics and the Cambridge debate in capital theory.

Marcel Boumans lectures on philosophy and history of economics at the University of Amsterdam. He is the author of *A Case of Limited Physics Transfer: Jan Tinbergen's Resources for Reshaping Economics* (1992).

A. W. Coats is Research Professor of Economics at Duke University and emeritus professor of economic and social history of the University of Nottingham. He has recently published the first of three volumes of his collected papers: *On the History of Economic Thought: British and American Economic Essays* (1992).

Avi J. Cohen is associate professor of economics at York University, Toronto. He is currently working on a book linking the Cambridge capital controversies with previous capital controversies involving Böhm-Bawerk, Clark, and Fisher, and Hayek, Knight, and Kaldor.

I. Bernard Cohen is Victor S. Thomas Professor Emeritus of the History of Science, Harvard University. His current projects include a new translation of Newton's *Principia* and a study of the role of science in the political thought of Benjamin Franklin, Thomas Jefferson, John Adams, and James Madison.

Neil de Marchi is professor of economics at Duke University. He is coauthor of a book on Milton Friedman and, more recently, editor of a volume entitled *Post-Popperian Methodology of Economics: Recovering Practice*.

Steve Fuller is associate professor of science and technology studies at Virginia Polytechnic Institute and founding editor of the journal *Social Epistemology*. His books include *Social Epistemology* (1988), *Philosophy of Science and Its Discontents* (2d ed., 1992), and *Philosophy, Rhetoric, and the End of Knowledge* (1993).

Clifford G. Gaddy is an economist in the Foreign Policy Studies Program at the Brookings Institution. He is the author (with Ed Hewett) of *Open for Business: Russia's Return to the Global Economy*.

D. Wade Hands is professor of economics at the University of Puget Sound. He is the author of *Testing, Rationality, and Progress: Essays on the Popperian Tradition in Economic Methodology* (1993).

Albert Jolink is senior research fellow of the Tinbergen Rotterdam-Amsterdam Centre for Economics and a research fellow of the Institute for Economic Research at Erasmus University in Rotterdam. He is the author of *The Evolutionary Economics of Léon Walras* (1991) and co-author of the forthcoming *Equilibrium Economics of Léon Walras*.

Arjo Klamer is associate professor of economics at The George Washington University. His most recent book is *The Making of an Economist* (with David Colander).

Robert J. Leonard is assistant professor of economics at the University of Quebec in Montreal and is primarily interested in the history of contemporary economic theory.

Philip Mirowski is Carl Koch Professor of Economics and the History and Philosophy of Science at the University of Notre Dame. His books include *More Heat than Light* (1989), *Against Mechanism* (1988), and a forthcoming edited volume, *Natural Images in Economics: Markets Read in Tooth and Claw*.

Theodore M. Porter is associate professor of history at the University of California, Los Angeles, and author of *The Rise of Statistical Thinking, 1820–1900*. He is now completing a book entitled *Cultures of Objectivity: The Quantification of Public Life*.

Margaret Schabas is associate professor of philosophy at York University, Toronto. She is the author of *A World Ruled by Number: William Stanley Jevons and the Rise of Mathematical Economics* (1990) but has now moved back to the eighteenth century.

E. Roy Weintraub is professor of economics at Duke University. Trained as a mathematician, he currently writes on the history of the interrelationship between economics and mathematics. Author of a half-dozen books and numerous articles, he offers in his most recent work, *Stabilizing Dynamics* (1991), one of the first constructivist accounts of economic analysis.